Literacy, Schooling and Revolution

Education Policy Perspectives

General Editor: Professor Ivor Goodson, Faculty of Education, University of Western Ontario, London, Canada N6G 1G7

Education policy analysis has long been a neglected area in the United Kingdom and, to an extent, in the USA and Australia. The result has been a profound gap between the study of education and the formulation of education policy. For practitioners such a lack of analysis of the new policy initiatives has worrying implications particularly at such a time of policy flux and change. Education policy has, in recent years, been a matter for intense political debate – the political and public interest in the working of the system has come at the same time as the consensus on education policy has been broken by the advent of the 'New Right'. As never before the political parties and pressure groups differ in their articulated policies and prescriptions for the education sector. Critical thinking about these developments is clearly necessary.

All those working within the system also need information on policy making, policy implementation and effective day-to-day operation. Pressure on schools from government, education authorities and parents has generated an enormous need for knowledge amongst those on the receiving end of educational policies.

This series aims to fill the academic gap, to reflect the politicization of education, and to provide the practitioners with the analysis for informed implementation of policies that they will need. It will offer studies in broad areas of policy studies. Beside the general section it will offer a particular focus in the following areas: School organization and improvement (David Reynolds, University College, Cardiff, UK); Critical social analysis (Professor Philip Wexler, University of Rochester, USA); Policy studies and evaluation (Professor Ernest House, University of Colorado-Boulder, USA); and Education and training (Dr Peter Cuttance, University of Edinburgh, UK).

Education Policy Perspectives

Literacy, Schooling and Revolution

Colin Lankshear
with
Moira Lawler

 The Falmer Press

(A member of the Taylor & Francis Group)
New York, Philadelphia and London

UK	The Falmer Press, Falmer House, Barcombe, Lewes, East Sussex, BN8 5DL
USA	The Falmer Press, Taylor & Francis Inc., 242 Cherry Street, Philadelphia, PA 19106-1906

Copyright © Colin Lankshear 1987

First published 1987

British Library Cataloguing in Publication Data

Lankshear, Colin
   Literacy, schooling and revolution.—
   (Education policy perspectives).
   1. Literacy
   I. Title II. Lawler, Moira III. Series
   302.2   LC149

   ISBN 1-85000-239-8

*Printed and bound in Great Britain by
Redwood Burn Limited, Trowbridge, Wiltshire.*

Contents

For the People of
Sandino's Nicaragua
and their friends throughout the world

This book is dedicated also
to the vision of
a just and free Aotearoa

Foreword

During the past two decades, we have become increasingly conscious of the way education functions in class, gender, and race terms. Not only have the outcomes of schooling been closely examined, by tracing out the relationship between schools and the reproduction of the social division of labour, but the internal practices that go on within educational institutions have been rigorously scrutinized as well. Questions concerning the content and form of the curriculum, the pedagogy, and evaluative mechanisms — and the social assumptions that lay behind all of this — have become even more powerful. Whose knowledge is considered legitimate? Why is it organized in this way? Why is it taught to this group? In this way? What is the relationship between 'cultural capital' and 'economic capital'?[1]

These are complicated issues, as you would imagine. Yet, they are among the most important questions one might ask. Education does not stand alone, a neutral instrumentality somehow above the ideological conflicts of the society. Rather, it is deeply implicated in the formation of the unequal cultural, economic, and political issues that dominate our society. Education has been a major arena in which dominance is reproduced *and* contested, in which hegemony is partly formed and partly fractured in the creation of the commonsense of a people.[2] Thus, to think seriously about education is also to think just as seriously about power, about the mechanisms through which certain groups assert their visions, beliefs and practices. While education is not totally reducible to the political, not to deal with the structural sources of differential power is not to deal with education as a cultural and social act at all.

These points may be clearer if we reflect on the recent efforts in countries such as the United States and Britain to bring education more closely into line with industrial needs. With the disintegration of the post-war social democratic accord, right-wing groups, capital, and a fraction of the new middle class have been able to shift the terms of the debate over education to the language of efficiency, standards, and productivity. The altered discourse of the debate has become part of the cultural production of a new hegemonic accord in which educational policies are rearticulated around rightist principles.[3]

A division between educational, cultural, and political processes is difficult to maintain here. Of course, one of our problems is that we tend to assume that such a distinction is easy to make. That there is a close connection between culture and power in the real world is well argued by Richard Johnson. As he states, there are three reasons for not making a hard and fast separation between the cultural and the political:

> The first is that cultural processes are intimately connected with social relations, especially with class and class formations, with sexual divisions, with the racial structuring of social relations, and with age oppressions as a form of dependency. The second is that culture involves power and helps to produce asymmetries in the abilities of individuals and social groups to define and realize their needs. And the third, which follows the other two, is that culture is neither an autonomous nor an externally determined field, but a site of social differences and struggles.[4]

These points bear heavily on the 'industrialization' and rationalization of education now under way, and especially in the discovery of what is seen as the vast public problem of 'functional illiteracy'. The current attempts by dominant groups to blame schools for the social and economic crises now besetting advanced capitalist nations are part of a longer historic tendency. Whenever dominant groups declare that there is a crisis, we must always ask 'Whose crisis is this?' and 'Who benefits from the proposed "solutions"?' The recent declarations of a crisis in literacy in a number of nations are not immune to these questions. It is possible to claim that by shifting the public's attention to problems of education, the real sources of the current crises are left unanalyzed. That is, the crisis of the political economy of capitalism is exported from the economy onto the State. The State then in turn exports the crisis downward onto the school. Thus, when there is severe unemployment, a disintegration of traditional patterns of authority, and so on, the blame is placed on students' lack of skills, on their attitudes, on their 'functional illiteracy'. The structural problems of poverty, of the de-skilling and elimination of jobs, of capital flight, of systemic racism and sexism, problems that are 'naturally' generated out of our current economic and political arrangements, are distanced from our discussions.[5]

This is not to say that the kind of reading and writing that goes on in our institutions of formal and informal education is always successful or politically wise. However, the unit of analysis is simply wrong. To the extent that we focus on educational practices as the fundamental source of the problem, we are merely supporting the hegemonic strategies of the powerful. Understanding how these concerns about literacy fit into such hegemonic strategies is immensely important in any attempt to turn education into a more democratically oriented set of practices.

The concern with literacy is not neutral, then. As the authors of *Literacy, Schooling and Revolution* remind us, literacy is 'a socially constructed form, shaped by and reflecting wider social practices, relations, values, goals, [and] interests'.

With this said, it is still important to remember that literacy — what it means, who defines it, to what social ends it is put — is not simply a reflection of dominant interests. Rather, it signifies a site of cultural struggle. The very meaning of the term itself represents a series of cultural, economic, and political conflicts between what I have called elsewhere the forces of property rights versus person rights.[6] Thus, while many of its current uses — especially in an era of conservative restoration — may support relations of domination, this does not mean that it cannot be turned toward more emancipatory means and ends. Literacy can be constructed and used in ways that transform existing relations of exploitation and domination. In Lankshear and Lawler's words, 'proper literacy' — that is, literacy that 'enhances people's control over their lives and their capacity for dealing rationally with decisions enabling them to identify, understand, and act to transform social relations and practices in which power is structured unequally' — is not only our aim, but it *is* possible to achieve if we take seriously the larger context in which educators (conceived very broadly) work.

Thus, one of their major questions, and justifiably so, involves the potential role of literacy within political struggle. As Lankshear and Lawler put it, they want to 'address ways in which educators have promoted and applied literacy with a view to tapping its potential to stimulate and guide political action aimed at overcoming structural domination and subordination'. Literacy, then, becomes in large part a political act. It is deeply rooted in democratic and collective sentiment and in the quest for cultural power by dispossessed groups.

In his own discussion of some of these issues, David Livingstone articulates the position well:

> Cultural power involves the capacity of social groups to convey notions of actual, possible and preferable social beliefs and practices to their own groups and throughout society as a whole. While declining sentiments of confidence in established institutions of advanced capitalism are now substantial among overlapping groupings of working class people, women, racial minorities and the young or old, the cultural power of such subordinated groups generally remains limited and fragmented. In order to gain greater control over their lives, subordinated people need to identify the abstractions underlying their commonsense knowledge and everyday practices and, through collective reflection on such abstractions in relation to their own concrete situations, to more clearly recognize their own interests as well as the roles of different social groups in constructing and reproducing what they previously regarded as a dense and impenetrable social reality.[7]

This is a very different way of thinking about literacy. Rather than seeing it as the personal accumulation of technical skills, literacy is situated in its larger social arena. This is a context in which the social definition of the content and form of literacy is seen as part of a larger conflict within and among classes (and, just as importantly, gender and race) to control the process of the formation of collective memory and the sense of collective and personal possibility.[8]

What makes *Literacy, Schooling and Revolution* valuable, however, is not only its exceptionally useful conceptual and political clarification of what literacy has meant and might actually mean in the search for what Marcus Raskin has called 'the common good'.[9] The volume goes considerably further. It provides us with a series of detailed pictures of significant historical and contemporary struggles to engage in 'proper literacy'. These include attempts by working-class movements in Britain to resist cultural incorporation and to find their own voice, and by people in the United States to politicize the teaching of reading and writing by focusing in a Freirian way on the social meanings of everyday objects. The book also provides a compelling portrait of the policies and practices of the Nicaraguan experience and its campaigns for mass literacy.

Lankshear and Lawler recognize the import of the active participation of all people involved in such educational and political work. Successful programs are not based on political and cultural passivity, but are organized — from the outset — around dialogue and mutual respect. What is also refreshing is their explicit focus on the experiences of women in the volume. Too often many critical studies in education have suffered from a form of class reductionism. Issues of patriarchal relations are seen as epiphenomenal. In this way, the experiences of women are marginalized.[10] This is not the case here. The authors take seriously the double oppression of women and, again by focusing on the Nicaraguan experiment, document some of the largely successful attempts to deal with the realities of women's lives in these literacy programs.

The recognition that literacy, like all schooling, is not neutral, that it must be situated within the ideological dynamics of the larger society, has implications not only for the Nicaraguan experiment so nicely described in this volume. It also has profound implications for our own work in the industrialized metropoles as well. The democratization of the cultural resources, the polity, and the economy now beginning in a number of previously colonized nations is partly dependent on altering the international economic and ideological context in which they exist. This means that part of our task must be to continue and broaden our own efforts to teach honest material to students within the advanced capitalist countries, to provide them with the resources necessary for truly democratic deliberation and for criticism of the ideologies which pervade their own schooling. Moves toward the establishment of a democratic curriculum at the 'centre' may aid in the continued growth of such models in those countries struggling to determine their own destinies in the Third World. At the least, it would make it much harder for colonial nations to impose their cultural and economic forms on these less powerful countries. 'Proper literacy' in the First World, then, would be more than a little helpful to the establishment and defence of proper literacy elsewhere. This very international context makes our own educational struggles in the United States, Britain, Australia, New Zealand, and elsewhere even more important.

Our own responsibilities in the capitalist metropoles make *Literacy, Schooling and Revolution* an even more necessary book. The volume is more analytic and historically based than that now classic account of how political education can go on — William Hinton's masterful description of the Chinese experience in *Fanshen*.[11] Yet by synthesizing a range of historical and current experiments and struggles and building a framework upon which we can evaluate both the democratic intent and means (and outcomes) of literacy programs, *Literacy, Schooling and Revolution* takes its place beside Hinton's more personal account. It assists us in seeing some of the elements that are necessary and are possible if we are to have an education that can 'resist the continual pressure to prepare students for [less than powerful] political and economic roles, and that, in the process, can stimulate a criticism of the system that makes such demands'.[12] By repoliticizing the issue of literacy, Lankshear and Lawler extend the path established by Hinton, Freire, and others and enable us to understand more clearly what is at stake in one of the most crucial arenas of educational practice.

Their book reminds us in eloquent ways that reading and writing, those apparently simple and fundamental acts, are in capitalism 'at one and the same times forms of regulation and exploitation *and* potential modes of resistance, celebration and solidarity'. This double movement echoes Caliban's cry: 'You taught me language; and my profit on it is, I know how to curse'.[13] Our task as educators is to help the cursers find their collective voice.

Michael W. Apple
The University of Wisconsin, Madison

Notes

1 For a discussion of this work, see Apple, M. (1979), *Ideology and Curriculum*, New York and London, Routledge and Kegan Paul.
2 See Hogan, D. (1982), 'Education and Class Formation', in Apple, M. (Ed.) *Cultural and Economic Reproduction in Education*, New York and London, Routledge and Kegan Paul, 32 – 78 and William Reese (1986), *Power and the Promise of School Reform*, New York and London, Routledge and Kegan Paul.
3 This process is analyzed in more detail in Apple, M. (1986), *Teachers and Texts: A Political Economy of Class and Gender Relations in Education*, New York and London, Routledge and Kegan Paul. One of the best discussions of the right's partly successful strategies to rebuild a hegemonic accord can be found in Omi, M. and Winant, H. (1986), *Racial Formation in the United States*, New York and London, Routledge and Kegan Paul.
4 Johnson, R. (1983), 'What is Cultural Studies Anyway?', Occasional Paper SP No. 74, University of Birmingham Centre for Contemporary Cultural Studies, 3.

5   Apple, M. (1985), *Education and Power*, New York and London, Routledge and Kegan Paul, revised ARK Edition.
6   Apple (1985, 1986), *op. cit.*
7   Livingstone, D. (1987), *Critical Pedagogy and Cultural Power*, South Hadley, Bergin and Garvey, 7.
8   On the relationship between cultural power and collective memory, see Centre for Contemporary Cultural Studies (1982), *Making Histories*, London, Hutchinson.
9   Raskin, M. (1986), *The Common Good*, New York and London, Routledge and Kegan Paul.
10 See Barrett, M. (1980), *Women's Oppression Today*, London, New Left Books, and Apple (1986), *op. cit.*
11 William Hinton (1966), *Fanshen*, New York, Vintage.
12 Jones, K. (1983), *Beyond Progressive Education*, London, Macmillan, 12.
13 Batsleer, J., Davies, T., O'Rourke, R., and Weedon, C. (1985), *Rewriting English: Cultural Politics of Gender and Class*, New York and London, Methuen.

Acknowledgments

Numerous people have made a special contribution to my education in recent years. I want to thank them for their efforts, while recognizing that they doubtless wish I'd learned more than I have.

First, I owe a special debt to Moira Lawler. This book could not have been written without her participation. Moira has made a major contribution to chapters 1 and 5, and has discussed with me the main points at each step in the argument. Despite the fact that the text reads as the work of a single author, much of it has been jointly conceived and written. I have, of course, learned a great deal from Moira that goes beyond what is reflected in these pages.

I want also to thank Chris Holland, Matt Robson, Robert Mackie, Eric Braithwaite, and Kevin Harris for helping me learn much that I am glad to have learned.

Mike Apple encouraged me to continue my early inquiries into literacy — for which I am grateful. Brian Street has provided valuable comments on chapters 1 and 2. His generosity is very much appreciated. I have tried to take account of his evaluative comments, but realize I have not succeeded entirely.

I am grateful also to Rosa Maria Torres and Eduardo Baez for the introduction they gave me to adult education within the Nicaraguan Revolution whilst I was in Managua and, in Rosa Maria's case, subsequently. Thanks are also due to Peter Sandiford and Fiona Taler for their translations of Rosa Maria's work. Without Peter's taped contributions from Nicaragua I could not have completed this book.

Among the many others who have helped me find my way in recent years, the following have provided much needed inspiration and/or support: my parents, Derry and Cicely Lawler, Alison Jones, Jack Shallcrass, Petronella Townsend, Jim Marshall, Jonathon Kozol, Ira Shor, Paulo Freire, Chris Searle, Harvey Graff and Kenneth Levine. Some of these people I know only through their work. I hope I have made acceptable use of their ideas and practices.

My thanks go to Ivor Goodson and Malcolm Clarkson for inviting me to think through my ideas on literacy, schooling and revolution. I hope they don't regret it.

Apologies are due to those students of 1986 who suffered my worst pedagogy while I was writing. I won't let it happen again.

Lastly, I want to thank the editors of *Discourse, Landfall, Educational Theory* and the *New Zealand Journal of Educational Studies,* for permission to reproduce material contained in our earlier work.

Colin Lankshear
Auckland, 1987

Chapter 1

The Politics of Literacy

Introduction

This book addresses educational policy from a particular standpoint: namely the politics of literacy. During the 1970s and 1980s a host of books, articles, university courses, seminars, and even publishing lists, emerged as so many 'politics of' this and that. Common examples include the politics of health, art, religion, gender, peace, poverty, education, knowledge, research and theory. The list also contains several closely related areas of interest allied to the politics of literacy itself. These include the politics of reading, the politics of literature, the politics of the curriculum, and the politics of publishing. [1]

But what, exactly, is meant by the politics of literacy? This question has two components.

(i)   What kind of investigation is it that addresses the *politics* of literacy?
(ii) What constitutes *literacy*? In other words, what is the politics of literacy a politics of? How is literacy related to, say, reading or literature? What is the relationship between literacy and the curriculum? Does 'literacy' refer to the possession of certain specifiable techniques and skills? If so, what are they? And can literacy be understood solely in terms of these techniques and skills, or does it necessarily refer also to the content and context through which they are acquired and exercised?

The wider argument in this book rests on the particular approach I take to these questions. I want, then, to spell this approach out at the start of my discussion. This opening chapter considers the nature of political inquiry generally, and the politics of literacy in particular.

Politics and the Political

First, then, what delineates a work in the *politics* of literacy? Given the way in which knowledge is officially organized and produced within settings like schools, universities, and research institutes, two alternatives immediately stand out as possible answers to this question. One is that the politics of literacy identifies a distinctive *mode* of inquiry into the phenomenon of literacy. The second is that it distinguishes a particular area, or *field* of interest within the overall investigation of literacy.

Politics as a Distinctive Mode of Inquiry

The possibility suggested here is that the politics of literacy can be understood analogously to the philosophy of science, or the sociology of religion, or the history of education. That is, the politics of literacy is seen to refer to a mode of inquiry in which the logic, concepts, methods of analysis, tests for truth or probability, etc., that are used, are distinctive to a primary or foundation discipline called politics. In this event, to undertake investigation in the politics of literacy would be a matter of applying a particular primary discipline, or what Hirst would call a form of knowledge[2], to some set of human practices and conventions collectively called literacy.

This possibility is given some credence by the recent upsurge of interest in the history of literacy as a form of academic endeavour. Graff argues that the history of literacy has a unique and important contribution to make to social understanding and social policy.[3] While literacy is without doubt very important for the pursuit of human goals within modern society, our understanding of what literacy is and how (far) it can contribute to achieving these goals is badly flawed. According to Graff, 'discussions of literacy suffer from serious confusion'. We have inherited 'a set of legacies' about literacy and its great importance within human life. This 'body of thinking' that we have inherited is 'a source of anxiety and confusion in a changing world', where grave concern and fears are today held for 'the condition of literacy among youth and adult populations'. It is also, however, 'a historical outcome that can only be understood in historical terms ... Contemporary understanding can be best advanced, in this case, as in many others, through a perspective grounded in history'.[4]

Perhaps, then, there are also aspects of contemporary understanding that can be best advanced through a perspective grounded, distinctively, in politics. In which case, the politics of literacy will be construed as a self-contained mode of inquiry, parallel and complementary to the history (and philosophy, etc.) of literacy.

We must, I think, reject this view. The underlying belief that there are certain primary or foundation disciplines, demarcated from one another by their own unique tools or instruments for gaining access to truth or knowledge, has in recent years been seriously challenged by a 'new', anti-foundationalist epistemology.[5] One implication of anti-foundationalism is that knowledge cannot ultimately be compartmentalized into logically different types — for example, historical, philosophical, mathematical, sociological, scientific, etc. — corresponding to so many autonomous, foundation disciplines. This is because, in the final analysis, the alleged boundaries and crucial methodological and conceptual distinctions between the (alleged) several foundation disciplines do not exist. According to anti-foundationalists, the traditional compartments — the foundation disciplines — reflect a misguided conception of knowledge and should be abandoned. If this argument is correct, history — and, therefore, history of literacy — cannot properly be regarded as a distinctive mode of inquiry. The same would hold for philosophy (and so for philosophy of science, philosophy of art, etc.) for sociology (and the various 'sociologies of') and all the other traditionally-acknowledged foundation disciplines.

Regardless, however, of whether or not the argument denying foundation disciplines is correct, two facts remain that bear directly on the issue here. The first is that, despite anti-foundationalism, academic study, training and research still largely proceed on the model of compartmentalized disciplines and foundations. Students are trained as historians and sociologists in order that they might do distinctively historical and sociological research. Secondly, it is true that within this model politics has not typically been regarded as one of the distinctive foundation disciplines anyway. By and large, political analysis has been seen as drawing upon logics, concepts, methods of analysis, and tests for truth or probability from various (foundation) disciplines: notably, mathematics, history, and sociology — with politics itself assuming the status more of what Hirst would call a *field* of knowledge, as opposed to a form.[6] That the politics of literacy is indeed parasitic upon conceptual frameworks, methodologies and findings, generally associated with primary disciplines, is clear from the literature.[7]

What this means is that if politics is to be regarded as in some way comprising a distinctive perspective on human practices and conventions such as literacy, it cannot be in respect of some conceptual framework and methodology uniquely employed in generating *political* knowledge. Consequently, the analogy between the politics of literacy and, say, the philosophy of science or the history of literacy, fails.

Despite this setback, there does seem to be some point in regarding politics, or the political, as a distinctive perspective — albeit not in respect of some unique means of access to knowledge. Perhaps what is distinctive about politics is the sphere of human life which is picked out for investigation via intellectual and theoretical tools derived from various disciplines. The idea here is essentially the same as Hirst's idea of a field of knowledge. Hirst identifies so many fields of knowledge demarcated from each other by their unique subject matter. What distinguishes economics from geography, for example, is that they investigate different subject matters; different phenomena seen in need of understanding and explanation. Neither economics nor geography enjoys a unique mode of inquiry of its own. Each is deemed distinct, however, in respect of its broad object of investigation. The question is, can politics be regarded as a distinctive perspective along these broad lines? And if so, does this provide a satisfactory account of the politics of literacy?

Politics as a Distinctive Field of Inquiry

As a matter of fact, Hirst himself identifies political inquiry as a field of knowledge.[8] He says virtually nothing, however, about what he thinks constitutes the distinctive subject matter of politics. Moreover, this issue appears to be a focus for considerable dispute. Raphael suggests that there are conflicting views among political theorists as to the sphere of the political.[9] Some favour a narrower view, according to which 'the political is whatever concerns the State'.[10] Others allegedly favour a much wider view, and 'define the sphere of the political either in terms of power or in terms of conflict'.[11]

Raphael presents these alternatives in a simplified and polemical way. I intend to adopt this framework here in order to work gradually toward the view of the politics of literacy that will underpin this book. Since Raphael himself supports the narrower view, it is convenient to address that first. He asks,

> How should one mark out the sphere of the political so as to distinguish it from the 'social', i.e., from all those activities in different forms of relationships between individuals which are not political? The old way of doing this is to say that the political is whatever concerns the State, and on the whole this way of delineating the sphere of the political still seems to me the clearest.[12]

Raphael, then, is suggesting that the political can be distinguished from other areas or spheres of human/social life — such as the economic, the cultural, the recreational, the religious, the educational, the personal and interpersonal, and so on — by reference to the domain and concerns of the State. Defining the domain and concerns of the State is itself, of course, a highly contentious business. How does Raphael conceive of the State and, hence, of politics?

Drawing on Tonnies' distinction between 'Gemeinschaft' and 'Gesellschaft', he identifies the State as an association rather than a community.[13] A social group is an association when, and only when, its members have a specified common purpose or set of common purposes, and are deliberately organized for the pursuit of that purpose.[14] What, then, is the specified common purpose of the members of the State, how are its members organized to pursue its purposes, and who are the members of the State?

The reason why Raphael believes he can distinguish as clearly as he does between the political and the various spheres of social life is because the modern State (excepting totalitarian States) makes no attempt to organize *all* social purposes. And so the purposes of the State are limited — limited, that is, to those purposes that are political by definition. According to Raphael, the State has two broad functions. Its primary function is negative: to keep order and maintain security. This is security within the community as well as security against injury from sources outside the community.

> Security within the community means security against deliberate infringement of rights in respect of person or property (e.g., against

assault or theft), and against non-deliberate damage (e.g., owing to negligence). Security against external injury likewise covers both deliberate harm (as in acts of war by other states) and non-deliberate damage (as when a home industry suffers from the dumping of excessively cheap foreign goods).[15]

The State's negative function is, then, essentially one of protecting established rights and existing well-being and opportunities. In addition to this negative function, modern States observe — to a greater or lesser extent — a positive function as well. This is the task of promoting welfare and justice. Positive justice goes beyond the (mere) preservation of established rights inherent in the State's negative function. It involves actively 'reforming the order of legal rights so that it will accord more closely with current moral ideas of justice (often called "social justice")'.[16] How far a State goes in this area varies from case to case. There is general agreement these days, says Raphael, that the State should assume responsibility for ensuring that at least 'some measure of material well-being is available for all its members, that, for example, no one should be left to starve by reason of unemployment or sickness'.[17] What this measure is seen to be varies greatly between states, and even (within a single state) between different political parties. And as far as promoting non-material well-being is concerned, virtually all states assume responsibility for providing at least some education — which, of course, is relevant to the issue of literacy.

So much for the common purpose of the State as an association. How are its members organized in order to pursue this purpose? The answer here also covers the question of who the members of the State are. In short, the basis of organizing the State for promoting internal security and welfare [18] is the legal system — that is, rules backed by coercive power. Organization of the State's members around the law entails legislative, executive, and judicial aspects.

> The Legislature makes the law ... The Executive (which in this context may be taken to comprise not only the Government but also the vast host of public servants, i.e., the civil service, the police and prison services ...) gives effect to the law by applying and enforcing it. The Judiciary interprets the law and also ... helps to make law in the field of common or case law.[19]

The members of the State comprise all citizens: i.e., those who are subject to the law by virtue of their legal affiliation to that jurisdiction, as opposed to being, say, a visitor to the country and under that State's legal jurisdiction only for the duration of the visit. For citizens and visitors alike, the law of the State is sovereign: State rules are the supreme rules within that territory.

For Raphael, then, the sphere of politics is that in which the State performs its function (and citizens are obliged to act accordingly) of maintaining order and security, and providing for such positive benefits as it takes upon itself to decree, by exercising jurisdiction through the law. Citizens participate in the State in one or more roles: as citizen *simpliciter*, as parliamentarian, cabinet minister, voter, State commissioner, civil servant, magistrate, lawyer, law enforcement officer, and so on. The political incorporates 'the institutional framework of rule in a state', plus 'the behaviour of groups and individuals in matters that are likely to affect the course of government' (and, thus, the law).[20] This latter aspect includes voting, forming and participating in political parties, and involvement in trade unions, lobbies, and pressure groups, with the aim of influencing parliamentarians, cabinet ministers, civil servants, or public opinion generally, so as to influence in turn legislation and/or application of the law. The political life of the individuals is that part of their life lived within the context defined by the State: within the context of 'making, applying, interpreting, or enforcing the law'.[21] The political dimension of human activities and practices is that pertaining to the purpose(s) and organization of the State. As such, the sphere of politics and the political seems to be very clearly, and quite narrowly, defined.

The alternative conception of politics recognized by Raphael is, by contrast, much wider and less clearly demarcated from other spheres of social life and activity. Raphael refers to a tendency among some people 'to define the sphere of the political either in terms of power or in terms of conflict'.[22] On this view, then, it is the operation of power or the presence of conflict that allegedly makes a relationship, situation, or activity, *political* — regardless of whether or not the power or conflict in question has anything to do with the State, or with the behaviour of groups or individuals in matters likely to affect the course of government.[23] The notion of power in question is very wide, consisting in 'the ability to get other people to do what one wants them to do'.[24] In order to rule out cases like muggers forcing victims to hand over wallets, or the school bully having the power to extract sweets from other pupils, some may want to confine this view of power (and, thus, the sphere of the political) to contexts in which some authority is involved — for example, where parents get children to obey their will, and where teachers have similar success with pupils. The notion of conflict taken to define the political is likewise wide. As an example of a person holding this position, Raphael mentions the case of a political scientist who maintained that 'if two friends proposing to take an afternoon trip together on a tandem bicycle disagree as to whether they should go north or south, they are engaged in political conflict'.[25] In this particular example there is no attempt to confine the idea of conflict — and hence that of politics — to contexts involving authority. Elsewhere advocates of the wider position are not as open, and harness talk of the political to conflict involving some form or bearer of authority.

What this second view of politics implies is that the relationship between, say, parents and children is political insofar as it is one where parents exercise power over children, or assert the right to control children's activity and development, or assume responsibility for making decisions which involve children's interests. Similarly, where a boss can control a worker's activity, or has the power to determine working conditions, hours of work, rates of pay, and whether or not union labour will be hired, there too we find the political. Other relationships, such as those within marriage or the household —

husband/wife — or within professional life — for example, doctor/patient — might also be deemed political in terms of the wider view, to the extent that power and control is exercised over one party by the other. Indeed, there are strands within the literature dealing with the politics of the family, gender politics, and the politics of health care, that may seem entirely confined to issues of power, control, or conflict, between agents engaged in quite specific domestic, familial, personal, or professional-client relationships. Not only are such cases seemingly removed from anything whatsoever to do with the State, they also appear to bring 'the political' firmly into the realm of 'the personal'. In fact, the slogan, 'the personal is political', is frequently invoked in such contexts. Furthermore, workers within organizations like women's refuges and women's health centres often see their work as the very essence of political activity when addressing, for example, the (apparently) personal case of a particular woman who has been physically assaulted by a particular man, or when recommending that a woman with a particular ailment — for example, cystitis — avoid the services of a certain doctor.

The two alternatives identified by Raphael clearly comprise quite different views of politics and the political. As such they give rise to rather different sets of possibilities for a field of inquiry called the politics of literacy. Before considering some of these differences, however, it is worth noting one consequence for political inquiry shared in common by these competing accounts of politics as a distinctive field of inquiry. This is that each view is compatible with a wide range of specific approaches to political subject matter. Regardless of whether the scope of political inquiry is restricted to matters concerning the State or opened up to more wide ranging contexts involving conflict or power, it can take many different forms. It can range from the essentially philosophical — for example, analyzing key concepts, clarifying distinctions, and assessing the validity and soundness of different arguments — to the overtly empirical or statistical — for example, measuring and describing voting patterns within a particular group or area, or case studying specific instances of conflict. It can range from the purely descriptive — for example, describing statutes binding within a given state and the process by which they were legislated, or locating sources, distribution, and patterns of power within some organization or institution — to the predominantly normative — such as critiquing the ideal of 'positive' freedom embraced by certain collectivist states,[26] or attempting to justify the use of power by appeal to principles and precedents. Inquiries may be quite specific and address single instances, or more general and, perhaps, include comparative analysis. Diverse techniques may be employed within either conception of the political. These include sampling techniques, questionnaire investigation, statistical analysis, biography, comparative analysis, case study, historical investigation, conceptual analysis, normative philosophical argument, a history of political ideas and theories, theory critique, theory construction, and so on. Moreover, and finally, those who conduct political inquiry, within either conceptual framework of the political, may proceed from diverse theoretical and/or ideological bases: for example, empiricists, political 'behaviourists' (in the tradition of David Easton), historians of political theory, philosophers of politics (largely in the tradition of the British analytical school), Marxists, post-Marxists, and so on.

The Politics of Literacy : Two Views

We may now consider what implications the two views of politics and the political have for the politics of literacy. In other words, what sorts of inquiries or studies will constitute the politics of literacy on each of the positions outlined? I will take the narrower view first.

Politics as State Jurisdiction

Conceived as a field of inquiry, politics picks out some distinctive sphere of interest rather than a particular mode or method of inquiry. On the narrower view of politics, the sphere of interest focuses on the State. Consequently, from this standpoint the politics of literacy addresses aspects of the human practice of transmitting, refining and enhancing literacy which, in one way or another, involve the State. To put it more specifically, the politics of literacy addresses matters connected with making, applying, interpreting, and enforcing law pertaining to literacy. Law pertaining to literacy can be approached in terms of the State's negative function — by considering the role of literacy in safeguarding existing rights, well-being and opportunities, and how the state facilitates this role — and/or in terms of the state's positive function — by considering literacy as a welfare or social justice concern, and the extent to which the state takes upon itself the task of ensuring provision through which people can become literate.

Given this approach to the politics of literacy, the specific issues and concerns addressed, and the manner in which they are addressed, might vary widely. They may include, for example, purely descriptive accounts of official State expectations in respect of literacy attainment, or of what the State legally requires each person to be exposed to in the way of literacy teaching. Other possibilities here would include investigation of legal definitions of literacy (such as those employed in state-provided or state-regulated adult literacy programmes); and description or evaluation of legislation enacted to address problems of illiteracy or issues relating to literacy teaching (such as legislation providing for adult literacy programmes, for remedial reading programmes in schools, or for facilities to promote literacy in English as a second language). Comparative analysis and evaluation of different requirements and provision between one state and others represents another viable exercise within the politics of literacy. So too would accounts and critiques of the philosophies and official pronouncements of Ministers of Education, school inspectors, commissions of inquiry, etc., on issues and difficulties relating to literacy, together with descriptions and evaluations of the ways in which official regulations are actually interpreted, applied and enforced.

Still further possibilities within the politics of literacy on the present view, include the following sorts of investigation: an analysis of activities by pressure groups — representing, for instance, employers, parents, teachers, racial or ethnic minorities — aimed at politicians, Education Department officials, local education authorities and school boards, on matters relating to literacy; accounts of how one political party used the failed or discredited policies (in the literacy field) of their opponents as an election issue; critical evaluation of education cuts and their (likely) effect on literacy levels, together with analysis of why cuts were made in one area rather than another; investigation of the State's role in encouraging or promoting attainment of a particular quality of literacy as opposed to others — such as an emphasis on a *basic* rather than a critical literacy; argument that the State effectively promulgates a certain doctrine through policies and procedures officially imposed on the teaching of literacy — for example, the choice of material through which children learn to read, the teaching syllabus, curriculum guidelines, and the kind of pedagogy employed. And many more examples besides.

Politics as Power and Conflict

From this standpoint the politics of literacy addresses issues and situations of power or conflict arising in relation to literacy. For example, matters of power or conflict may arise in relation to the various processes and settings in which literacy skills are transmitted and acquired. Equally, such matters may arise in relation to those agents and agencies responsible for defining and promoting literacy within a society, community or group. Finally, considerations of power or conflict may arise in relation to the use of literacy within the different settings that make up daily life. Some elucidation of these points is in order before turning to examples of specific kinds of investigation that might be conducted within this broad view of the politics of literacy.

Literacy may be transmitted and acquired in a variety of settings (for example, school classrooms, culture circles, a mass literacy campaign, within an adult literacy group, with a private tutor, etc.), via a variety of processes (for example, typical formal classroom methods, informal one-to-one pupil and tutor, informal peer learning approach, a Freirean literacy group, etc.). These differing settings and processes can have radically different implications for the degree and type of power exercised, the source and distribution of that power, and the amount, type, and locus of conflict that arises. Agents and agencies responsible for defining or promoting literacy may also vary markedly — and with these variations can come quite different outcomes in terms of power and conflict. For the purposes of simple illustration, we may contrast the example of informal, voluntary adult literacy learning, where pupil and tutor work out together the sorts of skills and content that will be undertaken (for example, 'just enough so I can sit my driver's licence'), with the typical school learning experience, wherein skills and content are officially and, as far as the pupils are concerned, impersonally defined. These in turn differ from historical examples, like that of Hannah More[27], who deemed that for pupils within her Sunday schools literacy would be confined to minimal reading skills, with writing prohibited. The ways in which literacy is actually used, and the effectiveness of its use, are also prone to the exercise of power and the possibility of conflict. Teachers, for example, may require pupils to write essays on certain topics, and/or to write them in a particular way. Such requirements are potential and actual sources of conflict. Teachers (and parents) are inclined to restrict the uses to which pupils (and children) may put their literacy skills: for example, no writing love letters or graffiti, no printing notices advertising a pupils' strike, no using Dad's chequebook, no reading war comics, pornographic magazines, or cheap romances. Again, such restrictions provide a context ripe for conflict. Within the wider social context there are numerous ways in which power or conflict is apparent in relation to the use of literacy. At an obvious level, certain publications get banned and prohibitive taxes are imposed on others, some advertisements are censored, printing presses have from time to time been confiscated and radical study/reading groups repressed. At a more subtle level, newspaper editors may refuse to print letters submitted for publication if they infringe the editorial line, and insist that reporters write certain kinds of stories or avoid given issues. Library staff influence the choice of reading material available to the public through their power to decide which books, journals, periodicals, and newspapers will be available on library shelves.[28] Publishing companies likewise wield considerable power over the kind of material people at large will read — through size and range of lists, pricing policies, etc. Local bodies which refuse to recognize petitions or written complaints thereby impose limits on a potentially effective use of literacy by their constituents.

There are, then, at least these dimensions within which issues and situations involving power or control may arise in relation to literacy. Moreover, the notions of power and conflict seen as defining the scope of politics here (see pp. 6 – 7 above) are very open. Consequently, if the politics of literacy is construed as a field of inquiry which addresses issues and situations of power or conflict arising in relation to literacy, the field itself will be enormous. All manner of investigations will fall within the ambit of the politics of literacy, thus defined. The following examples provide some indication of the range of possibilities here.

Classroom interaction research focusing on the dynamics of power or conflict between teachers and pupils involved in reading and writing activities would presumably fall within the politics of literacy on the present account. The object of investigation could be a single teacher with a single class of children. Alternatively, the sample could be larger and, perhaps, a comparative dimension added. The inquiry could be entirely descriptive. Equally, an evaluative emphasis could be included.

At roughly the same level, inquiry might be conducted into the control parents have, or lack, over children's reading material. Again such inquiry could be limited to studying a single family unit and still qualify as a politics of literacy on the account given here. Alternatively, some wider base — perhaps, even, a cross section of parents from the society as a whole — could be employed. Once more a political inquiry here could range across description, evaluation, comparative and non-comparative analysis, and so on.

A third possibility would be to case study a dispute between a teacher and a parent over a particular child's poor performance in reading and writing. This option could be varied to include conflict between an entire school staff and the parents whose children it serves. A larger scale example of this kind of politics of literacy would be to investigate a lobby or pressure group which seeks to impose its definition of sound literacy achievement on a community or a national education system. During the past decade employers, concerned parents' groups, conservative academics and politicians, and 'new right' lobbies, among others, have been vocal on the theme of promoting basic literacy and numeracy. Indeed, in the hands of such advocates this goal has often been elevated to the status of *the* end of education for many, if not most pupils (as in, for example, the 'back to basics' movement).

Equally, a politics of literacy might investigate conflict between different community groups and organizations involved in providing adult literacy programmes — where, for example, several groups offering different types of programme and instruction are in competition with each other for pupils and funding. In this situation the conflict could turn, specifically, into dispute about what *really* constitutes literacy, and hence which group is most deserving of funds and clients.

Within the very broad conception of the politics of literacy under consideration here, a further viable form of inquiry might be the biography of a Minister or Director-General of Education who exercised considerable power over methods and curricula for teaching literacy in schools. Variations on this theme include case studying the chain of power and decision-making resulting in, say, a change in the official reading primers to be used in classrooms. Alternatively, where there is some choice available to teachers in the classroom reading material they may use, there would be point to studying the power influenced by publishing companies/representatives over teachers' actual choice of resources.

Next, studies of official censorship and other forms of state prohibition could be undertaken as a politics of literacy here. These might be given an historical twist by examining, for example, such cases as state hostility toward certain working-class newspapers (and other publications) in Britain during the early and mid-nineteenth century, and the various means taken — for example, stamp taxes — to put such publications out of business.[29] This sort of study, which focuses on the exercise of power by the State, or on conflict between the State and particular social groups, overlaps with potential inquiry conducted from the standpoint of politics as state jurisdiction.

Finally, a politics of literacy could investigate the hypothesis that literacy — or certain forms of literacy — serve as an important means of maintaining existing power and control differentials within society, by diffusing an ideology that effectively bolsters the *status quo*. A study which investigated literacy as a tool of domestication in the service of ruling elites[30], or which located 'school literacy' within a theory of knowledge and social control, would be examples of such a politics of literacy.

The State, Power and Politics

In seeking to clarify the politics of literacy I began with two possibilities: that the politics of literacy comprises either a distinctive *mode* of inquiry or a distinctive *field* of inquiry. The first possibility is easily eliminated. Even if the epistemological argument (that identifying distinct and autonomous foundation disciplines is a misguided approach to the nature and production of knowledge) can be met, there is the fact that politics has not generally been regarded as a mode of inquiry anyway. Indeed, in my outline of politics as a field of inquiry, I have suggested that extant political investigation draws upon a range of techniques and theoretical frameworks that derive from a variety of disciplines.[31] We can, then, dispense with the idea that politics comprises a distinctive *mode* of inquiry.

This leaves the possibility that politics, and thus the politics of literacy, comprises a distinctive field of inquiry. At this point it might be asked whether there are not further possibilities besides these two that I have identified. Rather than address this question here and try to imagine what some other possibilities might be, I propose to take the shortest route and see whether a viable account can in fact be provided of the politics of literacy as a distinctive field of inquiry.

Two alternative accounts of politics as a field of inquiry have been identified and briefly outlined. The narrow view defines the political in terms of the State. The wider view defines the political in terms of power or conflict, disavowing any necessary connection with the State. Obviously, it is not possible for both of these views to be correct — since each explicitly denies the centrality of what the other takes to be the defining or necessary characteristic of the political.[32] At best, one or other of these alternatives will provide the basis for a viable account of the politics of literacy. In order to advance the argument further we may consider the relative merits of these competing views.

To look ahead a little, the position I will ultimately adopt is that neither of these alternatives is acceptable. Each captures something that is very important concerning politics and the political. Neither, however, satisfactorily grasps what is central to the political dimension of human life. Hence neither adequately grasps the nature of political inquiry. Fortunately, a viable account of the politics of literacy *does* emerge from the critique of these alternatives. I turn now to this critique, beginning with the view that defines the sphere of the political in terms of power and/or conflict.

Politics as Power or Conflict: A Critique

I presented this view, after Raphael, in rather broad terms. It was seen to be the operation of power or the presence of conflict that gives a situation, relationship, or activity its *political* nature. Power was taken to consist in the ability — especially of persons regarded as having some kind of authority — to get other people to do what one wants them to do. Conflict involves disagreement between parties with competing or differing interests, wants, values, goals, etc. This view of politics and the political contains an important insight as well as a crucial flaw. The insight is that it focuses attention on issues and instances of power and conflict in a way that defining politics by reference to the State does not. The flaw is that it blurs the very important relationship between what is personal (or otherwise social) and what is distinctively political. What does this mean?

Raphael himself broaches this critique. He dismisses as absurd the view that the conflict between his two tandem riders, one wanting to go north and the other south, is a political situation. He continues:

> We should similarly have to call political a disagreement between husband and wife whether they should spend a saved £50 on a washing machine or a carpet ... If every [such] disagreement ... is to be called a political conflict, the word 'politics' is robbed of its distinctive meaning.[33]

Let us presume that Raphael would regard the disagreement here as (merely) personal or domestic conflict, or something similar. The relevance of this example is that it is very close to some examples suggested above of situations that would fall within the scope of the politics of literacy: for example, conflict between a parent and a child over what kind of material the child is allowed to read, or what sorts of letters or notes they can write without fear of punishment.

In such cases we may feel some sympathy for Raphael's claim that it is absurd to describe these disagreements or uses of power as political, and that to do so robs 'politics' of its distinctive meaning. Moreover, there are further examples mentioned above, involving the exercise of power or the presence of conflict in situations pertaining to literacy, that seem also, and in a similar way, to lack *political* significance: for example, a dispute between a parent and teacher over a child's poor reading and writing skills, or the (idiosyncratic) dynamics of power and/or conflict between a particular teacher and a particular group of pupils. Is it not possible, even likely, that such isolated individual cases might speak more loudly to the personalities of the actors involved than to anything properly regarded as political?

Perhaps so. Nevertheless, there are dangers in trying to draw a hard and fast distinction between 'the political' and 'the personal' as autonomous realms of human life. Furthermore, an excellent way of capturing the core of what is political is by exploring the relationship between the two spheres. To do this, let us turn to some ideas advanced by C. Wright Mills, in the light of which we can return to the sorts of examples I have just mentioned.

In *The Sociological Imagination*[34] Mills notes the widespread feeling among people today in societies like our own that they are trapped; that the troubles they experience are beyond their capacity to overcome. They feel helpless — trapped in circumstances and caught up in processes of change they understand but dimly, and which they sense to be beyond their control. Ironically, the more information people have about their world — about the world beyond their immediate milieux of family, work, neighbourhood — the more power-less they typically feel; the less they seem to understand 'the meaning of their epoch for their own lives'.[35]

One reason for this sense of helplessness and entrapment, says Mills, is the failure of so many people to grasp the relationship between biography and history, between feelings of personal entrapment and 'the seemingly imper-sonal changes in the very structure of continent-wide societies'.[36] A precondi-tion for escaping such feelings of entrapment, and confronting realistically the possibilities for control in our own life circumstances, is a quality of mind that enables us to perceive clearly the relationship between what is going on in the world and what may be happening within ourselves.

There is, according to Mills, an intimate connection between history and biography, between social structures (and changes in these structures) and our private experience of life. This connection, I will argue, lies at the heart of the relationship between the political and the personal. Mills says:

> The facts of contemporary history are also facts about the success and failure of individual men and women. When a society is industrialized, a peasant becomes a worker; a feudal lord is liquidated or becomes a businessman. When classes rise or fall, a man is employed or unem-ployed; when the rate of investment goes up or down, a man takes heart or goes broke. When wars happen, an insurance salesman becomes a rocket launcher; a store clerk a radar man; a wife lives alone; a child grows up without a father. Neither the life of an individual nor the history of a society can be understood without understanding both.[37]

The quality of mind by which people understand this relationship, and apply it to their own circumstances, consists in what Mills calls 'the sociological imagination'. By this we are enabled 'to grasp history and biography and the relations between the two within society'.[38] Perhaps the most important intellectual tool afforded by the sociological imagination is the distinction between '"the personal troubles of milieux" and "the public issues of social structure"'.[39] What is this distinction, and how does it assist our understanding of politics and the political?

Troubles are more or less private matters, arising within the individual's personality and their immediate social context — i.e., the context of their direct personal experience, social relationships, and purposeful activity. A person experiences troubles when something they value is felt by them to be threatened. The nature and origin of troubles lie within the persons themselves and their direct sphere of social life: family, work, club, neighbourhood, classroom, circle of friends, etc. Resolving troubles involves looking to this limited context. Issues, by contrast, are public matters, arising within 'the larger structure of social and historical life'.[40] This larger structure is the overall organization of so many private social spheres (of so many people) into the myriad social institutions which overlap and interpenetrate to form an historical society as a whole.[41] The nature and origin of issues, and their resolution, lie within the wider network of institutional practices and arrangements. A public (or publics) experiences issues when something it collectively values is seen to be threatened.

The distinction is nicely illustrated by Mills' examples of (among others) unemployment and marriage. When just one person in a city of 100,000 is unemployed, that fact of unemployment is their personal *trouble*. To overcome that trouble we look to that person's character, their skills, and their immediate opportunities. It is different, however, when in a workforce of 50 million employees 15 million are unemployed. That is an *issue*. It is misguided to seek the solution to that issue within the range of opportunities available to any one (or other) individual, for

> the very structure of opportunities has collapsed. Both the correct statement of the problem and the range of possible solutions require us to consider the economic and political institutions of the society, and not merely the personal situation and character of a scatter of individuals.[42]

Similarly, marriage. A particular man and woman may experience personal troubles within their marriage. When, however, there is a divorce rate during the first four years of marriage of 250 out of every 1000 attempts, 'this is an indication of a structural issue having to do with the institution of marriage and the family and other institutions that bear upon them'.[43]

We may now advance from Mills' distinction between 'personal troubles of milieux' and 'public issues of social structure' toward a clearer understanding of the political in relation to the personal. This requires three things. First, we must broaden our concern from the essentially negative focus on troubles and issues (although these are both highly important and illustrative) to human *experience* more generally: i.e., private/personal and public experience alike. Second, we must clarify Mills' notion of history and history-making[44], and relate this to social structure. Third, we need to spell out the link between, on the one hand, history and social structure, and, on the other, consideration of power and conflict.

In the most simple terms history is what people do and what happens to them within the society of their times. Accounts of history are accounts of human affairs; of what happens, and why, in human life. To speak of making history is to speak of the ways in which humans decide and act (or omit to decide and act) with consequence for the shape and quality of human life. History is made within society and, thus, within some prevailing social structure. The particular kind and shape of history that is made within a given society is, then, a product of the social structure prevailing within that society. This social structure is itself, however, created and shaped by what humans do (or omit to do). In other words, the structure of society is both a shaper of the history that is made within a given place in a given period or epoch, and a product or outcome of the history-making capacity of human beings. To give a simple example, the institution of work — the way work is carried out within a society — has itself been shaped and modified by human decisions and activity within that society. The particular way work is performed as a social phenomenon is not fixed or given. People work differently in different epochs and different places. At the same time, however, the institutionalized structure of work within a society exerts a tremendous influence over the shape of daily life in that society; over the shape of that society's history. Work, then, as an identifiable set of institutionalized human practices and relationships within a given society, is both a product (or outcome) and a shaper of history. Likewise, the institutionalized structure of decision-making processes — for example, parliamentary democracy — is both an historical product and a shaper of the history that is made within a society and epoch in which people see themselves as making their most important decisions and policies through the practices and relationships of parliamentary procedure. When Mills refers to 'an historical society as a whole', he means, then, the total structure of all such social institutions (as work, parliamentary process, family, etc.), which are *historical* in that people have shaped them in the course of living social lives and they in turn have shaped the lives that people live within them. In short, to make history is to play an active part in shaping social institutions which, in turn, shape daily life and what people do and become.

Mills' example of large scale unemployment can be approached as an historically-created structural phenomenon. That fact of contemporary history which is (in the example) large scale unemployment, is at the same time a fact of so many personal biographies: the biographies of those 15 million unemployed. The historical fact itself results from decisions, actions, processes, etc., occurring within the social structure — within, specifically, the institutional arrangements of work, government, and the wider economy. Personal and public experiences of unemployment here are *structural* outcomes or consequences.[45]

Having located human experience — personal and public — within its historically-created structural context, we can now move directly to politics and the political. Politics, I suggest, pertains to the operation, exercise, and distribution of power — and the contest or struggle for power — within the social structure; which shapes human life within a society, having consequences for the interests and life possibilities of its members. It incorporates power expressed in more or less conscious action and decision-making within existing social structure which influences what people do and become, as well as the use of power to change — in significant ways — the social structure itself, and thereby produce consequent changes in human life. It also incorporates power expressed in the form of (often hidden) mechanisms operating to produce systematic or patterned consequences for different groups of human beings pursuing their interests and goals within daily life. This needs some elaboration.

When we consider large scale unemployment two facts about its structured character are readily apparent. First, it is structural in the sense that it arises out of changes, decisions, policies, and wider processes occurring within the social structure (for example, within a capitalist economy). These changes and their structural consequences may be more or less planned, calculated, foreseeable, anticipated, etc. Some are entirely deliberate and controlled; others much less so. Secondly, unemployment is often structured in the further sense that it is patterned rather than random and haphazard. At the level of biography, unemployment may tend to happen to some people rather than others; to affect systematically some groups or strata rather than others.

Take the case of women within societies like our own during times of economic recession. Where economic circumstances put men and women into competition for scarce employment opportunities, it is common to find mechanisms at work within the social structure — that is, within the institutions of social life — which systematically enhance the probability of men retaining work and women losing it. These mechanisms range from the overt policies of employers to retain men rather than women under conditions of equal pay for equal work, through to the more subtle operation of ideology: for example, a resurgence of belief that a woman's place is in the home, or of talk about the crisis facing the family as a consequence of both parents working, etc. Where the outcome of disproportionate female unemployment (underemployment, relegation to low status work, etc.) can be explained in terms of such mechanisms working systematically against women, we may talk of the operation of structural power — even though the mechanisms in question may largely be the hidden, often unconsciously-held ideologies of patriarchy. Structural power, in other words, goes far beyond the more or less overt processes of decision-making, planned action, and conscious policy formation, within the institutional structure of society. It also, and crucially, subsumes the functioning of ideological systems which produces systematic or patterned outcomes within the history that is made in that society. Much structural power *is* tangible, observable, consciously employed, and readily understood. Much, however, is intangible, largely hidden, unconsciously operated, and extremely difficult to recognize, let alone understand.[46]

Staying with our example, to speak of unemployment (or underemployment, marginalized employment, etc.) here as being a political rather than a personal matter is to identify it as a consequence of the operation, exercise and distribution of structural power, and not as a reflection of so many attributes of individuals. Likewise, to the extent that men and women — and their respective interests — are brought thus into conflict within the sphere of work, this conflict may be described as political: since it reflects underlying structural factors and processes rather than a confrontation or struggle between particular personalities — although, of course, in specific cases of competition for work in order to promote personal interests, particular personalities *are* in conflict. Such conflicts are, nonetheless, properly understood as political to the extent that they reflect the deeper workings of *structural* power.

When we speak, then, of politics as a (distinctive) field of inquiry, we refer to investigation into the nexus of power, social structure, and the process of making history. *Political* inquiry examines the location, distribution, and effect of structurally expressed power. It also identifies and examines the many means through which power operates within the social structure. As we have seen these include overt mechanisms, such as the creation of official positions of power and formal procedures of decision-making, as well as more hidden factors, such as the operation of ideologies — or systems of beliefs and lived practices which effectively direct the routines of daily life along some lines rather than others, and which facilitate and maintain certain modes of decision-making and control rather than others.[47] Identifying the various interests that are promoted or negated (and how) by the exercise of power within the social structure also comprises an important dimension of political inquiry.

There is, in addition, a central political concern with how power is distributed within the social structure. As a matter of fact, access to the means of power and decision-making by which history is created and personal experiences shaped, is far from equally distributed among individuals and groups within our society. As Mills puts it, humans are free to make history, but some humans are much freer than others.[48] Some people have much greater access than others to structural power. Patterns of differential power can be discerned within the social structure, and power 'elites' identified. Such power elites are obviously better placed to promote their own interests — through the history that is created — than are subordinate groups. This is not simply a matter of politicians or 'big business' having greater access to effective power than the average citizen or the unemployed — although it certainly *is* that. In addition, the view of politics and the political emerging here points towards such unequal patterns of power as exist between, for example, male and female — where social relations and ideologies of patriarchy are in evidence — and between black and white — where racist social relations and ideologies obtain. Increasingly, theorists who adopt something like the present account of politics identify structured power differentials — and, hence, structured inequalities in the capacity to shape or govern the nature, direction, and quality of human life — across cultural, racial, ethnic, and sex-gender lines, as well as across lines of social class. As Apple states it: 'society is structurally unequal, and this inequality by race, gender, and class *is* truly structural'.[49]

It is possible now to clarify the relationship between the political and the
sonal, with reference to examples offered earlier. We may first consider
\ael's example of disagreement between husband and wife over whether to

spend money saved on a washing machine or a carpet. He regards it as absurd to see this as an instance of political conflict. Rather, it is a form of *social* conflict: personal or domestic. The argument I have just presented, however, suggests that it is misleading to carve up human life into self-contained pockets such that the personal or the domestic can be rigidly separated from the political. The ideas advanced by Mills positively challenge us to consider how, and the extent to which, the political infuses or penetrates the personal.

There is, in fact, a very important political dimension to the disagreement over washing machine versus carpet. Consider the situation in terms of the relationship within the family in a patriarchal society between power, money and gender. Let us assume that in the family in question the husband works for a wage while his wife stays at home taking care of domestic chores and the children. While both work to maintain the home and family, the wife's work is not recognized with a wage, and so she is economically dependent upon her husband. The husband's wage confers upon him power within the family which his wife lacks: namely, the 'right' to the final say over how the family income will be spent, and even the option of withholding this income from his wife altogether. In contesting whether to buy a washing machine or a carpet, both wife and husband are (at least tacitly) aware that, whatever the final decision, it is ultimately made with the *husband's* consent. The fact that this reality of differential power is *structured* by institutionalized social relations — within the economy and the family — gives a political dimension to the situation in this example.[50] The more obviously personal dimension here includes such variables as whether the parties argue over washing machines versus carpets or, say, stereo speakers versus a puppy; whether these sorts of disagreements typically arise after the husband has been drinking or after the wife has had a night out with her friends, and such like.

Similar comments apply to the example of conflict between a parent and a child over what kind of material the child is allowed to read. The political dimension here pertains to the exercise of structural power: for example, power relations between parent and child based on the assumption that within the family parents have the power — indeed, the duty — to make responsible decisions in areas concerning the 'healthy' or proper development of their children, and that their responsibility here extends to controlling such things as what their children read. In some cases this may even involve parents ensuring that children's reading complies with legal restrictions (for example, by age) on certain material. Insofar as the conflict between parent and child here reflects institutionalized practices, norms, and expectations, about roles and responsibilities within the family — related, for instance, to ruling notions of what it means for children to grow into good citizens, with socially acceptable tastes and purposes — we may properly speak of a political dimension in this case. Where the conflict arises because, say, the parent is simply feeling obstructive, or happens to detest a certain popular children's author, we may identify a more obviously personal dimension.

The important point is that the political is tied to the role and use of power (and any consequent emergence of conflict) within the social structure which patterns human life within a society; thereby shaping the historical contours of life in that society. Consequently, while the wider view of politics and the political described by Raphael properly focuses on power and conflict, it errs in failing to specify the power in question as being distinctively structural.

Politics as State Jurisdiction: A Critique

Raphael is correct in identifying the State and state jurisdiction as important elements of political life, for these certainly comprise the *formal* dimension of politics.[51] In suggesting, however, that the political comprises an entirely distinct sphere from the social, and in arguing that it is to be defined by reference explicitly and solely to the State, Raphael both distorts and artificially restricts our understanding of politics as a field of inquiry. To make good these charges it is necessary to expand some comments advanced in the previous section. The comments in question relate to the alleged differential access of identifiable social groupings to structural power, and the implications such differentials may have for the interests of those within various groupings.

My position here is based upon acceptance of four points which need to be made explicit. Some of these are not at all contentious. Others may be more controversial. Rather than argue for them in detail here, however, I will leave it to the argument of the book as a whole to expand and confirm them. To begin with, I accept that society[52] is made up of persons all of whom have interests. By 'interests' here I mean things that are important or necessary for people's well-being or welfare, rather than pursuits or ends they just happen to be interested in.[53]

Next, I accept that various interest groups can be identified within society. A given interest group can be defined as such along either or both of two dimensions:

    (i)   a shared view of what they deem to be in their interests, or in the interests of people at large;

    (ii) a common social base from which they may pursue or seek to promote their interests.

A homeschooling lobby, demanding exemption from compulsory school attendance by their children and spanning diverse socio-economic, ethnic and religious backgrounds, is an example of (i), as is a broad-based lobby for prohibition, or for free tertiary education, or for lower teacher-pupil ratios. Interest groups identified solely by gender, race, or class, without reference to shared conceptions of what is in their interests as a group — i.e., women as such, Maori as such, employers as such — are examples of (ii). Interest groups defined in terms of both (i) and (ii) include: women seeking for all women the right to equal pay for equal work, or for paid maternity leave with guaranteed right of re-entry to the work force; Aboriginals pursuing land rights; workers pressing for better working conditions and increased wages.

I further accept that certain interest groups discernible within contemporary society are inescapably in conflict with others. That is, competing interest groups exist in the sense that interests of the one can only be promoted at the expense of promoting interests of the other. For example, in New Zealand the wish of the Ngaati Whaatua tribe[54] to regain control of land at Bastion Point has set them in conflict with successive governments (the Crown), as well as with the interests of several groups who stand to benefit from disposal of that land by the Crown. The Ngaati Whaatua claim that Maori land in the Bastion Point area was progressively alienated from them between 1859 and 1951. Since 1976 they have mounted a sustained campaign involving protest, physical occupation of Bastion Point, and legal petition, in an attempt to secure return of land to the tribe. This is but a single instance of a long-standing and deep-seated conflict between two competing forces, each with their own espoused interests, world-views, and ideologies centering on land: the indigenous Maori people of Aotearoa[55], for whom control of tribal land is absolutely essential to preserving and enhancing the culture of the tribe; and the tradition of the (Pakeha) colonists in which land is perceived as capital and property, and the right to acquire and dispose of land in accordance with legal procedures (established within *their* historical and cultural tradition) is regarded as basic and inalienable.

Marxist theory actually goes so far as to seek an understanding and explanation of the entire historical process in terms of conflict between competing interest groups — in the form of antagonistic social classes created by the prevailing mode of production. Each class is seen as striving to secure its own interests which, in turn, necessarily involves undermining the interests of the opposing group. According to Harris, lurking at the heart of what appears to be a cohesive capitalist society is 'basic antagonism manifesting itself in constant struggle between two opposed classes': capitalists and workers[56]. Again, feminist theory takes it as axiomatic that within a patriarchal society the interests of women and men are necessarily in conflict to some degree. For women to promote their interests as women inevitably brings them into conflict at certain points with men's interests.[57]

The fourth point accepted here is that certain interest groups are systematically better placed to promote their interests than are their competitors, and that this is because the former have greater access to structural power — both overt and hidden — than the latter. Recognition of this has led many theorists to speak of dominant and subordinate (interest) groups existing within society; of ruling interests which prevail over ruled interests; of ruling elites dominating over subordinate or subaltern social groups. Those groups seen as systematically 'disadvantaged'[58] in terms of access to power by which to promote and serve their interests, are properly described as being *oppressed* within existing power relations. Patterns of dominance and subordination are most commonly identified within the social relations of class, gender, race/ethnicity, culture and age. Among adherents to this general view there is debate between those who seek ultimately to reduce all such differentials to a single set of social relations (for example, class or gender), or else to argue the historical priority of a single set, and those who resist or otherwise refrain from defending any such reduction or priority. Marxists, with their emphasis on relations of social class, exemplify the first position; Paulo Freire, by contrast, takes the more eclectic option. The important point here is not so much which is the more defensible position within this debate. Certainly I will not pronounce on it here, although I deliberately refrain from any attempt at reduction. Rather, the important point is that notions of 'rule' (or rulership), 'dominance' and 'subordination' etc., which arise here provide the basis for extending our conception of politics and the political beyond an unduly narrow and distortive focus on the State alone.

When Harris, for example, claims that 'politics is a matter of power, and domination and subordination', he means that the processes and mechanisms by which some groups within society dominate (or rule) over others extend far beyond the formal rule of the State.[59] We have to consider also the many ways in which, and the multiple sites within which, structural inequality is 'rooted in and reproduced by the economic, political, and ideological forms which currently exist'.[60] In using 'politics' to transcend the purely *formal* processes and mechanisms of state rule, I intend that we should consider the total context and range of processes by which some groups are systematically empowered within the social relations, practices, institutions, and ideologies of daily life, relative to other groups which are subordinated. Consequently, in this wide sense politics subsumes relations, ideologies, and practices of economic and cultural domination, as well as political domination in the narrower sense. First, however, the assumption that competing interest groups in fact *have* differential access to power within the social structure, and thus to the means of promoting their interests, needs some elaboration.

Two brief illustrations must suffice here. Drawing upon earlier argument, we may consider the case of women seeking to promote their interests within gender relations pervaded by institutional arrangements — that is, material conditions and practices, as well as ideology — of patriarchy. Given that a wage confers power within the existing structural framework of economic and family life, women may well see their interests as best served by achieving economic independence through employment — as, indeed, many have. Within a patriarchal society, however, this brings women's interests into conflict with men's, insofar as men value and seek to preserve the advantages they derive from being the sole (or major) wage earner and having a wife in the home: such as the assistance it gives them in their career, or the psychological boost that comes from having a domain in which to exercise the final right to make decisions, or the opportunity to have children one can be proud of without having major responsibility for raising them, etc. Just as this conflict in interests arises within the very logic of patriarchal society, so too are women systematically disadvantaged under patriarchy in their pursuit of economic independence (not to mention independence from sole or major responsibility for domestic work and child-rearing, and freedom from unfulfilment resulting from lack of opportunity to pursue a personal career) through employment. This is, perhaps, most apparent in times of a shrinking job market.[61] But it applies generally. Legal requirements that there be no gender discrimination in job or employee descriptions in no way prevent discrimination along gender lines at the point of selection: any more than equal opportunity legislation has changed the reality that whilst the majority of primary school teachers in New Zealand are women, the vast majority of principals are men.[62] The many mechanisms working to such ends are beyond our scope here. The relevant — and well documented — point is that the history made within patriarchal society systematically disadvantages women *vis à vis* men in the pursuit of their interests, by positioning women 'on the wrong end' of structural power.[63]

A similar picture has been painted, by numerous writers and with many variations, concerning the situation of the working-class within the nexus of educational, economic, and cultural life under modern capitalism. It is widely argued that schools are institutions of economic and cultural reproduction (although the actual processes and mechanisms of reproduction are as yet imperfectly understood). As such they perpetuate social relations, institutional practices, and ideological forms, in which and by which working-class interests are subordinated — to the advantage of middle/ruling class interests. A mountain of studies has emerged during the past fifteen years exploring and documenting the role played by schooling within the overall process of reproducing a labour force stratified by class (and gender), and generally investigating the way education functions in forming social classes and legitimating the privileges of dominant groups.[64]

It is argued that schooling plays an important role in economic reproduction on two dimensions. First, school assists in reproducing the social relations of capitalism *per se*. That is, it is functional in reproducing a mode of production structured around hierarchical social classes. Within these arrangements the economic interests of the working-class are undermined, to the advantage of capitalists and the 'new middle-class'.[65] By comparison with the other classes workers earn less, experience less autonomy within the work process, enjoy inferior work conditions, etc. Second, there is much evidence — from Marxist and non-Marxist theorists alike — to suggest that school plays a major role in reproducing social class intergenerationally: working-class children tend to remain working-class (employed or unemployed), whereas children of the more dominant classes stand a disproportionately greater chance of ending up economically advantaged. Moreover, the rhetoric of equal opportunity and meritocracy surrounding education means that schooling serves, simultaneously, to legitimate the patterned inequality — reflecting differential access to power within the social structure — it is instrumental in reproducing (see chapter 4 below).

Within explanations of this outcome, economic and cultural themes often intersect. Bourdieu's work, for example, focuses on the relationship between economic (and wider social) advantage, educational credentials, and the cultural trappings of social class. He sees the process by which working-class children are systematically precluded from achieving the educational credentials which offer advantage as one of cultural domination. Within schooling middle-class culture dominates over working-class culture, as a consequence of school culture having become infused with distinctively middle-class values and cultural style — what Bourdieu calls 'habitus'. Successful academic apprenticeship, he says, 'depends upon the previous possession of the instruments of appropriation [of school culture]'.[66] These instruments, however, 'are very unequally distributed among children from the different social classes'.[67] Whereas through their class-cultural socialization middle-class children have been provided with the habitus, or cultural code, necessary for success in school, working-class children lack this habitus. Indeed, the habitus of the working-class child is positively *dysfunctional* within the culture of the school. While other writers concerned with cultural and economic themes, provide rather different accounts from Bourdieu of how the schooling process is involved in reproducing social class across generations, the view that it *is* (somehow or other) involved is itself well established within contemporary radical studies of schooling.

Sometimes the mechanisms by which schooling offers differential advantage to dominant classes at the expense of the working-class are quite overt. While Illich claims that so far as their phenomenology is concerned schools are all the same[68], the fact is that in their potential for allocating life chances individual schools can vary greatly. On this score there is all the difference in the world between a ghetto school and an exclusive private school; between under-equipped schools with high teacher turnover and low morale, and even an average school within a middling suburb. This simple reality underlies the practice of 'busing'. So too does a concern with 'standards' in the light of structured illiteracy. Kozol notes that with increased public perception of the extent of illiteracy in the US, a concern has been expressed by more affluent and mobility-conscious parents over academic standards.[69] Fearful that their children may receive an inferior education — and thus be ill-prepared for employment or higher education opportunities — on account of low standards or adulterated courses at their local or zone school, many parents seek to remove their children from this disadvantage by busing them out of zone, or else by purchasing superior private education. In this way it is possible for those who are already advantaged to secure future advantage for their child *via schooling*, by employing means that are simply not available to entire groups of people.

Elsewhere the mechanisms of differential advantage accruing from schooling are more subtle and hidden. In a study which we will investigate at greater length in chapter 4, Jones uncovered qualitatively different pedagogies operating within the same curriculum and syllabus between higher and lower stream groupings in the one school. These pedagogies had opposite outcomes in terms of promoting academic success. That practised within the higher stream, populated almost entirely by white middle-class pupils, accorded well with meeting the demands of public examinations. By contrast, that employed within a lower stream, populated by black working-class pupils, was poorly adapted to examination demands. Even the teachers themselves were largely unaware of the differences in their own pedagogical practice. In this way a well-concealed mechanism was at work within the classroom contributing to the reproduction of working-class disadvantage.[70]

The social class situation, as I have sketched it here, parallels the case of women mentioned previously. Within the social relations and practices of patriarchy the interests of men and women conflict. At the same time, however, women are systematically disadvantaged *vis à vis* men in the pursuit of their interests: by the structured practices, gender relations, institutional forms, and ideologies that prevail. Similarly, within the social relations and practices of capitalism, the interests of the different classes conflict. At the same time the working-class is systematically disadvantaged *vis à vis* the dominant classes in pursuing their interests. An ever increasing volume of evidence suggests that schooling comprises a major context of practice and ideology in which this pattern of advantage and disadvantage is structured: in which dominant class 'rule' is established and maintained. To put it another way, schooling is a major structural setting wherein those classes whose interests are already dominant have access to greater power by which to maintain their dominance at the expense of subordinate class interests.[71]

The general point I am seeking here is this. In our everyday thinking 'politics' is typically associated with the idea of rule, order, control, government, or regulation being established within the context of humans living lives in pursuit of their interests, goals, and general well-being. Given the potential conflict and disorder that could arise in this setting, we generally admit the need for some framework or order by which interest-serving activity is regulated. Establishing this framework is commonly regarded as the central task of politics. Not surprisingly, then, there is a tendency for many people — including Raphael — to fasten onto the State, and state legislation, as defining political control. They see the rule of the State, through state legislation, as establishing the regulations and patterns governing the pursuit of interests and well-being in daily life. The State exercises *power* through the law (including interpretation, application and enforcement of law) to regulate the sphere of social activity directed at promoting and serving interests and goals. As we have seen, Raphael focuses on state law ensuring a basic framework regulating this sphere of social activity. The law secures and protects established rights and existing opportunities — so that one person or group cannot serve their interests by illegitimately violating the rights or opportunities of others. There are certain ground rules that have to be obeyed. And lest, in the hurly burly of life, some people get left so far behind that they are in danger of being unable to ensure their interests and well-being at all, the State may also guarantee by law (its positive function) that some measure of well-being is available for all its members. For Raphael, this dual role and focus of the law together with the processes by which it is interpreted, applied and enforced, exhausts the political sphere of human life.

My argument here, however, suggests a much wider notion than this of order, rule, control, and regulation operating within the context of humans pursuing their interests and well-being in daily life. This is the notion that differential access to structural power establishes definite hierarchies and patterns within interest-serving activity. It is the idea that pursuit of interests and well-being is regulated, governed, ordered and, ultimately, *ruled* through power differences pervading the social relations and practices of daily life. Beyond and within the political framework governing social activity established by the State through jurisdiction, there exists a whole further *political* framework/order constituted by the structured power relations of daily life. And it is in relation to this wider notion that Raphael's view of politics as state jurisdiction must be judged unduly narrow and distortive.

By artificially restricting the scope of politics and the political to the sphere of state jurisdiction, Raphael thereby limits our view of politics as a distinctive field of inquiry. At worst, we are positively directed away from investigating the existence and consequences of unequal power relations — as we have seen in discussion of the personal and the political. At best, the exclusive focus on the State leaves us at the whim of the particular theory of the State we happen to hold.[72] Those holding to a liberal or 'orthodox' view of the State[73] will typically be blind to the pervasive operation of unequal structural power. Since their theory does not pick out this aspect of social structure they will have no conception of the State and its law functioning *within* this wider political frame. Hence while they may focus upon, say, state support for adult literacy programmes, they will almost inevitably overlook the extent to which the kind of literacy promoted in various programmes has ideological significance, and plays a crucial role in sustaining social relations and material outcomes of inequality within daily life. By contrast, a theorist who happens to view the State from some feminist and/or Marxist standpoint *will* tend to focus upon these things. My point is that a properly conceived politics of literacy necessarily calls them out, and any view of politics and the political that does not explicitly target them for investigation is lacking. The mistakenly restrictive account of politics as state jurisdiction is just such a view.

Furthermore, accounts of politics as state jurisdiction can be highly distortive.[74] This is so, for example, where the State is seen as an autonomous and impartial body, removed from the actual interest-serving pursuits of social life. In this case, state jurisdiction is seen to be neutral or impartial with regard to the actual interest groups existing within society. As Harris describes this view,

> The State is a neutral body, an honest broker, a 'Supreme Other' which, through its institutions, serves the people and the nation, looking after common interests impartially, and bending to the will of the people (often as expressed through the ballot box). And just as the State is represented as impartial and neutral, so too are its institutions. The law, for instance, is represented as favouring no person or group particularly; and the education system, as concretized in schools, is represented as offering equal opportunity for all, and as being neutral with respect to conflicts occurring elsewhere in society.[75]

Given the account of politics and the political I am suggesting here, however, we must reject this view of the State and state jurisdiction.

Instead, the State must be seen as located *within* and actively *shaped by* the wider operation of structural power within society at large. State jurisdiction is not an independent, neutral arbiter of the history that is made within society, and of the consequences of this history for the interests of different groups and individuals. Naturally, state jurisdiction *does* have particular structural outcomes. Economic policies, for example, have structural consequences in terms of employment/unemployment, levels and distribution of wealth, etc., and thus have particular consequences for different people's interests. But these are not reflections of autonomous state power. Neither are they expressions of neutral or impartial processes. For this state jurisdiction — and its consequences for different interests — is itself a reflection of, *a causal outcome of*, wider power relations (in, say, economic, educational, and domestic/family life) which ensure that some interest groups are systematically better placed than others to influence legislation, and its administration. Instead of seeing state jurisdiction as independent of, and impartial toward, struggles and conflicts occurring elsewhere in society, we must see it as actually formalizing and legitimating patterns of rule — hierarchies of domination and subordination within society at large.

Politics and the Politics of Literacy

I have identified and critiqued two broad views of politics as a sphere of human life. It is time now to consider the implications of this critique for an account of the politics of literacy as a distinctive field of inquiry. The main conclusions to be drawn from the critique are these:

(i) Politics pertains to the operation, exercise, and distribution of structural power, and the way in which this shapes human life within society. Structural power takes on forms that are more or less overt as well as forms that are largely hidden.

(ii) State jurisdiction comprises an obvious and very important dimension of structural power. (It may be regarded as the pinnacle of *formal* structural power, and the activities of State identified as formal politics). The operation and use of structural power, however, extends far beyond state jurisdiction.

(iii) Structural power functions within the context of human beings pursuing their interests, goals and aspirations, as members of a society. This is a context in which conflicting interests and competing interest groups are readily apparent. Moreover, some interest groups have greater access to structural power than others, and are thereby systematically better placed to promote their interests. As a result, dominant and subordinate interest groups exist within society, creating patterns of ruling and submerged interests.

(iv)   State jurisdiction is neither autonomous of nor impartial within this wider context of competition to promote interests under conditions of differential access to structural power.

Consequently, when we speak of politics or the political as a sphere of human life, we refer to the operation and exercise of structural power — including state jurisdiction — within the context of people pursuing their interests, goals and aspirations, as members of a society in which access to power within the social structure (by which to serve their interests) is unequally distributed. As a general field of inquiry, politics investigates this sphere of the political: having particular regard for the ways in which differential access to structural power is maintained, enhanced, modified and challenged, and the consequences of this for different interests. As a specific field of inquiry, the politics of literacy focuses upon the form or forms literacy takes and the role it plays within this process of humans pursuing interests, goals, and aspirations under conditions of unequal power.

There are two important general points to be made here about literacy in relation to structural power. The first is that literacy has a potential role within attempts by subordinate groups to engage in political action aimed at resisting present inequalities of structural power (and their human consequences) and bringing about structural change. This theme has important contemporary associations with Paulo Freire and numerous lesser known radical educators, as well as with a wide range of popular and community-based initiatives.[76] It also has important roots in the past, notably within self-education initiatives undertaken by working-class folk in England during the nineteenth century (see chapter 3 below). The significance of literacy here derives from the fact that existing patterns and consequences of unequal structural power are not inescapably fixed, or 'given'. They prevail only so long as people continue to live within established social relations, practices, and their supporting ideologies. Once people recognize that structured relations (and associated practices) of unequal power are *historical* outcomes — that they are the consequences of how humans have organized social life — the possibility arises of consciously challenging and seeking to change these relations. This is a process of coming to understand the nature and origin of existing social arrangements and confronting them with informed resistance and struggle for structural change. It is a major task within the politics of literacy — as I have presented it here — to investigate the potential role of literacy within political struggle, and also to document cases where this role has actually been realized.

Accordingly, much of this book will address ways in which educators have promoted and applied literacy with a view to tapping its potential to stimulate and guide political action aimed at overcoming structural domination and subordination. In some cases this has taken the form of trying to promote within the very process of transmitting literacy itself a critical awareness of existing power relations and the will to address them in action. Elsewhere it has involved drawing on literacy skills people already possess, to stimulate among them the kind of critical awareness and political will in question. Elsewhere again, it has taken the form of attempts on the part of literate (and, often, *highly* literate) people to produce critical analyses of the nature, operation, and consequences of power differentials, with a view to assisting these other processes of promoting critical awareness and commitment to change. There is, of course, a connection here with the concern of C. Wright Mills to enhance the sociological imagination. Mills' agenda for social science has very clear political implications.

Secondly, we must try to understand as clearly as possible the nature and role of existing forms of literacy within *established* patterns of structural power and the pursuit of human interests. This matter is very complex. The actual form (or forms) literacy takes in daily life is/are shaped and defined within the process of competing interest groups struggling to meet their respective interests. In addition, the way in which literacy is actually used — the way people are taught to use (and not use) reading, writing, publishing, etc. skills, conditions or restrictions imposed upon their use, prevailing conceptions of the proper uses of literacy, and so on — is an important factor in determining which/whose interests are (most or best) served and aspirations met within daily life.

For example, a dominant interest group would remain dominant (other things being equal) under circumstances in which the use of literacy by subordinate groups is rendered less effective than its own. This could come about in any or all of at least three ways:

(i)   subordinate groups may possess literacy that is inferior to that of the dominant group in the light of established institutions, practices, procedures, etc., and is thereby less effective as a means of promoting interests;

(ii)   the kind of literacy practised by subordinate groups may somehow actively undermine their own interests and/or positively promote those of the dominant group;

(iii) opportunities for the (more) effective use of literacy by subordinate groups may be precluded by the absence of institutional mechanisms to ensure that their 'voice' is heard, taken seriously, and acted on. Alternatively, use of literacy by subordinate groups may be channelled into unproductive or counter-productive activity.

(i) and (ii) could arise under conditions in which educational arrangements reflect structured inequality of power. Dominant groups have, from time to time, conspired — with state support — to provide subordinate groups with education for inferior (i.e., to their own) literacy. Even where there is no such contrivance, it is possible to note ways in which the literacy of subordinate groups is rendered inferior to that of dominant groups by institutional arrangements: for example, the literacy of non-standard English in contexts where standard English is the official norm. Similarly, to the extent that education is a *hegemonic* process, by which subordinate groups are inducted into a world-view or ideological perspective which reflects the interests of dominant groups (and, thereby, conflicts with their own), the literacy acquired by subordinate groups will necessarily work against their own interests, and in support of dominant group interests. We will be very much concerned with 'literacy as hegemony' in later chapters. In such cases literacy can be seen to be itself shaped and defined within the process of competing interest groups pursuing their respective interests under conditions of unequal access to structural power. At the same time, the very practice of literacy by subordinate groups becomes a factor in their own domination; a structural factor in the elevation of dominant group interests. Instances of (iii) might arise where correspondence, petitions, submissions, requests, etc., are effectively channelled into bureaucratic red tape, or else absorbed by government Commissions, Offices, or Ministries, whose power to effect genuine action is well and truly circumscribed.

These general points about literacy in relation to structural power can be well illustrated by reference to two letters and their respective historical contexts. Indeed, taken together they embrace many of the very elements of social reality which must, I believe, be investigated in the politics of literacy. The first comes from Jonathan Kozol's *Illiterate America*. I have extracted the letter, the historical context, and Kozol's comment, in full.

In 1972 black children in the segregated Boston schools were taught by texts and teachers to pursue a set of standardized curricular activities in seeking social change. One of these activities was a time-honoured ritual known as 'The Letter to Our Representative in Washington'. Our congressperson in that era was a woman named Louise Day Hicks, an undistinguished politician who had been elected in a gerrymandered district on her reputation as an adversary of school integration.

'Dear Mrs. Hicks: We are students of the fourth grade in the Wendell Phillips School in Roxbury. We have had seventeen substitute teachers this year. Last year we had twenty-four. Our books are old, our building is collapsing. Nobody is learning how to read and write and do arithmetic. We would like to go to better schools — the same schools that are serving children of white people. Please, Mrs. Hicks, will you do what you can to help us with this problem?'

Teachers who allow this kind of lesson to take place, and who pretend to children that by exercises of this kind they are engaging in 'collective processes of democratic practice', do not merely leave unchanged the impotence of children entrusted to their care. They *advocate* impotence. They *teach* futility. They train their pupils to accede to rituals of guaranteed debilitation. The lesson, once it has been taught, remains to curse the learner with a set of inhibitions that will guarantee a lifetime of surrender: 'Ask, try, plead, fail. Puzzle a moment on the reason for your failure. Maybe the letter was not spelled correctly. Maybe it was not properly addressed. Maybe your penmanship was poor. Now it is time to move on to your next surrender'.[77]

The second example, written in the aftermath of the Nicaraguan Literacy Campaign, is recorded by Rosa Maria Torres in her *Post-Alfabetizacion in Nicaragua*.[78]

> Sunday 12 October 1980.
> Conpanero Minister of Education
> Carlos tunnermann,
> (...) Conpanero
> I can't write verywell but with the little bit I've learned I feel happy and verygrateful and I'll tell you Conpanero that when I found out that myConpanera Brigidista called me and told me that I would be carrying on As a Coordinator for me it was something that surprised me because I never expected that I was going to be useful in anything to benefit my fellow Canpecinos but now I find out how useful it is to Be Able to read and write.
> and that's why ifeel happy and at the same time Committed To our Revolution. With the literacy Crusade new ideas and new hopes arise in the hearts of all my fellow Canpecinos ...
> Carlos and Sandino showed us the way
> (signed) *Castulo Olivas Castellon*[79]

During the Nicaraguan Literacy Crusade of 1980, over 400,000 previously illiterate adults acquired the basic rudiments of reading, writing, and numeracy.[80] The Ministry of Education (supported with the enthusiasm of the adult participants themselves) was determined to establish an on-going programme of adult education, through which to consolidate and build upon the skills attained during the Crusade. It was also hoped that on-going adult education would bring skills to those adults missed by the Crusade. There were, however, major obstacles to an on-going programme of adult education: in particular, a dire shortage of both teachers and money. It quickly became apparent that if there was to be any such education programme the people would have to take major responsibility for it themselves. Certainly, they would have to provide the great bulk of teachers and organizers.

It was decided to organize adult education around small learning groups (called Popular Education Collectives), each one led by a coordinator. In many cases the coordinator was a person who had been illiterate just a few months earlier. Thereafter, they would be responsible for leading the learning activities within a group of their peers. The letter reproduced above comes from one such coordinator-to-be. It is written to the then Minister of Education, Carlos Tunnermann, expressing commitment to taking up the task of leading a Popular Education Collective.

These two letters call out issues and themes that have obvious significance for the politics of literacy, as defined here. The first provides a classic instance of literacy becoming part of the process of subordination. Members of a demonstrably subordinate interest group — black poor — are encouraged here to see literacy as an effective and proper means for pursuing interests. Such is their perception of literacy, and their belief in its effectiveness as a tool for achieving objectives, that when their letter writing efforts fail they assume that this is because of faults or shortcomings in their own literacy skills. As Kozol points out, however, the real source of the problem, lies elsewhere: in structured impotence, disguised as proper participation in processes of representative democracy. The context in which the pupils acquire and practice their literacy skills here is, then, one in which they acquire specific beliefs about how to practise democracy. But in this case the learned beliefs are positively hostile to the interests — present and future — of these pupils. The roots of their disadvantage[81] really lie in the very political structures they are being taught — via exercises in reading and writing — to participate in. They lie in the political mechanisms by which the voices of middle-class white parents demanding superior schools for their children are heard and heeded, while those of working-class black parents (and children) are rendered silent. Now it is not just a matter of this fact being *masked* by the ideological context in which these black pupils practise and use literacy. In addition, literacy here is actually being made into a *means* of participating in unequal power structures. This works directly against their interests, and in favour of dominant groups whose interests *are* promoted within the existing structures of representative democracy.

The content and context of the second letter is almost precisely the reverse of the first. The writer has confidence that despite their strictly limited literacy skills — 'I can't write verywell' — their use of these skills will be a potent instrument for promoting 'canpecino' interests.[82] It *will* ensure a programme of adult education for those previously excluded from all forms of educational provision. Moreover, the potential effectiveness of literacy is seen here as having much more to do with its use inside political structures that are palpably sensitive to the interests of the user than with the inherent character of literacy itself: i.e., it has more to do with genuine channels of communication existing than with correct spelling, tight grammar, and sophisticated style.

On some conceptions of literacy, the author of the second letter might barely qualify as being literate at all. Conceptions and criteria of literacy vary enormously. Having said much about the *politics* of literacy, it is time now to consider the nature and practice of literacy itself.

Notes

1   See, for example, POSTMAN, N. (1970), 'The politics of reading', *Harvard Educational Review*, 40, 2, pp. 244–52; KAMPF, L. and LAUTER, P. (Eds) (1972), *The Politics of Literature: dissenting essays on the teaching of English*, New York, Pantheon Books; HOYLES, M. (Ed), (1977), *The Politics of Literacy*, London, Writers and

Readers; LAWTON, D. (1980), *The Politics of the School Curriculum*, London, Routledge and Kegan Paul; APPLE, M. (1984), 'The Politics of Text Publishing', *Educational Theory*, 34, 4, pp. 307–19; MACDONALD, G. (1976), 'The Politics of Educational Publishing', in WHITTY, G. and YOUNG, M. (Eds), *Explorations in the Politics of School Knowledge*, Driffield, Nafferton.

2   Compare, HIRST, P. (1974), *Knowledge and the Curriculum*, London, Routledge and Kegan Paul, especially chapters 3 and 4.

3   GRAFF, H. (1981), 'Introduction' to his (Ed) *Literacy and Social Development in the West*, Cambridge, Cambridge University Press.

4   *Ibid*, p. 1.

5   See, for example, RORTY, R. (1980), *Philosophy and the Mirror of Nature*, Oxford, Blackwell, EVERS, C. and WALKER, J. (1982a), 'The unity of knowledge', *Access*, 1, 2; EVERS, C. and WALKER, J. (1982b), 'Epistemology and justifying the curriculum of education studies', *British Journal of Educational Studies*, 30, 2.

6   HIRST, *op. cit.*, p. 46.

7   Compare here the various essays in HOYLES (Ed), *op. cit.*, which draw extensively on work conducted within history, sociology, psychology, literature, and literary criticism.

8   HIRST, *op. cit.*, p. 46

9   RAPHAEL, D. (1970), *Problems of Political Philosophy*, London, MacMillan, chapter 2

10   *Ibid.*, p. 27.

11   *Ibid.*, p. 30.

12   *Ibid.*, p. 27.

13   Compare *ibid.*, p. 32 and p. 39.

14   *Ibid.*, p. 33.

15   *Ibid.*, p. 46.

16   *Ibid.*, p. 48.

17   *Ibid.*

18   That is, the State's negative and positive functions respectively.

19   RAPHAEL, *op. cit.*, p. 50.

20   *Ibid.*, p. 27.

21   *Ibid.*, p. 28.

22   *Ibid.*, p. 30.

23   Compare *ibid.*, p. 27.

24   *Ibid.*, p. 31.

25   *Ibid.*, p. 32.

26   Compare, for example, BERLIN, I. (1969), 'Two concepts of liberty', in his *Four Essays on Liberty*, London, Oxford University Press, pp. 118–72.

27   See, SIMON, B. (1960), *Studies in the History of Education 1780–1870*, London, Lawrence and Wishart, p. 133.

28   LEVETT, A. and BRAITHWAITE, E. (1975), 'The growth of knowledge and inequality in New Zealand Society', *New Zealand Libraries*, 38, 2, pp. 50–73.

29   See chapter 3 below.

30   FREIRE, P. (1972), *Pedagogy of the Oppressed*, Harmondsworth, Penguin.

31   That is, of what have traditionally been defined as (the) disciplines. I do not want to pronounce here on the argument between foundationalists and anti-foundationalists.

32   As a contingent point, there *can* be some overlap of studies conducted from these alternative standpoints. Depending on their theory of the State, or of power and

conflict, theorists working from either standpoint could end up investigating, for example, questions about censorship and/or the ideological function of literacy. This in no way alters the fact, however, that the two views of politics are competing views.

33 RAPHAEL, *op. cit.*, p. 32.

34 MILLS, C. WRIGHT (1959), *The Sociological Imagination*, New York, Oxford University Press.

35 *Ibid.*, p. 5.

36 *Ibid.*, p. 3.

37 *Ibid.*

38 *Ibid.*, p. 6.

39 *Ibid.*, p. 8.

40 *Ibid.*

41 *Ibid.*

42 *Ibid.*, p. 9.

43 *Ibid.*

44 Compare *Ibid.*, especially chapter 10. It is interesting to note here the similarity between Mills' account of history and history-making and that of Freire. Freire's work provides a crucial underpinning for my argument in this book.

45 There are important matters of detail concerning the relationship between biography and structure which I cannot address here. For example, when does a number of personal difficulties *become* an issue or a special problem? In addition, there is the whole question of the reciprocity (in at least some cases) between biography and structure. That is, a structural change may be *constituted* out of biographies at the same time as it *causes* or shapes them. Such questions are important, but they are not to my immediate purpose — which is to clarify the idea of politics and the political that underlies my subsequent argument. The important point here, so far as structure and biography are concerned, is to note the two levels and that they are related; not to establish details of the relationship. Hopefully, my discussion as a whole will speak to some of these details. I am grateful to Eric Braithwaite for raising these questions.

46 Brian Street has suggested to me that in the context of the present economic recession in Britain ethnic minorities might provide a better illustration of my point here than does reference to women. He notes that there is a structural shift in UK employment toward a larger proportion of women in the workforce. While this does involve lower status and part-time jobs, it nevertheless reduces the force of my example — which may prove generally, and not simply in the UK, to have been more true of previous recessions than the current one.

47 Compare, for example, HARRIS, K. (1979), *Education and Knowledge*, London, Routledge and Kegan Paul, especially chapters 3 and 4.; and HARRIS, K. (1982), *Teachers and Classes*, London, Routledge and Kegan Paul.

48 MILLS, *op. cit.*, p. 181.

49 APPLE, M. (1982), 'Reproduction and contradiction in education', in his (Ed) *Cultural and Economic Reproduction in Education*, London, Routledge and Kegan Paul, 4. See also GIROUX, H. (1985), 'Introduction' to FREIRE, P. *The Politics of Education*, London, MacMillan.

50 Indeed, this argument holds even more strongly when we consider that the situation described in the example might not be significantly different were husband and wife both unemployed. I owe this point to Eric Braithwaite.

51 Compare, Education Group, Centre for Contemporary Cultural Studies (1981), *Unpopular Education: schooling and social democracy in England since 1944*, London, Hutchinson, pp. 30–31.

52 That is, any and every society — although my examples here are drawn from societies like our own: viz., liberal capitalist democracies.

53 Harris refers to this as the distinction between the normative and psychological senses of 'interests', (1979) *op. cit.*, pp. 64 and 196n.

54 One of the seven original Maori tribes. Whilst in the text I refer only to the protest since 1976, it must be noted that the Ngaati Whaatua have resisted and protested land alienation on many occasions since the 1860s.

55 Aotearoa is a recognized Maori name for New Zealand.

56 HARRIS (1982), *op. cit.*, p. 44.

57 There are different strands within feminist theory offering different accounts of the nature and extent of conflict between women's and men's interests. Some feminists argue that the interests of women always have been and always will be in conflict with those of men — under *any* conceivable form of social organization. Others, however, argue that outside of patriarchal forms of social organization it may be possible to promote women's and men's interests together, without the advancement of one lessening the other.

58 I put 'disadvantaged' in scare quotes here to signal my unease with talk of disadvantaged groups. Very often such adjectives as 'disadvantaged' and 'underprivileged' mask the fact that the groups thus described are systematically oppressed and exploited — and should be described as such.

59 Compare, HARRIS (1982), *op. cit.*, p. 75.

60 APPLE, *op. cit.*, p. 4.

61 Compare p. 17 above.

62 The gap between legislation and popular consciousness can be immense. It assists women seeking promotion to the position of principal very little to legislate against demonstrable gender discrimination if the dominant conception of 'a principal' remains defined by qualities typically associated with *men*. Where such stereotypes dominate popular consciousness, a powerful ideological mechanism works against selection panels recognizing that 'the best "man" for the job is often a woman' — equal rights legislation notwithstanding. 1984 figures for New Zealand show that 84.5 per cent of year one teachers in primary schools were women, while just 13.7 per cent of primary principals were women.

63 Compare, for example, DEEM, R. (1978), *Women and Schooling*, London, Routledge and Kegan Paul; DEEM, R. (Ed) (1980), *Schooling for Women's Work*, London, Routledge and Kegan Paul; KELLY, G. and NIHLEN, A. (1982), 'Schooling and the reproduction of patriarchy', in APPLE (Ed), *op. cit.*, pp. 162–80; MACDONALD, M. (1980), 'Socio-Cultural reproduction and women's education', in DEEM (Ed), *op. cit.*,, MACDONALD, M.(1981), 'Schooling and the reproduction of class and gender relations', in DALE, R. *et al* (Eds) (1981), *Education and the State*, Vol. 2, Lewes, Falmer Press: ROSALDO, M. and LAMPHERE, L.(Eds), (1974), *Women, Culture and Society*, Stanford, Stanford University Press.

64 Compare APPLE, P. (1982) *op. cit.*, p. 3.

65 See, for example, HARRIS (1982), *op. cit.*, pp. 59–65.

66 BOURDIEU, P. (1977), 'Cultural reproduction and social reproduction', in KARABEL, J and HALSEY, J. (Eds), *Power and Ideology in Education*, Oxford, Oxford University Press, pp. 493–4.

67   *Ibid.*, p. 494.

68   ILLICH, I. (1971), *Deschooling Society*, Harmondsworth, Penguin, chapter 2.

69   KOZOL, J. (1985), *Illiterate America*, New York, Anchor and Doubleday, p. 19.

70   JONES, A. (1986), *At School I've Got a Chance: ideology and social reproduction in a secondary school*, PhD thesis, University of Auckland.

71   For an introduction to this literature, see APPLE (1982), *op cit.* Compare also the work of Basil Bernstein, Pierre Bourdieu, Sam Bowles, Henry Giroux, Kevin Harris, Douglas Holly, Clarence Karier, Rachel Sharp, Ira Shor, Michael Young, Geoff Whitty, Paul Willis, among others.

72   On the importance and relevance of this matter see, MACPHERSON, C. (1977), 'Do We Need a Theory of the State?', *European Journal of Sociology*, 18, 2, pp. 223–44.

73   Compare, HARRIS (1982), *op cit.*, chapters 2 and 4.

74   While I do not have Raphael's account especially in mind here, his position does, in my view, have potential for precisely this kind of distortion.

75   HARRIS (1982), *op cit.*, See also, BENTON T. (1974), 'Education and Politics', in HOLLY, D. (Ed.), *Education or Domination? : a critical look at educational problems today.* London, Arrow Books, pp. 9–37.

76   Compare, for example, the work of teachers and groups identified in HOYLES (Ed), *op cit.*, KAMPF and LAUTER (Eds), *op cit.*, KOZOL, *op cit.*, SEARLE, C. (1975), *Classrooms of Resistance*, London, Writers and Readers, and SEARLE, C. (1977), *The World in a Classroom*, London, Writers and Readers. Note also the countless exercises in promoting revolutionary literacy among peasant fighters within popular liberation struggles — past and present — throughout the Third World.

77   KOZOL, *op. cit.*, p. 94.

78   TORRES, R. (1983), *La Post Alfabetizacion en Nicaragua*, Managua, INIES.

79   Cited *ibid.*, p. 13. In its original Spanish this letter is positively riddled with basic errors in grammar and spelling. Many of these — for example, misplacing capital letters, running two words together, and mis-spelling 'campesino' (peasant, or rural dweller) as 'canpecino', or 'companero' as 'conpanero' — reflect the phonetic approach taken to teaching literacy within the Crusade. See chapter 5 below. Despite many basic errors of this type, the message and spirit of the letter are absolutely clear and effective.

80   Developments in literacy within the Nicaraguan Revolution will be examined at length in chapter 5, and these introductory points elaborated.

81   See note 58 above. Here, disadvantage is really structured discrimination.

82   That is, *campesino* interests. See note 79 above.

Chapter 2

Understanding Literacy

Introduction

The study of literacy has become a major academic growth area in the West during recent years. In some ways this trend is not especially surprising. There are many aspects of the practice of reading and writing — social, cultural, historical, etc. — that are intrinsically interesting and, in their own right, offer the researcher wide scope for stimulating investigation. In addition, a powerful instrumental ground has emerged to encourage critical investigation of literacy and its importance for the lives of individuals and societies within (at least) the Western world. This is the fact that during the past two decades the existence of widespread adult and youth illiteracy has been proclaimed within a number of developed nations, including Britain, the US, Canada, Australia, and New Zealand. Dramatic claims have been widely publicized to the effect that in Britain the number of functionally illiterate citizens — excluding recent immigrants and the mentally handicapped — could be anything from around two million to between six and eight million, depending on which reading age is taken to define 'functional literacy'. And since 1975, estimates suggesting the existence of approximately fifty-four to sixty-four million functionally illiterate US adults have been widely reported 'amid cries of alarm'. These estimates follow the 1971 Harris study, commissioned by the National Reading Centre, which concluded that around 15 per cent of US adults — approximately twenty-three million people — 'have serious reading deficiencies'.[1]

While heightened academic interest in literacy may not in itself be surprising, one *may* be surprised at some of the questions which have emerged as key issues for investigation. These include such questions as: what *is* literacy?; what does it *mean* to be literate or illiterate?; what is it about literacy that makes it valuable, and for whom is it (most) valuable? Many people would no doubt regard such questions as pointless; as 'academic' in the pejorative sense of the term. After all, there is a pervasive folk wisdom about literacy. Surely we *all* know what it is and why it is so valuable and important. The crucial significance of reading and writing, for individual and social betterment alike, has been a largely unquestioned assumption in the West from the time that stirrings for mass education as a main ingredient of social progress and reform emerged in the eighteenth and nineteenth centuries.

Conventional wisdom assumes the necessity and value of literacy for social and economic development, for advancing and maintaining democratic institutions, and for individual betterment. What literacy is, and what it means to be literate (or illiterate), are likewise widely regarded as unproblematic. Graff, however, gives us cause for concern about conventional wisdom here. He contrasts our confident everyday assumptions about the nature and meaning of literacy and the value attaching to reading and writing skills with the confusion and ambiguity apparent in many actual discussions of literacy. He claims that almost all attempts to locate the meaning of literacy are shrouded in vagueness, and that there is surprisingly little agreement as to the precise benefits — individually or socially — of literacy. Furthermore, there is little specific evidence for the benefits that are in fact claimed. While the value of literacy

> for achieving fulfilling, productive, expanding, and participating lives of freedom in modern societies is undoubted and unquestioned ... literacy does not seem to be well understood, popularly or academically ... Whether seen as a concept; a skill, tool or technique; or expected consequences from possession of the tool, discussions of literacy suffer from serious confusion.[2]

Increasingly, scholars have seen a need to problematize conventional wisdom about literacy: to address basic questions concerning the nature, role, and significance of literacy within daily life, evaluate different answers that have been given to these questions, and straighten out what they regard as major confusions over literacy. In this chapter I draw on some of the recent work done in this area — particularly that of Harvey Graff and Brian Street[3] — in order to establish ideas about literacy that will underlie my argument in subsequent chapters.

Understanding (and Misunderstanding) Literacy

I will begin by spelling out three widely-held beliefs about literacy which I regard as mistaken and will refer to here as popular misconceptions. Having elaborated these beliefs I will consider some major arguments advanced against them — arguments I regard as successful. These arguments offer in place of our common misconceptions the basis for a more accurate understanding of literacy.

Educationists and lay persons alike are often inclined to think of literacy as something people either have or lack. Those who lack it are assumed to need it, and ought to acquire it. Once they have it they can employ it for all sorts of ends; they can put it to whatever uses they choose. The world is opened up to the literate person in a way that it remains closed to the illiterate person; literacy produces good consequences for and valuable qualities within the literate person — consequences and qualities precluded from illiterate folk.

At least three closely related misconceptions are often to be found lurking within this view: namely, that literacy is *unitary*; that it is a *neutral* process or tool; and that it is an *independent variable*. Let us take these in turn.

(i) The idea that literacy is unitary is simply the idea that literacy is a single 'thing'; that it is essentially the same 'thing' for everyone. Of course those who see literacy this way acknowledge that there exist (significant) differences between people as regards, say, their *level* of literacy and how they use it. That is, some people have more facility with literacy than others: they can read and write more words, or more complex words, or do so more fluently than others. They may be literate in more languages, or use their literacy in more sophisticated ways than other folk. But in the end, what literate people share in common, regardless of such differences in detail, is their possession of this 'thing' called literacy. What illiterate people share in common is the fact that they don't possess it at all, or else have so little of it that it doesn't count.

The basis for perceiving literacy as a unitary 'thing' typically lies in the belief that literacy is a *technology* or, alternatively, the *skill* to employ the technology of print. An analogy may be drawn here with computing. People are either in a position to use computers — they possess the technology and skills to use it — or they are not. Those who are can use the technology for quite different purposes, in more or less complex and sophisticated or more or less basic ways, within a wider or narrower range of purposes, and so on. In the end, though, the world can be divided into those possessing effective use of computer technology and those who lack it. And what it is that they possess or lack is essentially the same thing, whoever and wherever they are. When literacy is conceived in an analogous way, as a technology or the skill to use this technology, it is possible to observe and describe differences between those who use it whilst, nevertheless, regarding literacy as being the same unitary 'thing' in the end, despite these differences.

An influential example of this viewpoint to be found in recent scholarly research is provided by Goody and Watt, who focus on literacy as the technology of alphabetic writing.[4] They seek (for purposes of anthropological research and explanation) a distinction between literate and non-literate societies, and argue that it was only when the technology of alphabetic writing — 'letters' — became available in the Ancient Greek world that we find the emergence of institutions, social practices, and modes of thinking characteristic of all later literate societies. Goody and Watt introduce their idea of literacy by asking

> At what point in the formalization of pictographs or other graphic signs can we talk of 'letters', of *literacy*? And what proportion of the society has to be able to write and read before the culture as a whole can be described as literate?[5]

They suggest that it was only following the Greek adaptation of the Semitic alphabet — through the addition of vowels — during (probably) the fifth and sixth centuries BC, that 'anything like popular literacy, or the use of writing as an autonomous mode of communication by the majority of members of a society' emerged.[6] It is precisely this technology of alphabetic writing in its perfected form (i.e., with vowels added) that constitutes literacy for Goody and Watt. They do not regard the specific literacy *practices* actually engaged in by particular members and groups within given social contexts — i.e., the various ways the technology is used to pursue social goals — as intrinsic to literacy. Rather, it is the technology itself that constitutes literacy: the invention we call alphabetic writing. Behind all actual literacy practices and varying ideas about how reading and writing are to be used, to what ends, etc., there is seen to reside the technology itself — that unitary or singular thing which *is* literacy.

(ii) It is precisely the tendency to regard literacy as a skill or technology *per se* that encourages belief in its neutrality. For on such views literacy is seen as completely independent of specific social contexts.[7] It is seen, instead, as 'pure skill', or as 'a technology/tool purely and simply': as something to be distinguished in itself from the empirical forms it happens to take and the uses to which it is actually put within daily life. Literacy *in itself* is to be distinguished from the content it is used to acquire and convey, and from any advantages or disadvantages accruing from the particular ways it is used or the forms it takes. It is neutral in that it is detached from and impervious to the concerns, values, attitudes, trends, tastes, practices and patterns of power or influence to be found within given social settings.

There are two sides to this alleged neutrality of literacy. First, what literacy *is* in no way reflects matters of social context. Literacy is literacy is literacy. It is not shaped by the facts of particular social settings. As a tool or skill literacy is, of course, used to acquire and convey (certain) values, beliefs, opinions, traditions, etc; or, used to acquire and convey some values and beliefs rather than others. And so its *use* reflects details of social context. But according to those who accept the neutrality of literacy, 'use' is to be distinguished from 'the thing itself'. Literacy, as it were, remains aloof from the actual practices and processes in which it is employed and by which it is transmitted within varying social, political, cultural, etc., milieux.

The other side to this is that literacy does not of itself define, limit, or influence the use actually made of it, or the interests that are served or undermined by its actual use. Just as it is not up to the computer itself whether it will be used in producing an important breakthrough in medicine, or as an arm of Big Brother in the surveillance of citizens, or to guide nuclear missiles, so (allegedly) it is not a function of 'literacy itself' if people use it to read fine literature, or simply to scan magazine or comic stories, or to satisfy their lust by reading pornographic material; if it is employed to purvey false information or doctrinal belief, to transmit a systematically distorted view of reality; to serve the interests of some groups rather than others and keep 'ordinary citizens' at the mercy of 'the experts', rather than opening up important data and accurate information to people at large, thereby enabling citizens to participate in political processes and wider decision-making in an informed manner.

The belief that literacy is itself neutral with respect to the ways individuals actually use it, and to patterns of use that emerge within a given society or cultural setting, is widespread. Neil Postman describes this view, with specific reference to reading, as follows:

> One of the standard beliefs about the reading process is that it is more or less neutral. Reading, the argument goes, is just a skill. What people read is their own business, and the reading teacher merely helps to increase a student's options. If one wants to read about America, one may go to DeToqueville or *The Daily News*; if one wants to read literature one may go to Melville or Jacqueline Susann.[8]

Literacy, then, according to common opinion, has no 'favourites': it favours no particular content, view of the world, habits, practices, group interests, etc. It is simply 'there' for people to use however they choose. People's actual choices will, of course, be shaped by various factors and influences. These include such things as schooling, family background, peer interests, reading and writing models generally available to the individual, advertising, popular taste, social values, religious practice, the range and price of available reading material, and so on. On the view in question, however, such factors are no part of literacy itself. Rather, it is believed that literacy itself can be neatly distinguished — separated off from — all such particularities.

(iii) While literacy is often regarded as being completely independent of specific social practices, processes, values, interests and the like, it is nevertheless widely believed to be responsible for bringing about a number of general — and generally desirable — outcomes. In other words, while it is not in itself a consequence or reflection of outside influences and does not favour/champion one set of social values, interests or practices at the expense of others, it does produce some important outcomes in its own right. This is what is meant by speaking of literacy as an independent variable.[9] Consequences most commonly attributed to literacy as an independent variable (or cause) may be categorized as 'cognitive', 'economic-developmental', and 'social' respectively.

Those who attribute cognitive consequences to literacy argue that it is responsible for the emergence of key forms of cognition integral to rational thought and judgment. Street identifies (and challenges) theorists across different disciplines who claim that there are inherent differences between written and oral forms of communication. They see written language as freeing us from particularities of context to which humans are bound within oral communication. These particularities stand in the way of performing abstractions and other logical operations, making objective judgments, adopting a sceptical attitude toward information, and developing a concern for precision and avoiding ambiguity. With written language humans can transcend the particularities to which they are confined in oral communication, and develop these several dimensions of rational thought. On the basis of arguments about the special qualities of written communication, it is alleged that members of literate societies are enabled to perform logical-rational-cognitive feats precluded from members of non-literate societies.

Literacy has also been seen as responsible for economic-developmental outcomes. Anderson claims that

> there is convergent evidence that literacy of a large minority of males is a precondition for any significant transition of an underdeveloped economy to one marked by economic growth ... Very broadly, the data appear to support a generalization ... [that] about 40 per cent of adult literacy or of primary enrolment is a threshold for economic development.[10]

Writing in the same volume as Anderson, Kahan argues with regard to Russian agriculture at the turn of the century that the increased level of literacy among higher income groups of peasants and agricultural labourers became 'the precondition for introduction of machinery and more modern farming methods'.[11]

Often these claims that literacy has a causal influence on economic development seem to rest on little more than correlation: wherein the dates coinciding with a period of economic change and 'take off' correlate with literacy levels at or beyond 40 per cent. In some cases, however, more complex rationales have been advanced — as where the idea of a 40 per cent threshold rate of literacy is in turn 'explained' by theories of the type that allege the importance of literacy for the emergence of cognitive and personal qualities conducive, in turn, to economic development. Oxenham, for instance, suggests that the association of literacy with 'a modernization syndrome', 'the concept of modern man', and the development of such attitudes and dispositions as 'flexibility', 'adaptability', 'empathy', 'willingness to accept change' and 'proneness to adopt innovations', were guiding assumptions behind the trend to literacy campaigns in third world countries following World War Two.[12] In this vein, Hägerstrand claims that the demand for education is at times an innovation which must be introduced to a society in order to open it for further innovation. 'Literacy and other new skills', says Hägerstrand, 'eventually transform social communication and resistance' into patterns more susceptible to innovation and the progress that comes with it.[13]

In his book *The Literacy Myth*, Graff lists various social qualities and ends which are often alleged to flow from literacy. These include, for the individual, self-worth, social mobility, moral growth and personal achievement; and for the community as a whole, orderliness and a law-abiding disposition, cultural enrichment, and civilization generally.[14] It is precisely the belief in literacy as an independent variable having these alleged consequences that Graff labels 'the literacy myth'. His book is an attempt to demonstrate — by reference to specific case studies — the extent to which these beliefs are, collectively, in fact a myth: that the social reality is much more complex than the simple, one-way cause and effect relationship suggests, and that literacy does not produce on its own these outcomes at all.

I will turn now to making good the claim that the ideas about literacy outlined in this section are indeed misconceptions.

Toward Understanding Literacy

The three beliefs about literacy that I have just described are key tenets of what Street calls the 'autonomous' model of literacy. The general assumption behind this model is that literacy has autonomy from the particular social contexts in which it is employed. Its character is not determined by setting. Equally, it remains independent of and impartial toward the patterns and struggles of daily life. There is no conception of literacy being itself an important dimension of social practice: an integral part of the very social order itself — simultaneously *shaped* by wider social processes, and *employed* in defining, maintaining, transmitting, reinforcing, refining, or challenging various practices and values of daily life. Still less is there any idea that dominant forms of literacy may emerge as structured practices in the service of dominant interests.

Street rejects the 'autonomous' view of literacy and argues instead for what he calls an 'ideological' model. According to this view there is no such thing as a 'literacy essence' lying behind the actual social practices of reading and writing. Rather, the nature and meaning of literacy consists in the forms literacy practice actually takes within given social contexts. Those who espouse the 'ideological' view 'concentrate on the specific social practices of reading and writing': that is, on the forms reading and writing practice actually take, and the ways reading and writing skills are used, rather than on some abstracted technology.[15] In other words, what literacy *is* is entirely a matter of how reading and writing are conceived and practised within particular social settings.

Moreover, according to the ideological model, conceptions and practices of reading and writing evolve and exist within power structures and reflect tensions between competing power and interest groups. The views people have of what literacy involves, of what counts as being literate; what they see as 'real' or appropriate uses of reading and writing skills; the ways people actually read and write in the course of their daily lives; these all reflect and promote values, beliefs, assumptions and practices, which shape the way life is lived within a given society and, in turn, influence which interests are promoted or undermined as a consequence of how life is lived there.

Literacy is best understood as 'a shorthand for the social practices and conceptions of reading and writing'.[16] Indeed, for many social contexts we do better to think in terms of literacies rather than literacy. At any rate, literacy should be seen as an integral aspect — a dimension — of social practice as a whole, simultaneously reflecting and promoting certain beliefs, values and processes. And so it is directly linked to the actual consequences for the lives of individuals and groups of social activity and arrangements grounded in these same beliefs, values and processes. Far from being autonomous, or independent, of existing social values, trends and practices, and the consequences of these for people's interests, literacy is really an intrinsic dimension of them.

From the standpoint of the ideological model, the beliefs that literacy is unitary, neutral, and an independent variable, are readily seen to be mistaken. In this section I will employ a number of arguments which are advanced from the ideological perspective on literacy — or are otherwise consistent with this perspective — in order to critique these three beliefs.

(i) Against the view that literacy is unitary, it is apparent that quite distinct and different literacies exist in social practice. What researchers should do, accordingly, is identify and examine the character of these different literacies, and consider the roles they play within the functioning of the society as a whole and in the lives of various groups and individuals within that society. To establish this I will refer to historical and contemporary examples.

Cressy's investigation of illiteracy levels in England between 1530 and 1730 supports the view that a wide range of literacies was to be found during this period. He argues that a broad distinction between *passive* literacy — comprising 'an ability to read without knowledge of writing' — and *active* literacy — 'where writing as well as reading had been mastered' — can safely be assumed to have applied in England at that time. While available documents do not provide any conclusive evidence of the extent and distribution of active and passive literacy respectively during those years, the existence of a sector of the population who possessed a merely passive literacy seems an inevitable consequence of the way the curriculum was ordered in Tudor and Stuart elementary education.[17]

During the sixteenth century a system of 'charity' and 'petty' schools emerged, outside of the grammar and private school system which was available only to those of means. These former schools taught literacy skills in a strictly sequential manner. Mastery of reading was required before a pupil began learning to write. According to Schofield, within charity schools, 'writing was taught only to those who could read "competently well", and figures were taught only after the art of writing had been mastered'.[18] This sequence was still observed in the nineteenth-century monitorial schools, with the (by now measurable and documented) consequence of promoting a passive literacy among those working-class children who attended them. Thus the master in charge of the Borough Street School in London, which was the model school of the Lancastrian ... system, reckoned that it took twelve months to teach a child to read and between three and four years to teach it to write well together with some simple arithmetic. The average length of attendance at this school, which was well above the general average, was thirteen months, enough to acquire an ability to read, but not to write well.[19]

It seems both reasonable and historically edifying to acknowledge the existence of different literacies in this context — especially in view of the fact that the practice of teaching reading alone, to the point of positively *excluding* writing, was often a deliberate political ploy on the part of those people educating working-class children. The attitudes and practices of education providers like Hannah More and Andrew Bell — in the late eighteenth and early nineteenth centuries respectively — give force to the notion of a (distinctively) passive literacy, and reveal the acknowledged importance of promulgating such a literacy among the lower orders. Both understood very clearly the political value of promoting a limited ability to read among the labouring classes, while at the same time deliberately withholding writing skills.

Hannah More felt obliged to defend the Sunday schools she established in the Mendips during the 1790s against those who saw dangers of sedition resulting from extending learning to the masses. Her response was to assert 'the political value of religion', which value 'can never be too firmly believed, or too carefully kept in view'. The social order was indeed beautiful, 'When each, according to his place, pays willing honour to his superiors ... when high, low, rich and poor ... sit down satisfied with his own place'. Biblical text and religious tract offered powerful assistance in the service of this end. After all, was it not true that for 'the rich man at his castle [and] the poor man at his gate, God made them high and lowly and ordered their estate'? If the poor possessed rudimentary reading skills (acquired within an appropriate socialization process) they would be opened to such insights, and would constantly have positive affirmation of their proper attitude of passive resignation as close to hand as the nearest bible or tract. More was adamant: 'I allow of no writing for the poor. My object is not to make them fanatics, but to train up the lower classes in habits of industry and piety'.[20] The reference here to 'fanaticism' is revealing. It would appear that More feared the potential inherent in writing for fostering an active stance toward the world, to the extent that she doubted the capacity of Sunday school instruction and discipline to prevent an undesirable growth of religious fanaticism among the poor if they once acquired the art of writing. There was no such perceived danger, however, with a literacy that was confined to reading alone. The view of Andrew Bell, founder of the Anglican system of monitorial schools, was entirely consistent with More's sentiments. He wrote that with regard to the activities of National Society schools

it is not proposed that the children of the poor be educated in an expensive way, or even taught to write and cypher ... It may suffice to teach the generality ... to read their bible and understand the doctrines of our holy religion.[21]

What was being advocated here was the inculcation of *a particular literacy*. It was not simply a matter of offering the poor a strictly limited access to (the most minimal elements of) a *technology*. It was, more positively, to transmit to working-class children a definite conception of the bounds and uses of a reading practice appropriate to their class. Their literacy comprised a distinctive form, a coherent (and politically viable) 'package': a limited social practice and conception of reading, defined and rationalized by an ideology. As such it is properly to be regarded as a literacy in its own right; standing alongside other distinctive social practices and conceptions of reading and writing diffused among other social groups.

The research of Cressy, Schofield, and others demonstrates that quite different *literacies* were required — and, in fact, acquired — by people bearing different social class roles and status during the periods covered by their investigations. Cressy comments that during the seventeenth century

> clergymen, lawyers, and schoolmasters possessed a versatile range of reading and writing skills because that was a prerequisite of their vocation. Gentlemen too were expected to be fully and actively literate. Their education normally prepared them for the business of local administration, estate management, political gossip and civilized intercourse which went with their rank. Their literacy was appropriate to their needs.[22]

Between these groups and the working-class literate, as well as among these groups themselves, we are talking about literacies which are as distinctive as, *and commensurate with*, different social rankings and their associated occupations, pursuits, modes and styles of life. To reduce the practices and conceptions of reading and writing of these elite and professional classes to the idea of their having somewhat greater access across a wider range to *the same technology* as was available to the 'literate' portion of the labouring poor, is to grossly distort social reality. In every major sense other than the biological, these people *were* different from the masses. Their respective literacies were an intrinsic dimension of this difference, and integral to patterning relations between the various levels of the social order.

A further and particularly interesting case was that of the yeomanry — 'a thrusting, dynamic group, working hard, amassing land and profits, apeing their betters, and setting their sons up as gentlemen'. They practised a literacy attuned to their economic affairs, social aspirations, and, in the case of forty-shilling freeholders, the formalities of voting and being generally politically active and informed. Again, theirs was a distinctive literacy. It was, moreover, an integral aspect of a *distinctive mode of social being*. The yeoman's literacy was part of the very structure, the very patterning, of that distinctive mode of social existence which was the life and style of the yeomen. Their literacy was a social *form*: an identifiable set of reading and writing practices governed by a conception of what and how to read and write, when, and why. It was a lived practice symmetrical with the wider life lived by the yeomen, and a core part of the very *structure* of that life. To reduce the yeomen's literacy to a (particular) degree and range of access to a unitary technology is, once again, to dissolve away the utterly social character of literacy. Their literacy was inseparable from their very social being. Cressy makes an interesting comment, which feeds directly into the notion of the yeomen having a distinctive social practice and conception of reading and writing, when he notes that yeomen

> were the natural audience for certain types of printed material. Almanacs, guides to good husbandry, even books of etiquette, appear to have a yeoman readership in mind.[23]

The point I am seeking through these historical examples can, I think, be well made by means of an analogy with work. People down the ages and all over the world have engaged in work in order to sustain their existence. If we pose the question, 'what is the nature and meaning of work?', we could confront it in a manner analogous to treating literacy as a neutral technology lying behind the myriad actual social practices and conceptions of literacy. We could say something like, 'work is organized human activity directed toward producing items that are necessary or otherwise desirable for sustaining human existence'. Having grasped the 'essence' of work in this (or some similar) way, we might then suggest that while different people may participate in greater or lesser amounts of work, across a wider or narrower range of item production, employing more or less sophisticated methods of production, under one or other system or logic of producing their respective items (for example, process line assembly versus one person producing an entire item), they are nevertheless all ultimately engaged in the same 'thing': namely, *work*. In other words, work is the same thing in the end — people just happen to do 'it' differently, for different ends and under different conditions.

Clearly this is absurd. There is no single, unitary, unifying essence of work lying behind the myriad actual social practices and conceptions of work. The perceived essence exists as nothing more than a figment of the imagination of the 'essentializing' philosopher or social scientist. The reality of work — what work *is*: its nature; the meaning of 'work' — is what particular individuals and groups engage in as their structured social practice of work. And this social practice is carried out under governing conceptions of what it is they are (having) to do, how, and why. As for work, so for literacy. Both are dimensions, and interrelated dimensions, of human life: of social practice generally. The perceived unitariness of both is illusory.[24] The important thing so far as the social understanding of work and literacy is concerned, is the actual forms they take within and among particular groups and individuals, in particular times and places. The search for unitary essences directs our attention away from these matters and the many issues — social, political, ethical, cultural, etc. — that turn on them. It is a central virtue of the ideological model of literacy that it brings us back to these matters and their related issues.

There are also very important contemporary dimensions to the claim that we should identify and examine different literacies rather than assert or assume a single unitary literacy. We find present day writers distinguishing between 'basic' and 'critical' literacy, 'domesticating' and 'liberating' literacy, 'improper' and 'proper' literacy, 'functional' and 'full' literacy, and even between different 'functional' literacies. In addition, some identify and elaborate different literacies by social class, culture/sub-culture, ethnic group, etc.[25] Rather than consider such contemporary dimensions of the present issue here, I will offer later in this chapter a detailed analysis of two distinct *functional* literacies. This analysis will be advanced in the light of my arguments against literacy as a unitary phenomenon, as well as arguments which critique the further claims that literacy is neutral and an independent variable.

(ii) I want now to challenge the alleged *neutrality* of literacy. The arguments I have advanced against the view that literacy is unitary also have grave implications for the claim that literacy is a neutral technology or a neutral skill: i.e., that literacy does not itself determine the uses to which it is actually put and is not itself shaped by the uses made of it. This belief is readily shown to be mistaken once the view is adopted that literacy comprises actual social practices and conceptions of reading and writing.

It is helpful here to return to Neil Postman's consideration of reading as a neutral skill. Having acknowledged the common belief that reading is a neutral skill, that what people read is their own business — for example, on the topic of America they are free to read De Toqueville or *The Daily News* — and that the reading teacher, far from shaping in any way the pupils' worldviews, merely helps increase their options, Postman continues as follows:

> In theory, this argument is compelling. In practice it is pure romantic nonsense. *The New York Daily News* is the most widely read newspaper in America. Most of our students will go to the grave not having read, of their own choosing, a paragraph of De Toqueville or Thoreau or John Stuart Mill or, if you exclude the Gettysburg Address, even Abraham Lincoln. As between Jacqueline Susann and Herman Melville — well, the less said, the better. To put it bluntly, among every 100 students who learn to read, my guess is that no more than one will employ the process toward any of the lofty goals which are customarily held [such as opening students' minds to the wonders and riches of the written word, to give them access to great fiction and poetry, to permit them to function as informed citizens, etc.] The rest will use the process to increase their knowledge of trivia, to maintain themselves at a relatively low level of emotional maturity, and to keep themselves

simplistically uninformed about the social and political turmoil around them.[26]

Postman is describing here what literacy actually *is* for people in daily life. He is sketching — albeit in a polemical manner — the actual social practices and conceptions of literacy for the population in question. Literacy is largely seen as a means to information about the world via popular daily newspapers, and so people practise the reading of newspapers *en masse* — with only a tiny proportion turning to social or political theory and critique as a basis for interpreting and evaluating what they read about the world in newspapers, or for seeking a deeper and more accurate knowledge of social, political, and cultural reality. Conceptions of literacy include notions of what is to be read, what one can expect to get from particular print media (for example, 'you get the necessary current affairs information from the newspaper', 'you get a good story from Mills and Boon', 'you get interesting — important? — facts from *The Guinness Book of Records*'), and what the purposes or goals of reading are (to be amused, entertained, transported away, kept up to date, kept informed or in touch, etc.). These very conceptions guide our literary practice. And our practice in turn affirms these conceptions when we *are* amused, or *do* feel informed and kept in touch.

Now what Postman points to is that these conceptions and social practices of literacy are patterned. There are definite patterns, observable *structures* of reading behaviour. The same applies *a fortiori* to writing. To begin with, people are much more inclined to read than to write. Many people who read a great deal actually write only very occasionally. And what of the writing behaviour itself? Here I take licence to paraphrase Postman. My guess is that among every 100 students who learn to write in societies like our own, no more than one will use the process to write a reasoned and scholarly critique of a newspaper article, to research in any depth the logic and consequences of racist beliefs or sexist attitudes, or to critically examine the democratic assumption that our society successfully promotes equality of opportunity — or pursues this goal as fully as possible. Will one writer in 1000 ever seriously address such themes as whether schools *in fact* provide children with a genuine liberal education? Will one in 100,000 use their writing skills to consider whether schools might reasonably be expected to promote a truly critical, liberating education within capitalist society (or other themes of comparable sophistication)? By contrast, we write relatively many letters (and those addressing daily themes are often lamentable from a critical standpoint, as perusing 'Letters to the Editor' columns readily attests), cheques, shopping lists, notes to the children about when we will be back home, and so on.

These comments are not intended as value judgments — although Postman's values do come through clearly and, hopefully, mine will also in due course. Rather, they are intended to repudiate the myth that literacy is a neutral skill or technology. Literacy is not neutral. To use Postman's formula, literacy — that is, the actual social practices and conceptions of reading and writing —

is ninety-nine for *The Daily News* and one for De Toqueville. Literacy is aligned ninety-nine to one *against* critical in-depth, evaluative reading. It is aligned ninety-nine to one in *support* of 'increasing one's knowledge of trivia and remaining simplistically uninformed about the social and political turmoil around us'. It is similarly aligned *against* critical, penetrating, evaluative, truth-seeking writing; and *for* the minimal, routine forms and procedures typically followed in daily life.

Against the belief that literacy does not itself determine the uses to which it is put and is not itself shaped by the uses made of it, I argue that literacy *is* the uses to which it is put and the conceptions which shape and reflect its actual use. Once this is admitted we do more than merely achieve relief from the gross reification of literacy involved in the literacy-as-a-neutral-skill-or-technology view. In addition, we are freed to ask a whole range of questions that we are effectively discouraged from asking if we assume that literacy is neutral. For we can now entertain the possibility that the forms reading and writing take in daily life are related to the wider operation of power and patterns of interest within society.

The questions we are freed to ask include, for example: why is it that reading and writing practices are patterned in the way they are?; what forces or practices encourage this patterning?; why are the very options that are often held up as the *real* purposes of reading and writing conspicuous by their near absence?; what are the forces and processes that effectively close off these (pseudo) options from the great majority of readers and writers in our society?; are there particular interests served and/or undermined by the widespread tendency for actual reading and writing practices to be uncritical, superficial, trivializing, un- or mis- informative, etc.?; if so, what are these interests, and how are they related to those forces and processes that pattern literacy practices and their guiding conceptions?; what are the consequences, in historical and biographical terms, of literacy practices (habits?) being what they are?; are there ways of altering these patterns in a more critical direction?; should we attempt to?; when all is said and done, how free *is* the individual to choose for the sorts of options Postman seems to value most highly?

Against this background we can raise the possibility that belief in the neutrality of literacy is, in fact, an important ideological belief. For as long as literacy is presumed to be neutral, teachers and other purveyors of literacy are absolved from having to consider what the end consequences are of their activities. We can rest easy in the belief that it is none of *our* responsibility if learners just happen to end up choosing the more minimal options, and are left to grope their way through life systematically misinformed, as bearers of distorted or naive views of the world, even clinging to 'information' (myths) that undermine their own interests. We are given a moral and political 'holiday': left free to continue teaching under a comforting delusion, oblivious to the actual outcomes of our labours.

Only if we face up to the ways in which, and extent to which, reading and writing *are actually patterned* are we enabled to consider the wider scene in which we, as teachers of reading and writing, are key characters. Only then are we obliged to consider closely the extent to which it is responsible, *or irresponsible*, to continue teaching reading and writing skills without seeking knowledge and understanding of the full and real outcomes of the literacy we facilitate, and the ways in which we might strive to gain some control over and against such outcomes — and thereby bring the outcomes of our educational practice more closely into line with our liberal educational rhetoric. An important first step in this process is to discard the mistaken belief that literacy is neutral. Indeed, it is precisely this kind of belief that shields us from recognizing and questioning our role in a process that claims to educate people for liberal and liberating ends, but succeeds only in socializing generation after generation into uncritical participation in routine practices and beliefs: including routine practices and conceptions of reading and writing.

If it is true that within our own society the social practices of reading and writing are predominantly uncritical, within a world that positively calls out for sensitive critique of so many trends, practices and policies, perhaps educators should be asking whether there exist contemporary equivalents of Hannah More's Sunday schools: that is, forces and processes that effectively maintain a social order in which interests are served differentially, by systematically withholding skills, *including literacy skills first and foremost*, that enable critical investigation and evaluation of this social order. Do mass media networks, advertising, curriculum policies and practices, pedagogies, educational rhetoric, popular taste and opinion (already well and truly shaped by these other forces), play a role in shaping prevailing patterns of literacy? Or, perhaps, might work processes that in no way call for the critical use of literacy skills result in whatever skills people may once have possessed being extinguished, lost through lack of use, or positively discouraged? If so, can we detect interests which are systematically favoured or negated by the literacies (and illiteracies) shaped by these influences, and by the effective 'swamping' of more critical forms of literacy? The belief that we can in fact detect such interests underlies the claim that prevailing practices and conceptions of literacy — and, indeed, *all* forms of literacy — are ideological. It also underlies the claim that belief in the neutrality of literacy is an important ideological view.

(iii) Powerful arguments have been advanced against the alleged cognitive, economic-developmental, and social consequences deriving from literacy as an independent variable. Street provides a comprehensive coverage of the case against cognitive outcomes. Rather than deal with this here I simply refer readers to his work. I want briefly to survey some arguments against the claimed economic-developmental outcomes ·of literacy, since these will resonate with themes addressed later in reference to literacy and the Nicaraguan Revolution. My main interest here, however, is with a line of argument advanced by Harvey Graff against the alleged social consequences of literacy.

The belief that literacy, as an independent variable, produces important economic-developmental outcomes is readily dispensed with. According to

Hunter and Harman,

> mounting evidence suggests that literacy skills are not sought unless
> they are generally considered desirable within the culture — that is,
> unless 'literacy consciousness' is the norm.[27]

If this is true there are grounds for believing that 'literacy skills follow rather
than precede development' — including economic development. In other
words, perhaps some level of economic development (within wider processes
of development) is causally significant in promoting literacy as a relevant goal
and enhancing its attainment among the population, *rather than the other way
round*. This would certainly help explain some of the massive failures of literacy
campaigns within a number of radically 'underdeveloped' countries. Whatever
the precise relationship actually is between literacy and economic dimensions
of development, it is obviously more complex than the simple 'literacy
causes/produces development' view suggests.

Moreover, insofar as the diffusion of literacy among a population does
help enhance development, this will not be literacy as an abstracted, autonomous technology. Only particular forms of literacy — particular practices and
ideals of reading and writing — will have significance: namely, forms attuned
to the real needs, interests, and perceptions of local people. Just what these
forms comprise will be largely determined by factors extrinsic to the mere
technique(s) or technology of reading and writing. Street makes precisely this
point in a brief but penetrating attack on the ethnocentric mentality of those
developmentalists who — albeit with good will — foist literacy programmes
(and other development 'initiatives') on third world people without due regard
or respect for them and their reality. With reference to the pilot scheme for a
literacy project in Tanzania (during 1971), Street notes:

> the literacy that was provided for local farmers was not ... 'rooted in
> their daily work' [although those promoting the programme believed
> it would be]: indeed, since the local farmers had no integral use for
> what they had been taught it soon began to 'atrophy' and the project
> staff had to construct an artificial 'literacy environment' to try and
> sustain it.[28]

The message here is that for literacy to assist in promoting or enhancing
development it must be grounded in the real development needs of the people
concerned, and be seen by them to have this grounding. This, however, will
necessarily make it a *particular literacy*, not some contingent application of
universal abstracted literacy. If literacy is to continue enhancing development
once it has already begun, it must remain open to refinement, alteration, and
redefinition in the light of altered circumstances, local experiences, priority
shifts, etc. Revised conceptions and practices of reading and writing may prove
necessary to maintain development impetus. To repeat, this is in no way the
idea of an independent variable acting unilaterally to bring about desirable (or
desired) consequences. Literacy and local circumstances are interwoven. We

should, of course, expect this since literacy is *used*. And for it to be used it must have a form that is usable and useful within its specific context. It was because the literacy foisted on the Tanzanian farmers had no use for them that it 'atrophied'. To conceive literacy (indeed, *literacies*) this way is to see it as interwoven with wider social practices, goals, interests and processes: as an organic part of a social order and social practice; not as an independent, detached variable producing its own causal outcomes on an external reality. To a large extent literacy is a dependent variable — shaped by the wider social life within which it evolves and is practised.

Let us now turn to arguments advanced by Harvey Graff which bear on the alleged (important) social consequences of literacy. Graff focuses on the everyday belief that literacy is a very important tool for ensuring fulfilling lives and productive citizenship: that literacy brings, simultaneously, advantages to the individual — in terms of personal development, happiness, equal opportunity to pursue advantage, social mobility, job satisfaction, economic reward, personal enrichment and fulfilment — as well as to society — in terms of enlightenment, social cohesion and harmony, respect for the law, enhanced democratic practice, orderliness, variety, enriched institutional life, etc. He takes our largely uncritical belief in the power of literacy to bring about such wide ranging social outcomes and subjects it to close empirical scrutiny, by means of historical case study and analysis. His investigation centres on three cities in Ontario, Canada, during the mid-nineteenth-century. Hamilton, London, and Kingston all had high rates of literacy — in excess of 90 per cent — as defined and measured by census, and documented records for these cities offer good data for analysis.[29]

Each town had a high proportion of migrant citizens: notably, Irish, English, and US born — with many of the latter being black. Graff identifies the (90 per cent) literate and (10 per cent) illiterate populations, observing that

> the ascribed characteristics of Irish birth, Catholicism, colour, and
> female sex, as they intersected with age, constituted the dominant
> forces among the origins of illiteracy.[30]

At this time a well developed rhetoric of achievement was espoused at official levels within the province by such people as Egerton Ryerson, Ontario's Chief Superintendent of Education. Literacy was widely acclaimed as necessary, and even sufficient, to enable those who possessed it to overcome ascribed handicaps and achieve social mobility. Literacy, it was claimed, was not merely instrumental in overcoming inherited economic disadvantage. It would also enable individuals to overcome 'other ascribed characteristics, including those stemming from ethnic origins, family and class backgrounds, and sometimes sex and race'.[31]

To test for the alleged 'personal benefits' outcome of literacy Graff compares the literate and illiterate populations in terms of occupation and income level (the most readily measurable forms of benefit) for the year 1861. He also adds a temporal dimension to the argument by assessing the fortunes ten years on (i.e., in 1871) of those illiterate adults who remained in the one town, and also considers the economic fates of their children. His findings suggest that there is no basis for the view that literacy functions as an independent variable to bring about personal benefits in occupational and economic terms.

He finds that many literate workers shared occupations with illiterate folk — indeed, 75 per cent of unskilled labourers and 93 per cent of semi-skilled workers were literate. On the other hand, almost 20 per cent of illiterate males obtained artisan or skilled work across a wide range of occupations. Moreover, some illiterate adults actually found work within commercial, clerical, and professional pursuits. For many adults, then, being literate provided them with no advantage over others who were illiterate. In fact, significant numbers of illiterate adults actually enjoyed occupational advantage over their literate peers. This advantage was almost entirely the result of ascription: especially the fact of being English and Protestant. More than 50 per cent of illiterate English Protestant males obtained skilled or non-manual work. By contrast, for many Irish Catholics, women generally, and Blacks,

> the achievement of education brought no occupational rewards at all; inherited factors cancelled the potential of advancement through literacy.[32]

The significance of literacy for personal benefit was small, if not negligible, here. Graff claims that the one context in which being illiterate was a disadvantage and being literate an advantage in occupational terms was where an individual *already had* the 'right' ascribed characteristics. Illiteracy seems to have imposed an important barrier against an English Protestant moving upward into skilled labour; but its significance for an Irish Catholic was virtually non-existent. Substantially the same patterns are reflected in income levels. Where being literate *did* intersect with higher income — for example, in gaining skilled work which brought with it higher pay, plus the fact that literate skilled workers earned more than illiterate skilled workers — the major factor operating seems again to have been ascribed characteristics.

Adding the temporal dimension makes no real difference to the overall picture. Ten years later, illiterate adults who had stayed in the same town revealed some modest success in improving their occupational status, wealth, and ownership of property — despite the fact that emerging industrialization might have been expected to call for enhanced skills (including literacy skills) in order to maintain one's occupational standing and economic level, let alone improve it. Illiteracy seems not to have been a disadvantage in these terms to adults who had learned to 'read' their city through experience. Interestingly, by 1871 not a single illiterate English Protestant in the sample remained poor. All had achieved what Graff calls a middle-class economic standing. By contrast, many literate Irish, Catholics, and Blacks remained poor. A generation on, many literate sons of illiterate fathers enjoyed some measurable mobility over them. Even so, these sons remained within the working-class itself. They moved upward relative to their fathers, but only *within* the working-class. Interclass mobility, says Graff, was 'quite exceptional ... literacy and education did not have *that* kind of impact on the social structure.'[33] In brief, Graff's study suggests that, with regard to personal benefit (defined in quantifiable terms), 'literacy's role was neither as simple nor as direct as contemporary opinion would predict'. There is no basis to be found here for the belief that the role of literacy is 'central and deterministic ... a requirement, in fact, of development ... in respect of individuals'. Far from operating as an independent factor, let alone a major determining factor,

> literacy interacted with ethnicity, age, occupation, wealth, adjustment, and family organization, reinforcing and mediating the primary social processes that ordered the population, rather than determining their influences.[34]

What, then, of the alleged consequences of literacy as an independent variable for society more generally? Graff proceeds here by identifying the social benefits that were explicitly sought by those people who promoted education and literacy in mid-nineteenth century Ontario, and considers the nature and role of literacy in relation to achieving these benefits. Once again his argument suggests that literacy did *not* function as an independent causal factor in the achievement of social benefits. Rather, it functioned as an integrated and highly conditioned component within a very complex process of schooling. When examining literacy in relation to occupation and income, Graff found it impossible to isolate the effect of literacy from that of ascribed characteristics where literate workers did well or improved their circumstances. Similarly, when examining literacy in relation to achieving social goals Graff finds it impossible to isolate the operation of literacy from that of, say, the process of maintaining control in the school. Moreover, he finds that school literacy — the literacy transmitted in school — cannot be understood as a pure skill or technology. Rather it can only be understood as a complex *form*, conditioned and shaped by a 'hidden' curriculum, a definite pedagogy, sector interests, and a valuative position consistent with those sector interests. Far from being an independent variable, the school literacy of working-class youth in Ontario was very much a dependent, conditioned variable.

Three closely related themes run through Graff's argument pertaining to the alleged social consequences of literacy.

(i) Promoting literacy for its own sake, or for whatever ends the individual might choose to employ it, was never on the agenda of those who advocated mass schooling for universal literacy in nineteenth-century Ontario. Indeed, 'literacy alone ... — that is, isolated from its moral basis — was feared as potentially subversive'.[35] *The Christian Guardian* stressed the need to control the use of literacy, in school and home alike. 'No part of education is of greater importance than the selection of proper books'. Especially feared were 'exciting books of fiction', along with the works of such authors as Tom Paine and Voltaire. *The Christian Guardian* insisted that novels be proscribed for young and unmarried women. A religious newspaper was recommended for the needs of all — especially of poor families. The Bible was seen as the best of all possible literature for guiding the new social order. The views of the *Guardian* assume special significance when it is known that Ryerson edited that paper before becoming Education Superintendent.

(ii) A schooling based upon literacy was seen as important for efficiently adjusting working-class children to the social order and for establishing a hegemony attuned to the emerging industrial capitalist society.

> The literacy of properly schooled, *morally restrained* men and women represented the object of the school promoters. As Susan Houston summarizes, 'The campaign against ignorance (and the mandate of the school system) encompassed more than reading; illiteracy was deplored, but more as a visible sign of that other ignorance that was the root of personal and social deviance', and a threat to the emerging capitalist order.[36]

In other words, it was the achievement of 'moral' development and social control, to be effected through school learning, discipline and order, *mediated by literacy* (since literacy is the inevitable medium of education within a print society), that underlay the strong commitment of the school promoters to ensuring universal literacy.

Ryerson's own view was that education should promote principles, habits, and character, in an apprenticeship for life and eternity. Christian duties and discipline were to be central in education. After all,

> high intellectual and physical accomplishments may be associated with deep moral and public debasement. It is the cultivation of [our] moral powers and feelings which forms the basis of social order and the vital fluid of social happiness.[37]

Literacy was to be the medium of an educational process leading to correct moral development and the growth of discipline and social control. The morality in question would be a shared morality — a morality common to all social classes, drawing them together in social cohesion. It would simultaneously shape a responsible, obedient workforce, and mask the conflicting interests of different classes within the social order by uniting them under a common conception (ideology) of a benign society functioning in the interests of all equally. In Graff's words,

> Community and oneness, the basis for cohesion and hegemony, would be well advanced in common and correct schooling. The classes — rich and poor alike — would share habits and values once more, respect one another, and the lower-class would become respectable and self-respecting. Of course, neither the social classes nor the social order need be disturbed.[38]

(iii) The actual physical characteristics and dynamics of the classroom, together with the pedagogy employed and a hidden curriculum associated with reading, contrived to produce a learning context admirably suited to promoting that 'moral' development and social control sought among working-class children through education. Graff notes, for example, that classrooms were typically crowded — with teacher-pupil ratios of 1:100 by enrolment and 1:70 by typical attendance being commonplace. As a result, maintaining order in the classroom was a major priority. The heavy emphasis accordingly placed on sheer classroom management had obvious implications for the sorts of attitudes and habits each child had to develop in order for learning to proceed. Children were obliged to be quiet and docile, to the point of being virtually inactive, other than when called on to recite the ABCs. Classroom learning effectively became an apprenticeship in passivity and resignation: an exercise in social control. In addition, the pedagogy employed was highly conducive to promoting obedience, quietness and discipline. The dominant method of rote repetition of letters or words actually militated against reading or writing with genuine comprehension. Consequently it was 'safe' in the sense that it was impotent to generate a critical literacy that might in turn encourage questioning of social practices and arrangements, or the values of the hegemony sought by ruling interests. This method did, however, assert the teacher's authority, establish the values and habits of drill, and promote passive attitudes and responses on the part of pupils.

The implications of Graff's inquiry are obvious. To the extent that literacy played a role within educational processes leading to moral development, social control, and cohesion built around a shared view of society as promoting the interests of all, it is clear that literacy did not function as an independent variable. To begin with, it would be impossible to separate off the contribution of literacy *per se* from that of the control mechanisms employed, the pedagogy that operated, or the other components of the schooling process (overt and hidden) as a whole. Moreover, the idea of a socially detached, free-ranging technology of reading and writing giving rise to social (or personal) benefits is entirely out of place here. The literacy sought by those who promoted and controlled education in Ontario was a thoroughly conditioned variable. The social practices of reading and writing they envisaged were grounded in an ideal which was ideological through and through — immersed in the interests of those who stood to gain from maintaining and consolidating existing social relations. Literacy was intended to offer access to moral instruction — which promised social control and cohesion in addition to (though very much informed by) Christian rectitude. Moral instruction and judicious control of reading matter would, in turn, eliminate the risk of potentially 'dangerous' uses of literacy — including those which might lead to critiquing and challenging existing social arrangements. Furthermore, the actual literacy acquired and practised in the classroom (that is, the specific form it took, or the form that it *was*) incorporated the pedagogy itself. In other words, what literacy very largely *was* reflected and embodied the distinctive pedagogy by which it was acquired (as a rote form) and employed by the pupils (in repetition on demand).

This is quite alien to the idea of literacy as an abstracted, socially/culturally disembodied technology. It is, rather, the idea of literacy as ideological: as a socially constructed *form*, shaped by and reflecting wider social practices, relations, values, goals, interests, etc. This is precisely the view of literacy I am recommending here.

It follows from what I have argued that to misconstrue literacy as an independent variable is to mystify and distort what actually goes on in education. Furthermore, such confusion is interest serving, as can be illustrated by reference to Graff's study. For in this context it would suggest that social cohesion, orderliness, and 'moral propriety' were the fortunate but spontaneous/uncontrived outcomes of a neutral technology or process — namely, literacy. In fact these outcomes reflect the way in which educational practice was socially constructed and maintained. What is more, these outcomes were especially beneficial to (and desired by) particular sector interests. Cohesion, harmony, obedience, and acceptance by all of the status quo, serve the interests of those who do best out of existing social arrangements. Their interests are doubly served if such social 'values' are seen to result from literacy itself rather than from socially constructed and maintained (educational) practices: since the true origins of advantage and disadvantage, *in social practice*, are masked. What is really socially constructed advantage appears instead to be the natural outcome of a neutral process.

Literacy: A Summary Statement

I see the major points about literacy to have emerged thus far as these:

(i) Literacy is best understood, in Street's words, as a shorthand for the social practices and conceptions of reading and writing. There is no single, unitary referent for 'literacy'. Literacy is not the name for a finite technology, set of skills, or any other 'thing'. We should recognize, rather, that there are many specific literacies, each comprising an identifiable set of socially constructed practices based upon print and organized around beliefs about how the skills of reading and writing may or, perhaps, should be used.

(ii) The *form* that particular literacies take reflects aspects of the wider social reality within which they are evolved and practised. These aspects include values, goals, beliefs, assumptions, ideals, traditions, interests, institutional procedures, patterned power relations, etc. We have seen, for example, that the school literacy described by Graff reflected social relations of authority and control; patterns of domination and submission. These relations characterized the pedagogy by which reading and writing were taught/acquired, and within which they were employed in the classroom. And so the distinctive practice of school literacy here was *structured* around these relations. The practice of reading and writing actually reflected hierarchical social relations. As such, this particular school literacy accorded well with the views of dominant interest groups as to how life should be lived — for example, harmoniously and obediently within established social goals and hierarchies of power, control and authority — and with the existing hierarchical class, gender, and racial relations of that society.

This does not mean, however, that literacies are merely passive, conditioned reflexes of wider social reality. The relationship between literacy and social beliefs, values, and practices more generally, is dynamic and dialectical. Literacies 'act back on' social reality as well as 'being acted on'. Indeed, as we will see, some practices and conceptions of reading and writing are consciously constructed and practised with a view to transforming existing social reality.

(iii) A given literacy is, then, a *representation* of reading and writing practice. It is a form that reading and writing *can* take and, as a matter of historical fact, *has* taken. As such each form is a response to some values, assumptions, practices, etc., rather than (or more than) others. Literacies are not neutral. They are ideological forms with profound significance for how human life is lived and whose interests are most served by the way life is lived. One literacy may favour engagement with serious literature for contemplation; another with light reading for amusement or diversion. One favours critical investigation and analysis; another is entirely uncritical. These dispositions must be seen as integral to the literacies themselves; not as (merely) contingent features of them. As structured practice, one literacy (or form) *is* critical; the other *is* uncritical. They have different implications for how people approach their world.

(iv) Within a given society definite *patterns* of literacy practice may be apparent. Postman, for example, suggests that the dominant reading practice within the US is superficial, unreflective and uncritical — to the point of promoting *un*awareness. Reflective, evaluative, and genuinely informative reading practice is, in his view, hopelessly marginalized. If this is a reasonable assessment, important questions arise as to how such patterns emerge, and why they emerge: especially in view of our official educational rhetoric which stresses the importance and value of literacy for critical enlightenment, informed participation in democratic processes, etc. In particular, are certain interests served by the patterns of literacy that emerge? And if so, what possibilities exist for those whose interests are undermined by prevailing literacy practices to create new ones which better reflect and promote their interests?

Given the argument in chapter 1, the view that literacies are socially constructed has important implications for the question of literacy and human interests. For if literacy is socially constructed we should expect some people or groups within societies like our own to have greater influence than others in the process of determining what will count as literacy within that social-historical setting. Moreover, this should in turn result in their interests being better served by the literacy which evolves than those of groups with lesser access to power by which to shape social practice.

In the remainder of this chapter I will address the relationship between literacy and human interests, and consider the implications of my account for the politics of literacy. Before turning to this task, though, I want to comment briefly on the emergence of *patterns* of actual literacy within a society, by reference to Graff and the school literacy of nineteenth-century Ontario.

School Practice and Uncritical Literacy

Postman presents us with a contradiction. We 'customarily hold' a whole range of 'lofty goals' for literacy. In fact these goals are negated by the actual reading and writing practice of the overwhelming majority of citizens. How does this come about? How are we to explain the dominant pattern of literacy, in which uncritical and unreflective practice prevails? Graff's work again provides a clue here. If we take his description of classroom practice in the common-schools of Ontario we can see how the practice of a distinctively *uncritical* — even uncomprehending — literacy would become the norm, almost inevitably, for those pupils. Unless there were powerful countervailing influences in their adult lives the only literacy available to them would have been the minimal form acquired in their schooling. Whether or not there *were* countervailing factors is not an issue here. We have already seen, however, that influential opinion at the time stressed the importance of controlling literacy outside school as well as within it. Such control would have worked against the emergence of critical literacy had their been an inclination toward it. What though, of school literacy itself?

In chapter 7 of *The Literacy Myth* Graff inquires into the quality of literacy promoted by Ontario's common-schools during the 1850s – 70s. The evidence he musters suggests that the quality of literacy achieved by most pupils was low. There was generally a minimal comprehension of what was read in class, and minimal ability to actively employ the mechanical skills of reading and writing. Graff notes several factors contributing to this outcome, all of which were *structural* characteristics of the school. These include: the impossible physical conditions teachers and pupils alike had to contend with in the classroom—overcrowding, poor ventilation, freezing conditions in winter, etc.; the fact that most teachers were of low ability and/or poorly trained, and the few good teachers that did exist were so poorly paid and otherwise rewarded that they soon left teaching; a way of organizing the curriculum which inevitably resulted in superficial coverage of the various branches of knowledge — and, thus, of the content that was read and written; and the methods of instruction and classroom management that were employed.

These latter warrant further description. Inadequacies in prevailing methods of teaching reading were recognized by education officials at the time. In the 1850s the dominant method was to teach the alphabet first, and then move to spelling syllables of two or three letters — rather than using whole words as the unit of instruction. Ryerson, for one, found this method inappropriate (favouring an approach based on words). He described the method used as tedious to the teacher, stultifying to the student — 'protracted for many months' in its purely mechanical process. Lacking were, in his opinion, meaning, ideas, and applications. Indignantly, Ryerson asked, 'Is it not calculated to deaden rather than quicken the intellectual faculties? Is not such irrational drudgery calculated to disgust the subject of it with the very thought of learning?' In the rote repetition of the letters, sometimes extending to years, the intellectual side—the meaning of what was read — was neglected; obscured were 'the meanings of the words used, the facts narrated, the principles involved, the lessons inculcated'. Children learned neither useful skills nor fluency; they learned little more than indifference or aversion to reading, and with 'so few pleasant recollections, that they engaged in it with reluctance, and only from necessity'.[39]

Other failings in methodology noted by Graff include an overemphasis on enunciation — in the mistaken belief, perhaps, that it correlates with comprehension — and the failure to take due account of the fact that the style and diction of school and book might be very different from that of home and street — with obvious implications for the transferral of literacy skills outside a classroom setting.[40] Finally, the practices of classroom management were hostile to any desire (let alone propensity) to learn. The schoolroom became

'a prison from which [the child] gladly escapes and to which he unwillingly returns'. The children dared not speak or ask questions; this would violate classroom order. 'His active little mind, playing in his healthy body, looking for and desiring knowledge, is curbed, depressed, broken, under the discipline of the present system'. Fondness for learning and study were presumed to depend on the nature of early encounters with the school. From the beginning, then, desire was being crushed.[41]

The point I am seeking here is this. Given that Graff is describing something like the norm for common-school practice and pupil experience at the time, we would expect the majority of those emerging from the schools to indeed possess a low quality, uncritical literacy. This school literacy would become patterned practice — if reading and writing were kept up to any significant extent at all upon leaving school. The higher the proportion of the population for whom this formed the experience of reading and writing, the more dominant this particular practice of literacy would be. Interestingly, Graff comments that high degrees of literacy skill were not required by most people, for work or welfare alike, in Ontario at this time. The culture simply did not require it. Even among non-manual workers — in clerical work, say — '"automatic responses" and "rule of thumb techniques" may well have played a more common role than higher, more advanced literacy skills' (let alone a genuinely critical literacy).[42] What is more, the culture *did not desire* a higher literacy for, as we have seen, it was believed that unless literacy was controlled it was potentially subversive. Now it is precisely out of such an interplay as that between structural aspects of schooling hostile to the emergence of high quality critical literacy, and the fact that the culture 'neither required nor desired it', that patterns of literacy practice evolve. When faced with the situation described by Postman, we may ask: what are the contemporary social forces that are the equivalents of those described by Graff for mid-nineteenth century Ontario? I will address this issue in chapter 4.

Literacy and Human Interests: Two Models of Functional Literacy

In this section I will outline two competing models of functional literacy and spell out the very different implications these models have respectively for serving human interests. The first is a model which emerged as an official response (a policy) to the discovery of widespread adult illiteracy in the US during the 1960s and 1970s. The second comprises my own view of how functional literacy *ought* to be understood and approached in practice: an ideal to be pursued in preference to the first model.

'Official' Functional Literacy

In both Britain and the US, official policy responses to evidence of widespread adult illiteracy saw *functionality* adopted as the appropriate standard of attainment to be pursued by literacy programmes. The US Office of Education defined the literate person as 'one who has acquired the essential knowledge and skills in reading, writing, and computation required for effective functioning in society, and whose attainment in such skills makes it possible for him to develop new attitudes and to participate actively in the life of his times'.[43] In Britain

> *A Right to Read* ... quoted with approval the US National Reading Center's (USNRC) definition: 'A person is functionally literate when he has command of reading skills that permit him to go about his daily activities successfully on the job, or to move about society normally with comprehension of the usual printed expressions and messages he encounters'.[44]

While the latter statement is explicitly minimal in its vision of attainment, the US Office account — which allows for a level of literacy skill making it possible for individuals to *participate actively* in the life of their times — has more expansive potential. Whether this potential is actually realized is, however, another matter altogether. Clearly, the important issue is how official policy is in fact defined and implemented — in theory and practice. There is no doubt that, within Britain particularly, but also within Australia and the US,[45] some of the adult literacy programmes to emerge in the wake of official recognition of adult illiteracy do pursue learning goals which are pedagogically sophisticated and critically demanding. Nevertheless, the best known attempt to date to define in empirical terms what it means to be functionally literate within a modern western society promotes an unacceptably minimal vision of attainment. This is the model of functional literacy advanced by the Adult Performance Level Study (APL), which was undertaken by the Office of Continuing Education at the University of Texas on behalf of the US Office of Education.

In *Adult Functional Competency: a summary*, APL constructs a model of functional literacy on two dimensions: content and skills. Content refers to the kind of information the individual needs access to and the knowledge they must be able to generate in order to function competently in daily life. APL defined five general knowledge areas which, for them, comprise the *content* of functional literacy. These are consumer economics, occupationally related knowledge, community resources, health, and government and law. On the *skills* side, APL claims that the great majority of requirements placed on adults are accounted for in four primary skills: communication skills (reading, writing, speaking and listening); computation skills; problem-solving skills; and interpersonal relations skills.[46]

Content and skills intersect to provide an empirical account of what is required for functional literacy. For each content area a broad *goal* is specified. To achieve these goals is to be functionally literate. The five goals, by content area, are:

1. consumer economics — to manage a family economy and to demonstrate awareness of sound purchasing principles;
2. occupational knowledge — to develop a level of occupational knowledge which will enable adults to secure employment in accordance with their individual needs and interests;
3. health — to ensure good medical and physical health for the individual and his family;
4. government and law — to promote an understanding of society through government and law and to be aware of government functions, agencies, and regulations which define individual rights and obligations;
5. community resources — to understand that community resources, including transportation, are utilized by individuals in society in order to obtain a satisfactory mode of living.[47]

Each goal statement is then defined more specifically in terms of detailed empirical *objectives*. Within consumer economics twenty objectives are identified. There are ten for occupational knowledge, thirteen for health, six for government and law, and sixteen for community resources (of which nine relate to transportation). Examples of these objectives are revealing.

For example, *consumer economics* objectives include: being able to count and convert coins and currency and to convert weights and measures using mathematical tables and operations; understanding the concepts of sales tax and income tax; developing an understanding of credit systems. *Occupational knowledge* objectives include: being able to identify sources of information — radio, newspapers — which could lead to employment; knowing how to prepare for job applications and interviews; being aware of vocational testing and guidance methods which may help one recognize job interests and relevant qualifications; knowing which attributes and skills may lead to job promotion and the standards of behaviour for various types of employment. And objectives relating to *government and law* include: developing an understanding of the structure and functioning of the federal government; understanding the relationship between the individual citizen and the government and between the individual and legal system; and exploring the relationship between government and the US tax system.

At the most specific level, functional literacy is defined in terms of situation-specific requirements called *tasks*. APL did not publish examples of tasks in *Adult Functional Competency*, partly because they were revising them at the time and partly because it is 'the *objective* that is the most important element in the requirements for functional literacy'.[48] Explicitly stated tasks would be guidelines at most, rather than fixed and final requirements: examples of how objectives *might* be met, allowing for the considerable variations that may exist within the nation between the detailed circumstances and needs of different people.

To be functionally literate in this sense comprises a minimal, essentially negative, and passive state. The functionally literate person can at best *cope* with their world. They manage to fill in job application forms, having read the advertisement for the job. They may even get the job and, in that event, survive in it assisted by the ability to read bus and train timetables, job instructions, order forms, and the like. To be functional here is to be *not unable to cope* with the most minimal routines and procedures of mainstream existence in contemporary society. (Though, of course, being able to read and write hardly bestows the power to create jobs where none exist, or a livable income where jobs attained are very poorly paid.) It is, then, a negative state — avoiding failure to cope — rather than any optimal achievement, or a *positive* achievement of human capacities. It is, moreover, passive. Functional literacy equips the person to respond to outside demands and standards, to understand and follow. There is no suggestion here of leading, commanding, mastering or controlling.

Indeed, there are good grounds for arguing that this allegedly functional literacy is in fact *dysfunctional* for disadvantaged illiterate adults[49], and functional instead for those people whose interests are best served by maintaining the social relations and practices of the society by which they are already advantaged. For the APL approach to functional literacy is a potent ideological mechanism which, in its content and process aspects alike, affirms the disadvantaged in a view of the world that leads them to accept as inevitable, and to participate actively in, the very practices and relations that disadvantage them.

Three aspects of this ideological role, by which elite interests are served at the expense of those of subordinate groups — subsuming the illiterate themselves — may be identified. First, the very *logic* of the APL approach to functional literacy is ideological. It operates on the model of donating 'competencies' to passive recipients. The latter are thereby invited to perceive themselves as deficit systems, presently struggling because of their own personal deficiencies. A series of messages is powerfully conveyed to the illiterate adult by this logic, with the net effect of adjusting them to the *status quo* in which they are disadvantaged, rather than challenging and enabling them to question it. Consider, for example, the following sequence of assumptions or beliefs transmitted by the logic of donated 'competence':

1. 'the problem is within me. If I can't get a job, or the job I want, that is because of my personal inadequacy rather than a fault or weakness in the system' (such as a crisis in capital, a depressed job market, an ever-shrinking number and range of skilled and interesting jobs, etc.);
2. 'others do better than I do because they *are* better. There is nothing wrong with the "game" itself. I'm just not a sufficiently skilled "player"';
3. 'to do better I must be assisted by others who will diagnose my problem and provide the assistance I need'.

This, clearly, is a powerful initiation into passivity and political impotence — into accepting unquestioningly personal responsibility for conditions and circumstances which may well have their real origin in, say, the economic, political, and social (including educational) structures of daily life. For the potentially disaffected and politically active to become bearers of such beliefs and assumptions is greatly to the advantage of those whose interests will continue to be privileged so long as existing social arrangements are not challenged and transformed.

This outcome of serving elite interests at the expense of subordinate interests is further enhanced by a second aspect of the ideological role of the APL model of functional literacy. The point here is that the very process leading to successful acquisition of the various skills and content specified by APL is at the same time a thorough immersion in the values and practices of a capitalist-consumer society. It is a process by which disadvantaged adults are 'hooked' even more deeply (and irretrievably) into the very 'game' — the social relations and practices of capitalism and consumerism — in which they are objectively disadvantaged. This is because they are actively involved in 'playing the game' in the very process of learning those rules, skills, beliefs, and values which are held up as the means to successful participation in mainstream society — but which, of course, are in no way *sufficient* means to success. The point here can be demonstrated by building on an idea advanced by Neil Postman.

Postman claims that in a complex society people cannot be *governed*, and so cannot be 'good citizens', if they cannot read rules, signs, regulations, forms, directions, directives, etc.[50] Teaching illiterate adults reading skills in this context, however, goes far beyond the mere mechanics of controlling their *behaviour*. Citizens who are enabled to obey regulations and meet required standards by learning to read are, simultaneously, inducted into a set of values and norms: namely those underlying the regulations, directions, standards, and requirements themselves. Their consciousness, their perception of the world and *what it is to live in the world*, is shaped in this same process. And so, by extension of this argument, to attain the objectives specified by APL is precisely to be inducted into the values and practices of a competitive capitalist-consumer society. (Compare, 'to be aware of the basics of consumer decision-making', 'to know the attributes and skills which may lead to promotion', 'to know basic procedures for the care and upkeep of personal possessions', etc.). Since the minimal skills offered by such a functional literacy cannot possibly transform all — or even many — who acquire them into 'successful' people in capitalist-consumer terms, the act of engaging disadvantaged adults in these values and practices can only further enhance the interests of those who *are* successful within existing social arrangements. Such literacy is, then, *dysfunctional* for those people for whom it is alleged to be functional; and functional for others instead.

Finally, the APL model transmits a particular conception of literacy, which masks from learners the potential reading and writing have for developing critical acumen and stimulating effective political action aimed at promoting the interests of one's group. There is, for example, a minimal emphasis placed on active *writing* skills by APL. The act of merely teaching people to read, as opposed to (also) teaching them to write competently, has important consequences for 'domesticating' a population.[51] Levine argues that, on the whole, it is

> writing competencies that are capable of initiating change. Writing conveys and records innovation, dissent, and criticism; above all it can give access to political mechanisms and the political process generally, where many of the possibilities for personal and social transformation lie.[52]

The functional literacy proposed by APL actively inducts learners into a world view and set of practices which work *against* their interests, while at the same time denying them access to dimensions of literacy with the potential to stimulate informed resistance against processes and circumstances oppressing and otherwise disadvantaging them. In transmitting a set of essentially passive skills and 'knowledges' in the name of literacy, APL assists in defusing potential disaffection and effective transforming action. For one of the 'lessons' learned by clients of such a functional literacy programme is that literacy (thus construed) has no political significance. Or to put it the other way, the insight that literacy *can* have real political significance — opening up a new view of human options, and stimulating active organized pursuit of these options — is systematically withheld from learners here.

Consequently, what APL proposes as functional literacy is, in fact, a classic instance of a literacy which negates personal control and critical, informed, rational engagement with one's world. Instead of enhancing control and understanding, it offers a deeper induction into and further affirmation of that very (distorted) consciousness of daily life which maintains and reinforces social relations and practices of structured advantage and disadvantage. The irony here is that it is precisely these social relations and practices that yield (among other ills) structured adult illiteracy in the first place. Thus a deep paradox emerges: whereas functional literacy is presented as being functional for illiterate disadvantaged persons it appears, rather, to be *dysfunctional* for them, *and functional instead* for those persons and groups whose interests are best served — at the expense of the disadvantaged — by maintaining the economic, political, social, and cultural status quo. Adjusting and accommodating potentially disaffected and politically active people to the status quo is precisely what such (official) functional literacy achieves.

Optimal Functional Literacy

To describe a form of literacy as *functional* is elliptical. It is an abbreviation. If we are to understand and assess a given description of functionality we must ask: 'functional for whom, and for what, and in what ways or by what means, etc.?' Promoters of such minimal functional literacies as that advanced by APL would fill out the ellipsis/abbreviation by claiming that the literacy they offer enables presently illiterate adults to function more effectively in society, to develop attitudes and skills conducive to achievement and personal success, and to participate actively in the life of their times. If pushed further, as we have seen, they cash these values out in terms of being able to gain employment and to function smoothly within the established workforce, make their (often meagre) income run as far as possible in satisfying objective life needs, to adopt sound purchasing habits tailored to their means, to fill in the myriad forms one faces in daily life, to learn of one's rights *and duties* as a citizen, to be able to cast a vote in an election, and such like.

Now the point is that there is no necessary reason to fill out the ellipsis in this way. There are all sorts of other values that can be used to fill in the 'for whom?', 'for what?', and 'in what ways, or by what means?' variables. Opponents of the APL (or any similar) approach are free to contest the particular values assigned to these variables. They may reject the association of functional literacy with a specific population: namely, illiterate adults within societies where universal literacy is the expectation. Rather, they might argue, a truly functional literacy is what we should be aiming at on behalf of *all* people. Likewise, the assumption that what is to be provided in the way of (functional) literacy should aim at successfully accommodating illiterate adults to established relations and practices of capitalist production and consumerism, is open to challenge. So too is the idea of achieving this accommodation by means of transmitting a set of minimal reading and (perhaps) writing skills employing content and reflecting concerns steeped in an ideology of capitalism and consumerism.

The fact that a given conception and practice of functional literacy is open to challenge, and *is* challenged, in no way guarantees that a single shared alternative will emerge in its place. Competing views as to what comprises an optimal or ideal functional literacy seem inevitable. Rather than enter into lengthy debate here about the relative merits of potential alternatives to the APL model, I intend simply to identify the approach to literacy taken by Paulo Freire as encompassing an ideal of functional literacy.[53] This involves some licence on my own part, since Freire does not himself speak of functional literacy in respect of his theory and practice. Yet, I believe, a notion of functionality is entirely appropriate here: an idea of being functional, however, which has no connotations of being merely (or narrowly) instrumental, minimal, or otherwise 'second best'.

There is neither space nor need here to spell out Freire's conception and practice of literacy at any length. Details of an attempt to implement a functional literacy along broadly Freirean lines will emerge in chapter 5. For my present purposes a brief outline of how the variables involved in talk of functional literacy may be filled out by reference to Freire's work must suffice. As far as the 'functional for whom?' variable is concerned, the point to be noted is that this will be a universal ideal. Given what counts as being literate on Freire's view, the rightful possessors of a genuine functional literacy will be *all human beings*. This is because the achievement of literacy — as understood by Freire — is a necessary aspect of functioning as a human being. Since functioning as a human being is a calling for all humans equally, it follows that a literacy which enables us to function cannot be reserved for a special or limited group targeted to receive distinctive treatment.

For what ends, or to what purposes, may Freirean literacy be regarded as functional? The short answer is that the kind of literacy promoted by Freire's pedagogy is functional in respect of enabling human beings to pursue their common ontological and historical vocation of becoming more fully human, on a basis of equality with one another.[54] According to Freire, to become more fully human is to become ever more critically aware of one's world and in creative control of it. The more one engages in conscious action to understand and transform the world — one's reality — in a praxis of reflection and action, the more fully human one becomes. As human beings our shared vocation is to each become an active *subject* engaged on an equal basis with others in the process of creating (or 'naming') the world — that is, creating history and culture — rather than existing merely as passive *objects* accepting reality/the world as ready-made by other people. The key point here is Freire's belief that in creating history and culture humans do not merely create and recreate social reality, but simultaneously create their own *being* in this process. In speaking of our vocation as one of becoming more fully human, Freire means that we are to be ever more fully present in determining what we become as human beings. Each of us, equally, is to become more and more a shaper of the form our humanity takes. To live in a world which is ready-made by others is to accept the personal being that is shaped by the processes of living in that world; by the social structures that operate within that world. It is to surrender to others the power to make of ourselves what we become: to surrender our agency, our supreme (human) power of self-creation. To use Freire's language, it is to be dehumanized: to be reduced to an object that is shaped and made, rather than to express our uniquely human potential to be actively involved in creating what we become.[55] Becoming literate, as Freire conceives it, is a necessary part of pursuing our human vocation.

The ways and means by which Freirean literacy is functional for the universal human pursuit of our common vocation are bound up with its character as a distinctive *praxis*. Freire insists that literacy be acquired and employed within an on-going process involving both action and reflection directed at our world. Freire not only identifies a common human vocation to become more fully human. He also recognizes the existence of structured practices and relations of unequal power — of domination and oppression — which deny for many people the pursuit and attainment of their human vocation. These include oppressive practices and relations patterned along lines of gender, race, class, age, ethnicity/culture, etc.[56] If humans are to pursue their vocation on equal terms with one another they must break down these structures of domination and oppression, and increasingly replace them with social arrangements which positively enable all humans to participate in creating history, culture and, ultimately, human *being* itself. This process involves confronting the reality of oppression and dehumanization, identifying those social relations and practices (grounded in structured power differentials) that thwart and deny the human vocation, and proceeding to recover and express our humanity by building enabling alternatives in the place of existing oppressive structures.

A truly functional literacy is both a means and an outcome of this very process. To understand our world as oppressive, and to act to transform it, requires a praxis of reflection *and* action. We come to know our world more critically, more accurately, not merely through reflecting upon it but, rather, by reflecting upon it and acting upon it in the light of our reflection. Conversely, we cannot act meaningfully on our world to transform it into a context in which all humans can equally pursue their vocation unless we act on the basis of critical reflection. Action without reflection is not merely blind; it is also mere *behaviour* and, as such, appropriate to the animal rather than the human world. Human praxis involves a unity of conception and execution, action and reflection, consciousness and expression of that consciousness in action.

Freire proposes that literacy be learned and practised in such a way that humans achieve a progressively critical consciousness of their world and become involved in acting upon it. The *words* that people learn to read and write must stimulate critical investigation of oppression, and enhance the possibility of liberation from this oppression through a process of cooperative human action. Mechanical literacy skills are, then, to be acquired within an expressly ideological context — key words providing the medium for learning are words which call out critical themes for discussion and analysis of the learners' social reality. This discussion and analysis will then suggest possibilities for collective action addressed at overcoming some oppressive aspect of social reality. The *process* by which literacy is transmitted and employed in the praxis of critical reflection and transforming action must itself be non-oppressive: it must be democratic and liberating. According to Freire, the literacy process must be a dialogue: a pedagogical engagement among equals which partakes of the very character of humans, equally and in community with one another, pursuing their vocation of becoming more fully human. In other words, the literacy process must itself be characterized by social relations of equality and liberation, reflecting the values of trust and respect for persons.

Consequently, in Freire's approach humans learn to read and write within an overtly political process: a process aimed at enhancing our understanding of how and where oppression operates, and stimulating informed commitment to overcoming it. The learning context is explicitly ideological. Literacy is acquired in the process of understanding one's world from a particular theoretical perspective. This is a perspective which positively *assumes* the operation of structured oppression. People uncover oppression and become committed to overcoming it in the very process of overcoming the tyranny of illiteracy — which they come to understand as being itself a symptom of oppression. The literacy process itself, and the wider cultural action for freedom born in the context of learning to read and write, reflect the values of equality and activity rather than hierarchy and passivity. Moreover, the literacy which comprises reading and writing words is seen, ultimately, as an intrinsic part of a much larger literacy: the act of 'reading' and 'writing' the world itself. 'Writing' is the act of creating history, culture, and human *being*, in the light of "reading" the text of social reality through the act of critical reflection. The values involved here are, then, the precise antithesis of those inherent in approaches to functional literacy which, in one way or another, effectively adjust and accommodate human beings to a ready-made world in which adult illiteracy is just one symptom of oppression and structured disadvantage.[57]

Kozol provides an example of this ideal in practice by reference to a community-based literacy programme with which he was involved. During the operation of this programme

> at least 200 persons nightly filled the basement of our church and overflowed into a network of apartments that we rented in the ... neighbourhood in which we worked. [M]ost of us (teachers and learners both) were also taking action on the words we learned and on

the world of anguish and injustice which those words revealed. Literacy sessions that evolved around such words as 'tenant', 'land-lord', 'lease', 'eviction', 'rat', and 'roach' led to one of the first rent strikes in our city. Words connected to the world, led — not in years but in a matter of days — to the reward of a repainted building, the replacement of illegal exits ... and the reconstruction of a fire escape that served the tenants of a building of five storeys but could not be used because it had rotted into empty air above the second floor.

He adds that none of the adults he worked with in such programmes was prepared to settle in their learning 'for the "functional abilities" of bottom level job slots in available custodial positions'. Many of them became leaders in struggle for structural change, notably involvement in action to desegregate the Boston schools. Employment-wise, some became community advisers, others gained degrees from the Harvard Graduate School of Education (despite lacking a college education), and another became 'a mortgage officer in Boston's largest bank'.[58]

I have contrasted these two models of functional literacy with a view to indicating how they are entirely different literacies, with opposite implications for serving human interests. The APL model is intended to promote the work and welfare interests of people seen as presently disadvantaged in these respects by their illiteracy. But immersed in an ideological perspective which does not recognise the *structured* nature of advantage and disadvantage, 'success' and 'failure', and oblivious — it seems — to their own ideological trappings, the creators of APL come up with a conception and practice of reading and writing that can only reinforce and deepen the disadvantage and powerlessness of those millions in the US who are illiterate.[59] APL ultimately serves the interests of those who benefit most from ensuring that all citizens participate smoothly and unquestioningly in the routines of work and consumerism within a modern capitalist society. In terms of its uncritical character, the social 'benefits' it helps promote, and the interest groups to whom its *real* benefits accrue, APL literacy has much in common with the school literacy described by Graff. Both are literacies which accommodate people to existing circumstances in which the interests of some are systematically elevated at the expense of others. Impotent to address (or even identify) the structures in which such advantage and disadvantage originate, APL literacy effectively serves the interests of elites at the expense, ironically, of precisely those subordinate interests it is intended to benefit.

By contrast, the second model *begins* from the assumption of structured domination and subordination, advantage and disadvantage. As a definite theory and practice of reading and writing it promotes understanding of these structures and, ultimately, their transformation into more truly democratic forms: in which the interests of (class, race, gender, ethnic, etc.) groups disadvantaged by current economic, social, cultural and political arrangements, are promoted to a position of equal status with those of all other human beings, and pursued on that basis. To engage in this literacy *is* to engage in the process of understanding and transforming social relations and practices of oppression and inequality. Accordingly, it works in exactly the opposite historical direction to APL.[60]

Literacy, Politics and Policy: Proper versus Improper Literacy

The political significance of literacy has to do with the form it takes and the role it plays within the process of humans pursuing interests, goals, and aspirations under conditions in which power is distributed unequally within the social structure. Given the argument in this chapter we are now in a position to clarify this further. It has been shown that literacy is not singular. A wide range of practices and conceptions of reading and writing exists. Both historical and contemporary examples of different literacies have been sketched here, and some aspects of their connection with human interests and aspirations noted. This question of relationship between specific literacies and the interests of various social groups will be considered in greater detail in chapters 3 and 4. Enough has already been said, however, to suggest the manner in which and extent to which particular literacies may systematically favour the interests of some groups over others by legitimating, maintaining, and strengthening social relations and practices in which power is structured unequally. Conversely, a given literacy may — as in the case of the second model of functional literacy — play an important role within activity aimed at identifying, understanding, and challenging social arrangements in which unequal access to power is patterned along class, gender, race, cultural, ethnic, etc., lines. Different literacies, then, may have very different *political* implications.

I want to apply these ideas to Wayne O'Neil's distinction between being properly and improperly literate: that is, between practising a proper or an improper literacy.[61] As amended here, this distinction will offer a useful criterion with which to assess, from a political point of view, educational policies and practices centering on literacy.

O'Neil's original distinction has to do with whether or not a person has control over their life and world and is able to deal rationally with their life and decisions. Proper literacy enhances a person's capacity for genuine control and rational decision-making. Improper literacy reduces and destroys it — offering a mere illusion of control in place of genuine control. One may be able to read and write and yet be improperly literate, says O'Neil.

> Make a distinction: being able to read means that you can follow words across a page, getting generally what's superficially there. Being literate means that you can bring your knowledge and your experience to bear on what passes before you. Let us call the latter proper literacy; the former improper.[62]

An unfortunate feature of our modern schooled society is that 'we have too much improper literacy at the expense of properly literate folk'.[63] And yet it is clearly in people's interests to be properly literate, and against their interests to be improperly literate.

O'Neil believes the way we teach reading in school inevitably leads to many people becoming improperly literate. By the time a child begins school they have already achieved a solid basis for proper literacy. Their ability to 'construct coherence around experience', and to 'deal in words and action with [their] experience' is already well-developed. Unfortunately, the teaching of reading in school destroys this basis for proper literacy: for control and understanding mediated by reading and writing. In place of genuine control it promotes a superficial pseudo-control. What happens is that school reading replaces the child's initial *depth* understanding of the world — their under-standing of the layers and complexity of experience — with linear, surface, 'understanding'. Experience of the world is reduced to the surface linear arrangement of letters on a page. 'Knowledge' becomes shallow; instead of the deep and complex process it really is (and is seen to be by children before they are inducted into school reading). Within school, reading is treated 'as if it were another language, another world, not as if it were a highly abstract represent-ation of the world the child already has tacit knowledge of'. Reading is pushed 'into context-less space': the first step in destroying coherence and, with it, the chance for genuine control of and rational dealing with the world.[64]

The subsequent practice of reading and writing within school completes the process of obliterating genuine understanding of and control over experi-ence. Knowledge is still further reduced to superficiality and misunderstanding through the curriculum: by which the child is made to 'review what [they] already know' and to 'learn anew the surfaces of knowledge.' The curriculum reduces geography to a catalogue of names, products and capitals, history to 'a linear succession of dates and events', science to taxonomy, and literature to a chronologically ordered set of the best thoughts humans have uttered. Finally, improperly literate adults take effective control of school administration, and ensure that 'impropriety' is maintained by stamping out any serious attempts made by teachers to actually foster some proper literacy. The remedy for all this, in O'Neil's view, is to let children *learn* to read, by allowing reading to emerge in the context of children and adults talking and telling of the riches youngsters already possess. To promote proper literacy we must 'keep all the words and the world together and [children] involved in it'.[64]

O'Neil's discussion is brief and intentionally schematic. It is suggestive rather than exhaustive. The point to be noted here is that, as far as he goes, O'Neil may have put his finger on a symptom rather than a cause. There are no grounds for believing that if children are somehow helped to 'keep all the words and the world together and themselves involved in it', they will inevitably overcome existing structural impediments to genuine control and rational decision-making in their lives. It can be argued that typical school reading practices have evolved and are maintained (for example, by focusing on problems of quantity rather than quality, on remedial reading rather than promoting critical literacy) *precisely because* they have no significance for identifying and addressing structured inequalities of power and, consequently, for overcoming barriers to the kind of understanding and control that enable people to pursue their interests and aspirations on an equal basis with others. The world in which children are to be kept involved, and with which all the words are to remain connected, is at present a world in which class, gender, race, age, cultural, and ethnic relations reflect differentials of power: where access to the means by which to articulate and promote individual or group interests is patterned unequally. Achieving genuine control over our lives and the capacity to deal rationally with decisions presupposes coming to understand and transform existing *structural* barriers to these ends.

This suggests a necessary modification to O'Neil's distinction between proper and improper literacy, to invest it with *political* force. Proper literacy enhances people's control over their lives and their capacity for dealing rationally with decisions by enabling them to identify, understand, and act to transform, social relations and practices in which power is structured unequally. For it is in this inequality that the real barriers to understanding and control originate: including the power to foist upon others ideological positions which shape their understanding of the world against their interests, and lead them to make decisions to their own disadvantage. Improper literacy either fails to promote, or else actively impedes, such understanding and action. It follows from this that the functional literacy promoted by APL is an improper literacy: since it further immerses people who are currently disadvantaged in the very ideologies and practices that disadvantage them in the first place. Similarly, the common-school education of working-class children in mid-nineteenth century Ontario made them improperly literate. By contrast, those members of oppressed groups who practise reading and writing along the lines described (and practised) by Freire, are properly literate.

We come, finally, to the implications of the argument in this chapter for educational policy specifically. Here I want to make three brief points. First the distinction between proper and improper literacy, as I have amended it, provides a criterion by which to assess the *politics* of particular educational policies concerned with literacy. That is, one way of describing and evaluating such policy is in terms of whether it enhances or impedes the achievement of genuine control and rational decision-making in people's lives.

Second, the range of policies that may be considered is very wide. Relevant policy is by no means confined to the sphere of formal education. Indeed, some of the most important policy developments concerned directly and explicitly with literacy in recent years have been pitched outside formal education — notably, informal literacy programmes for adults. Moreover, it will be clear from earlier argument that a good deal of policy which is pertinent to literacy is not actually couched or presented as literacy policy *per se*. In many cases, policies addressing school curricula and pedagogy cannot be fully understood and appraised without considering their implications for promoting one or another form of literacy: for example, critical or uncritical?; proper or improper?; etc.

Finally, there is no need to limit discussion to policies framed and enacted by such official organs as ministries, departments, or offices of education, local education authorities, education commissions, etc. In addition, policies, manifestos, recommendations, ideals, and demands advanced by lobbies, pressure groups, political parties, and even revolutionary fronts (as we will see) fall within the legitimate scope of investigation here.

Notes

1 With regard to the British estimates see HARGREAVES, D. (1980), *Adult Literacy and Broadcasting; the BBC's experience*, London, Frances Pinter, 1. The lower estimate is based on a reading age of nine years, and the higher on a thirteen year reading age. For the US reference see HUNTER, C. ST.J. and HARMAN, D. (1979), *Adult Illiteracy in the United States*, New York, McGraw Hill, pp. 26–30.

2 GRAFF, H. (Ed), (1981) *Literacy and Social Development in the West*, Cambridge, Cambridge University Press, p. 1.

3 GRAFF, *ibid.*, and (1979), *The Literacy Myth: literacy and social structure in the nineteenth-century city*, New York, Academic Press. STREET, B.V. (1984), *Literacy in Theory and Practice*, Cambridge, Cambridge University Press. The framework of my discussion in the next section owes much to Street's account of the autonomous model of literacy.

4 GOODY, J. and WATT, I. (1968), 'The Consequences of Literacy', in GOODY, J. (Ed.), *Literacy in Traditional Societies*, London, Cambridge University Press, pp. 27–68.

5 *Ibid.*, my italics.

6 *Ibid.*, p. 40

7 Compare STREET, *op. cit.*, Introduction.

8 POSTMAN, N. (1970) 'The politics of reading', *Harvard Educational Review*, 40, 2, pp. 247.

9 Compare here Street's reference to the tendency on the part of some theorists to isolate literacy as an independent variable and claim to be able to study its consequences, in *op. cit.*, Introduction.

10 In ANDERSON, C.A. and BOWMAN, M. (Eds), (1966), *Education and Economic Development*, London, Frank Cass, pp. 345 and 347.

11 KAHAN, A. (1966), 'Determinents of the Incidence of Literacy in Nineteenth-Century Rural Russia', in *ibid.*, p. 302.

12 Compare STREET, *op. cit.*, p. 185. The reference is to OXENHAM, J. (1980), *Literacy: writing, reading and social organization*, London, Routledge and Kegan Paul.

13 HÄGERSTRAND, T. (1966), 'Quantitative techniques for analysis of the spread of information and technology', in ANDERSON and BOWMAN (Eds), *op. cit.*, p. 244.

14 GRAFF, H. J. (1979), *op. cit.*, Compare XV and 19.

15 STREET, *op. cit.*, p. 2.

16 *Ibid.*, p. 1.

17 See here CRESSY, D. (1981), 'Levels of literacy in England 1530–1730', in GRAFF (1981), *op. cit.*, pp. 105–6.

18 SCHOFIELD, R.S. (1968), 'The Measurement of literacy in pre-industrial England', in GOODY (Ed), *op. cit.*, p. 136.
19 *Ibid.*, p. 137.
20 Hannah More cited in SIMON, B. (1960), *Studies in the History of Education 1780–1870*, London, Lawrence and Wishart, p. 133.
21 Cited *ibid.*
22 CRESSY, *op. cit.*, pp. 109–110. Note that I am speaking here of different literacies and not, merely, of varied skills.
23 On the yeomen, compare *ibid.*, p. 110.
24 This perception may, however, perform a very important ideological function: suggesting that, in the end, all humans are equally workers. We are all workers and, therefore, all really *the same*. This deflects critical attention away from such matters as the fact that some workers get more pay than others, enjoy better working conditions, have more control over their work, etc. Often the better-off 'workers' are more accurately described as capitalists.
25 Of the many references possible here, compare the following as selected examples: BERNSTEIN, B. (1971), *Classes, Codes and Control*, 1, London, Routledge and Kegan Paul; FREIRE, P. (1972), *Pedagogy of the Oppressed*, Harmondsworth, Penguin, (1974), *Education: the practice of freedom*, London, Writers and Readers, (1985), *The Politics of Education*, London, MacMillan; KOZOL, J. (1985), *Illiterate America*, New York, Anchor and Doubleday; LABOV, W. (1973), 'The logic of non-standard English', in KEDDIE, N., (Ed), *Tinker Tailor ... the Myth of Cultural Deprivation*, Harmondsworth, Penguin; O'NEIL, W. (1970), 'Properly literate', *Harvard Educational Review*, 40, 2, pp. 260–3; POSTMAN, N. (1970), *op. cit.*; ROSEN, H. (1972), *Language and Class: a critique of Bernstein*, Bristol, Falling Wall Press; SEARLE, C. (1975), *Classrooms of Resistance*, London, Writers and Readers; (1984), *Words Unchained: language and revolution in Grenada*, London, Zed Press.
26 POSTMAN, *op. cit.*, p. 247.
27 HUNTER and HARMAN, *op. cit.*, p. 15.
28 Compare STREET, *op. cit.*, chapter 7, especially pp. 186–94. The quotation is from p. 190.
29 GRAFF (1979), *op. cit.*, pp. 17–19.
30 *Ibid.*, p. 65.
31 *Ibid.*, p. 71.
32 See *ibid.*, pp. 75–7.
33 See *ibid.*, chapters 3 and 4. The quotation is from p. 189.
34 *Ibid.*, p. 56.
35 Compare *ibid.*, p. 23.
36 Cited *ibid.*
37 Cited *ibid.*, p. 30.
38 *Ibid.*, p. 34.
39 *Ibid.*, p. 279.
40 *Ibid.*, p. 275.
41 *Ibid.*
42 *Ibid.*, p. 303.
43 Cited in LEVINE, K. (1982), 'Functional literacy: fond illusions and false economies', *Harvard Educational Review*, 52, 3, p. 256.
44 Cited *ibid.*
45 In the case of Britain compare, for example, the work of ALBSU, the Friends'

Centre, and see also MACE, J. (1979), *Working with Words*, London, Writers and Readers/Chameleon. With regard to the US, compare KOZOL, *op. cit.* Within Australia some very interesting developments in adult literacy have emerged out of the ESL Programmes, 'Women's Work, Women's Lives' and 'Migrant Women and Work', written by Barbara Bee for the Outreach Project at Randwick Technical College, Sydney.

46 Adult Performance Level Study (1975), *Adult Functional Competency*, Austin, University of Texas, 2.

47 *Ibid.*, appendix.

48 *Ibid.*

49 With regard to the relationship between being illiterate and being disadvantaged more generally, compare HUNTER and HARMAN, *op. cit.*, chapter 2.

50 POSTMAN, *op. cit.*, p. 246.

51 Compare FREIRE, (1972, 1973, 1985) all *op. cit.* See also, BERGGREN, C. and L. (1975), *The Literacy Process: a practice in Domestication or Liberation?*, London, Writers and Readers.

52 LEVINE, *op. cit.*, p. 262.

53 Compare FREIRE's various works, *op. cit.* See also his (1973), *Cultural Action for Freedom*, Harmondsworth, Penguin.

54 Compare FREIRE (1972), *op. cit.*, chapter 1. See also my (1986) 'Humanizing functional literacy: beyond utilitarian necessity', *Educational Theory*, 36,4. Much of the argument in this section originally appeared in my article in *Educational Theory*. I am grateful for permission to reproduce that material here.

55 Compare FREIRE, *ibid.*, chapter 1.

56 Compare GIROUX, H.A. (1985), 'Introduction' to FREIRE, *op. cit.*

57 Specifically, Hunter and Harman explore the intersection between being illiterate/educationally deprived, being unemployed and otherwise poor, belonging to a racial or ethnic minority group, having a prison record, and being female. While they do not draw hard and fast conclusions, they produce figures which, for all their incompleteness, are strongly suggestive. Compare HUNTER and HARMAN, *op. cit.*, chapter 2.

58 KOZOL, *op. cit.*, pp. 44–5.

59 O'NEIL, *op. cit.*

60 That is to say, other things being equal. Brian Street reminds me that at least some learners are likely to see through the hidden logic and ideology of a text like APL, and transcend passivity.

61 O'NEIL, *op. cit.*, p. 262.

62 *Ibid.*, p. 263.

63 *Ibid.*

64 *Ibid.*

Chapter 3

Literacy and the Politics of Daily Life

Introduction

In this chapter and the next I will examine a range of historical and contemporary cases of literacy with a view to adding an empirical dimension to what has so far been a mainly theoretical discussion. Part of my purpose will be to further develop two points argued in chapter 2. These are:

(i) literacies are social constructions forged in the process of humans pursuing values, goals and interests, under conditions where some groups have greater access to structural power than others; and

(ii) literacies can be assessed as proper or improper, according to whether they extend people's control over their lives and environment and enable them to deal rationally with decisions and experiences which face them, or hinder these ends.

In addition my argument will address two points which turn on the historical and ideological nature of literacy, and which are embryonic in ideas raised in chapters 1 and 2. These are:

(iii) distinct and competing literacies evolve as dimensions of struggle between competing interest groups. They are *shaped* within the process of competing interest groups pursuing their goals and, at the same time, are important factors in *influencing* whose interests are actually promoted/served and which goals met. Hegemonic forms of literacy will operate as mechanisms of ideological domination, enhancing the interests of dominant groups and undermining those of subordinate groups. Against these, counter forms of literacy may well be developed by subordinate interest groups as a means to challenging existing inequalities of power, privilege and opportunity. In many cases such counter forms emerge as part of, or within, a wider programme of political action; and

(iv) within societies like our own there is a tendency for forms of literacy to prevail which effectively maintain patterned inequalities of power within the social structure, and thereby bolster established patterns of domination and subordination, privilege and denial. To put it another way, within (so called) liberal capitalist democracies there is a tendency for improper forms of literacy to prevail among groups which are disadvantaged in terms of access to structural power, and whose interests are to that extent subordinated. Moreover, institutional barriers — coercive as well as ideological — stand in the way of promoting proper forms of literacy among members of subordinate interest groups.

The discussion in this chapter centres on literacy and working-class struggle in England between 1790 and 1850. In chapter 4 I will consider literacy in the context of contemporary mass schooling. The argument in these chapters will provide a basis for comparing practices and conceptions of reading and writing (including policy considerations) from our own social-historical tradition with those in a society currently undergoing a process of revolutionary change: namely, Nicaragua.

Literacy and Working Class Struggle in England, 1790 – 1850

Throughout this period the English working people bore a triple yoke of oppression. They were oppressed politically (in the *formal* sense, within the sphere of formal politics), economically, and culturally. Organic working class struggle against oppression emerged on all three fronts between 1790 and the 1830s — the decades which, according to E.P. Thompson, witnessed 'the making of the English working class'.[1]

There were two major dimensions to this 'making' : the growth of working-class consciousness, whereby the diverse groups of working people began in numbers to perceive an identity of interest among themselves, as distinct from and opposed to the interests of other classes; and the emergence of distinct forms of political and industrial organization corresponding to and reflecting this perceived identity of worker interests.

> By 1832 there were strongly based and self-conscious working class institutions — trade unions, friendly societies, educational and religious movements, political organizations, periodicals — working-class intellectual traditions, working-class community patterns, and a working-class structure of feeling.[2]

Thompson stresses the importance of recognizing the active role of working-class people in making themselves as a class. The working-class was not *forged*, in the manner of a casting, in the crucible of the Industrial Revolution — with external forces operating on inert human raw material, pressing it into shape, and turning it out 'ready made' at the other end. Rather, the making process was one in which working people acted and created, as well as being acted upon and responding to externally imposed economic, political, and cultural forces. 'The working class made itself as much as it was made'.[3] Moreover, the pursuit, attainment, and practice of proper forms of literacy was a vital galvanizing element within the active role played by working folk in making themselves as a class.

If the period between 1790 and 1832 saw the essential making of the English working class, the period to 1850 saw a first full expression of this achievement in the Chartist Movement. As for the earlier period, so for the later : the creation and practice of a proper literacy was a key to the dynamism of the Chartist Movement, as we will see.

What, then, of the tripartite oppression of working people throughout the period in question, and their active response to it? Politically the working class was bereft of formal power in 1790 and remained in precisely the same circumstances in 1850 — without the vote and without any authentic voice to express their interests in parliament. The 1832 Reform Act, which followed more than fifty years of middle- and working-class agitation for political reform, actually eroded the very few working-class rights to vote 'as had existed ... for instance, in the relatively democratic constituencies of West-minster and Preston'. In fact, the Reform Act 'specifically excluded the working class from any part in electing representatives to Parliament'.[1] Prior to 1832 the middle class had scarcely greater voting rights than working people. By a combination of voting qualifications and distribution of seats, the electorate in England and Wales was confined to some 11 per cent of adult males (approximately 366,250 out of 3,463,795 adult males in 1831 were entitled to vote). The 1832 Reform Act redistributed seats to give greater representation to the towns, but imposed an 'intentionally stiff' property qualification on borough voters. This 'kept out non-property owners who were deemed unworthy to be trusted with the vote'. Clearly, the government of the day 'wished to preserve above all things ... the continuance of government by men of property'.[5] And so, for example, the new electorates of Leeds, Birmingham and Manchester, with a combined population of 451,000 admitted just 25,000 voters among them. While the proportion of adult males in England and Wales entitled by the Act to vote increased from 11 per cent to around 18 per cent, this did not include working folk — who, predictably, could not meet the voting qualification of owning or occupying property worth at least £10 per year. The increased electorate, rather, was accounted for almost entirely by middle-class urban dwellers; which was the express intent of the legislation.

From an economic standpoint the circumstances of working people varied significantly : between artisan and labourer, rural and urban workers, one trade and another, from one harvest to the next, from north to south, etc. We cannot do justice to detail here. Even so, enough of the scale and dimensions of working-class oppression to meet our purposes can be briefly and generally indicated here without undue distortion. The demonstrable truth is that working folk were economically oppressed on several dimensions. Income levels — for all their vagueness and indeterminacy — testify to a grossly unequal distribution of the nation's wealth. Low wages made the working class absolutely vulnerable to the effects of slumps, failed harvests, labour market fluctuations, excessive taxation to finance wars and support corrupt economic administration, Corn Laws, and so on. At their worst, conditions resulting from low wages, unemployment, abysmal housing and urban squalor, were abominable — as reflected, for example, in measures undertaken for Poor Relief during the period in question, and captured in Engel's *Condition of the Working Class in England*.

There was more, however, to economic oppression than income levels alone. Agricultural workers had been driven off the land by enclosures. Independent skilled workers had been transformed into dependent factory workers. Working conditions were often harsh and the work itself monotonous. And everywhere workers were faced with the reality that the profits from their toil were accruing to others rather than themselves. In general terms the economic condition of the majority was bad in 1790 and remained bad in 1830. The decades from 1830 to 1850 were characterized by boom and bust fluctuations. Over the whole period 1790 — 1850 'there was a slight improvement in average material standards', but at the same time 'there was intensified exploitation, greater insecurity, and increasing human misery'.[6] The slight material gains for working people, largely confined to 'more potatoes, a few articles of cotton clothing for the family, soap and candles, some tea and sugar', were offset psychologically by the experience of exploitation. In Thompson's words,

> the 'average' working man remained very close to subsistence level at a time when he was surrounded by the evidence of the increase of national wealth, much of it transparently the product of his own labour, and passing, by equally transparent means, into the hands of his employers. In psychological terms, this felt like a decline in standards.[7]

The cultural oppression of the working class is exemplified by educational arrangements. There are several counts on which working folk were oppressed educationally. There was considerable opposition among the better-off classes to the poor being provided with any form of instruction whatsoever, lest they become discontent with their lot. This opposition gradually declined during the nineteenth century. The decline, however, was offset by the belief that such instruction should be provided for working-class children as would effectively make them 'beings for others' — by reconciling them to their station in life, teaching them respect for their betters, and promoting respect for (others') private property. The poor should be educated, according to the new view. But they should be educated in the interests of others; not in their own.[8]

By a combination of conscious policy and heuristic incompetence, this principle was in fact met through the minimal forms of educational provision actually available to the poor. In the late eighteenth and early nineteenth centuries provision for the poor was pretty well confined to the activities of Charity, Dame and Sunday schools, with a few poor having access to endowed schools and small private fee-charging schools. After 1810 there were, in addition, the monitorial schools. Most Sunday schools taught little more than reading, and what they did teach was typically attuned to their original guiding ethos : 'to educate the poor in the principles of religion and the duties of their lowly status in life'.[9] Dame schools taught at best the rudiments of reading and, occasionally, writing. Many, as Simon observes, taught little or nothing at all. And the dubious quality of much monitorial schooling is well documented by the Hammonds in their *Age of the Chartists*. Even the more elaborate and extended forms of provision for working-class children were severely limited. In his *Recollections*, John Binns describes his formal education (which lasted until he was fourteen) as defective in that it lacked any systematic course of study. Those working men, like Binns and Francis Place, who *did* engage in serious reading and reflection prior to involvement in cooperative worker education activities, had done so almost entirely at their own initiative rather than as part of their schooling. All in all, the forms of instruction available to the poor 'provided little enough education, but at least it was possible to learn to read and write'.[10] That is, if one's parents could afford to pay whatever fees were involved and forego what little income one might earn in child labour. There is no doubt that many working-class children were denied instruction because the family economy could not afford it. Finally, where the working class *was* successful in evolving educational forms which promoted their own class interests, they met severe and highly effective opposition through the exercise of state power or, otherwise, through various counter activities of the middle and upper classes.

While state jurisdiction was a major factor contributing to working class oppression during this period — compare, for example, legislation countering working-class attempts to win the vote, laws against establishing combinations (such as trade unions) to protect and promote working class economic interests, etc. — the politics of daily life comprised much more than the formal power relations between citizen and state. For working people the politics of daily life consisted in the experience of powerlessness in economic, cultural, and social relations generally : powerlessness which was, to be sure, formalized, legitimated, and reinforced by legislation (or absence of it), but which was actually *lived* within the daily routines of economic, cultural, and social life. The conditions and circumstances of work, together with wage levels, were matters wholly determined by employers and the vagaries of the economy. Between employer and worker, economic power resided almost entirely with the former. Within social life the working class had a well-defined station to observe and maintain. Relations of deference, acceptance of authority, and willingness to be controlled by one's betters, were culturally enforced. These relations extended to education as well. Whether or not the poor received education, what they received, and under what conditions, were details that were largely outside the power of the working class to determine: although rather less so than workers often perceived them to be, as will be shown.

If working-class struggle between 1790 and 1850 was very much centred on winning the vote and, thus, on *formal* politics, it was nevertheless with a view to transforming the unequal social relations of daily life as a whole. As a *political* struggle it transcended the purely formal dimension. This is especially evident with regard to developments and trends in literacy. In examining the social construction and practice of literacies within the context of working-class struggle against the oppression they experienced in daily life, I will focus on three cases of worker initiative and the forms of opposition (mounted on behalf of competing class interests) met by workers in the course of their activity. These cases are the Corresponding Societies of 1792–99, the struggle for a working-class press, and the theory and practice of Chartist education.

The Corresponding Societies : Working-Class Literacy and Political Reform

Stimulated by middle-class initiatives for political reform and radical currents engendered by the American and French Revolutions — including the work of Thomas Paine and the reactionary backlash to his *Rights of Man* — the London Corresponding Society was founded in January 1792 by eight men seeking a political association which would represent the working classes. The Society's general aim was to arouse nationwide commitment to pursuing political reform and to establish links between groups throughout Britain involved in reform struggle. Its specific goals were universal suffrage and annual parliaments. Membership was open to any man who, being proposed by two members, affirmed their belief that every adult had the right to vote and vowed they would promote the cause of parliamentary reform 'by all justifiable means'. Subscription was by payment of one penny per week, and the resulting income was used to foster correspondence with other societies and to publish literature which would promote political reform[11]

The underlying assumption was that common people could make their aspirations and grievances known, and force them to be acknowledged by parliament, if — and only if — they would unite. When the right to popular participation in government was realized and popular control of parliament established, existing political evils would be overcome. This would in turn bring economic and cultural amelioration. Winning this right called for information and discussion, unity and communication, mobilization and appropriate action. It would be essential to educate the people so that they understood their political rights, and then to organize 'hundreds of thousands of these men throughout the kingdom' to demand parliamentary reform.[12] *Educational* activity was to have two main aspects. Members would read and discuss political works in order to develop political awareness and commitment. Secondly, the Society would publish and distribute (on a large scale) copies of their official addresses as well as other relevant tracts and manifestos. The goal of *organizing* the people would be pursued through establishing and maintaining an extensive and efficient correspondence network.

Limiting the subscription to a penny per week opened membership to workers and effectively introduced the cause of political reform to the working class. The London Corresponding Society truly emerged as a 'poor man's society'.[13] Other similar groups soon emerged — in Bath, Bristol, Birmingham, Cambridgeshire, Derby, Hereford, Leeds, Manchester, Norwich, Nottingham, Sheffield, Strathaven, Stockport, and elsewhere. Many of these were predominantly, if not almost exclusively, working-class in membership. Even within societies of mixed middle- and working-class membership it was generally working folk who assumed leadership roles. This leadership experience was crucial for building trade unions in later decades.

The London Corresponding Society (LCS) is the best known and was probably the most sophisticated of the corresponding societies. It offers an excellent example of a distinctive literacy being constructed and integrated into a wider set of practices through which people actively pursued greater understanding and control of their world and their own circumstances. Of particular interest is the way in which a democratic and empowering form of literacy was constructed within the process of struggling for popular empowerment and a more democratic approach to government in Britain. Moreover, the same commitment to democratic process and values was writ large in the organization and government of the LCS itself.

The LCS operated in accordance with the very values its members aimed to promote within parliamentary government: active popular participation, accountability, responsibility, minimal factionalism, and an optimal blend of efficiency, order and freedom. Members were organized in divisions (ideally) of thirty, with each division electing a chairman who served as delegate and treasurer for his division. The body of delegates from the various divisions formed a delegates' committee. They centralized and administered the Society's accumulated funds, and held weekly meetings to conduct business and correspond with other reform groups. The power, however, rested ultimately with the members — in the divisions themselves. They were 'the final source of authority'[14], having to be consulted on all questions of principle and holding the right to recall delegates.

The internal government of the Society, then, involved members in actively practising political relations and practices of democratic participation and control — whether as delegates or ordinary division members. This was a key aspect of the educative life of corresponding societies generally: learning to *practise* democracy in the process of pursuing a democratic state. According to Thale, the written constitutions of corresponding societies were very important expressions of their nature and existence.

To the LCS a constitution was not only a way of establishing orderly procedures for meetings, but also a way of educating the members so that they could exercise their rights responsibly when parliament and society were reformed and a way of showing the world a model of a just society.[15]

Literacy was crucial to the Society's government in several ways. Minutes were recorded faithfully, accounts kept, constitutions written and revised, notices distributed to members, correspondence conducted with other societies and visits arranged, etc. It is evident that an active purposeful literacy was practised and refined by delegates in transacting business, finance and correspondence. There is a noteworthy comparison here with the literacy of CEP coordinators in Nicaragua, mentioned in chapter 1. The literacy skills of delegates were often far from 'perfect'. The early recorded letters of Thomas Hardy, founder of the LCS, are replete with errors of spelling, grammar and punctuation. The message, however, like that of Nicaragua's CEP coordinators, was always clear. In the early life of the Society members benefited from valuable literacy assistance offered by well-educated sympathisers from other social classes. Self-sufficiency, though, was soon achieved.

To understand more fully the nature and role of literacy within the work of corresponding societies we must turn to their more overtly educational activity : in discussion meetings and publishing. The LCS provides the model here. Each division ran weekly discussion meetings. After new members had been admitted, the delegates had reported on the last delegates' meeting, and the division had voted on questions directed by the delegates' committee to the membership at large, members would listen to a reading of a reform pamphlet or newspaper article. (Many members were, of course, unable to read). Discussion would follow. In addition, political broadsides, pamphlets, and books were sold and circulated, and reform songs sung. This form of organized cooperative self-education was complemented by Sunday evening reading and discussion meetings and regular debates.

The nature and educational quality of the division meetings and Sunday evenings varied considerably. At their 'roughest' they seem unlikely vehicles for reflection and close analysis. 'Almost everyone speaks and there is always a great noise, till the delegate gets up. People grow very outrageous and won't wait, then the delegate gets up and tries to soften them'.[16] At their most sophisticated, though, they reflect a unique and powerful pedagogy. Francis Place offers an inspiring account of the division meetings and Sunday evenings in which he personally participated. According to him the discussions and debates opened to members 'views which they had never before taken'. Members were compelled by these discussions 'to find reasons for their opinions and to tolerate others'. Sunday evening meetings were often held in members' homes and, in Place's view, 'were very important meetings and the best results to the parties followed'. These meetings followed a typical pattern.

> The chairman (a different man each Sunday) read aloud a chapter of a book. During the ensuing week, the book was passed around for the men to read at home. The next Sunday the chairman read the chapter again, pausing three times for comments. No one was to speak more than once during the reading, and anyone who had not spoken during the first two pauses was expected to speak at the end. After that there

was a general discussion during which no one could speak on a subject a second time until everyone who wished to had spoken once.[17]

The material read and discussed had a definite radical and liberating flavour. Paine was a favourite author, although any work asserting the political and social rights of citizens, and analyzing how and why these were denied in daily life, was considered appropriate. In the words of a member of the Sheffield Society, reading and discussion were intended

> to enlighten the people, to show the people the reason, the ground of all their complaints and sufferings; when a man works hard for thirteen or fourteen hours of the day, the week through, and is not able to maintain his family; that is what I understand of it; to show the people the ground of this; why they were not able.[18]

Out of the reading, discussion, and analysis undertaken by LCS members there emerged frequent official addresses. These were steeped in the political theory of Paine, Voltaire, Rousseau, and the like — proclaiming the political rights and duties of individuals and lamenting that these were denied to the great majority of 'free-born Englishmen'[19] by corrupt government. These addresses demonstrate a powerful and penetrating clarity; the message was readily accessible and arousing. In its first address to the nation at large the LCS explains its *raison d'etre*, lays out its constitution, and documents examples of gross parliamentary misrepresentation. It is stated, for example, that a mere 354 electors in twenty-eight Corporation towns returned fifty-six members to the House of Commons, while 'the towns of Sheffield, Manchester, Birmingham, Leeds, Wolverhampton, etc., containing above 300,000 people, have no electors or representatives whatever'. So much, says the address, for the House of Commons, 'which is so frequently and so falsely called the Democracy of the Nation'.[20]

The Corresponding Societies were also heavily involved in publishing. Webb speaks of the astonishing range of material which has survived, and produces evidence that publishing was on a very large scale. It is estimated that 200,000 copies of Paine's *The Rights of Man* had been sold before 1794. This massive circulation was assisted by the creative active literacy of corresponding societies. In Manchester, for instance, a radical leader was asked to abridge the book so that it could sell for less than a shilling. The Sheffield Society produced an edition for sixpence. Besides such larger works societies published their official addresses, pamphlets, radical newspapers and magazines, collections of political ballads, periodicals, satirical pieces, broadsides, printed handbills, and even catalogues of low priced reform publications.[21] The outcome of this indigenous publishing activity was that working people had access to an enormous body of critical, innovative, (often humorously) penetrating, politically enlightening and inspiring literature. This freed working-class readers from the ideological grip of the upper class — whereby workers were immersed in a view of the world that reflected and enhanced the interests of their oppressors.

Unfortunately it is impossible to do justice here to the complexity, vitality, and richness of the Corresponding Societies. They merit study in their own right. Sufficient has been said, however, to situate empirically two central ideas. First, we have seen in the life and work of Corresponding Societies a literacy being forged in the context of a group (in this case a social class which was becoming increasingly conscious of itself as a distinct class) pursuing its interests and aspirations under conditions characterized by extreme inequality of access to structural power. Indeed, it was precisely the awareness of being completely excluded from formal political power by which to exercise some control over their social and economic conditions, and thereby promote their class interests, that drove these working men to actively pursue political reform: to get a hold on some formal power as a means to confronting and redressing their oppression. The conception and practice of literacy which emerged was tailored to pursuing the political enlightenment, organization, and mobilization of a social class.

Second, the literacy that evolved was a proper literacy: indeed, it was a properly functional literacy in the manner of Freire (see chapter 2). The form and content of reading and discussion — the *pedagogy* — was, at its best, a powerful force toward working people assuming greater control over their circumstances and destiny, and doing so in a rational and informed manner. 'Here were methods devised by a workers' society, of a kind to encourage self-confidence, clear thinking, and the capacity for self-expression'.[22] There may not have been much in the way of creating original abstract theory, as Brown notes. (This, of course, is hardly surprising given that the working class was systematically denied all but the most minimal forms of formal instruction and intellectual development. Quite simply, working people lacked an organic intellectual tradition, a basis, from which to develop their own original theory.) There was, however, a genius for transforming theories, ideas, beliefs, and arguments into active pursuit of class interests; a gift for political organization which gave material substance and real political force to newly won ideas.

These ideas, and the organized forms of political practice and activity — mediated by literacy — through which they were simultaneously acquired and expressed, became the basis of the working-class movement itself: the early foundations of political consciousness, organization and sustained struggle, which bore tangible fruits in the latter half of the nineteenth century and the early decades of the twentieth. Brown claims that the same practical genius which built up the trade unions in the nineteenth century is evident in the educational movement of the Corresponding Societies: in the system of division meetings, delegation and correspondence, as well as in the organization and control of mass meetings, and the adept use of the press, sympathetic booksellers and friendly publishers.[23] Literacy — proper literacy — was both a vehicle and an outcome of this genius.

In fact the literacy conceived and practised by Corresponding Societies helps us to specify more closely the ideal of proper literacy as extending people's control over their lives and enhancing their ability to deal rationally with their life decisions. Here we can draw on ideas developed earlier in my argument. Within Corresponding Societies literacy promoted what Mills calls 'sociological imagination' or, more comprehensively, what Freire calls 'critical consciousness'. It enabled working people 'to grasp history and biography and the relations between the two in society'[24], and thus to understand the relationship between social structures (relations and practices) and their own personal experiences of life. The comment of the man from the Sheffield Society attests to this. In the light of this critical understanding of history and biography, working people were moved to activity aimed at critiquing and changing existing practices and relations of oppression. In addition to involvement in discussion, correspondence and publishing, members of Corresponding Societies organized mass meetings and demonstrations, hosted Conventions, and undertook 'missionary' tours to drum up zeal for political reform throughout Britain and to consolidate fledgling and otherwise struggling societies. By this activity they consciously sought change from circumstances and arrangements in which 'humans are free to make history, but some humans are much freer than others'[25], to circumstances in which humans are ever more equally free to 'participate in creating history and culture' — history and culture in which the interests of all are served more equally. These are precisely notions of control — i.e., actively shaping the very social forces and processes, institutions and practices, which in turn influence how human interests are served — and rational dealing with one's life and decisions — i.e., in achieving a more accurate, critical, and informed awareness of oneself in relation to the wider social reality.

Of equal importance to the present argument is the response of the state and of civilians representing ruling class interests to the Corresponding Societies. Hitherto, those who saw their class interests vested in maintaining the existing social and political order had adopted one or other of two positions with regard to working-class education. They either opposed the poor being provided with any instruction whatsoever lest they become discontent with their lot or, like Hannah More, emphasized the important hegemonic value of a properly controlled and dispensed 'education'. Those who supported the latter position could be reasonably satisfied with existing forms of working-class provision — for example, Sunday schools, Charity schools — insofar as these taught minimal reading skills to the poor in conjunction with explicitly religious content and attitudes of deference.

The emergence of Corresponding Societies, however, utterly contradicted both positions by providing an educational setting and a pedagogical form in which the ability to read and write became an instrument for stimulating radical political thought and activity. Suddenly the rudimentary literacy skills transmitted by established purveyors of working-class education acquired highly subversive potential — regardless of the ideological setting in which these skills were originally acquired. The Corresponding Societies positively wrested ideological influence over their members *away* from the champions of the existing social and political order and, with the help of radical theorists from other classes, developed a counter hegemony. They offered an opportunity to achieve a systematic, coherent, and critical understanding of working-class life within the existing order; to understand the way in which social, political, and religious values and beliefs preached by representatives of other class interests and imposed upon the consciousness of working people, effectively adjusted (or *domesticated*) the working class to its own domination and oppression. Moreover, this learning opportunity was equally available to literate and illiterate workers alike, since the skills of literate members opened viewpoints, theories, and critiques to scrutiny by those who could only listen and discuss, as well as to those who could also read and write.

Opposition to the Corresponding Societies was swift, intense, and backed with the full power of the state. The response makes two things perfectly clear. First, it becomes clear just how far the literacies evolved by Corresponding Societies and their opponents respectively were key factors in a *struggle* between competing interest groups — indeed, they were products of as well as forces in this struggle. Second, we have here a classic instance of distinct literacies emerging and taking on polarized roles within a struggle taking place under conditions of (nakedly) unequal access to structural power.

The reality and importance of the struggle is demonstrated by the lengths taken on the part of ruling interests to defeat the Corresponding Societies. Two approaches were taken simultaneously: coercive and hegemonic/ideological.

The State took four major coercive steps against corresponding societies:

(i) In May 1792 a Royal Proclamation was issued against seditious meetings and publications. Magistrates threatened tavern keepers with the loss of their licences if they allowed their premises to be used for Society meetings. Taverns were a logical and popular base for such activity, since many members lacked homes sufficiently large to accommodate meetings. The societies themselves were infiltrated by spies who informed authorities as to meeting places and society proceedings, thereby aiding the official tactic of intimidating taverners and members alike. This tactic was successful in containing membership as weaker brethren and potential members were frightened off. In addition, authors, publishers, booksellers, newspaper vendors, and even bill posters were prosecuted for sedition. Thomas Paine fled for France before he could be tried. Many others endured prosecution. Legal agents were appointed in most districts

> for the special task of prosecuting acts of sedition, and particularly to indict booksellers who had been guilty of selling the works of Paine. An official heresy hunt was soon on foot in almost every town from Portsmouth to Newcastle and from Swansea to Chelmsford.[26]

Society correspondence was threatened with interception in the post, and a bill poster 'appointed by the LCS to post the "Answer to the Place and Pension Club" was hauled off to Bow Street and committed to Tothill Fields for six months'.[27]

(ii) Following state trials against reformists in Scotland (where defendants, including members of the LCS in Scotland for a convention, were sentenced to transportation for fourteen years), English law moved against reform societies in May 1794. Seven members of the LCS were arrested (together with six from the London Constitutional Society). In October three of the defendants were tried. Each was acquitted, at which point further prosecutions were abandoned. Between the arrests and the trials membership of the LCS alone had fallen by several hundred. While it rose again, dramatically, after the acquittals the respite was brief. The State moved more effectively in 1795.

(iii) By the Treason and Sedition Acts of November-December 1795, 'almost every possible form of agitation, or indeed of political action', was outlawed. 'At the same time Habeus Corpus was suspended and many reformers were arrested and sent to prison without trial'.[28] Memories of the state trials were still fresh, and the effect of the Treason and Sedition Acts was devastating. Membership of corresponding societies fell away, never to regain earlier levels. In fact this was the beginning of the decline to eventual extinction.

(iv) In 1799 a series of acts of parliament placed all secret associations, federations, and (fledgling) trade unions under a ban. Special legislation was enacted 'utterly suppressing and prohibiting' the LCS by name.[29] Although there is evidence that it at least among the Corresponding Societies continued to operate in some formal — albeit minimal — capacity through 1800, the first organized working-class experiment in knowledge-as-power was effectively eliminated by 1799.

It is impossible here to communicate the full force and extent of state coercion directed against the Corresponding Societies. This can be gleaned from several sources recommended to the reader.[30] Suffice it to say that the coercion was intense, reflecting on the part of ruling interests a clear awareness of what was at stake if such forms of working-class organization and education — and the distinctive literacy it involved — were not destroyed.

The coercive power of the state was backed by hegemonic activity directed at the working classes against the ideological impact of Corresponding Societies. One line of attack was by establishing clubs and associations committed to maintaining dominance of the prevailing church and king hegemony among the working class. This movement began with the Crown and Anchor Association, instigated in November 1792 when one John Reeves issued the prospectus of an association 'for protecting liberty and property against republicans and levellers'. The objectives of this association were

to suppress seditious publications, to convince the public that the measures being canvassed by perverted men were not applicable to this country, and to promote similar societies throughout the country.[31]

With respect specifically to countering the reform literature and theory propagated by Corresponding Societies and other groups, the prospectus expressed the intention 'occasionally to explain those topics of public discussion, which have been so perverted by evil designing men, and to show, by irrefragable proofs, that they are not applicable to the state of this country, that they can produce no good, and certainly must produce much evil.'[32] Reeves' initiative was highly successful, and associations with a church and king flavour based upon his model soon emerged in almost every district of England. The activities and propaganda of these associations provided powerful ideological support for the more overtly repressive measures taken by the state.

The ideological role of church and king clubs was complemented by a major publishing initiative designed to counteract the burgeoning literature of reform and equal rights. Much of this publishing was, in fact, financed — on the model of Corresponding Societies — from subscriptions to church and king clubs. It built on work begun in the 1780s by Sarah Trimmer, which aimed at providing the poor with 'safe' reading matter. In the tradition of Trimmer — whose *Family Magazine* presented instructional tales designed to 'help' the poor, with appropriate assistance from their social betters, to correct many of those faults peculiar to their humble station in life — Hannah More and her sisters began (in the mid 1790s) publishing tracts intended 'to answer Voltaire and Paine, to counteract French Revolutionary ideas, and to promote a proper regard for the social order'. The Mores' work included the *Cheap Repository Tracts* and Hannah's (anonymously published) *Village Politics, Addressed to All the Mechanics, Journeymen, and Labourers in Great Britain, by Will Chip, a Country Carpenter.* Webb describes *Village Politics* as perhaps the most celebrated of the anti-reform tracts. It is written in a style intended to instruct and amuse a working-class readership — although More clearly underestimated many of her intended audience who grappled with the most sophisticated theories of their time.

> In form it is typical: a dialogue in which the solid blacksmith inevitably wins the argument over the silly radical mason ... The laboured humour, the contrived heartiness, the identification of dissipation and radicalism, and the notion of leaving politics to one's betters are common to the species.

Other works published in opposition to the reform press included *Strictures on Thomas Paine's Work and Character* (anonymous), Chalmers' *Life of Pain*, William Vincent's *Short Hints Upon Levelling*, Paley's *Reasons for Contentment: Addressed to the Labouring Part of the British Public, The Englishman's Political Catechism*, and very many others. According to Webb, such material was published as low priced pamphlets, broadsides, and handbills to be stuck on walls (with impunity, of course — only reform posters were seditious) and distributed in alehouses: clear evidence that 'the supporters of the status quo were worried indeed'.[33]

In the end coercion and hegemony prevailed. The Corresponding Societies were defeated. The distinctive literacy and pedagogical form devised and practised in this working-class association was driven out by a combination of legal repression, organized opposition, and stark political reality. The reference to 'stark political reality' is important. For all the ideological work undertaken by Corresponding Societies and their efforts to diffuse a proper literacy among the working classes, the established hegemony of church and king prevailed and continued to dominate *among the lower* as well as the higher social rankings. When it came down to it the majority of working-class people were aligned against reformers; even working-class reformers. The Corresponding Societies began the process of developing a consciousness among working people grounded in their own interests as a class rather than in the interests of classes which oppressed them. But it was just a beginning. Most of the working class remained immersed in a consciousness quite contrary to their own interests. That is, they remained hegemonized. And so, for example, Francis Place had no doubt that the Treason and Sedition Acts were extremely popular among oppressor and oppressed alike.

> Infamous as they were, they were popular measures. The people, ay, the mass of the shopkeepers and working people, may be said to have approved them without understanding them. Such was their fear ... that 'the throne and altar' would be destroyed, and that we should be 'deprived of our holy religion'.[34]

If one literacy — namely, the proper literacy practised in Corresponding Societies — was a key element in giving rise to fears for the social and political order in the first place, a second literacy — practised in the original Sunday schools and enhanced by anti-reform tractarians — ensured that working-class sympathies were predominantly aligned *against* those who challenged the established order.

Literacy and Struggle for the Working-Class Press

While precise figures are not available, the working class was increasingly a reading public from the late eighteenth century.[35] Furthermore, the Corresponding Societies had demonstrated that, through association, individuals did not personally require reading skills in order to gain access to ideas and critiques through which to achieve enhanced understanding of their circumstances and pursue greater control over their lives. The end of the war with France, in 1815, ushered in a period during which the battle for access, via print, to the minds of working people once again assumed major proportions and significance. With this renewed battle came a revisiting of the broad themes considered in the previous section — this time in the context of struggle for a popular press.

Wickwar identifies 1816 as a landmark in the struggle for freedom of the press. The peace with France had brought continued economic distress rather than improvement to the lower orders, and fanned disillusionment within the middle class. Politically aware critics identified a government which had palpably failed to promote the welfare of its subjects. They saw electoral corruption in 'borough mongering, pensions, sinecures and patronage'. They saw general political and economic corruption, privilege, and vested interest in

> a corn law passed to keep the price of wheat up to eighty shillings a quarter, on the assumption that rents would thus be kept high and that the high rents were necessary to keep up the landed interest on which the government of church and state was assumed to depend.

Political malcontents again turned their attention to reform. Change to the constitution was the precondition of improved social and economic conditions, they argued. Unless the people shared the power of government, they could scarcely hope to share its benefits.[36]

Under conditions of intense and prolonged economic hardship, discontent had become widespread among the working class, and 1811 brought violence with the outbreak of the Luddite Revolts. Initially much of the violence was directed against machinery and industrial property, in the belief that machines and profiteering were the source of economic distress. There were, in addition, sporadic food riots and outbreaks of mob violence triggered by unemployment, high prices, and wage reductions. Commentators generally describe the widespread and regular outbreaks of violence and disorder between 1811 and 1816 as spontaneous and unorganized — in the sense that they were not individually parts of a unified, informed, orchestrated programme of political agitation. Moves were taken to alter this in 1816 when, under two main influences, political reform re-emerged as a unifying theme and educational activity aimed at promoting widespread commitment to the reform cause was once more in evidence.

The first influence was the revival of reform societies in the wake of a reform tour by Major Cartwright. In the tradition of corresponding societies the Hampden, Union, and Spencean Clubs promoted discussion and political activity within regular class meetings.[37] This initiative was soon accompanied by the development of radical Sunday schools — secular and political in nature and focus. The second influence was the emergence of a politically critical popular press directed specifically at working people with the intention of educating them as to the real cause of their distress: namely, political and constitutional evils. It is with the emergence of the popular press that I am mainly concerned here.

Three points can be made by way of background to trends which evolved in popular publishing from 1816.

(i) Since 1712 publications had been subject to tax. In that year parliament taxed printed papers, pamphlets and advertisements, and required a stamp to be placed on anything it deemed to be a newspaper. During George II's reign the stamp on newspapers was set at a penny per sheet, and penalties for transgressions of the Stamp Tax were extended from publishers to include vendors as well. In 1815 the Stamp Tax was set at fourpence per newspaper. Clearly, the cost of the tax had to be included in the sale price of newspapers, unless publishers and vendors chose to risk publishing and selling unstamped papers. The Stamp Tax thereby placed legitimate newspapers beyond the pockets of working class individuals.

(ii) Strict legislation to control the content of publication was in place. This began in 1637, when all books and papers were required by law to be licensed and registered before publication. During the eighteenth and early nineteenth centuries tough laws governing sedition and libel were added. As Wickwar summarizes:

> The publication of anything with a malicious intention of causing a breach of the peace was a misdemeanour at Common Law. Anything that it was thus illegal to circulate was called a criminal libel, and the same term was commonly applied to the act of circulating it. Criminal libels were distinguished as defamatory, obscene, blasphemous or seditious libels, according to as they treated of personal, sexual, religious, or political matters.[38]

Of particular relevance here is seditious libel. This law legislated against public expressions of discontent with the established government. A publication was a seditious libel if it (i) tended to bring into contempt or hatred either the monarchy (including heirs and successors), the government and constitution, parliament, or the administration of justice; or (ii) tended to incite subjects of the realm to attempt to change any matter of church or state by other than lawful means. Given that there was no provision for popular participation in government, there *were* no lawful (or, by definition, peaceful) means by which the people could change either government or constitution. Hence the law covering seditious libel presented a powerful and wide-ranging control on the political content of the press. Since Britain's rulers in the early nineteenth century 'were generally satisfied with the working of the constitution and the Christianity of the day', and 'saw no reason why the whole nation should not be united in ... respect for Christianity and in contentment with the constitution they had inherited', there was both an incentive and a tendency for the laws covering libel and sedition to be employed — particularly when public unrest reached crisis point, as it did frequently between 1790 and 1816 (and after).[39]

(iii) By 1815 an impressive range of types of publication existed for middle and upper class readers. Besides books, these included newspapers—containing national, local, and foreign news, and comprehensive reports of legal and parliamentary proceedings — monthly and quarterly reviews and magazines, and an increasingly popular (typically) weekly form known as political registers. Together with certain books and pamphlets, these registers mainly fell outside 'the respectable part of the press'.[40] While some had a literary and dramatic focus, most were political in content and anti-establishment in bias. They were usually published by a single individual and reflected that person's viewpoint. Whereas newspapers sought to describe or record events, registers aimed explicitly to shape them. And whereas monthly reviews and magazines reviewed general policies, the registers reviewed and evaluated current events. They evolved as potent instruments of political and, often, religious critique. And they were subject to the Stamp Tax.

Perhaps the most celebrated of the register genre was *Cobbett's Weekly Political Register*, founded by William Cobbett in 1802. Cobbett reflects *par excellence* the spirit and intent of the register writers as described by Wickwar. These individuals expressed in their publications what they 'took to be the interests of the otherwise unrepresented people' — and particularly the working class. For Cobbett, the ills of the working class flowed from political corruption; their interests called for parliamentary reform. But if Cobbett argued and agitated on behalf of the interests of others, he required in turn their support. 'He had to try to make his opinion their opinion, so that they might together accomplish what he could never do alone'.[41] The way in which Cobbett sought to make his opinion working-class opinion led to a further chapter in the chronicle of literacy as a force and an outcome of struggle between competing interest groups.

Because of the heavy stamp duty Cobbett's *Register* sold at 1s 0½d — with only 'a very small portion ... left to the author'. Despite the high price it was read by workmen who grouped together to buy copies and read them in public-houses. When Cobbett heard of publicans objecting to 'meetings for reading the *Register* being held at their houses for fear they should lose their licences', he decided to make available a cheaper edition. He was (legally) able to do this by means of a loophole in the Stamp Tax law. Printing on open sheets (i.e., sheets printed without the intention of folding them) required no stamp. And so 'the whole of one of my *Registers* might be printed in rather close print upon the two sides of one sheet of foolscap paper ...'[42]

Cobbett's unstamped version of the *Register* sold for twopence — the original 'Twopenny Trash'. It sold 44,000 copies inside a month, and more than 200,000 in all. A score of political periodicals followed Cobbett's lead: notably, Wooller's *Black Dwarf*, Sherwin's *Political Register* (later transformed by Richard Carlile into the *Republican*), and the penny *Gorgon*, edited by John Wade. Political corruption and the pressing need for reform was the central theme of the twopenny trash. This theme was expressed in articles analyzing and commenting upon current circumstances and events, exposing the motives and interests of opponents of reform, advocating and documenting the advantages of lawful association, and generally expounding elements of radical political theory. The politicizing influence of this literature upon the working class was enormous. It performed a role akin to that of the literacy engendered by Corresponding Societies, providing a focus for class meetings within the Hampden Clubs and other reform societies. The role of Cobbett's work in particular was widely acclaimed. According to Samuel Bamford, Cobbett's writings were

> read on every cottage hearth in the manufacturing districts of South Lancashire ... Leicester, Derby, and Nottingham ... Their influence was speedily visible; he directed his readers to the true cause of their sufferings — misgovernment; and to its proper corrective — parliamentary reform. Riots soon became scarce, and from that time they have never obtained their ancient vogue with the labourers of this country ... Instead of riots and destruction of property, Hampden Clubs were now established in many of our large towns ... The labourers read [Cobbett's works] and thenceforth became deliberate and systematic in their proceedings.[43]

Thompson cites a reformer who attributed the emergence of political knowledge and fixed political principles among Manchester's poor to 'Mr. Cobbett's masterly essays, upon the financial situation of the country, and the effects of taxation, in reducing the comforts of the labourer'.[44]

Cobbett's original twopenny *Weekly Political Pamphlet*, 'Address to the journeymen and labourers', is an exemplar of the genre. Cobbett argues that despite being smaller in population and poorer in soil and climate than many other countries, England was (in 1816) the most wealthy and powerful nation in the world. This wealth and power, he says, springs from the labouring classes. Moreover, the same labouring classes as produce the nation's wealth also secure its safety. While military and naval commanders receive the titles and the financial rewards, it is the people who actually win the victories. What do working people receive in return for producing wealth and ensuring security? They are denegrated by their 'betters' — referred to as the Mob, the Rabble, the Swinish Multitude — and reduced to abject misery.

Cobbet asks after the cause of this misery and how it might be remedied. The main cause, he says, is excessive taxation. But do 'the friends of corruption' recommend reduced taxes for the poor? Not a bit. Instead they complain about being levied for the Poor Rate. They would seek even to deny poor relief to the labouring classes — despite the fact that poor relief is the only tangible return workers might see for the taxes they pay. Even less do these friends of corruption propose political reform which would admit the real creators of wealth and security to the body politic. The same political corruption that reduces the poor to misery ensures that sinecure placemen and pensioners receive from twenty to forty thousand pounds a year — in return for producing and securing nothing! Having attacked Malthus' 'remedy' for the situation, Cobbett proceeds to his own. The only remedy is to give every person who pays direct taxes the right to vote for MPs at annual elections. A reformed parliament would redress economic injustices and ensure the most democratic electoral procedures. He ends by exhorting working people to pursue political reform with zeal and resolution — by peaceful and lawful means. And

> if the *Skulkers* will not join you, if the 'decent fireside' gentry still keep aloof, proceed by yourselves. Any man can draw up a petition, and any man can *carry* it up to London, with instructions to deliver it into trusty hands, whenever the House shall meet.[45]

The revival of reform societies, initiated by Major Cartwright, had its heyday between 1816 and 1823. The twopenny trash was an important part of the literature read and discussed by working-class folk in the various Hampden Clubs, political Protestant Unions, secular Sunday schools, and other reform associations. The literacy practised within the class meetings of these societies reflects pedagogical approaches and a range of educational concerns which are interesting and important in their own right.[46] Unfortunately, they are beyond our scope here. For my concern in this section is not with the overall context and practice of a particular literacy — as it was with the Corresponding Societies. Rather, I wish to focus more narrowly on the emergence of an important *medium and expression* of working class literacy: namely, the working-class press. In this I will emphasize the dynamic between efforts and initiatives taken to establish a distinctively working-class press and the many obstacles presented to these efforts.

The twopenny trash was the first step toward a genuinely working-class press. By 'a working-class press', I mean (i) a press which offered working people access to information and comment on their daily reality at a price (more or less) within their economic grasp; and (ii) a press which reflected working class interests and was committed to promoting those interests. This, of necessity, was a press increasingly under the control of working people themselves.[47]

We may think of (i) and (ii), crudely, as cost and content dimensions. Pursuit of a working-class press involved *struggle* against oppositional forces on both of these dimensions. The Stamp Tax militated against a working-class press on the cost dimension. Laws covering sedition and libel imposed powerful obstacles on the content dimension. So too did initiatives undertaken by representatives of middle and upper class interests to make cheap literature available to working-class readers with the intention of diverting them from authentically working-class critiques of social, economic, and political conditions, and accommodating them to the status quo — thereby promoting the interests of the privileged at the expense of working-class interests. To carry this part of the argument forward it is necessary to outline some key aspects of the struggle which ensued following Cobbett's intervention in 1816. Once again, my description here is intended to be illustrative rather than exhaustive, and will be limited to selected aspects of struggle between 1816 and 1836.

The struggle for a working-class press echoes the earlier struggle for *proper* worker literacy within the Corresponding Societies, in that it too was confronted by both coercive and ideological/hegemonic forms of opposition. Examples of coercion include the 1819 legislation covering Stamp Duty and Sedition, and measures employed against Hetherington and others in the 1830s. Hegemonic opposition is represented in attempts by various publishers, organizations, and even the government itself, to 'write Cobbett down' and establish a cheap anti-reform literature. It is also to be found in the activities of such organizations as the Society for Promoting Christian Knowledge and the Society for the Diffusion of Useful Knowledge.

COERCION

In the midst of heightened and critically informed activity for political reform, the government passed the notorious Six Acts of 1819. Two of these were explicitly directed against the low cost reform press. The 'Act for the more effectual prevention and punishment of Blasphemous and Seditious Libels' reminded the public of what constituted criminal libel (as outlined above), and established mechanisms for administering the law more effectively than before and for frightening would-be offenders. Greater powers of search and arrest were given to magistrates and constables, and penalties for a second offence under the Act included banishment from the Empire or, alternatively, transportation for up to fourteen years. The 'Act to subject certain Publications to the Duties upon Newspapers, and to make other Regulations for restraining the Abuses arising from the Publication of Blasphemous and Seditious Libels' (or Publication Act, for short !), closed Cobbett's loophole by bringing the twopenny trash within the definition of a newspaper, thereby subjecting all such publications to the Stamp Tax of fourpence per copy. The complex definition of a newspaper written into this Act — that is, the lengths the Act went to in order to prevent the proliferation and accessibility of the reform press to working people — is recorded by Wickwar.[48]

The two Acts, then, undermined a free press in two ways: by economic constraint and by controlling content. The battle for the free press during the 1820s was mainly a battle against the restriction on content. It was not, to this extent, a battle for a working-class press *per se*. Rather, people like Richard Carlile, his shopmen, and his army of vendors, fought for the right to express political beliefs and criticism freely. While the battle was fought on this front the twopenny trash collapsed. Wooller, Cobbett, and others conformed to the Stamp Tax requirement, and their circulation fell away under the resulting price increase — with Wooller folding in 1824. A system of reading rooms, coffee shops, and other networks, at which people could peruse papers they could not afford to purchase, continued throughout the decade. In general, however, 'the working-class press struggled under the crushing weight of the stamp duties' until 1830.[49] In the meantime the most authentic expressions of working-class interests available in print had been effectively moved beyond the economic means of individual working-class readers.

For a decade the Publication Act of 1819 checked development of a cheap popular press. The legislation of that year brought in its wake prosecutions for seditious publishing rather than for defiance of the Stamp Tax. But in 1830 the struggle moved to the other front, with the battle of the 'great unstamped'. By 1830 the battle for free expression had been largely won. The courage and defiance of Carlile's army of persecuted and punished had defeated — morally and practically—those who would suppress political critique in the name of preventing sedition. The barrier which remained against a politically informed and critical working-class press was the Stamp Tax — which remained at the prohibitive level of fourpence set in 1815.

After several years of relative quiet, clamourings for political reform broke out anew in 1829, when 'the widespread depression afflicting various sections of the community found voice and passion'.[50] A host of political unions quickly emerged, based upon the principle of middle and working-class collaboration in the pursuit of reform. Some working-class leaders, however, anticipating the subsequent betrayal of working-class efforts for reform in the 1832 Reform Act, formed associations explicitly concerned with promoting working-class interests. The most important of these was the National Union of Working Classes and others — formed in early 1831 when London workers broke away from the middle-class dominated Metropolitan Political Union. Its leaders included a printer named Henry Hetherington, and it was he who became the central figure in the struggle against the Stamp Tax on behalf of a working-class press.

Through October and November 1830 Hetherington published a series (twenty-five in all) of penny daily papers, entitled *Penny Papers for the People*. These were written in letter form, addressed to their intended audience, in an attempt to evade the Publication Act (and, thus, the Stamp Tax) whilst at the same time providing 'cheap political information for the people'. The first *Penny Paper* was addressed to the people of England, and subsequent issues were addressed to such as the Duke of Wellington, the King, and the Archbishop of Canterbury. In December 1830 Hetherington shifted to a weekly format with *A Penny Paper for the People* by the *Poor Man's Guardian*, containing 'a comprehensive digest of all the political occurrences of the week'.[51] This new format brought Hetherington to court, and to conviction, for defiance of the Stamp Tax. He was sentenced to six months imprisonment, appealed, but had the appeal disallowed. Hetherington's response to his conviction and sentence was to produce (on 9 July 1831) the first issue of *The Poor Man's Guardian*. Instead of the official stamp it bore the emblem of a hand-press. Its motto was 'Knowledge is Power', and it was headed 'Published contrary to "law" to try the power of "Might" against "Right"'.

Hetherington was uncompromising; his aim in defiance of the law was absolutely explicit. His opening address stated the intention to protect and uphold the freedom of the press, 'the press, too, of the ignorant and the poor'. He served notice that *The Poor Man's Guardian* will contain 'news, intelligence, and occurrences', and 'remarks and observations thereon' and 'upon matters of church and state tending to excite hatred and contempt of the government and constitution of the tyranny of this country, as by law constituted'. One by one he cited the clauses of law his paper was to defy.[52] Gone was any attempt to evade the law by loopholes — as in the earlier format of a letter addressed to an 'intended' audience. Hetherington was confronting the Publication Act head on in the cause of a working-class press.

Other unstamped newspapers appeared, including Carlile's *Gauntlet*, Hobson's *Voice of the West Riding*, Doherty's *Poor Man's Advocate*, O'Brien's *Destructive*, and a paper called the *Working Man's Friend* which, together with Hetherington's *Poor Man's Guardian* became the voice of the National Union of Working Classes. The working-class press was born: a press by working-class people, for working-class people, expressing and promoting working-class interests, and at a price working people could reasonably afford.

Some appreciation of the quality of ideas and thought accessible to working-class readers via their own press can be gleaned from a typical example taken from the *Poor Man's Guardian*, 17 November 1832. The background to this particular article concerned the formation of a separate Union of the Working Classes in the Midlands. Faced with this development a council member of the Birmingham Political Union claimed that no sufficient reasons had been given which would justify the formation of a distinctively working class union. The *Poor Man's Guardian* published a reply to this charge. In it five grounds were advanced for establishing the new organization.

(i) Leaders of other political unions simply could not represent working class interests because their own interests conflict with those of workers. For example, men of property who live off rents would have an interest in preserving the Corn Laws. Yet abolition of the Corn Laws was absolutely basic to working-class interests.

(ii) The most active members of existing political unions were interested in securing representation of *property* rather than of human beings. As with ruling classes from time immemorial, they seek power to make laws which will promote their own ends. It is precisely the creation of such interest-serving laws which has yielded 'extreme wealth on the one hand, and the destitution and starvation of the artisans of our own town on the other'.

(iii) Working class distress has resulted from displacement of manual labour by machines and other inventions, which have forced workers to compete with each other for employment. This has resulted in low wages. Since masters and capitalists have an obvious interest in further mechanization if it brings still cheaper labour, they could hardly be expected to exercise power — inside or outside of parliament — with due consideration of working-class interests.

(iv) Those 'above' working-class station seek to avoid involvement in productive labour. Consequently, they have an interest in securing privileged positions in the army, navy, church, or excise, for themselves, their families and connections. This makes them part of the very problem producing the heavy taxes which cripple working people. To this extent they cannot represent working-class interests, which directly conflict with their own.

(v) The working classes are sufficiently intelligent to discuss issues concerning their best interests, their rights and liberties, and to acquire enhanced knowledge of these matters, *among themselves* — without being dictated to or controlled by persons with opposing interests.[53]

In purely economic terms, then, the working class had access through the work of Hetherington, Hobson, Doherty, and others to properly literate publications at a price they could afford. At a different level, however, the price of such publications was extremely high. As is self-evident from the article I have just described, it was very much in the interests of the ruling classes to have strong coercion brought against the development of a cheap press which politicized working people. Were such ideas to become prevalent among the masses, the social, economic and political order would surely be overthrown. And so the law moved against the working-class press. Hetherington served multiple six month terms of imprisonment, and between these spent considerable time (publishing) on the run from the law. Watson served six months. A veritable army of vendors responded to Hetherington's advertisement calling for 'some hundreds of poor men out of employ who have nothing to risk, some of those unfortunate wretches to whom distress has made prison a desirable home', to sell the *Poor Man's Guardian* in the face of the law. They sold; they were prosecuted in large numbers — up to 750 prosecutions according to one reliable estimate; they were jailed. Shortly after the *Poor Man's Guardian* finally ceased publication, at the end of 1835 with its 238th number, the Stamp Tax was reduced to a penny, 'and the way had been opened for the Chartist press'.[54]

The role of legal coercion against the working class in their struggle for a press which authentically expressed and aimed to promote their class interests is accentuated by the fact that publications reflecting ruling class interests, *and which ought to have been stamped but were not*, remained free from prosecution. This patently class-interested operation of the law, which opposed worker initiatives in search of a proper literacy and sided with church and state sponsored activities to perpetuate improper literacy among working people, is best articulated by Simon.

> Sellers of the *Poor Man's Guardian* were unmercifully persecuted up and down the country; James Watson was jailed with Hetherington, Cleave and his wife seized, Heyward of Manchester, Guest of Birmingham, Hobson and Mrs Mann of Leeds, and about 500 others suffered imprisonment, as sellers of the unstamped press. Yet at the same time prominent members of the government unctuously promoted the activities of the [Society for the Diffusion of Useful Knowledge] whose *Penny Magazine*, which had been launched in 1832 as part of the policy of providing innocent amusement for the

workers, but which should equally have been stamped, circulated unchallenged.[55]

This biased application of the law did not escape working class notice. And in the best tradition of informed struggle the National Union of Working Classes and the worker press together treated it as an issue through which to further politicize working people. As an example of this we may consider a letter from the Leicester Branch of the National Union of Working Classes to the *Poor Man's Guardian*. The branch formally expressed its 'detestation and abhorrence' at the 'base spite and vindictive malice' by which Hetherington had been singled out for persecution

> whilst Brougham, and a whole host of *lying* editors, proprietors, and publishers of the *Penny Magazines, Omnibus*, and others too numerous to mention, all equally offending against the *damnable and detestable taxes on knowledge*, are suffered to go on with impunity, and even rewarded with honour, expressly because they either basely abuse and deceive the people, or attempt to divert their attention from their true state, and the cause of their distress, instead of showing these.[56]

The letter ends by expressing the Branch's resolve to continue their efforts until tyranny is overthrown and Equal Rights and Equal Laws established.

Besides denouncing selective coercion against working-class publishers, this correspondence draws our attention to the role of popular publication as an ideological tool for preserving ruling class interests by fostering improper literacy among worker readers. To follow this theme further I turn now to the hegemonic dimension of the struggle surrounding the emergence of a working-class press.

HEGEMONY

The state was actually involved in activity against the twopenny trash and those associated with it prior to the Acts of 1819. In part this was coercive activity. A Shropshire magistrate, for example, 'caused two men to be apprehended under the Vagrant Act for distributing *Cobbett's Political Register*, and had them well flogged at the whipping post'.[57] Elsewhere hawkers were detained, prosecuted and, in some cases, fined with the option of imprisonment for non-payment. In addition, however, the state was implicated from 1816 in an extensive ideological campaign against Cobbett and others who published reform literature at working-class prices. The primary object of this campaign was hegemonic: to maintain support — especially among the working class — for the existing political order by creating a cheap anti-reform press centreing around a concerted anti-Cobbett campaign. The focus on Cobbett stemmed from the fact that he was universally acknowledged as the most effective and, therefore, most dangerous communicator of radical ideas to working-class readers.

Following a four column assault on Cobbett published in *The Times*, and subsequently republished for sale at 'a penny singly, or 6s. per 100', a correspondent of the *Morning Post* recommended that bastions of the status quo adopt the same approach to influencing political consciousness as that taken by their opponents. After all,

> if Cobbett's poisons are circulated in short pamphlets, at the expense of Jacobins, why not make their antidotes be circulated, in the same manner, at the expense of loyal men who can afford to give them away?

This correspondent recalled that during the 1790s 'many excellent pamphlets were circulated by government and by individuals, *which gave a just tone to the public mind*', and was at a loss as to why the same measures were not being adopted in 1816.[58]

In fact they were. Aspinall claims that the government was involved to the limits of its financial resources in assisting the publication and distribution of pamphlets 'calculated to counteract the mischief done by "incendiary" publications'. Indeed, government thought so well of an anti-Cobbett pamphlet published in 1819 (called *The Beauties of Cobbett*), that it printed thousands of copies and assisted in its circulation. Lord Sidmouth, the Home Secretary, received much correspondence seeking subsidies for such anti-reform publications, and personally issued the challenge (in 1818) that Cobbett 'must be written down'.

Anti-reform publication generally, and anti-Cobbett initiatives in particular, extended far beyond government activity. Webb notes that, in addition to the government, numerous publishers and organizations were involved. Cobbett's work and character were attacked in a host of low cost pamphlets, including *Anti-Cobbett, The Political Death of Mr William Cobbett, Politics for the People by William Cobbett*, and the *Letter to William Cobbett* published by the Birmingham Association for the Refutation and Suppression of Blasphemy and Sedition. Wooller's *Black Dwarf* was countered with Merle's *White Dwarf*. And W.H. Shadgett published a *Weekly Review of Cobbett, Wooller, Sherwin, and other Democratical and Infidel Writers*, 'designed as an antidote to their dangerous and subversive doctrines' and to disseminate 'just and sound principles, on all popular subjects'. The wider body of anti-reform literature included a refurbished *Village Politics* and more than a dozen new tracts from Hannah More. Activity was feverish in the towns as well as the provinces.

> London publishers, like Hatchard and Seely, turned out numbers of cheap anti-reform pamphlets. George Cayley, a physician, published two addresses to pitmen and keelmen at Durham ... Edward Walker in Newcastle published *A Word from the Other Side, The Friendly Fairy* . . . and reprinted Paley's *Reasons for Contentment* . . . The *Leeds Intelligencer* in 1819 published a penny *Reformers' Guide* and also issued a loyal paper called *The Domestic Miscellany*, and *Poor Man's Friend* . . . [In Manchester] a periodical called *The Patriot* appeared after Peterloo . . .

> The Pitt Club in 1817 distributed two [dialogues] by Canon C.D. Wray . . . and in the same year Francis Philips wrote *A Dialogue between Thomas, the Weaver, and His Old Master.*[59]

This literature aimed to counter directly the reformist flavour of material which had become increasingly accessible to working people after 1816. It confronted the ideology of radicalism and reform with an ideology grounded in the beliefs and values of the established order: that is, in the worldview of those whose interests were best served by existing political, social, and economic arrangements. It is true that the Publication Act of 1819 had been largely successful in restricting working-class access to radical ideas in print. As we have seen, however, seditious libels continued apace, and despite their reduced circulation among working-class readers it was clear that they would continue to exert upon working-class consciousness an influence hostile to ruling interests. After all, ideas in currency could be communicated orally, from those with direct access to published opinion to those without — providing a basis for discussion and further development of these ideas among those penalized by taxes on newspapers. Since the cause of reform embraced (to 1832) both middle-class and working-class activists — and radical societies with mixed class membership continued into the 1820s, and were revived again after 1829 — dissemination of radical critiques among the working class would (and did) continue. Hence the considerable activity on the part of supporters of the status quo to develop and communicate as widely as possible a direct counter to reformist ideas: one reflecting their own interests and ideological position.

The policy of publishing a direct counter to reformist ideas was an *overtly* political strategy — an exercise in consolidating active support for maintaining the status quo by shaping and controlling political consciousness. This, however, was only one line of ideological attack available to the ruling classes. A second approach involved a more *covert* strategy, but one which would equally preserve the status quo. This was to make 'safe' literature available at low cost to working-class readers. 'Safe' literature was of two main types: religious tracts, and material intended to inform, interest, and amuse, but which was powerless to stimulate political critique. Religious tracts would secure loyalty to Christian doctrine and, to that extent, help maintain the hegemony of church and state. Informative literature would operate (in political terms) on the logic of diversion — it would deflect the reading habits of workers out of the political field altogether; whether the politics of reform or anti-reform. It would effectively depoliticize working-class readers by channelling their reading energies into politically impotent content, with the effect of maintaining the status quo by failing to stimulate opposition to it.

Among the leading groups to employ the strategy of providing cheap but safe literature for worker readers were the Society for Promoting Christian Knowledge (SPCK), and the Society for the Diffusion of Useful Knowledge (SDUK).

The SPCK was formally established in March 1699. In part it was a response to its founders' perception of the deplorable moral and religious situation in England. More broadly, however, it was concerned to promote christian knowledge at home as well as in His Majesty's Dominions. A subscription society, its major activities at home during the eighteenth century included promoting charity schools with a catechetical flavour, formulating policy (communicated by the bishops) for charity schools under the trusteeship of Anglican churchmen, publishing religious literature for sale at subsidized prices and for use within charity schools, establishing libraries for poor clergy and religious services for prisons, and producing bibles, prayer books, liturgies, etc., in Irish, Welsh and Gaelic. Records from 1815 establish that at this time the Society recognized three main tasks: missions abroad; distribution of the Scriptures, the prayer book, and religious tracts; and the education of the poor 'in the principles of our faith'. Its publishing activities were conducted under eighteen separate headings, with major priorities including printing and distributing bibles, prayer books, commentaries and explanations (pitched at different levels for different readerships), sermons and tracts on catechetical themes, books for public and private devotion, guides to confession and absolution, and works concerning duties, vices, and the evils of popery.[60]

In the midst of the political turmoil of 1819, however, a new dimension was added to the work of the SPCK, and its activity took on a special urgency. 'Viewing with much concern and dismay the efforts which the enemies of Christianity were making in disseminating the poisons of infidelity', and believing it proper to employ all its available means to counteract the evils being done by radical publications, the Society appointed a special committee charged with countering the infidel influence. This committee had instructions 'to publish in a more popular form, and at a diminished price, suitable tracts then on the Society's Catalogue', and also to publish 'such other works as might be deemed necessary'.[61] Large print runs were made of several existing works, and more than thirty new tracts were produced. According to SPCK records more than a million copies of books and tracts 'against infidelity and blasphemy' were printed and distributed in less than a year — with expenses being met from the £7000 raised by appeal to supporters.

Webb suggests that this attempt (during 1819–20) to counter the influence of the emerging radical press on working-class readers brought some disappointments to the SPCK. Reports from Manchester, Bolton, and London's East End expressed great difficulties in getting the poor to take the tracts, even where the original policy of selling them cheaply was waived in favour of distributing them gratis in order to reach an audience. While sales were good in better off areas, such as London's West End, the Society's real concern was to have an effect in the poorer neighbourhoods. Whatever its true degree of success may have been, the SPCK expressed satisfaction 'that the measures . . . pursued were productive of much good'. So much so that the work of the anti-infidel committee was reactivated in 1830–31 when, once more, 'the infidel press teemed with the bitterest invectives against religion and the ministers of Christ', and publications 'of the most pernicious kind, full of blasphemy . . . were circulated with unceasing activity'.[62]

This was the era of Hetherington and defiance of the Stamp. The SPCK again raised funds for publication. Many of the earlier tracts were reprinted and distributed, and no less than twenty-nine new titles were produced. Together these comprised *A Library of Christian Knowledge*. In 1832 the Society's rejuvenated publishing programme took a further step with the formation of a Committee of General Literature and Education. This was a response not only to the 'evil opinions being inculcated' in some parts of the popular 'penny literature', but also to the fact that in other parts (where opinions were not in themselves 'evil') the knowledge being diffused among the masses was 'studiously separated from religion'. Under the auspices of the new committee the SPCK entered popular publishing on several new fronts, including historical and biographical series, a scientific series with a 'decided bias' towards revelation, and a penny weekly called the *Saturday Magazine*.[63] Together with the work of the Religious Tract Society, the activities of the SPCK represent the most impressive attempts to foster safe literature on the model of religious content. On a political level their work was complemented by the efforts of publishers specializing in essentially secular knowledge. Foremost among these was the Society for the Diffusion of Useful Knowledge.

The major figure behind the formation of the SDUK (in 1826) was Henry Brougham, a leading Whig and, subsequently, Lord Chancellor. Brougham's *Practical Observations upon the Education of the People* had been published in 1825. In this he noted two main impediments to a sound working class education. First, working people could not afford the books and instructors available to more affluent citizens. Second, even had they been able to afford the expense, workers lacked the necessary leisure time to plough through the kind of learning material as did exist within such areas of knowledge as science, literature and the arts. To overcome these impediments facing the provision of a sound education for the working class, Brougham advocated making available cheap publications adapted to the special learning circumstances of workers: this material to be available in the fields deemed useful knowledge. Even earlier, in 1821, Charles Knight had expressed his hope that 'ignorant disseminators of sedition and discontent' — i.e., people such as Cobbett — would be 'beaten out of the [publishing] field' by opponents with 'better principles', who would thereafter 'direct the secret of popular writing to a useful and righteous purpose'.[64] The sentiments of Brougham and Knight (who became the main publisher for the SDUK) were reflected in the official aim of the Society: namely, 'the imparting of *useful* information to all classes of the community, particularly to such as are unable to avail themselves of experienced teachers, or may prefer learning by themselves'.[65]

The ideological purpose of such activity was expressed very clearly by Knight himself, some years after the SDUK was founded. He insisted that

the object of the general diffusion of knowledge is not to make men dissatisfied with their lot — to make the peasant yearn to be an artisan, or the artisan dream of the honours and riches of a profession — but to give the means of content to those who, for the most part, must necessarily remain in that station which requires great self-denial and great endurance; but which is capable of becoming not only a condition of comfort, but of enjoyment, through the exercise of those very virtues, in connection with a desire for that improvement of the understanding which to a large extent is independent of rank and riches.[66]

The early publications of the SDUK kept clear of explicit political themes, including political economy. The *Library of Useful Knowledge* specialized in biography and natural science. It was supplemented by the *Library of Entertaining Knowledge* which, as its title suggests, offered amusement on less esoteric matters. The two *Libraries* appeared in monthly issues and 'were filled with miscellaneous scientific and cultural information, ranging from Lepidophera to "Autumnal Customs in Kardofan"'.[67] In 1832 the *Libraries* were joined by the *Penny Magazine*, edited by Charles Knight. Knight aimed to produce 'a safe Miscellany, in which all classes might find much information and some amusement'. Webb suggests that the proportions were rather more the reverse. The *Penny Magazine* was largely a compilation of 'quaint facts and descriptions of various animals, buildings, and natural phenomena', with much of its initial popularity doubtless due to its woodcut illustrations. Even so, it was by no means entirely bereft of political implication. Consider, for example, the ideological message conveyed in 'The Weaver's Song', published in an early number of the *Magazine*.

Weave, brothers, weave! — Swiftly throw
   The shuttle athwart the loom,
And show us how brightly your flowers grow,
   That have beauty but no perfume!
Come, show us the rose, with a hundred dyes,
   The lily, that hath no spot,
The violet, deep as your true love's eyes,
   And the little forget-me-not!

Sing, — sing brothers! weave and sing!
   'Tis good both to sing and to weave:
'Tis better to work than live idle:
   'Tis better to sing than grieve.

Weave, brothers, weave! — Toil is ours;
   But toil is the lot of men:
One gathers the fruit, one gathers the flowers,
   One soweth the seed again!
There is not a creature, from England's King,
   To the peasant that delves the soil,

> That knows half the pleasures the seasons bring,
>   If he hath not his share of toil!
> So, — sing, brothers! etc.[68]

Despite such excursions into thinly veiled political comment on the virtues of accepting one's station with grace and serenity, comforted by the 'insight' that toil is the lot of (all) men, the content of the *Libraries*, the *Penny Magazine*, and the *Penny Cyclopaedia* was diversionary rather than explicitly political in nature; an exercise in covert rather than overt strategy. This material was attacked from all sides: by tories, middle-class radicals, and the working-class press itself[69]; and from 1830 the SDUK published in addition to its programme of safe literature a number of works steeped in the political economy of the bourgeoisie.

While there is not the space to develop the theme here, it is worth noting that the attempt by the SDUK to diffuse political economy as useful knowledge among working-class readers involved a shift to an overtly hegemonic strategy. Such publications sought to shape the consciousness of working-class folk in accordance with an ideology grounded in middle-class interests and which directly contradicted the interests of workers themselves. Quite simply, there is no other way in which to understand Charles Knight's *Results of Machinery*, Brougham's arguments on wages, consumption levels and employment, presented in the *Companion to the Newspaper*, or the SDUK's *Short Address to Workmen on Combinations to Raise Wages* — all of which insisted that attempts by workers to force higher wages through combined activity were futile. According to these arguments, the inexorable operation of supply and demand meant that wages must inevitably be set by market forces. The economy simply could not sustain wages above the level fixed by the labour market. The real choices facing labourers were, according to SDUK theory, strictly limited. They must either accept the fortunes (and misfortunes) of the labour market and learn to live within them, or escape by becoming themselves capitalists. Those labourers who did not choose to become capitalists could, at best, hope to make the most of their earnings (whilst employed, that is) by practising thrift and sound economic management. And so, says the *Short Address to Workmen*,

> 'when labour offered for sale is plentiful its price [i.e., wages] will be low, when it is scarce it will be high. This is a law of nature against which it is vain to contend'; only 'forbearance, management, and economy' could alleviate the inevitable lot of human life, as revealed in the iron law of wages. Active protest was out of place. 'Your complaints [labourers were informed] are sometimes exaggerated and were they better informed than they are, you would not have chosen [protest and combination as] the remedy to remove them'.[70]

The working class press was severe in its treatment both of overt and covert approaches to ideological domination by such organizations as the SPCK and the SDUK. In penetrating and revealing these strategies, working-class writers exposed attempts on behalf of opposing class interests to foist an improper literacy onto workers. In the same process by developing their critiques they helped positively to enhance proper literacy among their readers. Against the political economy of the SDUK, such working-class writers as William Longson, Bronterre O'Brien, William Carpenter, and numerous economic commentators for the *Poor Man's Guardian*, produced compelling yet entirely accessible rebuttals.[71] Some of the most scathing comment, however, was reserved for the exponents of diversion: for those who would neutralize workers' critical potential by channelling their reading energies into safe literature and, thereby, turn hard won skills against the interests of those who had managed to acquire them.

The SPCK was denounced for aiming 'to prop up the "present cannibal order of things" by reconciling the poor to poverty'. O'Brien referred to those who circulated the Society's tracts as 'canting vagabonds' with 'hypocritical pretensions to religion', lamenting that the hold they had over weak minds made it even 'more difficult to break through their slimy meshes' than to overcome the persuasive powers of the stamped press.[72] In more moderate vein, Cobbett exposed the SPCK as hoping to prevent the people from reading and thinking politics.

The working-class press similarly denounced 'useful knowledge' as patronizing, hypocritical, and hostile to the people's interests. The kind of knowledge truly required by the people — that is, the content of a proper literacy — had nothing to do with the number of humps on the back of a dromedary, the number of transmigrations in the life of a caterpillar from chrysalis to butterfly, or with how a kangaroo jumps. It had, instead, to do with their rights as citizens; with why the class that actually produced wealth was the most degraded, while that which produced nothing was elevated; with why working people were denied a vote and any say whatsoever in legislation, while the 'idle and mischievous' exercised complete power in political and legal matters; with why those whose acts revealed that they were really without religious conviction had control of the nation's religion.[73]

Critiques published in the working-class press of the literacy fostered by the SCPK and the SDUK came from rank and file readers as well as from the editors and other established writers. Hollis cites a labourer's assessment (published in the *Poor Man's Guardian*) of the 'useful knowledge' purveyed by the *Penny Magazine*.

> Useful knowledge, indeed, would that be to those who live idly on our skill and industry, which would cajole us into an apathetic resignation to their iron sway, or induce us to waste the energy and skill of man for them all day, and seek relaxation of an evening in the puerile stories or recreations of childhood ... This first number of their *Penny Magazine*, insinuates that poor men are not qualified to under-stand the measures of government. 'Every man is deeply interested in

all the questions of government. Every man, however, may not be qualified to understand them'. My fellow-countrymen, I beseech you now do be modest, do be very diffident, — pray do distrust the evidence of your reasons — submit implicitly to the *dicta* of your betters![74]

This writer shows a profound understanding of the distinction between proper and improper literacy; of reading and writing that promises enhanced control over and genuine understanding of one's daily life, and that which effectively negates them in the interests of others. The self-conscious aim of those who produced the working-class press was to advance proper literacy among their readers. Nowhere is this expressed more clearly and directly than by O'Brien.

> Some simpletons talk of knowledge as rendering the working classes more obedient, more dutiful — better servants, better subjects, and so on, which means making them more subservient slaves, and more conducive to the wealth and gratification of idlers of all description. But such knowledge is trash; the only knowledge which is of any service to the working people is that which makes them more dissatisfied, and makes them worse slaves. This is the knowledge we shall give them ...[75]

The battle for the working-class press between 1816 and 1836 provides an excellent illustration of distinct and competing literacies emerging as social constructions within the context of struggle between competing interest groups. The polarized conceptions of Charles Knight and Bronterre O'Brien capture this in microcosm. From a working-class standpoint, the form of literacy promoted on behalf of ruling class interests for worker consumption must be adjudged *improper* — and, in fact, was assessed as such by the working-class press. Against this hegemonic literacy the working-class press battled to create and transmit a proper literacy: a truly counter-hegemonic form which would focus workers' attention upon those structured inequalities of power and control within economic, political, and social life, that were the *real* causes of their condition.

Proper Literacy in Chartist Practice and Theory

A rich and complex movement, Chartism was characterized by considerable regional and local diversity and beset with some massive internal divisions. While the broad objectives of political reform — as defined in the six points of the People's Charter — and economic improvement for working people were kept in focus throughout, an intricate array of more specific aims existed, and a variety of methods were employed in pursuing them. Consequently, there is a risk of distortion in referring to 'Chartist practice and theory', insofar as this may suggest a degree of unity and uniformity that simply did not exist.[76] Nonetheless, those aspects chosen for discussion here belong unmistakably to the Chartist movement, and offer some valuable perspectives on the politics of literacy generally and the pursuit of proper literacy in particular.

The Chartist movement was very much an outgrowth of earlier working-class organization and struggle. Five of the six points contained in the Charter had been discussed and adopted by the London Working Men's Association eighteen months before the final terms were published in May 1838. There is some evidence that the Working Men's Association had themselves taken these points from the London Radical Association. Wearmouth traces the origins of Chartism to 'the political associations of 1831–1835, the radical agitation of 1816–1823, and the Reform Societies of the eighteenth century'. Indeed, he goes so far as to say that Chartism derived from these origins 'a political programme somewhat fully developed and defined'.[77] Not surprisingly, then, we find that Chartism has some notable points of connection with themes already addressed in this chapter.

In the first place, it was very much involved in consolidating and developing the working-class press. The dominant Chartist newspaper was the weekly *Northern Star*, which at its zenith achieved a very high circulation — especially in view of the fact that it was a stamped paper (the duty having been reduced to one penny in 1836; low enough to make defiance of the tax inexpedient for publishers, but high enough to keep the *Star* beyond the means of many potential readers). In terms of circulation, the *Charter*, *People's Paper*, and *Beehive*, also ranked as major publications — although falling well behind the *Star*. To these must be added scores of other papers and periodicals (often short-lived) which were established or otherwise employed in the Chartist cause. These included, for example, the *Northern Liberator, Scottish Patriot, Chartist Circular, The People*, the *Democratic Review*, Ernest Jones' *Notes to the People*, and others such as Thomas Cooper's *Rushlight, Extinguisher*, and *Midland Counties Illuminator*, which today are mentioned in only the most specialist studies. Many publishers, editors, and correspondents of the Chartist press began their careers with the unstamped, providing direct links between Chartism and the earlier era.

The Chartist press maintained the educative tradition established by Hetherington and other publishers of the unstamped, emphasizing a proper literacy that was functional to the pursuit of working-class objectives. In addition to keeping readers informed of Chartist activities — reporting speeches, covering meetings and conventions, etc. — and providing comment on immediate political issues, newspapers and periodicals also contained 'much cultural and scientific material which provided matter for reflection and discussion'.[78] Simon notes the comprehensive offerings of papers such as the *Northern Star* and *People's Paper*. These, he says, devoted 'a great deal of space to educative articles on economic, cultural and scientific subjects'. The *Northern Star*, for example, ran a 'series of twenty-four articles ... on socialist theory and practice ... in 1842–3'. In addition, it covered in detail 'the hard fought political debates between Owenites and Chartists, or between the Owenites and [the Chartist] J.R. Stephens on religion'. Literature was well represented, with the work of major poets like Burns, Shelley, and Byron featuring along with verse written by Chartists themselves. Furthermore, entire pages were regularly given over to reporting foreign news, and the proceedings of parliament and parliamentary commissions. 'There is no doubt', concludes Simon,

> that the cultural standard maintained by [the Chartist] press was extremely high, and this must have had its effect on the discussions and debates held in the Chartist meeting rooms and halls.[79]

One example must suffice here for providing more detailed illustration of the efforts by the Chartist press to promote a proper literacy among the working class. The issues of the *Northern Star* for April 1 and April 8 1848, featured letters by Ernest Jones and John H. Mackay on the theme of soldiers in relation to the working class and worker agitation for political rights. These letters appeared at a time when the Chartists were preparing for renewed mass agitation and, therefore, when it was to be expected that troops would be used against demonstrators. In his letter Jones exposes the logic of divide and rule employed by 'class government'. Since bestowing privilege is in the hands of government, each of the divided groups

> crawls more abjectly than his neighbour to the footstool of power — asking for advantage over those less forward. Government thus pulls the leading strings of its political puppets, playing a few off against the rest; and as long as it can maintain the invidious distinctions, so long will it have the bayonet of one Englishman against the breast of another — and be able to stop a people on the highway of progression, crying: 'Stand and deliver, poor rates and taxes'.[80]

Jones' response is to try and demonstrate the identity of interests between soldiers and the working class generally: indeed, between all sections of the community and the working class, since it is in the interests of no one to be divided, ruled, and degraded by a tyrannical power. He spells out several respects in which soldiers at the time were oppressed, degraded, and exploited as 'a tool of faction'. He decries this abuse of soldiers and submits that his sentiments would prevail among Chartists at large. In this way Jones sought to enhance class consciousness across groups of working-class people (namely, soldiers and Chartists) who were regularly brought into conflict with each other in accordance with the interests of other classes. By advocating the principle of 'fraternity' over that of 'divide and rule', Jones was seeking to unite Chartists and soldiers — equally bearers of working-class interests and equally objects of oppression — under a more accurate understanding of their mutual circumstances, and thereby increase the possibility of working people winning greater control over their lives and the conditions in which they lived. If class cohesion between soldiers and Chartists could be achieved, a major impediment to working people winning the political demands of the Charter — i.e., the use of crushing State violence — would be removed.

Mackay's letter appeals even more directly to soldiers that they not allow

themselves to be used to put down Chartist agitation for political reform. He
was confident that 1848 would bring the 'death knell' to despotism on the
continent, and that it should soon resound throughout Britain as well. To
Britain's soldiers he says,

> then . . when you shall see the toiling millions assembled in their might
> — when they shall rise *en masse* and steadily demand their birthright —
> freedom! Then shall you prove to the world that you are truly worthy
> of being called defenders of *your country*, to the dismay of the tyrant
> and the oppressor.[81]

Here Mackay effectively identifies 'your country' with 'the people', or 'the
toiling millions'. This makes an important ideological point. We have noted
Francis Place's observation that the Treason and Sedition Acts of 1795 were
popular measures among the working class, where they were seen as important
for defending the nation's security. Here, of course, 'the nation' implies those
interests protected under the hegemony of church and state. By this definition,
working–class interests fall outside the interests of 'the nation'. Consequently,
for a majority of workers to support the Treason and Sedition Acts (and their
supporting sanctions) against advocates of political reform in the name of
national security was precisely for them to defend ruling class interests against
their own class interests. The situation was exactly the same for soldiers called
to put down Chartist demonstration. By insisting that 'the country' (or nation)
refers properly to 'its people as a whole', and *not* to a single minority class,
Mackay counters a major component of ruling class hegemony — clearing the
way for working people to identify securing the interests of the nation with
securing *their own* interests. To convey this idea in print to working-class
readers is of the very essence of enhancing proper literacy.

   Secondly, in maintaining the tradition of class meetings, and establishing
their own halls, schools, and Sunday schools, Chartists kept alive pedagogical
activities practised in the earlier reform organizations. The class meetings,
modelled on the Methodist system, functioned only very briefly during the
Chartist period: during 1839–41 and, momentarily, during 1848. Their
legality was questioned by certain Chartist leaders whose opinions carried the
day. As with the divisions of the Corresponding Societies, Chartist classes
performed several functions: to spread the cause and maintain solidarity, to
circumvent the ban on open air meetings, provide a network for organizing
effective forms of agitation and a medium for raising revenue through
subscriptions and contributions, as well as to educate. 'Moral force' Chartists,
in particular, gave tremendous emphasis to education as a means for effecting
political reform. This education, of course, had to promote *really* useful
knowledge[82] : a *proper* literacy; an understanding of the world that would
enhance worker interests and not, like the offerings of the Useful Knowledge
Society, undermine these interests. Teaching literacy skills remained an
important task, and Wearmouth notes that in the classes many Chartists
learned to read. In addition, they learned to 'discuss, speak [publicly], debate,

instruct; they grew wise and skilled in "promulgating truth"'.[83] Class members were urged to make the best educational use of the organized classes. The *Northern Liberator* communicated an appeal to Chartists throughout the land to make the class meetings

> as much as possible, a medium for the diffusion of intelligence, and not, as is often the case, meeting merely to enter into light conversation, pay the penny [subscription], and go home. [Members should pay careful attention to the] works of history, and especially the history of our own country, discussing its great events philosophically, not as matters of fact, but noting their bearing on our present state ...[84]

The ideal implied here is one of proper literacy. Reading and writing should yield much more than a mere acquaintance with 'matters of fact' — in the manner of the 'diffusion of useful knowledge'. Whereas absorbing 'useful knowledge', through that Society's publications, was a passive affair — confined to reading for amusement or 'interesting' information — the Chartist class ideal involved an *active* pedagogy. History, for example, was to be *discussed* and *interpreted*, with particular attention to the bearing of historical developments on the present conditions of working people. The awareness sought was of how existing conditions came about: how structures of domination and exploitation were established historically, legitimated through law and the constitution, maintained through traditions and practices, and defended against the just demands of the people. How widely this educational ideal was actually realized within the Chartist classes is unclear, although it can be safely assumed that many classes did in fact approximate to it during their brief existence.

Various modes of Chartist education existed besides the press and the class meetings. Chartists established halls and meeting rooms, many of which housed small libraries. The facilities were used for a wide range of educative activities, from lectures to dramatic productions, evening debates to the operation of Sunday schools for adults and children and so on. In some areas Chartists actually established radical day schools for children. Simon records several cases, in all of which there was an expressed concern to promote forms of understanding and commitment that presupposed a *proper* literacy. The aim of Chartists opening a school at Yew Green is typical. They hoped their undertaking would

> receive the support of the Chartist body, for most desirable it is that the rising generation should receive instruction (afforded them by no sect or party under the present system) which will bring them up in the nurture and love of the principles of liberty, and fit them in after years to 'know their rights, and knowing dare maintain them'.[85]

The deployment of literacy skills by Chartists in the interests of enhancing class consciousness and exposing the true causes of oppression and misery took some highly creative turns. In his autobiography, Thomas Cooper mentions a good example. He encouraged two men who belonged to his Association in Leicester, and who had occasionally shown him their verse, to write hymns for the Sunday meetings. The hymns were published in the *Extinguisher*, and eventually collected in the local Chartist Association's hymn book. John Bramwich (a stocking weaver) produced fourteen hymns, and William Jones (a 'glove hand') sixteen. The best received effort of Bramwich, who died 'of sheer exhaustion, from hard labour and want' in 1846, was entitled 'Britannia's sons, though slaves ye be'. It contains the following thoughts (among others)

> Britannia's sons, though slaves ye be,
> God, your Creator, made you free;
> He life and thought and being gave
> But never, never made a slave!
>
> All men are equal in His sight,
> The bond, the free, the black, the white:
> He made them all — them freedom gave;
> God made the man — Man made the slave.[86]

Chartist learning was by no means confined to overtly political themes — although development of a sound political consciousness set the parameters within which learning was conceived and conducted. Cooper tells of forming a Sunday school, 'for men and boys who were at work on the week days', and how additional meetings on one or two weeknights were later added. When there was not 'some stirring local or political topic' for discussion, Cooper

> lectured on Milton, and repeated portions of the 'Paradise Lost', or on Shakespeare, and repeated portions of 'Hamlet', or on Burns, and repeated 'Tam O'Shanter' ... or I took up Geology, or even Phrenology, and made the young men acquainted, elementally, with the knowledge of the time.[87]

The obvious differences between Cooper's attempt to acquaint working men 'elementally' with the knowledge of the time and the activities of the SDUK were differences of context and milieu. The wider context of Chartist education was politicized; educational activity was situated within struggle for political, economic, and social rights. While Milton could be enjoyed for his own sake, and aspects of geological knowledge entertained as being of interest in their own right, ultimately the awareness of Chartist learners was integrated in a politically informed way. Their information was not inert. Neither was it random. And the pedagogical milieu in which they acquired and developed their understanding of the world was active. The emphasis was on discussion and interpretation; not on passive absorption.

Much more could be said on the theme of proper literacy and the educational practice of Chartists. This, however, is not my sole concern here. I am equally concerned with ideas contained in Chartist theory which relate to the rightful provision and control of education for children. The emphasis in this chapter so far has been largely on adult literacy initiatives during the period before mass schooling emerged in Britain. In chapter 4, however, the focus will shift to literacy in the context of contemporary mass schooling, and forms of literacy transmitted and employed in school will be assessed in terms of their politics. This assessment will, of course, be made in light of the fact of mass schooling. Judgements will relate to the actual practice of state-provided and regulated schooling. Before turning to what will be, as it were, an assessment from hindsight, it is interesting to consider various arguments that were advanced by Chartists in foresight: that is, *before* the fact of mass schooling. For these arguments emphasize the necessity of education being genuinely under popular or democratic control, so that it can truly reflect and promote the interests of people equally, if (what might be called) proper forms of literacy are to emerge and improper forms be avoided. Given the argument in chapter 4 it will be clear that Chartist aspirations for proper literacy — and proper education more generally — have not been realized, and that their fears for the outcome of a national system of education not genuinely under popular control have been vindicated. In what follows I refer to three elements of Chartist educational theory. These are the *Address on Education* of the London Working Men's Association (LWMA, 1837), William Lovett and John Collins' *Chartism: a new organization of the people* (1840), and occasional writings on education by Ernest Jones (1851–2).

The background to these Chartist writings is important, although there is not the space to detail it here. The early years of the nineteenth century saw growing interest in the principle of a national system of elementary education. Attempts within government to move in this direction — such as the initiatives of Whitbread and Brougham — had, however, been comprehensively defeated. At the advent of Chartism, such schooling as *did* exist for working-class children was provided on a voluntary basis and, in the case of Dame and Common Day Schools, required fees. Estimates suggest that in the 1830s approximately one tenth of the total population of England and Wales attended some form or other of day school. In its report of 1838 a parliamentary committee urged that provision be made available for 'one in eight of the population in great towns'.[88] At this time an important incentive for government initiatives to extend educational provision among the working classes was the growing conviction that an ignorant populace was a dangerous populace. Over the next decade, of course, this belief was fuelled by the existence of the Chartist movement itself!

> The uneasiness caused by the Newport Rising of 1839 and by the Chartist agitation in general, [was] increased by the riots of 1842 ... [Against this background] education was regarded as a means of enabling the working classes 'to govern and repress the workings of their passions'.

Indeed, a letter from the Education Committee of government to Monmouth Mining Proprietors, encouraging them to establish schools in their districts, made direct reference to the idea of education as a form of insurance. If the proprietors did not feel the weight of moral considerations in the matter of providing education, surely they would sense the dangers of

> leaving their wealth exposed to ... popular tumults and secret violence [and see the prudence of investing] a comparatively small annual expenditure ... in introducing the elements of civilization and religion [which] would render society harmonious and secure.[89]

Despite the growing beliefs in some quarters that an appropriate form of educational provision for all working-class children was essential for national peace and security, during the period from 1833 into the 1850s successive governments failed in their attempts to improve the quantity and quality of education available. At government level both the quantity and quality of existing provision were recognized as problems. Between 1833 and 1843 major reports were submitted by the Manchester Statistical Society, the Children's Employment Commission, and at least three separate government committees. All drew attention to the inadequacy of existing provision in numerical and qualitative terms. In addition, reports made by school inspectors provided graphic evidence of gross pedagogical shortcomings in the monitorial schools subject to government inspection. Inspectors' reports along with those of the Children's Employment Commission pointed out, moreover, the atrocious conditions in which 'education' was often conducted.

To a large extent, the lack of quantity and quality could be traced to the fact that educational provision was widely seen to be properly the business of voluntary organizations, and under these arrangements the major tendency was toward monitorial schooling under the auspices of two rival religious societies: the National Society, representing Church of England interests, and the British and Foreign Schools Society, representing nonconformists. In 1833 government had succeeded in legislating a grant in aid of £20,000 per year for building schools. Grants from this fund could be claimed by the two religious societies to subsidize monies raised from supporters' subscriptions, subject to meeting certain conditions. Rivalry between the societies was intense, and provided the major obstacle to government initiatives in respect of the amount and quality of provision available during the Chartist era. In 1839 Russell proposed an education plan allowing for increased grants, the provision of teacher training schools, opening up eligibility for grants in aid to non-religious bodies, and creating a committee to consider 'all matters affecting the education of the People' (including administering grants). Opposed vehemently by both societies the plan was abandoned. All Russell achieved was a watered-down committee and an addition of £10,000 to the annual grant. Subsequent initiatives by a tory government in 1843 and a whig government in 1846 were defeated by opposition from the religious societies, each of which perceived damage to their own interests and advantage to the other's in what government was proposing.

In qualitative terms, shortcomings were observed on two levels. First, the pedagogy of monitorial schools was criticized by inspectors. Secondly, even in terms of the minimal goals sought by these schools their results were poor. (NB. It is generally acknowledged that children learned considerably more in monitorial schools than in Dame and Common Day schools!) With regard to results, reports cited by the Hammonds are revealing. One inspector estimated that three-quarters of the children he inspected would leave school unable 'to read the scriptures with tolerable ease or correctness' — the Bible being the main, and often the sole, text in monitorial schools. Meanwhile, the Children's Employment Commission complained that many children deemed able to read by the monitorial schools were found, when examined, to know only the letters of the alphabet. Only a small proportion were able to read an easy book competently. And of those who *could* read fluently,

> very few, when questioned, were found to have any conception of the meaning of the words they uttered, or were able to give any intelligible account of what seemed to the examiners to be simple and easy terms and things; so that, as far as regards the acquisition of any useful knowledge ... these children ... were as little benefitted, after years of so-called tuition, as if they had never been at school.[90]

Given the pedagogy employed — and largely employed of *necessity* given a monitorial setting — it is difficult to see how knowledge that was useful for preserving social order, let alone the kind of awareness afforded by proper literacy, could have emerged from the monitorial system. The Manual of the British and Foreign Schools Society stipulates the following question and answer sequence to accompany the reading lesson based on the first verse of Genesis.

Monitor   Who created the heavens and the earth?
Pupil   God.
Monitor   When did God create the heavens and the earth?
Pupil   In the beginning.
Monitor   What did God do in the beginning?
Pupil   He created the heavens and the earth.[91]

In response to the quantitative and qualitative limitations of existing educational provision, the incidence of crime and the obvious inadequacy of punishment to deter it, and the heightened opposition of working-class organizations to existing political and economic arrangements, 'speculative philanthropists [were] urging an inquiry into the merits of *national education* as the most efficient cure for [Britain's] national evils'.[92] This gave Chartists cause for alarm, since 'speculative philanthropists' represented the very class interests which had dictated the educational fate of working-class children to that time. In advancing their views concerning the rightful provision and control of education, Chartist theorists rejected outright the assumptions, 'principles', and practices advocated and employed by ruling interests, which had so far produced educational outcomes harmful to working-class interests.

Against the principle of developing a national system of education to promote and maintain upper- and middle-class interests, Chartist writers urged the necessity of working people playing a full and equal part in determining the education their children would receive. Their guiding thought was, perhaps, best expressed by Ernest Jones when he wrote:

> There are few things of greater importance than the education of the people. But it must be remembered that *a people's education is safe only in a people's own hands.* [93]

In their *Address on Education* the LWMA denounced the attitude of those members of other classes who effectively viewed working-class children as mere objects to be controlled and manipulated for the advantage of others: to be educated not at all, or else taught in accordance with the interests of property, religious sects, or both. The assumption that religious doctrine must form the basis of education for the poor negated the possibility of genuine education. Moreover, the LWMA observed that religious squabblings actually hindered the process of providing *any instruction at all* — good or bad — for many children. The actions of 'selfish and bigoted possessors of wealth' had convinced the LWMA that the ruling classes

> still consider education as their own prerogative, or as *a boon to be sparingly conferred upon the multitude*, instead of a universal instrument for advancing the dignity of man, and for gladdening his existence. [94]

Against the provision of a *partial* system of education, through charity or otherwise on the cheap, the LWMA asserted the principle of 'publicly extending an equal education to all; not as a charity, *but as a right*' deriving from society itself. Since society implies 'a union for mutual benefit', it must 'publicly provide for the ... proper training of all its members'. Far from leaving educational provision to whim or charity, government has a positive *duty* to ensure that education is available. Education free from religious squabbles, and free from religious teaching. [95]

The LWMA were clear as to the nature and control of education. Regarding control they deemed it the duty of government to raise money — through taxes or otherwise — for education, to distribute this money so that a sufficient number of suitable schools are built, and to oversee the management of schools to ensure that the people's educational objectives are truly being met. Government must not, however, have the power to select teachers, books, or the type of instruction to be given, or be directly involved in school management. While government must ensure that education is conducted in accordance with the will of the people, it is not itself to determine what that will is, or to discharge it directly. Rather

> the selection of teachers, the choice of books, and the whole manage-ment and superintendence of schools in each locality should be confined to a SCHOOL COMMITTEE, elected by *universal* suffrage

of all the adult population, male and female. And to prevent local prejudices or party feuds from being prejudicial in the choice, the district for selecting the committee should be extended beyond the locality they [are] called on to superintend. [The committee] should ... be responsible at all times to the majority of their constituents.[96]

In place of the stupefying pedagogy practised in monitorial schools, and typically confined to transmitting the narrow tenets of a particular creed or sect, the LWMA envisaged a rational, secular, and comprehensive education. All children should receive — free — an infant, preparatory, and high school education. In addition, a college education in the higher branches of knowledge should be available free to all who sought it. All teachers would have to be properly trained and qualified, through normal schools established for this purpose. At all levels the principle of education would be the same: namely, the harmonious and optimal development of the physical, moral, and intellectual powers of each child, so that each may enjoy their own existence and contribute the greatest amount of benefit to others. The object of education should be to make each person 'politically free, morally honest, and intellectually great'.[97]

For all its lack of detail, the LWMA statement has definite implications for literacy. The literature to be used in schools, and the kinds of instruction built around that literature, must be under democratic (and hence popular) control. This would be necessary in order to 'guard against the influence of irresponsible power'.[98] Without popular control of education being established, government would inevitably favour practices of reading and writing reflecting the interests of those classes who themselves control government through their greater access to political power. After all, in 1837 the working class was still without the vote. But even *with* the vote, as the LWMA clearly realized, an improperly literate working class would be unable to implement its real interests through the ballot box. The important goal identified by the LWMA was to prevent any national system of education becoming a mechanism for implementing forms of literacy which would effectively and irretrievably hegemonize the working class. The best (albeit slim) chance of averting this lay in establishing national education on a truly democratic basis at a time when working people had access to authentic working-class theory (including educational theory!) and were increasingly organizing around the pursuit of their demonstrable class interests: political, social and economic. In other words, a properly literate working class would, by virtue of being the majority of the population, be able to ensure that its interests were served in education, if education was under democratic control. At the same time, however, proper forms of literacy — indeed, a proper education *in toto* — would only be available to the working class in the first place if education was under popular rather than upper- and/or middle-class control. The LWMA *Address on Education* laid out the broad educational goal to be pursued alongside more specifically political and economic goals. Moreover, the educational,

political, and economic objectives were mutually interdependent: each
depended on the others for its coherence and attainment.

For a more detailed picture of the implications for literacy of Chartist
views concerning the rightful provision and control of education we must turn
to the work of Lovett and Collins and Ernest Jones. In the view of Lovett and
Collins, the hallmarks of a *proper* literacy are that it is active, critical, integrated
with daily life, politically and morally enlightening, and conducive to the
interests of humans as humans rather than as the bearers of privilege or class
affiliation. Their ideal contrasts simultaneously with the constraining
pedagogy of the monitorial schools and the class-interested objectives of those
'education-promoters' who are 'but state-tricksters seeking to make [edu-
cation] an instrument of party or faction', eager 'to mould the plastic mind to
their own notions of propriety', and willing to sacrifice 'the great principles of
human nature, social mobility, and political justice' to the end 'of promoting
their own selfish views and . . . interests'.[99]

The active and integrated aspects of literacy are to be stressed from the
very beginning of education, in the infant school. Children should be taught

> by the most simple explanations and experiments to perceive and
> discover the use, property, and relationship of every object within
> their own locality, and learn to express in writing, and in correct
> language, the ideas they have received.[100]

Children are to acquire knowledge 'of things as well as of words'. Indeed,
words and things are to be learned as far as possible in conjunction with each
other, in a process that involves maximum activity on the learners' part. We
may compare here the technique of using a 'case of moveable types' in
conjunction with objects and pictures of objects, as described by Lovett and
Collins. Their emphasis on integrating literacy with the child's own reality is
evident in, for example, the recommendation that history and geography
should begin with study of local events and phenomena and proceed outward
to encompass other countries. The implication is that sound judgment is best
developed by proceeding from what is more familiar toward that which is less.
Furthermore, since the true purpose of education is to promote maximum
happiness for the individual and society mutually, it seems reasonable that
instruction should be tied first and foremost to the individual's personal and
social circumstances.

The critical dimension of a proper literacy is emphasized by contrast with
the passive, unreflective, rote methods employed at the time by teachers in all
types of school, and which were actually endorsed by such eminent philosophers as James Mill. Lovett and Collins insist, by contrast, that *real* knowledge
can be attained only through the exercise of 'the perceptive, comparative and
reflective powers'. If children merely absorb words and phrases 'without
inquiry or knowledge of the reality', their information can form 'no real basis
for reflection or judgment [and] cannot, therefore, be properly designated real
knowledge'. Given the predominance of passive, uncritical modes of teaching

is it any wonder, they ask, that so many scholars 'have so little practical or useful knowledge, are superficial in reasoning, defective in judgment, and wanting in their moral duties?'[101] Lovett and Collins stress, as a cardinal principle, that children should not merely be given a taste for reading (and writing), but should also develop the power of *understanding* what they read (and write). And the pedagogy they advocate is in complete accord with this principle.

The conduciveness of proper literacy — ranging over moral understanding, political awareness, and intellectual attainment in the many branches of human knowledge — to the interests of humans *as humans* is implicit in the metaphysic espoused by Lovett and Collins. While all people are not 'gifted with great powers of intellect' all are, nevertheless,

> so wisely and wonderfully endowed, that all have capacities for becoming intelligent, moral, and happy members of society; and if they are not, it is *for want of their capacities being ... properly cultivated.*

They add, in similar vein, that to give a person knowledge is to give them

> a light to perceive and enjoy beauty, variety, surpassing ingenuity, and majestic grandeur ... Enrich [their] mind and strengthen [their] under standing, and you give [them] powers to render all art and nature subservient to their purposes.[102]

This is *every* human being; not merely a privileged minority of them. The key that unlocks these treasures is *real* knowledge. And real knowledge presupposes proper literacy: literacy which affords an accurate and critical understanding of human life, social and political circumstances, the relationships between people, and the true values and objectives of human existence. Such knowledge, according to Lovett and Collins, comes only with political and moral enlightenment. If literacy fails to promote such enlightenment it is not educative; it is not proper.

Here we glimpse the boundless faith Lovett and Collins had in the power of real knowledge, fostered by proper literacy, to redress the social, political, and economic ills of the time. All classes, they said, are morally and politically ignorant. This ignorance was the underlying cause of existing troubles. To the extent that real knowledge could supplant ignorance these troubles would be overcome. Among the working class a deep political ignorance was manifested in their willingness to submit to arrangements whereby a small minority of the population monopolized political power, and used this power to make laws which advantaged their own 'order' but were 'inimical to the interests of the many'. This general ignorance was compounded by a special ignorance, through which large numbers of those who are excluded from political power to the detriment of their own interests nevertheless 'readily consent to be drilled and disciplined, and used as instruments to keep all the rest in subjection'[103] Equally destructive of human interests was the ignorance and moral poverty of the ruling classes. Surely it is the lack of information with which to understand their true interest, and the lack of moral motives to pursue it,

> [that] induce the wealthier classes of society to perpetuate a system of oppression and injustice which ... fills our gaols with criminals, our land with paupers and our streets with prostitution and intemperance.

Likewise, ignorance and lack of moral culture causes the middle class to worry their way through life, pursuing wealth or rank 'through all the soul-debasing avenues of wrong' — only to find happiness escaping them. [104]

The human interests of all would be enhanced through the pursuit, by all, of a true understanding of 'the social and political relations that exist between [each child] and their fellow beings'; a knowledge of 'the conditions of social and political life, and the rules of conduct on which their well-being chiefly depends'. Through this knowledge, 'a love of justice, truth, benevolence, firmness, and a respect for whatever is great and good' emerge as cardinal principles. Attainment of political and moral knowledge would reveal to all the futility of existing forms of education, which train the powerful in contempt for all useful labour while making them content to live on the toils of those who perform it, and submerge the poor in a false conception of their legitimate entitlements as human beings and of the causes of their present misery. The practice of a critical, *proper* literacy was seen here as an essential aspect of the pursuit of political and moral enlightenment. This, however, presupposed popular control of education — as we have seen.

Ernest Jones echoes the theme of proper literacy and popular control being cornerstones of a socially and politically just system of education. The people's education, he argues, cannot be entrusted either to government or to church. The problem with government-controlled education is that it becomes an ideological instrument of the dominant class. Children's minds become warped and distorted under the pressure of ruling class ideology. The risks of narrow mindedness and distortion are even greater, he says, if education is controlled by religious bodies. Rightfully, government has a duty to provide the *means* of education, but is not entitled to influence the *character* of education. It must provide resources for the exercise of the mind, but cannot direct the way in which children's minds are actually exercised. In Jones' words:

> Government is bound to open the page of history impartially to the people, to unroll the long catalogue of facts, but must then leave it to the people, or their *spontaneous* teachers, to point the moral, and pronounce the judgment. [105]

Jones is clear that if working-class children are to receive an education that promotes rather than undermines their interests, working people themselves must assume ultimate control over the teaching and learning of their class. 'If education is to be safe, the people must become their own educators'. This demand called out, according to Jones, an important immediate task: namely, providing a democratic literature for children. If working-class children were to achieve proper literacy they would require appropriate reading matter — a democratic literature. 'While the class-books of the rich are the exponents of class government, ours must be the exponents of popular sovereignty'. Unfortunately, says Jones, the democratic literature that exists is entirely written for adults. There is a desperate need for a literature written expressly for working-class children. While pressing his readers to address this task urgently, Jones acknowledges that a proper working-class literacy will of necessity be ideologically loaded. His approach is uncompromising.

> It may be said: 'Are we then going to fall into a similar course with our rulers?' 'Are we, too, going to *bias* the mind?'
> Yes! in self-defence. If a young tree has been drawn crooked, it needs drawing the other way, even BEYOND the perpendicular, so that, when arrived at sufficient stamina to stand of itself, the one-sided growth may have been outbalanced and the stem may grow erect.[106]

Clearly, if working-class children were to become capable (as adults) of making judgments and decisions, and undertaking courses of action, in accordance with their real interests, the ideological perspective informing such judgments, decisions, and actions would have to cohere with their interests being served rather than being undermined. To Jones, this meant that their framework for interpreting and understanding the world must be grounded in an ideology of popular sovereignty, rather than in some classist ideology of a ruling elite. The relationship between literacy and one's interpretation and understanding of the world is powerful and dynamic. Literacy, as we have seen, is inescapably ideological. Consequently, the literacy a person practises is a powerful influence upon their consciousness: upon their beliefs, assumptions, values, and related activity (or inactivity). At the same time, consciousness acts back upon literacy, influencing a person's literacy practice — for example, maintaining, reinforcing or, perhaps, modifying it — with further consequences for consciousness.

These ideas help clarify Jones' reasoning and establish it as basically sound. He is aware of the (inherently) ideological nature of literacy and understands the dialectical interplay between literacy and consciousness. As a result he grasps the potential that exists in creating a genuinely democratic children's literature for effecting a political intervention on behalf of working-class interests. The theory and practice of popular sovereignty coheres with promoting working-class interests, whereas the theory and practice of class government is hostile to these interests. A children's literature grounded in the ideology of popular sovereignty would tend to promote working-class interests both indirectly and directly. Indirectly, it would work to remove working-class children from the grip of ruling class hegemony — hence, they would be inclined *not* to interpret their life circumstances and possibilities in terms beneficial to elite interests at the expense of their own. More directly, it would positively provide working-class children with an ideological perspective enabling them to understand, interpret, and act upon their world in a way that accords with their interests.

In this context Jones' treatment of the question of *bias* is reminiscent of Freire, for whom literacy (like education generally) cannot be neutral but must, within existing relations of differential power and opportunity, be a medium either of 'domestication' or 'liberation'. The educational choice facing the working class in 1852 was clear cut. They could consent to their children being instructed via literature which reflected and bolstered a ruling class view of the world; or they could create a children's literature reflecting a view of the world conducive to worker interests, and make that literature a key medium of education. The choice for literacy was not: 'to bias or not to bias?' Rather, it was a question of whether the education of one's children should be biased in *favour* of their own objective present and future interests or *against* them. And given existing trends in ideological control, Jones actually saw a need to 'overcompensate' on the side of fostering a distinctively working-class ideology among workers' children.

The hope expressed by Ernest Jones and other Chartist theorists was that if education could be brought under popular democratic control, as part of a wider programme of democratizing social/cultural, economic, and political life generally, the outcome would be a proper literacy that was functional for working-class interests: indeed, for the interests, ultimately, of all humans *as humans*. How has this hope fared after a century of (compulsory) mass schooling funded and controlled by the state? What are the contemporary politics of literacy as shaped, maintained, and reinforced by school practice within our own society? These questions underlie the discussion in chapter 4.

Notes

1 THOMPSON, E.P. (1963), *The Making of the English Working Class*, Harmondsworth, Penguin.
2 *Ibid.*, p. 213.
3 *Ibid.*
4 SIMON, B. *op. cit.*, p. 163.
5 EVANS, E.J. (1983), *The Great Reform Act of 1832*, London, Methuen.
6 THOMPSON, *op. cit.*, p. 231.
7 *Ibid.*, p. 351.
8 NB. The ruling class did not, of course, articulate it to themselves in these blunt, exploitative terms. Their own ideology 'softened' and distorted their conception of the situation. In defending a God-given social and political order they were — in their eyes — actually *promoting* the interests of the poor, by helping them to perform their proper duty: shaping them as God's servants within the station and duties that God Himself had ordained, and protecting them from evil influences that would deflect them from these duties. If in this life the working class were, effectively, 'beings for others', this was their divine calling. Hannah More offers an excellent example of someone whose ideological position enabled her to undermine working-class interests in the belief that she was actually promoting them. She agreed with Burke that 'good order was the foundation of all good

things [and] to achieve it the people must be tractable and obedient'. On the other hand, 'her humanity made it impossible for her to despise them or to refer to them in [Burke's] unhappy phrase as the "swinish multitude". Her respect and affection for the poor was in marked contrast to his contempt (such are the deep workings of ideology! — C.L.). The people were ignorant and childish, easily excited by wicked men for their own ends; they must be taught, she held, where truth lay in the great debate of the day' (JONES, M.G., (1952) *Hannah More*, Cambridge, Cambridge University Press, p. 135).

The fact remains, however, that ideology (and rationalization) notwithstanding, the 'education' proposed for working people was such as would make them beings for others; educated in the interests of others and against their own — given that a divinely ordained social and political order is a myth!

9 SIMON, *op. cit.*, p. 183.
10 *Ibid.*, p. 184. See also HAMMOND, J.L. and B. (1930), *The Age of the Chartists*, London, Longmans Green, ch. 11.
11 See BROWN, P.A. (1918), *The French Revolution in English History*, London, Allen and Unwin, ch. 3.
12 THALE, M. (Ed), (1983), *Selections from the Papers of the London Corresponding Society 1792–1799*, London, Cambridge University Press., xvi.
13 BROWN, *op. cit.*, p. 56.
14 *Ibid.*, p. 57.
15 THALE, *op. cit.*, xxviii.
16 Cited THOMPSON, *op. cit.*, p. 170.
17 THALE, *op. cit.*, xxvi.
18 Cited BROWN, *op. cit.*, pp. 62–3. For typical examples of the literature fostered by Corresponding Societies, see WEBB, R.K. (1955), *The British Working Class Reader*, London, Allen and Unwin, ch. 2.
19 Compare THOMPSON, *op. cit.*, p. 213.
20 Reprinted in THALE, *op. cit.*, pp. 11–14. The quotation here is from p. 13.
21 See WEBB, *op. cit.*, ch. 2.
22 SIMON, *op. cit.*, p. 181.
23 BROWN, *op. cit.*, pp. 73–4.
24 MILLS, C. WRIGHT *op. cit.*, p. 6.
25 *Ibid.*, p. 181.
26 BROWN, *op. cit.*, p. 85.
27 WEBB, *op. cit.*, p. 41.
28 WALLAS, G. (1898), *The Life of Francis Place*, London, Allen and Unwin, p. 25.
29 THOMPSON *op. cit.*, p. 191. See also THALE, *op. cit.*
30 Compare especially THALE, BROWN and THOMPSON, all *op. cit.*
31 BROWN, *op. cit.*, p. 83.
32 Cited WEBB, *op. cit.*, p. 13.
33 For ideas and references contained in this and the previous paragraph, compare *ibid.*, pp. 42–5. There are, however, alternative interpretations. Pedersen, for example, recommends that we do not interpret the Cheap Repository Tracts *in toto* as being political in intent. Rather, they should be read as an attack on popular culture. This, of course, does not negate the particular reference here to 'Village Politics'. See PEDERSON, S. (1986), 'Hannah More meets Simple Simon', *Journal of British Studies*, 25, pp. 84–113.

34 PLACE cited in WALLAS, *op. cit.*, 25n.

35 See WEBB, *op. cit.*, p. 167, note 34.

36 WICKWAR, W.H. (1928), *The Struggle for the Freedom of the Press*, London, Allen and Unwin, p. 49.

37 Compare WEARMOUTH, R.F. (1948), *Some Working Class Movements of the Nineteenth Century*, London, The Epworth Press, chs. 1 and 2. See also SIMON, *op. cit.*, pp. 186–9, and THOMPSON, *op. cit.*

38 WICKWAR, *op. cit.*, p. 19. See also pp. 18–20 for legal descriptions of malicious intent, breach of the peace, etc.

39 *Ibid.*

40 Compare *ibid.*, p. 51.

41 Compare *ibid.*, p. 52.

42 COBBETT cited in *ibid.*, pp. 53–4.

43 BAMFORD, S. (1984), *Passages in the Life of a Radical*, Oxford, Oxford University Press, pp. 13–4.

44 See THOMPSON, *op. cit.*, p. 679.

45 COBBETT cited in COLE, G.D.H. and M. (Eds), (1944), *The Opinions of William Cobbett*, London, The Cobbett Publishing Co., p. 216.

46 See, for example, SIMON, *op. cit.*, pp. 186–93. THOMPSON, *op. cit.*, pp. 712–36, and WEARMOUTH, *op. cit.*, pp. 31–49. An especially interesting development was apparent in the growth of secular Sunday schools, where a major concern was to free working people from the ideological influence of the church. This influence was seen by many working-class leaders as 'the chief means whereby the people were held back from action'. The reform groups established in Royton maintained that there was no hope of a more liberal form of government while priests were able to awe the people with fears of being damned to eternity. Antireligious literature and discussion was a feature of reform activity in Lancashire. This concern with undermining the unwanted ideological influence of religion extended to promoting a proper literacy among working-class children as well as adults. Lancashire reformers 'endeavoured to replace the religious indoctrination of children with a rational education in the Sunday schools they promoted, as part of the union movement for parliamentary reform from 1817 onwards'. The underlying assumption was that instruction in an ambiguous, doubtful, and contradictory religion cramped children's understandings, and baffled their judgments. It made for uncritical, irrational, and distorted thought. When people were trained to think rationally, and to distinguish critically between right and wrong, it would be impossible for any king or government to tyrannize over them and deny them their rights. See SIMON, pp. 187–8.

47 It is, for example, debatable how far Cobbett's concern for political reform was grounded in authentic commitment to working-class interests. In the *Address to Journeymen and Labourers*, for instance, we find him recommending the principle that the right to vote be extended only to those who pay direct — as opposed to indirect — taxes. This would have denied the vote to vast numbers of working people. In acknowledging this, the best Cobbett offers is the assumption that a reformed government could very easily hit upon an optimally just arrangement . . . (compare COLE and COLE, *op. cit.*, pp. 214–5). The relationship between journalism and authentic commitment to working class interests is much less ambiguous in Hetherington and *The Poor Man's Guardian* and later, in the Chartist press.

48 WICKWAR, *op. cit.*, p. 137.
49 THOMPSON, *op. cit.*, p. 799.
50 WEARMOUTH, *op. cit.*, p. 50.
51 BARKER, A.G. *Henry Hetherington*, London, The Pioneer Press, pp. 5–6. See also LOVETT, W. (1920), *The Life and Struggles of William Lovett*, London, Bell and Sons, p. 60.
52 BARKER, *ibid.*, pp. 8–9. See also COLLET, C.D. (1933), *The Taxes on Knowledge*, London, Watts and Co., ch. 2.
53 The Address is reproduced in HAMPTON, C. (Ed) (1984), *A Radical Reader*, Harmondsworth, Penguin, pp. 458–9.
54 THOMPSON, *op. cit.*, p. 800.
55 SIMON, *op. cit.*, p. 227.
56 Cited *ibid.*, p. 228.
57 ASPINALL, A. (1949), *Politics and the Press, 1780–1850*, London, Home and Van Thal, p. 47.
58 *Ibid.*, p. 155, italics mine.
59 WEBB, *op. cit.*, p. 52.
60 See CLARKE, W.K.L. (1959), *A History of the SPCK*, London, SPCK, ch 11, especially pp. 148–52, and ALLEN, W.O.B. and McCLURE, E. (1898), *Two Hundred Years: the history of the SPCK*, ch. 5, especially pp. 188–9.
61 ALLEN and McCLURE, *ibid.*, p. 189.
62 *Ibid.*, p. 190.
63 WEBB, *op. cit.*, p. 73.
64 KNIGHT cited in SIMON, *op. cit.*, p. 159.
65 Cited WEBB, *op. cit.*, p. 67.
66 Cited in HOLLIS, P. (Ed) (1973), *Class and Conflict in Nineteenth Century England 1815–1850*, London, Routledge and Kegan Paul.
67 SIMON, *op. cit.*, p. 160.
68 By Barry Cornwall, *Penny Magazine*, 7 July 1932, cited in HOLLIS, *op. cit.*, p. 53. See the reply, 'The weaver's song not by Barry Cornwall', *Poor Man's Guardian*, 3 November 1832, cited in HOLLIS, p. 54.
69 See, for example, SIMON, *op. cit.*, pp. 160–1, and HOLLIS, *ibid.*, pp. 334–5, for reference to tory and middle-class attacks.
70 SIMON, *ibid.*, p. 162.
71 See HOLLIS, *op. cit.*, pp. 64–9.
72 Cited in *ibid.*, p. 144.
73 HOLLIS, P. (1970), *The Pauper Press: a study in working-class radicalism in the 1830s*, London, Oxford University Press, pp. 20–21.
74 Cited *ibid.*, pp. 143–4.
75 Cited *ibid.*, p. 20.
76 See BRIGGS, A. (Ed) (1959), *Chartist Studies*, London, Macmillan, ch. 1.
77 WEARMOUTH, *op. cit.*, p. 85.
78 SIMON, *op. cit.*, p. 250.
79 *Ibid.*, pp. 250–51.
80 JONES cited in SAVILLE, J. (1952), *Ernest Jones: Chartist*, London, Lawrence and Wishart, p. 99.
81 Cited *ibid.*
82 On the theme of *really* useful knowledge, see JOHNSON, R. (1979), 'Really Useful Knowledge: radical education and working-class culture, 1790–1848', in

CLARKE, J. CRITCHER, C. and JOHNSON, R. (Ed), *Working Class Culture: studies in history and theory*, London, Hutchinson.

83 WEARMOUTH, *op. cit.*, p. 142.

84 Cited *ibid.*

85 Cited SIMON, *op. cit.*, p. 252.

86 Cited in COOPER, T. (1971), *The Life of Thomas Cooper*, Leicester, Leicester University Press, p. 166.

87 *Ibid.*, p. 169.

88 See HAMMOND, *op. cit.*, p. 183.

89 Cited *ibid.*, pp. 191–2.

90 Cited *ibid.*, p. 210.

91 Cited *ibid.*, p. 173. This is from the Manual of 1816. Later editions did not significantly alter the pedagogy — compare *ibid.*, pp. 174–6. For references to and critiques of the National Society approach, see *ibid.*, ch. 10.

92 LOVETT, op. cit., p. 138. *The Address on Education* is reprinted in full in Lovett, pp. 138–50.

93 Cited SAVILLE, *op. cit.*, p. 157.

94 Cited SAVILLE, *op. cit.*, pp. 140–141.

95 *Ibid.*, p. 142n.

96 Cited *ibid.*, p. 144

97 Compare *ibid.*, pp. 144–8.

98 *Ibid.*, p. 143. By 'irresponsible' the LWMA clearly meant the exercise of power in their own interests by the wealthy classes.

99 LOVETT, W. and COLLINS, J. (1969), *Chartism: a new organization of the people*, Leicester, Leicester University Press. pp. 74–5.

100 *Ibid.*, p. 39.

101 *Ibid.*, p. 81.

102 *Ibid.*, p. 67.

103 *Ibid.*, p. 71.

104 *Ibid.*, p. 70.

105 Cited SAVILLE, *op. cit.*, p. 158.

106 Cited *ibid.*, pp. 158–9.

Chapter 4

Schooling, Literacy and Subordination

Introduction

As Michael Apple notes, radical critique of education undertaken during the past fifteen years or so has made us more sensitive to the role played by schooling within the process of 'reproducing a social order that remains strikingly unequal by class, gender and race'. That the educational and cultural system is a major factor in maintaining existing relations of domination and exploitation within modern capitalist societies is a belief shared by 'individuals as diverse as Bourdieu, Althusser, Baudelot and Establet in France, Bernstein, Young, Whitty, and Willis in England, Kallos and Lundgren in Sweden ... Bowles and Gintis, [Apple himself] and others in the US'. Now while these people may disagree, even markedly, as to *how* the process actually occurs, 'none would deny the importance of examining the relationship between schooling and the maintenance of these unequal relations'.[1]

This provides the broad frame for my discussion in this chapter. I accept that the thesis of a relationship between schooling and reproduced inequality is well enough established to justify examining it further. My particular focus here will be on the extent to which, and the manner in which, transmission and practice of literacy in school contributes to maintaining patterns of unequal power and advantage within the social structure. For in our own day, school is the (sole) social-cultural setting officially charged with promoting universal literacy.

Two central themes are discussed in the body of this chapter. First, I will identify the social production of structured *illiteracy* within modern capitalist society, and locate this process within the politics of daily life. In this I will draw mainly on material relating to the US — where the most readily accessible research has been done. The point I work toward here is that school has become a site on which structured inequalities of economic, cultural, and political power intersect, to produce illiteracy which is patterned by race/ethnicity and class.

The second theme concerns elements of school practice, and its supportive rhetoric, which undermine pursuit of proper literacy and, instead, engage pupils in acquiring and employing improper forms of reading and writing.[2] Discussion here will include reference to a recent ethnographic study of classroom activity, in an attempt to preserve some balance between theoretical discussion and the empirical elaboration of school literacy. After all, school literacy comprises the forms of reading and writing actually practised within empirical classrooms. There is, I believe, a need for close examination of daily classroom practice in terms of the distinction drawn here between proper and improper literacy. The study referred to below provides some indication of how ethnographic research can contribute to our grasp of the politics of literacy.

In the last part of this chapter I locate a thread that links continuing (albeit marginalized) activity within formal educational settings to the tradition of working-class education described in the previous chapter. I consider briefly the attempts of two contemporary educators to foster proper forms of reading and writing within school among students from subordinate social groups.

School and the Social Production of Structured Illiteracy

Considerable adult illiteracy was discovered in Britain and the US during the 1970s. This discovery was quickly replicated in Australia, Canada, New Zealand, and elsewhere. Figures cited for the US vary from twenty-three million to almost eighty million adults who, relative to some set of criteria or other, may be judged illiterate. Kozol advances a figure of sixty million (or more than one third of the entire adult population). Leading researchers in the field agree that his estimate is cautious.[3] British estimates, as we have seen, range as high as 6–8 million, depending on the reading age employed. Some Australian estimates suggest that 10 per cent of adults there may have serious difficulties with reading and writing. Figures produced for New Zealand in 1977 — based on a reading age of $9\frac{1}{2}$ years on standardized PAT Reading Tests — indicated that 50,000 – 100,000 adults (from a total of 2,200,000 aged 15 and over) were in trouble.

Of particular interest to me here are two quite different responses to have emerged among writers with an undoubted concern for issues of oppression and social justice to this discovery of large scale adult illiteracy. On one side, Kozol embraces the discovery and uses it as a pad from which to launch a demand for an all-out assault on adult illiteracy in the US. He attacks measurement procedures by which official census figures (and other statistics) had for decades 'verified' near universal literacy in America. The 1970 Census had claimed that 99 per cent of US adults could read and write. The 1980 Census increased this figure to 99.5 per cent. Kozol's attack on the statistics supports the view that had people seriously been looking for adult literacy prior to the 1970s they would have found it.[4] The important thing, as far as Kozol is concerned, is that now the 'discovery' *has* been made it should be put to positive use as a wedge for tackling social injustice.

By contrast, Ira Shor concentrates more on the extent to which the Literacy Crisis was *invented* rather than discovered. This invention, in Shor's view, formed a necessary part of the 'conservative restoration' agenda for education.[5] 'Without a literacy crisis', says Shor, 'there would have been no cause for launching a traditionalist crusade for the basics'.[6] He notes how the *Newsweek* story which made the alleged crisis into a major public issue in 1975 was grounded in a highly selective reading of SAT scores and of National Assessment of Educational Progress findings. The Literacy Crisis is seen by people like Shor as a timely invention to underpin attacks on the more emancipatory, egalitarian, liberal curricula and pedagogies of the 1960s. It opens the way for attacking liberal trends in education on the grounds that they are a prime cause of current social and economic woes. The logic underlying such attacks is simple — and simplistic. Introduction of mass schooling was widely presumed to have done away with illiteracy. According to the rhetoric, schooling promotes personal benefit and fulfilment, equalizes opportunities, transmits socially useful skills and knowledge, and preserves the most worthwhile forms of thought humans have evolved.[7] These claims positively *assume* universal literacy as the minimum, taken-for-granted base from which all other educational goods flow. Official statistics had 'confirmed' near perfect literacy in the US. Now, suddenly, there was large scale illiteracy evident. This could be passed off as a new phenomenon. New phenomena are readily associated with recent events and causes. And the openly liberal approach to education which characterized the period from the mid 1960s was a trend ripe for being blamed and eliminated, so far as opponents of more expansive and egalitarian educational ideals and practices were concerned.

In addition to the conservative restoration agenda identified by Shor, there are further advantages for dominant interest groups and other reactionary elements to be had from the discovery of widespread adult illiteracy. Some of these will surface in the argument which follows. My main concern at present is to identify two responses to the Literacy Crisis which come from people sharing a common political vision of liberation from oppression, but which are seemingly in tension. For I have sympathy with both responses. With Kozol, I believe we have to be prepared to 'name victims'.[8] And as we will see, those who are adjudged illiterate within American society are, overwhelmingly, *victims*. At the same time I am well aware of risks involved in publicly admitting the existence of large scale illiteracy: particularly when illiteracy is assessed relative to the kind of narrowly functional criteria employed in many US measurements. The challenge, as I see it, is to understand the alleged Literacy Crisis in a way which dissolves any apparent tension between the emphases and commitments of people like Shor and Kozol respectively. This calls for a politically informed account of adult illiteracy. In particular, it requires us to consider illiteracy as being *socially produced* and *structural*, and to clarify the position of schooling within this social process.

To begin with it is necessary to elaborate the estimates of illiteracy. What do the figures mean? My argument in chapter 2 alerts us to the fact that the meaning of illiteracy figures will not be self-evident. Since 'literacy' itself does not denote any single state or phenomenon, neither does 'illiteracy'. People are adjudged literate or illiterate relative to some standard or other of the many that are possible: relative to some social practice and conception or other of reading and writing. The question is, which one has been used in making a particular assessment? Moreover, since notions and practices of literacy vary markedly over time within a single society, it cannot be assumed that illiteracy rates or figures produced at one time relate in any direct or clear way to those produced at another time. What, then, do recent figures mean?

Kozol's account of the US situation provides the most lucid, comprehensive, and up-to-date statement available to me. The figure of sixty million illiterate American adults put forward by Kozol is relative to a conception of minimum *survival* literacy within contemporary US society. It is not a measure of absolute illiteracy, or total unfamiliarity with print; although, of course, it subsumes this.[9] The figure of sixty million comprises twenty-five million adults 'reading either not at all or at less than a fifth grade level', and a further thirty-five million 'reading at less than ninth grade level'. These are estimates of *actual performance* rather than data referring simply to school attendance.[10] Kozol provides clear examples of what these levels mean in empirical terms.

> It requires ninth grade competence to understand the antidote instructions on a bottle of corrosive kitchen lye, tenth grade competence to understand instructions on a federal income tax return, twelfth grade competence to read a life insurance form. Employment qualifications for all but a handful of domestic jobs begin at ninth grade level. I have argued, therefore, that all of these sixty million people should be called 'illiterate in terms of US print communication at the present time'.[11]

What was discovered in the 1970s, then, was illiteracy relative to a particular (social) conception of the skills needed by people in order to survive or function at a minimally adequate level, within the America (or an equivalent society) of the 1970s and 1980s. This was a social setting in which competition for employment — *any* employment — had increased sharply, and the general sophistication of daily life had raised the minimum level for print competence greatly over that of earlier times. Furthermore, the minimum level will continue to rise. One expert has claimed that 'anyone who doesn't have at least a twelfth grade reading, writing, and calculating level will be absolutely lost' by the 1990s.[12] Had assessments of adult illiteracy been made some decades earlier the criteria employed would have been quite different. In times of full employment, with considerable face to face communication and ample opportunities for purely manual labour, a person might need only to be able to sign a pay slip in order to obtain work. Today, however, it is typically necessary to be able to read advertisements, fill in forms, make written applications, etc., for even the lowest status jobs. Similarly, the transition from corner store to supermarket, and from the sale of fresh or open goods to sophisticated packaging, has increased consumer reading needs exponentially.

Between such social contexts, conceptions of the minimum competence required in order to count as being (functionally) *literate* alter accordingly.

There is an important implication here for the question of schooling in relation to measured illiteracy: namely, that recent estimates of illiteracy reflect the operation of much wider social processes and trends than the performance of schools alone. Even if we accept that rates of measured illiteracy are higher now than they were a generation ago, it does not follow that schools are producing less in the way of reading and writing skills than they were then. Neither does it follow that standards have slipped, nor that progressive pedagogies and curricula yield lower levels of attainment than more traditional or basic forms. In fact, according to Kozol, during the past two decades

> the number of those who cannot read at all has either diminished slightly or remained unchanged. It is functional illiteracy which has increased; this is the case because the term is, in itself, a 'function' of the needs imposed upon a person by the economic and the social order. The economy and the society have changed in every age. It is the rate of change, and the degree to which it may outpace the literacy level of the nation, that determine what part of the nation is unable to survive and to prevail within the context of its times. The speedup in the rate of change, especially within the past two decades, is well known.[13]

What this means, in colloquial terms, is that during the past two decades schools have had to run in order simply to stand still. They have been, and are being, required to produce ever higher averages of minimum attainment in order simply to sustain previous rates of literacy. Even if schools improved their current performance to the point where they matched the functional demands of the present day, changes occurring *outside* the school — in technology, economic production, commerce, communications, consumerism, cultural life, etc. — would tend toward creating a rate of illiteracy in the future by simply continuing to raise the minimum required level of print competence. Off-setting this tendency would pose strain enough on schools. And this is to leave out of the picture completely all those learnings school is called upon — or *ought* to be called upon — to instil in order that young people maintain mental, physical, emotional, and spiritual well-being within an environment that is increasingly hostile to these ends.

The argument so far suggests two (related) things. First, the connection between schooling — including curricula, pedagogy, teacher effectiveness, etc. — and measured levels of adult illiteracy is much more complex than those who urge a simple back-to-basics would have us believe. Second, illiteracy should be seen as socially produced, in the sense that (increased) requirements for print competence reflect the way life has been, and is being, constructed historically within a society. In other words, the way modern society has been made, and what it has been made into, has much to do with the *creation* of large numbers of adults who fail to meet proclaimed minimum demands for print competence within that society.

To move further toward the idea of socially produced *structured* illiteracy, we must note how illiteracy is *patterned*. There is nothing new in the fact of patterned illiteracy. By whatever standard or criteria illiteracy rates for the nineteenth century are assessed, illiteracy occurred disproportionately by social class, race/ethnicity, and gender, at that time. With regard to national illiteracy rates for the US in the nineteenth century, Tyack claims that

> The aggregated data ... mask very important variations in [school] attendance and literacy by region (the South lagged far behind the rest of the nation); by ethnicity (commonly forbidden to read under slavery, Blacks were 90 per cent illiterate in 1870; and foreign-born adult whites were considerably less literate than native-born); and by other factors such as social class and urban or rural residence. [14]

The same broad patterns are apparent today, despite the intervention of more than a century of compulsory mass schooling. In their extensive survey of present day illiteracy in the US, Hunter and Harman establish that those persons who lack sufficient reading and writing skills to function effectively in mainstream American society

> are found in large numbers wherever there are poor people and whenever there are congregated racial and ethnic minority groups. They are found in city ghettos and doing hard physical labour on unmechanized farms. [15]

Illiteracy is found disproportionately among the unemployed or those employed in low status work (for example, unskilled and migrant workers), among the imprisoned and, in the case of Hispanics at least and possibly blacks as well, among women. [16] Kozol notes that while white native-born Americans comprise the largest single group of illiterate adults, the figures in proportion to population are much higher for blacks and Hispanics than for whites. Whereas 16 per cent of white adults are functional or marginal illiterates, the rate is 44 per cent and 56 per cent for black and Hispanic citizens respectively. Moreover, among the younger generation of black adults the proportion is increasing, with 47 per cent of all 17 year-old blacks being functionally illiterate. It is predicted that the figure will reach 50 per cent by 1990. Kozol also confirms the correlation between illiteracy and social class claimed by Hunter and Harman. By Kozol's reckoning,

> Half the heads of households classified below the poverty line by federal standards cannot read an eighth grade book. Over one third of mothers who receive support from welfare are functionally illiterate. Of eight million unemployed adults, four to six million lack the skills to be retrained for hi-tech jobs. [17]

How are these patterns to be understood? The explanation I offer here is that patterned illiteracy is grounded in tendencies, practices, and processes inherent in the social structure. Both the scale and the distribution of illiteracy, then, are largely consequences of the kind of history we have made and are making within our society. This approach to explaining the broad patterns of illiteracy that occur contrasts with others which attribute correlations primarily to alleged traits, attributes, general characteristics, etc., of *individuals or groups themselves*. A simplified, but commonly heard, example of this latter approach goes as follows. Some people are just dumb, lazy, come from 'deprived homes', or simply do not value education. As a result they do not get out of schooling what it has to offer them — notably here, literacy. Failing at school and, therefore, missing out on skills and qualifications, they get only low status jobs or else no job at all. They end up, consequently, as working class (or unemployed) on low incomes (or welfare). Illiterate and poor, they make ineffective parents and pass on their own disadvantages to their children. This 'cycle of disadvantage' begins from their inability to provide the kind of home background, support, stimulation, materials, experiences, and other conditions through which children are enabled to acquire the skills and other learnings school offers them. These children end up illiterate ... (and so on for another cycle). Thus is patterned illiteracy and wider disadvantage commonly 'explained'.

A problem with this kind of explanation is that it has sufficient plausibility to convince those who do not (and have never been taught to) think seriously and in structural terms about their world. To spot the weaknesses in such explanations calls for a sociological imagination. For there *is* an element of fact in the above 'explanation'. While parental illiteracy 'does not "breed" illiteracy' and thereby *cause* existing patterns of disadvantage to be reproduced in the new generation, it *does*

> set up the preconditions for the perpetuation of the lack of reading skills within successive generations. Illiterate parents have no way to give their children preschool preparation which enables them to profit fully from a good school or — in the more common case — which will protect those children, by the learning that takes place at home, against the dangers of the worst of schools. Where schools are relatively effective, the children of illiterate adults may forfeit much of what is being offered. Where schools are bad, the children of illiterate adults cannot draw upon the backup education which is present in the homes of people who can read and write.[18]

In such cases, wider complicating factors — like poverty, high levels of local unemployment, race or ethnic minority status, having English as a second language, general feelings of powerlessness and estrangement from school culture — intermesh with parental illiteracy to reinforce the greater likelihood of illiteracy, subsequent school failure, poverty and unemployment, and so on in the next generation of adults.

While it is true that parental illiteracy, feelings of powerlessness and futility which are interpreted as laziness, and other personal attributes *are* apparent within the patterning of illiteracy, the 'explanation' from personal failings is woefully superficial and distortive. To get closer to the truth of why illiteracy is distributed in the way it is, we must consider some of the ways in which social practice generally is structured within our society, and note their implications for persons acquiring or failing to acquire literacy skills. Consider, for example, the following facts concerning the structuring — or systematic organization — of daily life within our society.

(i) Economic life is organized around policies, practices and relations which produce markedly different outcomes at the level of personal economic destinies. The fact that some work pays very well while other works pays very badly, or that a level of permanent unemployment — sometimes higher, sometimes lower — has been a feature of some national economies for generations, reflects the way economic life is structured. Given certain policies, practices, economic principles, and relations of power within the framework of capitalist production, it is inevitable that *some* proportion of the population will be unemployed, or will earn at or below the poverty level. As a matter of fact, economic policies in the US have long maintained levels of unemployment which have effectively imposed pressure (through competition on the job market) to keep wages down, reduce the bargaining power of labour unions, etc. In other words, unemployment has been a structured fact of life for a proportion of American (and British) citizens for generations now. While particular economic policies, practices, and relations *per se* may not determine exactly who the individuals are that will be unemployed or poor, they *do* ensure that some — even large numbers — will be. Within Australia, Britain, New Zealand, the US, and elsewhere, economic life is currently dominated by policies which may broadly be termed 'monetarist'. These policies structure economic life and produce systematic outcomes: for example, increased levels of unemployment; an increased proportion of deskilled and lower paid jobs on account of greater investment in capital-intensive high-tech industries; the greater likelihood for more and more people of temporary employment interspersed with periods of unemployment, stints on 'job training schemes', etc.; welfare cuts; 'user pays' principles, etc. Under such policies competition for work, and material life chances generally, intensifies. For an increasing proportion of the population, future economic prospects will objectively diminish under the continuation of these or similar policies. Consequently, we may speak here of economic poverty or insecurity, unemployment, low-skilled/boring work (and the like), which exist at the level of personal experience, as *structured economic outcomes*. Given the way economic life is structured, they are inevitable for many people. To change this reality at the level of personal experience for the numbers concerned would necessitate addressing the very structure of economic life. That unemployment, poverty, large income differentials, and so on, *do* originate very largely in the social structure — in the unequal distribution of economic power, and the power to make unequal economic policies — rather than in the traits or inadequacies of individuals, can be seen by reference to, say, Cuba: where policies have reduced income differentials greatly, reorganized the basis of production (away from the creation of surplus value for private and corporate capitals), and almost entirely eliminated poverty and unemployment.

(ii) Educational practice has become increasingly identified with and monopolized by schooling. School is accepted as *the* agency which educates: attainments considered *educational* are (to be) acquired in school. The rise of school has seen the corresponding demise of the variety and number of educational forms and organizations of earlier times — such as the kind of organized working-class education sketched in chapter 3. Because of the progressive structuring of educational practice around schooling, we now find that for many people if they fail to acquire those skills and learnings deemed educational (including skills of reading and writing) within school, then they do not acquire them at all: because alternatives sites for gaining them are largely non-existent. In New Zealand at present we find strong and increased support for special reading programmes in schools, whilst adult literacy schemes struggle for funding and paid full-time personnel are few and far between.

(iii) The practice of selecting employees for the workforce is structured around reference to individuals' school attendance and performance. 'Employers ... tend overwhelmingly to select employees according to length of schooling and certification'.[19] As a consequence, schooling has come to be very largely valued on instrumental grounds: in terms of its significance as the accepted route to a desirable, or at least viable, economic future. There is, however, a twist to this. Schooling has also come to be strongly *disvalued* by many who sense that it is a route to inevitable failure. With reference to the US setting, Hunter and Harman link this to Collins' notions of education as a market for cultural goods and the inflation of education credentials since the mid-nineteenth century.[20] They note that groups at the bottom of the social and economic heap in America last century were led to believe that literacy and other educational achievements would enhance their life opportunities. But as the number of people within these groups gaining educational credentials increased, so too did the level of qualifications demanded for the same jobs.

Each time competing ethnic minorities reached the educational levels they had been told would lead to economic success and prestige, the game rules were changed ... [Given] the resulting inflation of educational credentials ... disillusionment is likely among those who purchase such credentials through school attendance when the promised pay-off fails to materialize. The disappointed groups may drop out of the difficult process of schooling.[21]

They *do* drop out: and, in many cases *tune* out from an early stage. Moreover, the actual disvaluing of school commonly takes more extreme forms than tuning and dropping out alone. Arson and vandalism of school buildings and property is most marked within areas where patterned educational and economic 'failure' is to be found. Without in any way condoning such acts, one can note, sadly, a certain realistic and objective basis to them.

(iv) School practice is itself structured around a particular and narrow selection of pursuits and values. The curriculum, for instance, draws on but a tiny sample of the endless variety of activities potentially available.[22] Moreover, within the curriculum offerings themselves some subjects enjoy recognized higher status than others. This hierarchy and, indeed, the original selection of 'worthwhile activities', are seen by many writers as reflecting the cultural dominance of particular (and minority) interest groups — for example, white middle-class, male, etc. — over others. A large literature now exists which points to school practice and its underlying values as reflecting the greater power of some groups than others to influence the character of schooling.[23] The education shaped by these power elites — through their disproportionate involvement in policy-making, places on commissions, superior articulation, appreciation of how (best) to make submissions, connections with official power, influence on or over school boards, and the fact that *their* voices tend to be heard and heeded — reflects their own values, concerns and interests. These come to dominate within schooling over the values and interests of other, and invariably more populous, groups. The latter are properly described as subordinate interest groups within education.

Where, for example, does 'popular culture' find anything like equivalent educational validity with that 'higher' culture represented by, say, serious music, or discussion in French of French life and customs?; or technical-trade subjects with science and pure mathematics? — despite the fact that many more people in our society follow football or baseball teams than ever develop an interest in the cello or Chopin; that many more end up tinkering with cars and motorbikes than ever visit France and engage in the French way of life. Witness also the official recognition of standard English over non-standard forms.[24] For many, and probably *most*, pupils the values and pursuits that are seen *really* to define education (and which comprise gateways to the highest forms of certification) are culturally, experientially, and existentially alien. This structured cultural dominance within education is intensified to a large extent by the attitudes, preferences, and very *being* of the teaching profession itself. Teachers are very much bearers of the ruling habitus.[25] This fact fosters stereotypes, ensuring which children are listened to, taken seriously, have their cultural style and experience most appreciated; it influences which children are picked out as likely failures or trouble-makers; and it helps determine which children will be equipped to make the teacher (and school as a whole) 'work' for them.[26] This idea of school practice being structured, and structured in accordance with the culture of particular elites, goes a long way toward explaining (for example) the fact that in Australia children of professional parents 'have a twenty-seven times greater chance of entering law school and a twenty times greater chance of entering medical school than children of the working class'. Yet there is absolutely no evidence 'to indicate that for each intellectually gifted lower class child there are twenty or twenty seven similarly gifted children whose parents are professionals'.[27]

By recognizing these (and similar) dimensions of structured social practice we can begin to see how the patterning of illiteracy has considerably more to do with social structure than with the sorts of characteristics ascribed to individuals and groups that underlie 'blame the victim' approaches to explanation. Quite simply, a child is more likely to live in a neighbourhood served by badly equipped schools, with a high teacher turnover and low morale, where school is widely viewed as a route to almost inevitable failure, where minimal alternative educational resources and models are available outside of school, and where school experience is culturally alien, if born into a family that has known unemployment and poverty for years (or, perhaps, generations). Such factors are highly conducive to learning failure, yet they are entirely outside the child's sphere of personal control and, in all likelihood, the parent's as well. For these factors reflect the operation of social structure. The personal here is well and truly conditioned by the political.

Despite concern for their child's educational future, parents here will very likely lack the economic means to provide them with 'better' schooling. If culturally estranged from schooling they may not even know what it would mean to seek 'better' schooling. And if illiterate they may be unable to act effectively on a felt concern. Yet they, as much as the child, may have been victims of similar structural factors operating in the previous generation. The fact that a particular child is 'bright' and motivated to learn may pale into insignificance alongside the reality of a poor learning environment resulting from regular changes in teacher; compounded by irregular attendance on account of responsibility for minding younger siblings, and the occasional change of school when parents are forced to find new rented accommodation; and capped by disruptive classroom behaviour stimulated by attitudes of learned futility stemming from the fact of high permanent unemployment in the area, coupled with frustration created by the distance between subject matter and children's experience, cultural tradition, etc. Add to this parental illiteracy and we have a virtual guarantee of (school) learning failure. Add further the operation of racism, classism, and/or sexism — however subtle and unintended — and the likelihood of learning failure is sealed. At the same time, the average *minimum* demands for print competence are soaring: a fact which has everything to do with structured social practice (within the economy, commerce, bureaucracy, communications, etc.) and nothing to do with the personal traits of those who remain illiterate.

By comparison, a child enjoying the advantages of average to high family income, literate parents, a 'good' school, personal congruence with school culture, and so on, may be seen to enjoy all the benefits of being born 'on the right side of social structure'. For such a child, relative educational success may follow *despite* strictly average 'ability' or considerably less than optimal effort. Other things being equal, this child's chances of ending up illiterate are undeniably lower than those of the child whose circumstances approximate to the description in the previous paragraph. Patterned illiteracy is the net outcome.

By focusing on these sorts of ways in which social practice is structured, we can identify a wide range of factors which contribute greatly to individuals and groups being what they are (or are not) and acting as they do (or fail to do); and where these modes of doing and being have definite implications for whether or not a person becomes literate. We can understand the phenomenon of patterned illiteracy more fully and accurately *only* if we give a central place within our explanation to structural factors. To do this is precisely to speak of the social production of *structured* illiteracy. Once we begin thinking about patterned illiteracy in structural terms — and my account here is at least an attempt to make a beginning — we can see the extent to which, and why, it is inappropriate to attribute this to personal or group traits. We can, moreover, extend this kind of reasoning beyond the fact of patterned *illiteracy* to patterned disadvantage/oppression more generally.[28]

The social production of structured illiteracy is a very important *political* process: a key factor in reproducing hierarchies of domination and subordination. There are two related dimensions to this. First, to produce illiterate people is very much to produce human beings whose interests can be readily and systematically subordinated to the interests of others. I will return to this point shortly. Second, the reality of patterned illiteracy which correlates highly with wider patterned disadvantage is readily misconstrued in ways which serve the interests of dominant groups. By confusing causes and symptoms it is possible to 'legitimate' and explain away existing inequalities. It also encourages us to seek solutions to social problems in the wrong places. Both tendencies serve dominant interests.

In the first step, patterned material disadvantage — such as unemployment or low status, low paid work — is attributed to illiteracy: i.e., 's/he's unemployed because illiterate'. Illiteracy may in turn be easily reduced to a matter of personal failing given the influence of wider ideologies: notably, ideologies that link learning to school, and school to equal opportunity and meritocracy. For according to these ideologies, if people fail to do well in life it is because they personally, and/or their family, have failed to take the chances for success offered by school. All people, allegedly, have the equal chance to acquire literacy in school. Where individuals fail to do so the problem is seen to lie with themselves, or their family, group, etc., and not with the way society is organized. And so we talk about incompetence (whether of individual, family, group, teacher, school, and so on), but not about injustice; about personal failure, but not about oppression; about being a loser, but not about being a victim. In this way, the disadvantage of some/many is not seen as a consequence of the very structures by which others are advantaged and enabled to perpetuate their advantage.

At the same time, misperceiving personal failings as the *cause* of illiteracy, and (thus) of unemployment, poverty, etc., we seek *solutions* in the personal sphere: by fixing people up, through such mechanisms as Headstart, intervention programmes in school, remedial reading and psychological services. To this extent attention is diverted away from the structures of daily life; and so solutions are not sought via genuine *structural* change. This clearly benefits those who prevail within existing structural arrangements. Whilst they continue to benefit, the main factors contributing to patterned advantage and disadvantage, domination and subordination, are left untouched.

Let us turn now to my initial point about the political significance of structured illiteracy. In what ways can the social production of structured illiteracy be seen as part of the process of maintaining the dominance of certain interest groups over others? I will argue that illiterate persons are situated at the wrong end of structural power with respect to their economic, political, and cultural interests. I will take these in turn.

Within employer-employee relationships the fact of illiteracy can (and often does) make employees virtually powerless to promote, or even protect, their own economic interests. Under prevailing economic and technological conditions within our society, illiterate persons are prime candidates for the now permanent reserve army of unemployed labour. Moreover, the increasingly impersonal nature of work relations makes print competence essential for even the most mundane and low status jobs. 'I've lost a lot of jobs', says one illiterate man quoted by Kozol. 'Today, even if you're a janitor, there's still reading and writing ... They leave a note saying "Go to room so and so". You can't do it. You can't read. You don't know'.[29] Where employment opportunities *do* remain open to illiterate people they are within an increasingly narrow range of tasks, typically poorly paid and with otherwise low status, and within which the illiterate employee has absolutely minimum negotiating strength: the 'choice' generally being to put up, or else leave and face the probability of unemployment. The labour market is entirely a buyer's market at present — and given economic restructuring under free market policies will remain so for the foreseeable future. Under such conditions the situation is ripe for enhanced economic exploitation and oppression.[30] The illiterate are especially vulnerable here.

While the fact of structural illiteracy systematically undermines the economic interests of those who are illiterate, it also works positively to reinforce the position of groups who are already economically advantaged. I have hinted at aspects of this already. To begin with, given that illiteracy (and employment consequent upon it) is strongly patterned, an obvious economic advantage exists for children of present elites. The greater the level of structural illiteracy the better the chances of those who *are* (deemed) literate to obtain work, or higher status work: within a shrinking labour market which is being polarized increasingly into unskilled versus highly technical and otherwise skilled or expert-based work. Given the correlation between economic advantage and the likelihood of becoming literate and educationally qualified, the implications of the social production of structured illiteracy for reproducing existing advantages across generations are clear.

In addition, and very importantly, structured illiteracy reduces the chances of penetrating critique of existing economic arrangements on the part of those who are most disadvantaged by them. Literacy is essential for generating and transmitting information and criticism, and for organizing opposition, lobbying, articulating grievances, and so on. At precisely the time when grounds for economic grievance are increasing for more and more people, we find these very people being systematically denied a crucial weapon for understanding and expressing their grievance, and organizing to do something about it. The other side to this, as we have seen, is the fact that structured illiteracy appears to explain and legitimate (to dominant and subordinate alike) those very inequalities and disadvantages that exist. Attention becomes focused on the idea that people are economically disadvantaged *because* they lack basic skills. To this extent attention is directed *away* from structural trends and changes within the economy: such as increased unemployment and deskilled work consequent upon economic policies. During the current crisis within a number of capitalist economies, large scale illiteracy and perceived weaknesses in basic literacy have helped centre debate around the idea of *unemployability* instead of around the facts of economic restructuring. (This is another point at which we have to recognize the relevance of Shor's notion of the Literacy Crisis as an invention.) And so what is precisely a structural question has been distorted and defined as a problem with educational standards, failure to teach the basics, and other weaknesses within schooling itself. The attack on schooling here nicely complements 'blame the victim' reasoning directed at individuals and groups, so far as promoting elite interests is concerned. 'Solutions' are sought within education rather than within the economy. This clearly serves the interests of those who benefit from the economic restructuring that is going on at present, and undermines the interests of those whose failure to secure non–existent jobs is blamed on their unemployability. Within this distortion of economic and social reality, schools — like individuals — become to some extent a victim: blamed for problems originating in the economic structure.

In formal political terms the illiterate are effectively disfranchised. At the most fundamental level this is a matter of sheer inability to complete a voting paper by those without reading skills at all: quite independently of how any preference they may have (but cannot express in a ballot) was influenced in the first place. But even where someone's literacy skills *are* sufficient for casting a formal vote, they may be quite inadequate for gleaning relevant information via print by which to make an *informed* vote — that is, a vote that is actually in their own interests. This would be so where one votes for a candidate on the strength of their presentation on visual media, without realizing that the policies they represent are in fact hostile to one's own interests. Kozol captures both dimensions of illiterate citizens being disfranchised as follows.

> Illiterate citizens seldom vote. Those who do are forced to cast a vote of questionable worth. They cannot make informed decisions based on serious print information. Sometimes they can be directed to their interests by aggressive voter education. More frequently, they vote for a face, a smile, not for a mind or character or body of beliefs.
>
> The number of illiterate adults [in the US] exceeds by sixteen million the entire vote cast for the winner of the 1980 presidential contest. If even one third of illiterates could vote, and read enough and do sufficient math to vote in their self-interest, Ronald Reagan would not likely have been chosen President ... Democracy is a mendacious term when used by those who are prepared to countenance the forced exclusion of one third of our electorate.[31]

It is, of course, rather more complex than this. Even if people can read fluently there is no guarantee that the kind of material affording information by which they can vote in their own interests is readily available. Indeed, there may not even be *candidates* or *parties* available in an election that can be said genuinely to represent the interests of large numbers of subordinated people (as many New Zealand voters have discovered recently). Ensuring the effective availability of such candidates and parties within the electoral structures that prevail in our society requires much more than literacy alone! This, however, is not quite the point. The point is, rather, that structured illiteracy can only reinforce and maintain the process by which groups of people become and remain politically marginalized and excluded. While literate people may not necessarily (or even typically) use their skills to vote in their own interests, there is at least the possibility that they can and will; or that they can organize appropriate candidates, political tickets, etc. By contrast, illiteracy virtually *guarantees* that they cannot and, hence, will not.

Moreover, illiterate folk are systematically disempowered in political terms outside the process of voting itself. They are marginalized and excluded by other structures which define formal political practice. Making submissions, lobbying, petitioning, organizing, and the process of information gathering, analysis, and articulation which are basic to doing these other things effectively, are rendered extremely difficult — if not practically impossible — for illiterate people. In all, political subordination intersects with subordination more widely along economic, gender, race/ethnic, and cultural lines, to compound structured disadvantage. Unable to vote for candidates and policies that truly represent their economic, gender, or ethnic group interests, or else 'enabled' to vote for candidates who actually represent policies hostile to these interests, illiterate citizens are made doubly powerless relative to dominant interest groups.

The same reasoning extends to cultural subordination, whereby superior literacy becomes a factor intersecting with superior economic, political, and social power generally, to reproduce the dominance of a particular cultural style and set of cultural values through education. At the same time, the cultural dominance established and maintained in this way acts back on processes within the economic and political spheres of life to further undermine subordinate class, gender, and race/ethnic group interests.

Ira Shor provides a compelling account of this process in operation within the US during the 1970s and 1980s. His book *Culture Wars* documents at length the way in which school culture has been reshaped — via reactionary ideologies, policies and practices — to restore conservative, hierarchical, and anti-democratic values, at the expense of the more radical and egalitarian values and practices that characterized education in the 1960s. The net effect of this process has been the transformation of school culture from being a force of relative sympathy for egalitarian ideals and social justice demands (during the 1960s), to a culture which openly champions values and practices of hierarchy and inequality. Within the transformed school culture such themes as justice, equality, and community have given way to those of competition, elitism and authority. The implications for human interests are clear. 'Making inequality legitimate again after the strong egalitarianism of the 1960s ... helped restore the authorities who sat on top of the social hierarchy'.[32]

As far as structured illiteracy is concerned, the main point to be noted here is that illiterate people are as much excluded from this process of determining school culture — and, thus, from the process of shaping a school culture consistent with promoting their interests and those of their children — as they are from the process of shaping economic and political life. They are as disadvantaged (and for precisely the same reasons) within the school culture that has been made during the period from the mid 1970s as they are within the economic and political history that has been made in the same period.[33] The economic, the political, the cultural, and the educational are all dialectically interwoven here. Within each interacting dimension the structural contours are identical. Superior power is exercised by dominant groups, within structures which facilitate this, to establish ideologies, policies, and practices in the service of their own interests, and at the expense of the interests of those groups who are thereby (further) subordinated. The social production of structured illiteracy is simultaneously a symptom of this exercise of unequal power, *and* a vital contributing factor to its continuation and 'legitimation'.

Schooling and the Social Production of Improper Literacy

The vision of people like Lovett, Collins and Ernest Jones, more than a century ago, of democratically controlled and liberating education being a major force for progress toward a truly democratic and egalitarian society has not materialized. Education has become identified almost exclusively with school-ing, and school itself has become a site wherein wider power differentials (economic, political and cultural) intersect to produce the ultimate form of educational anti-democracy: namely, structured illiteracy. This, however, is only half the story so far as schooling, literacy, and the politics of subordi-nation is concerned. In addition there is the fact that while educational activity results in by far the majority of citizens becoming literate, this literacy is overwhelmingly *improper*. The social production of improperly literate people complements structured illiteracy in reproducing patterned domination and subordination.

To the extent that school is involved in the social production of improper literacy it disables subordinate social groups from pursuing informed political action in order to establish their interests on equal terms with others'. For it is (only) in practising *proper* literacy that subordinate groups achieve a rational understanding of their circumstances and are able to pursue genuine control over their lives.

Fostering proper literacy within groups of subordinated people requires that we conceive and practise reading and writing under the guiding idea that domination and subordination, advantage and disadvantage, are socially created and structured. Proper literacy involves practices of reading and writing that enable subordinate groups to achieve a *critical* understanding, in Freire's sense, of social reality and their circumstances within it. This implies, minimally, that they learn to relate biography and structure, in sociological imagination. Such critical understanding is central to the rationality com-ponent of being properly literate. Only when subordinate social groups can understand their circumstances in structural terms, and as being historically created, can they make informed decisions and embark upon courses of action that will truly enhance the control they have over their destinies. Critical understanding, however, comprises much more than a merely intellectual, abstracted grasp of the biographical in relation to the structural. Freire speaks to us again here with his idea of conscientization.[34] For subordinate groups to achieve a literacy which enhances their *control*, it must necessarily assist in the process of carrying ideas and beliefs into effective action aimed at transforming existing social practices and their inherent relations of unequal power into more democratic forms. An essential part of this process involves subordinated groups learning to practise democratic social relations and to structure their own social activity along lines of (more) equalized power and active partici-pation by all. We saw this crucial aspect of proper literacy writ large in the activities of Corresponding Societies, and it will emerge again in chapter 5. If pupils from subordinate social groups are to become properly literate we must bring words/print and the world together in pursuit of a critical understanding of structured domination and oppression, and do this within curriculum activities and pedagogical forms which equip them to apply ideas and understanding in transforming social action.

There are two parts to my argument in this section. The first takes an indirect approach to the claim that schooling promotes improper literacy. It identifies general features of the theory and practice of liberal academic education that undermine pursuit of proper literacy, and thereby *withhold* from subordinate groups access to proper literacy. The second approach is more specific and direct. It draws on an ethnographic study of classroom practice to suggest how educational activity in that particular instance *positively engages* pupils from a subordinate social group in practising improper literacy.

Schooling as Withholding Proper Literacy

Much that is important and relevant to the ways in which schooling subverts proper literacy has been written recently in critiques of 'basics', 'the standards debate', 'concern for preserving "excellence"', increased emphasis on careers education and vo-tech, and demands that schools prepare pupils for our high-tech society.[35] Arguments about curriculum, pedagogy, and improper literacy can be generated out of this literature (and the reality behind it), that would parallel closely my description and critique of APL functional literacy in chapter 2. Rather than develop *these* arguments here — although they are important — I want to take somewhat higher ground and argue that pursuit of proper literacy is actually subverted by ideas and practices of schooling which lay claim to the status of a liberal academic education. In other words, I believe that a powerful tendency to withhold proper literacy exists not only within the kind of curricula and pedagogy associated with basics, career education, and the like, *but also* within what many people would regard as sound — even *high quality* — learning experience in the liberal academic tradition.

This argument focuses on the intersection of classroom practice with a set of philosophical ideas about the nature and organization of knowledge, and their implications for a liberal education based on studying 'the disciplines'. Perhaps the most explicit, comprehensive, and accessible statement of the broad philosophical view in question here is provided by a group of educational philosophers whom I identify as liberal rationalists. Hirst, Peters, and Scheffler are among the best known of these.[36]

According to liberal rationalists, the aim of a liberal education is to develop autonomous persons who can arrive at their own critical beliefs, judgments and evaluations, and act on the basis of principles, standards, and a set of values which they prescribe and justify for themselves.[37] The key to autonomous thought is that it is rational. And so for liberal rationalists, the development of autonomous persons through education is essentially a matter of developing *rational* persons. Of particular importance here are their ideas of what it is to be rational, the process by which people become rational, and the curriculum pursuits which are central to this process.

Thinking and acting rationally is seen to involve the use of concepts, criteria, methods, standards, procedures, and tests which humans have evolved over the millennia as intellectual tools. These are embodied *par excellence* within academic disciplines, or what Hirst calls the 'forms and fields of knowledge'.[38]

Hirst identifies seven *forms* of knowledge: mathematics, the physical sciences, the human sciences, history, religion, literature and the fine arts, and philosophy. A *form* of knowledge comprises a distinct theoretic framework, or structure, through which a particular type of knowledge (for example, mathematical, historical, etc.) is generated, and within which people think rationally (about mathematical, historical, etc. matters). Each form has its own distinctive and defining concepts, logical structure, expressions and statements, and techniques by which to appraise, understand, and explain experience. A *field* of knowledge is defined by its subject matter rather than by a distinctive approach to understanding and explanation, or by a distinctive *type* of knowledge. Geographers, for example, draw on mathematics, physical sciences, human sciences, etc., in order to deal rationally with geographical phenomena and discover truths about them.

Given this view of rationality, it is argued by liberal rationalists that humans are not innately rational. They are neither born rational, nor do they naturally or automatically become rational. Rather, becoming rational is a matter of being taught to think and inquire in a rational manner. It involves 'being initiated into' the forms and fields of knowledge.[39] Those concepts, procedures, standards, and so forth, that define and govern rational thought, are public possessions that have to be acquired from others who already possess them. In Hirst's words,

> The art of scientific investigation and the development of appropriate experimental tests, the forming of an historical explanation and the assessment of its truth, the appreciation of a poem: all of these activities are high arts that are not in themselves communicable simply by words. Acquiring knowledge of any form is therefore to a greater or lesser extent something that cannot be done simply by solitary study ... it must be learnt from a master on the job.[40]

This is seen to entail a strong notion of academic authority. Indeed, the educator/teacher is taken to be *in* authority largely because they are *an* (academic) authority. They possess mastery of the tools for rational judgment and belief which pupils are in the process of acquiring. It is only through education that pupils eventually become authorities in their own right within various spheres of inquiry. Until they reach a level of competence by which they can proceed to rational judgments on their own, pupils are rightly subject to the academic authority of the teacher. The latter alone has authority to make judgments on matters of truth and interpretation, to correct mistakes, and decide what is the best or appropriate way to proceed — since they, and not the pupils, are already on the inside of the disciplines and, thus, of rational inquiry.

One further aspect of liberal rationalist theory is of special concern to us here. This is the idea that the various rational disciplines have their own distinctive 'literatures', as well as their own distinctive 'languages'.[41] The *language* is what we have already looked at: the concepts, tests and procedures, etc., and their organization into frameworks by which we think historically, scientifically, and so on. The *literature* of a given discipline comprises the attainments to date of people working within that form or field of knowledge, who have remained faithful to its language. Learning the 'language' of a rational discipline — and thus learning to think rationally within that area of inquiry — is seen by liberal rationalists as requiring initiation into the 'literature' of that discipline.[42]

While much more could be said about this epistemology — which is an important part of the supporting theory of liberal education — the brief sketch provided here is adequate for my purposes. For I want just to note the potential of this epistemology for underwriting educational activity which systematically withholds (or subverts) the pursuit and practice of proper literacy. When we turn to a discussion of typical classroom practice we will see, unfortunately, that this potential is very largely realised: within schools and tertiary institutions alike. Some of the more obvious and central aspects here are as follows.

(i) The kind of emphasis given to academic authority within the educational process by rationalists may undermine the pursuit of proper literacy in at least two ways. First, it lends itself to conceiving and practising reading and writing in a manner better adapted to *absorbing* information than actively generating knowledge. A reverence for expertise — whether in the person of the teacher, or in the texts and theorists the teacher looks to — may well emerge, disposing pupils to abdicate control over knowledge production altogether: with recourse to authoritative texts and opinions being seen as the appropriate route to uncovering truth or reasoned opinion via print. To acquire the control necessary in effecting structural change, however, presupposes learning how to take control in producing information. At the same time, of course, producing sound information calls for rigour, concern for relevance, and other rational virtues. The pedagogical secret is to foster these virtues alongside pupils learning to assume some genuine control within the process of generating knowledge. Such a heavy emphasis on academic authority as found in rationalist theory readily underwrites a 'banking' approach to education at the level of practice.[43]

Secondly, the model of academic authority involved here is hostile to conceiving and practising reading and writing within a context of learning to live (more) egalitarian and democratic social relations. Liberal rationalist theory legitimates hierarchical social relations of learning. As a result, it underwrites a process wherein pupils learn to practise literacy skills within a context of structured overt inequality of power. In other words, the practice of reading and writing in accordance with this epistemology becomes itself a thorough initiation into the very social relations (of unequal power) that a proper literacy is concerned to challenge. This clearly works against the ideal of pupils acquiring rational understanding of socially produced domination and subordination, and seeking to this reality through informed political action.

(ii) As numerous writers have noted in recent years, the separation of knowledge into so many discrete, autonomous 'forms and fields' encourages the fragmentation of inquiry and awareness. If we *begin* from the assumption that, say, historical knowledge is distinct from and autonomous of sociological, literary, ethical, etc., knowledge, the barriers to achieving an overall integrated view of social reality (drawing on ideas, theory, and evidence from these wider inquiries) become great. In principle liberal rationalist epistemology may well seek the active relating of one kind of knowledge with another in an attempt to build the big picture. In practice though, once made, the split is very difficult to overcome — especially when reinforced by timetable slots within school. The study of discrete school subjects quickly becomes an exercise of reading and writing to produce *parts*, with little or no chance to integrate them seriously into *wholes*. Such a partial, fragmented approach to understanding the world represents a poor basis from which to frame courses of transforming social action that stand a reasonable chance of being effective.[44]

(iii) It is a necessary feature of proper literacy that social practices of reading and writing bring words and the world together around the pursuit of an ever enhanced understanding of the relationship between biography and structure. This understanding must transcend the merely theoretic or intellectual, to embrace aspects of people's own lived reality. For this to happen, however, they have to *learn* how to organize, interpret, and explain their experience in the light of such ideas as social class, differential power, competing interests, social relations, gender conflict, patriarchy, racism, ideological domination, the history that is made, and so on. That is, people have to *learn* to think in structural terms. But there is nothing in liberal rationalist theory to suggest that the language and literature of the disciplines need include initiation into a structural approach to thought. On the contrary, the work of people like Hirst, Peters, and Scheffler is notable for its overtly non-structuralist tone. As far as their theory goes, there is no requirement that the 'languages' and 'literatures' within which pupils employ reading and writing in pursuit of rationality provide opportunities for learning how biography and structure are related. Insofar as the liberal rationalists themselves provide an index of what counts as disciplined inquiry, we would expect curriculum activities to ignore the challenge to foster a sociological imagination. This would be to withhold proper literacy.

(iv) There seems every possibility that curricula and pedagogies grounded in a liberal rationalist approach to knowledge will positively drive a wedge between critical inquiry and the world itself, such that critical reflective energies make no real contact with daily reality. This is because the 'literatures' of the disciplines may readily become themselves the focus of reflection and inquiry, rather than the reality they (allegedly) depict. Consequently, reading and writing may be deflected entirely into addressing words and theories, without directly touching the world at all: whether in structural terms or otherwise. There are important implications here for evaluating (or, more accurately, for *failing* to evaluate) social reality. Given rationalist theory, a piece of literature or a geographical description *can*, in principle, provide a catalyst for analysis and critique of pupils' social reality. There is, however, no requirement that it must, and every likelihood that it will not. Within literature, for example, critical energies and literacy skills might be entirely directed into assessing the plot of a novel, or the depth and quality of its character development, or else into describing and, perhaps, evaluating various critics' interpretation of the work. In this event inquiry and focus would effectively be removed from evaluation of one's social reality and place within it: reading and writing would be perceived and practised as activities without any potential as instruments for social transformation.

(v) There is, in addition, the possibility of those 'literatures' employed as the medium by which pupils learn and practise the 'languages' of rational inquiry being thoroughly hegemonic. Given an epistemological demand that history be taught — since it is a form of knowledge — we might well ask *'which* history?', or *'whose* history?' Which of the various conceptual and methodological approaches to history will be employed in school history texts? From whose point of view (for example, colonizer or colonized, black or white, male or female, bourgeois or worker) will the history found in school books be written? Should the prevailing ideological perspective within the literatures of school subjects be that of a class, gender, or race/ethnic elite, subordinate groups will thereby be engaged in practising improper literacy: since the understanding of the world they acquire through reading and writing within curriculum activities will conflict with their interests as a subordinated group and, indeed, present a powerful barrier to their developing an informed view of what their interests as a group actually are and how these interests are subverted by current social practice.[45]

So much for the theory of liberal academic education. What, now, is to be said about the typical everyday practice of school literacy in relation to my remarks about the potential of rationalist theory to underwrite denial of proper literacy? It is important to recall that I am concerned here with at least a good average of liberal education — of the kind of thing that goes on within typical academic streams of our schools and tertiary institutions — and *not* with vo-tech, basics, careers education, and other forms which are more readily identifiable as domesticating. Given the liberal rhetoric of education — including elements of curriculum theory — it is within the more self-consciously academic strands of schooling that we would best expect to find critical inquiry with potential for the practice of proper literacy occurring.

Mounting evidence of actual classroom activity, however, points toward denial of proper literacy. As typically taught, the rational disciplines present reality as essentially something to be *discovered* rather than evaluated and transformed or made. The object of scientific inquiry is nature: eternally fixed to physical, biological, chemical, etc., laws. Scientists seek to discover and confirm these governing laws. Critical inquiry in the aesthetic and moral domains also largely takes discovery of 'truth' as its object: compare, 'which interpretation is the most accurate?', 'which theory of ethics involves least contradiction?', and so on. We are faced daily with many undesirable applications and side effects of science. These include nuclear weaponry and waste, pollution, surveillance, and the use of technology to protect elite interests. Yet the forms of critical inquiry championed within academic school learning are not well suited to performing this evaluative role. Certainly, within the study of science as a discrete, fragmented branch of knowledge, it is not seen as the task of the scientist *as scientist* to evaluate these applications. Where evaluative issues *are* taken up in the classroom it is generally within marginalized timetable slots – such as liberal studies — with low status and/or no serious prospects for certification. Furthermore, the topics discussed are more likely to cover issues of pollution, peace and the threat of nuclear war, environmentalism, and the like, than the lived reality of racism, class division and patriarchy. And where issues of race, gender and class do get addressed, depth of *structural* critique is often conspicuous by its absence. After all, where are the teachers who have themselves been prepared and encouraged by their academic studies to identify and address issues through a sociological imagination?[46]

The problem for proper literacy, consequently, goes deeper than whether or not reading and writing are applied to understanding and evaluating social reality in structural terms. For social reality, to a very large extent, is not seriously evaluated in any terms at all. Critical inquiry is systematically directed away from generating commitment to social appraisal and action, and especially so from a structural point of view. This theme pervades a collection of dissenting essays on the teaching of English, edited by Kampf and Lauter.[47] The concern for what I have called proper literacy, and frustration that literary criticism and the teaching of literature in schools, colleges, and universities is not promoting it, lies at the heart of these essays. After all, the teaching of literature represents a key place within the curriculum where proper literacy might be undertaken.

In their introduction to the collection Kampf and Lauter argue that recent trends in literary criticism related to the massive growth in tertiary educational provision since World War Two have had major consequences for the teaching and study of literature: from school to university. They contrast the role and activity of literary criticism as a central part of the education of middle-class children in the nineteenth century with what literary criticism had become by the 1970s. During the earlier period, they argue, middle-class children engaged literature critically as part of their preparation for positions of economic, political, cultural, and social dominance within daily life. To evaluate literature critically was, for those children, to understand and evaluate aspects of daily life and their place within it. The role of literary criticism in 'civilizing' middle-class children and 'providing a cultural overlay' distinguishing them (in their own eyes) from their social subordinates, meant that the link between literary criticism and the hierarchical relations of daily life was tight and explicit — albeit not in a way that is endorsed here!

Kampf and Lauter claim that literary criticism had assumed a very different role and focus by the 1970s. According to them, the main function of 'the vast bulk of criticism and literary scholarship being ground out today' is to 'certify college and university teachers of English'.[48] Those thousands of people teaching literature in English and foreign language departments at tertiary level must publish in order to secure tenure, gain promotion or, even, to maintain self-respect and a sense of purpose in their work. Aspiring teachers must publish in order to get a job in the first place: obtaining a doctorate, while necessary, is no longer sufficient here. The historical trends plotted by Kampf and Lauter can be seen to have negative consequences for the practice of proper literacy in schools.

To begin with, literary criticism became increasingly divorced from the lived experience and appraisal of daily life. As a case in point, Ohmann's paper in the collection shows how the influential school of New Critics generated an entire theory — an ideology — of literary criticism which systematically directed critical attention *away* from concern for and appraisal of social reality. Indeed, he says, New Criticism represents a flight from politics altogether.[49] The net effect of such theory production, and the general drift of literary criticism away from the concerns of daily life, is that literary study as an academic discipline has been effectively denied an official 'literature' which models commitment to, and skills of, social appraisal.

In addition, intense specialization has developed within professional literary scholarship, and the study of literature has been fragmented from other areas of formal study. Literary study has become structured as an autonomous, self-contained inquiry. From the point of view of professional specialists with occupational needs to establish expertise through regular publication, this structuring is 'convenient, even necessary'. After all, how are specialists

> to master Spenserian prosody and allegory ... if they must also understand the underlying economic and social struggles of Renaissance Europe, the balance of political forces in Elizabethan England, the ideological functions of *The Faerie Queene* in those struggles? ... Or what can Engels tell them of the conditions of English workers that is significant in understanding Dickens' characters in *Hard Times*? Why, then, study Engels if you have Dickens in a nineteenth-century novel course?[50]

The problem for us here is that the historical trends and processes identified by Kampf and Lauter have not been confined to shaping the production of literary *scholarship* alone. They have been important also in structuring the very *teaching* of literature. Within the school curriculum — and also, to a great extent, within that of the university — literature has been made into an object of narrow and formal study. Literature is *studied* as a self-contained, isolated field within a wider body of formal knowledge. According to Kampf and Lauter, while this

> does not always kill the possibility of experiencing books ... [it does] remove the experience of literature from the here and now to some realm of fantasy, or to the realm of an autonomous, disinterested aesthetic.[51]

They note that, as a matter of fact, most teachers accept one or other of these options for literary study, 'not merely as legitimate pedagogical objectives, but as laws of nature'. Such acceptance can be seen as simultaneously influenced and legitimated by such theories as New Criticism. More generally, however, it is entirely consistent with, and legitimated by, liberal rationalist epistemology itself.

What this means is that genuine opportunities to develop and practise proper literacy are systematically withheld from pupils and students in schools and 'in the highest academies of the Empire' alike, by the way literature is conceived and taught.[52] The practice of reading and writing with a view to relating biography and structure, and learning how to appraise and address daily life through a sociological imagination, remains very much a minority option for the study of literature within tertiary institutions. Within schools — where curriculum, syllabus, and pedagogy, are subject to close definition and control by Ministries and Offices of Education, curriculum developers, inspection processes, teacher grading, and the like — the option is more marginal still. When we observe the central place assumed by literary study within the ideal of a liberal education — let alone within the core curriculum of school — this argument takes on special significance.

What is more, and what is already well documented, the 'literatures' of school subjects generally — i.e., textbooks — comprise a powerful mechanism of ideological domination on behalf of ruling interests over children from subordinate social groups.[53] In part, ideological control is a matter of textbooks representing social reality as fixed and immutable: as essentially incapable of being transformed in accordance with an ideal (or ideals), despite its many obvious imperfections. Gerard Macdonald describes the ideological position presented by textbooks as 'the politics of stasis', in which the existing social order appears as an 'exterior fatality'. The extent to which the world is 'a human project' is glossed or ignored by textbook knowledge, which 'does not help towards either real understanding or real alternatives'.[54] Harris refers to a study of English literature texts used in high schools in Victoria, according to which 'the overwhelming majority of books chosen for study have been written under capitalism', but that even those which are critical of capitalism accept it 'as a necessarily given "deep structure" rather than a historical mode'.[55] All of this accords very well with my earlier claim that within a 'forms and fields' approach to knowledge and curriculum, emphasis is placed on reality as something to be *discovered*, rather than appraised, transformed, made.

As well as communicating the general message of resigned quiescence, school texts can be viewed as inducting children from subordinate groups into a view of the world that positively reflects the ideas, beliefs, values, ways of seeing and being, and (thus) the very interests of those who dominate them. And so, for example, the individual rather than the collective is presented consistently as the basic social unit, and the struggles of daily existence portrayed as personal/individual rather than (class, gender, ethnic, etc.) group struggles. According to the study cited by Harris, the vast majority of the texts examined have as their central theme 'the struggle of an individual with a complex and/or unintelligible society in an apolitical context [i.e., a context which is patently *not* portrayed in structural terms] where the only intermediary group between the individual and society is the family'.[56] In this particular example it is more the *form* than the explicit content of the texts which is identified as transmitting an ideological perspective grounded in the world-view of power elites. The same is true of the dominant tendency of history texts to portray historical events as so many deeds of great men.[57] What comes through is a persistent message of history being the outcome of individual agency: of events being brought about by a minority of special persons, almost entirely male, who were/are beyond the rung of ordinary folk. History, in effect, becomes the study of powerful individual men. As the old example puts it: we all know of Napoleon; but name one of his troops! Yet it was the troops (on all sides) who did the fighting and, to that extent, made the history.[58] Before we even arrive at addressing the explicit *content* of school texts, we can see their very *form* presenting a formidable barrier to children attaining a sociological imagination; let alone to their subsequently taking up an informed commitment to engaging in collective action aimed at transforming oppressive social relations and practices of daily life.

Focusing on aspects of content, Anyon argues that even 'up-dated' social studies texts used in US schools portray native Americans, blacks, women, and the working class, in terms that reflect and favour the interests of those who dominate over these groups. Texts are replete with interest-serving omissions, stereotypes and distortions. History texts, for example, consistently promote the idea that there is no working class in the US. According to Anyon,

> the schoolbooks provide no label with which to unify as one group with a set of distinct concerns all those wage and salaried persons who are industrial labourers, craftspersons, clerical workers, or service, sales, and technical workers. Without such a label, workers are not easily called to mind as a group, and the objective fact of the working class has no subjective reality. In this way the textbooks predispose workers and others against actions on behalf of the interests working people have in common. Predictably, then, we will not find school

textbooks that are written from the point of view of the working class. Textbook economics that discusses or promotes management techniques or ways of increasing worker efficiency is socially legitimate; textbook economics that identifies or promotes working-class resistance to these activities is likely to be regarded as politicized or ideological.[59]

Madeleine MacDonald has surveyed numerous studies which examine the ways in which gender, and women in particular, are represented by school and university texts in such areas as domestic science, history, literature, sociology, political science, anthropology, psychology, and community studies. While acknowledging the exploratory and mainly descriptive nature of these investigations, she claims that they nevertheless paint a consistent and significant picture. They indicate that the general impression conveyed by school textbooks

> is one of woman's inferiority, her domesticity, her lack of intelligence, ability, sense of adventure or creativity ... There is a consistent distorted model of woman which not merely misrepresents her activities in social life but does nothing to correct the social patterns of discrimination. From the fantasy world of children's books to the male bias of academic disciplines which purport to be 'value-free', one finds a persistent pattern which can only be construed as the ideological wing of patriarchy.[60]

MacDonald identifies three pervasive elements within this ideological bias. Women are rendered 'invisible': they are largely 'absent actors in the histories of Western civilization', and the appearances they *do* make are mainly as individuals — rather than as collective agent of shared struggle and maker of history — and within passive roles. Occupationwise, women are strongly identified with 'low status or "second rate" jobs'. They are most likely to be portrayed as filling traditional occupations which are 'limited in prospect and narrow in range'. There is, finally, a dominant emphasis on women's domesticity: a message that comes through with 'a degree of repetition that can only be described as ideological bombardment ...'[61]

Even allowing for the valid comments of Whitty and others regarding limitations within existing studies of school texts[62], we can draw a safe conclusion from the evidence sampled here. Studies of the form and content of textbooks suggest that the practice of reading and writing within the academic curriculum of school, by pupils from subordinate (class, ethnic, gender) social groups, is built upon material which systematically withholds from them the ideas, visions of possibility, concepts, interpretive frameworks, role models, historical cases, and information necessary for engaging in proper literacy. The situation of, for instance, a working-class pupil reading texts, writing essays, and preparing for exams in history or literature, contrasts markedly with the practice of their forebears in Corresponding Societies, Chartist halls, reading rooms, and the like. The literature of Correspondents and Chartists was a literature of social critique which advocated the possibility and desirability/necessity of social change — of *structural* change. It was a literature of shared interests and concerns; it exposed structured domination, upheld the values of organization and democratic participation, and called for collective struggle. It portrayed history as a social construction in accordance with particular interests and at the expense of others. It was steeped in sociological imagination and, conceiving of history as capable of being controlled and changed in line with the interests of people at large, reflected the *will* to organize, struggle and change. Engaging this literature — within the distinctive pedagogical forms employed in settings like Corresponding Societies — offered to many working-class people a stimulus and an intellectual framework for understanding their daily reality in a critical manner, and powerful incentives to engage in collaborative action on the basis of that understanding. The prevailing literature of school study today, by contrast, is conserving, partial and fragmented, oriented towards the individual (and atypical) agent, and otherwise steeped in the worldview of existing elites. It has little or no potential for fostering group consciousness and a structural understanding of society, and is largely bereft of models for collective activity around shared perceptions of a need to address the discriminatory social relations and practices of daily life. Barring exceptional teaching on the part of those rare educators who combine a truly critical consciousness with the pedagogical skill to foster it in others as well, engagement with this literature will be an experience which can only thwart the development and practice of proper literacy.[63] Moreover, I find little (if anything) within the influential theory of liberal rationalism to challenge these trends, and much — unfortunately — that has the potential to legitimate them.

Schooling and the Practice of Improper Literacy

During the past decade there have been frequent calls for researchers engaged in radical analysis and critique of education to give greater emphasis to investigating actual educational reality/practice and, perhaps, to indulge rather less in the kind of essay writing rehearsed in the previous section. I want now, briefly, to consider a single case of classroom practice which speaks directly to the claim that school learning actually engages children from subordinate social groups in the practice of *improper* literacy. In an ethnographic study of two streams within a New Zealand all-girls secondary school, Alison Jones produces data and arguments which bear directly on the social production of improper literacy in school.[64] Her study is *not* specifically concerned with literacy. Rather, it is concerned much more widely with education and social reproduction. In my account I aim to extract just those aspects relating directly to the practice of literacy in the classroom without violating the integrity of the study as a whole.

Reference to a lone study cannot, of course, establish much about the social production and practice of improper literacy in general. On the contrary, the account which follows illustrates something of the distinctiveness and particularity of one social practice and conception of reading and writing. It is important to recognize that although schooling overwhelmingly involves students in practising improper literacy, this does not happen in the same ways or involve the same things for all those who belong to subordinate groups within societies like our own. 'Improper literacy' does not refer to a single or unitary form of reading and writing. Quite different detailed practices and notions of reading and writing may be judged improper by the criteria I am using here. In referring to Jones' study I will be noting some features of *one* specific social practice and conception of literacy that can be deemed improper because (of the ways) it immerses pupils from a subordinate social group in an uncritical and distorted view of their social reality and personal circumstances within that reality. Moreover, the practice of literacy by these pupils has the effect of undermining their potential for future control over their individual and collective destinies. The study suggests how within one particular setting, under certain cultural, ideological, and pedagogical conditions, the organization of school learning in discrete bodies of formal knowledge under the accepted academic authority of a teacher, reinforces an authority dependence which promotes an approach to reading and writing that is tailor made for reproducing subordination. It is only through many such studies that we can develop more general, empirically-based accounts of how improper forms of literacy are produced and practised within school, and how this contributes to social reproduction.

'At School I've Got a Chance' is an attempt to understand how elements of classroom practice — especially pedagogy — intermesh with wider economic, cultural, and ideological factors to reproduce social class across generations. Jones' primary focus is on a middle-to-low stream class, Five Mason. These pupils are almost entirely from Pacific island families (settled in New Zealand) and are working-class. Her secondary focus is on a top stream, comprised almost entirely of white middle-class pupils, Five Simmonds. Much of the explanatory power of Jones' work rests on dramatic differences between the pedagogies practised in the Five Mason and Five Simmonds classrooms respectively, and the wider factors influencing those differences. I am concerned here only with Five Mason.

The Five Mason girls uniformly accept the ideology of meritocracy and equal opportunity to secure life chances through education. They want to avoid ending up with the kind of 'stink jobs' their parents, siblings, and friends commonly have — for example, shop assistants, factory work, cleaning, etc. — and set their sights instead on becoming secretaries, accountants, teachers, police, etc. They see success in school as the route to good employment prospects. In their view as much as that of the Five Simmonds girls, 'school success' means passing examinations. As fifth-formers they are faced with their first national examination, the School Certificate, and are eager to acquire the school knowledge necessary for passing this exam. They believe that acquiring the relevant knowledge and passing the examination involves a combination of ability and hard work, and accept that failure is essentially an outcome of either personal inability or laziness, or both.

Unfortunately for them, their notion of what counts as doing school work, and the very considerable effort they put into doing it, are quite inappropriate for obtaining school knowledge — that is, the kind of knowledge prescribed by the fifth-form syllabus and examined in School Certificate.[65] They have a completely different idea from the Five Simmonds pupils of what counts as doing the right work for passing school exams. It is Five Simmonds' idea and practice of school work that is the correct one, so far as scholastic rewards are concerned. The Five Simmonds girls succeed at school; the Five Mason girls fail — despite their genuine commitment to succeeding and real effort they make. The important point for us here is the conception and practice of reading and writing involved in the school work of Five Mason. To understand *their* (distinctive) school literacy is to see how it is shaped and reinforced by the interaction between *their* cultural perception of and response to schooling and the pedagogy employed in *their* classrooms.[66]

For Jones, 'culture' incorporates aspects of social class and ethnicity. She argues that, as members of the working class *and* of Pacific island ethnic groups, the Five Mason girls acquire an approach to obtaining knowledge which is grounded firmly in dependence on the teacher. Learning is perceived as getting (i.e., receiving) the teacher's knowledge, rather than engaging in elaboration, exploration, and evaluation of content relevant to a subject area via discussion and print (in addition to merely receiving information). The teacher is seen as having the relevant knowledge (= content). She is recognized and respected as *the* authority on all matters of school knowledge. Moreover, she is seen as the primary *source* of this knowledge. It is her job to provide content. This is what Five Mason expect of her. For her to initiate discussion or to try to draw knowledge out of the pupils is seen by Five Mason as irrelevant or bad teaching. Educational process is culturally perceived here as rigidly hierarchical. The teacher is authority and source: pupils are recipients of content.

In accordance with this culturally shaped perspective the Five Mason girls conceive 'school work' essentially as note-taking and, later, learning these notes. They define 'appropriate school work' as getting the teacher's *words* transferred into their own books. Note-taking is overwhelmingly their main form of school *work*. Indeed, they positively demand that their teachers give them copying work. Their notes are almost always neat and complete and teachers are evaluated according to whether or not they give good notes.[67] Consequently, copying notes — either at the time they are given or at some other time (including during a different class in a different subject altogether) — comprises the essence of their school literacy. This is how and what they predominantly read and write. And practising their school *literacy* largely exhausts their school *work*.

This is consistent with the Five Mason girls engaging a good deal in forms of classroom activity that are quite inappropriate and, moreover, counter-productive given what appropriating school knowledge *really* involves: while all the time perceiving themselves as working hard at what is required. Common examples of such activity include not following (or even trying to follow) the lesson, chatting, refusing and otherwise failing to *discuss* issues or think around a topic, and so on. It can all, seemingly, be left to getting the teacher's notes or copying material from texts on her recommendation — and swotting it up later. Even following written instructions in formal class activities — such as doing experiments — is only a way station to the real thing: getting the notes. The following is typical and informative of Five Mason's school literacy in relation to their school learning as a whole. The context is a science lesson.

> ... The teacher writes on the blackboard 'Magnetic Forces'. She writes underneath instructions for two experiments which the students must perform this period.
>
> By the time everyone has found their books and put their bags under their desks more than five minutes have passed Malia, sitting next to me, has no book. 'I've finished it. Forgot to get another one. I'll borrow Sina's'. She settles down with a *Cleo* magazine.
>
> 'Copy this down. It's clear enough what to do', says the teacher. Everyone is quiet as they copy down the instructions for the experiments. 'What do we do?' asks Sina. 'Read your instructions', the teacher sounds weary and sarcastic. The instructions tell them to tie a magnet with cotton and hang it from a stand. They manage to get the correct equipment from the front, and tie their magnet at one end so it hangs down. 'Tie it at the centre', says the teacher after a while. They do so, it takes some time to untie and retie the magnet. As only one or two girls in each group are doing the tying, others lose interest and chat together.
>
> The question they are supposed to answer is, 'Does the magnet stay still and face one direction?' 'It doesn't, says Sina, unsure. 'What's supposed to happen?, Lee is totally bemused. The teacher comes up and holds the magnet to stop it swinging. It hangs nearly motionless. Malia has temporarily abandoned her magazine.

> | | |
> |---|---|
> | *Malia* | What's it doing, Miss? |
> | *Teacher* | It is pointing North-South. |
> | *Lee* | Where's the North-South? |
> | *Teacher* | There's North, there's South (pointing). |
> | *Malia* | Is it to do with the stand? |
> | *Teacher* | No. |
> | *Malia* | What, then? |
> | *Teacher* | You know when you use a compass, it points to the north, doesn't it? |

Lee	How does the compass know?
Teacher	It's the magnetic field. I'll tell you about that later. Now, answer your question. (Goes to another group).

Some girls write in their books, 'points North–South'. Now they must put iron filings on paper, and put a magnet under the paper, and draw what they see. Inevitably the filings get stuck to the magnet, but eventually Lee and Sina manage to set it up as instructed. There is no apparent clear pattern on the paper. Sina draws what she sees, but it makes no sense in terms of magnetic concepts. The others play with the filings and stab each other with magnets and stands. A small crowd gathers round a nude male centrefold in Malia's *Cleo*. The bell goes, there is chaos as everyone rushes to leave. The teacher asks for all the magnets to be put back in their boxes, but as I leave I notice empty boxes and iron filings on the floor.

The following day, at the next science lesson, the teacher goes over yesterday's experiments. She draws the equipment and explains what the hanging magnet 'was supposed to do', saying she will give them 'some notes on the Van Allen belt and the global magnetic forces next lesson'. She writes down what the magnet did. Everyone copies what she has written . . . The teacher asks someone to draw on the board what they saw with the iron filings on the paper. Ruth draws some lines on the blackboard, but they are 'incorrect'. 'I'll have to draw it'. The teacher rubs Ruth's lines off, and draws the 'correct' diagram. Everyone copies the teacher's diagram and sentences attentively. 'Lucky I never wrote it in yesterday', says Lee. I asked her why the lines look like that, but she does not know, although the sentences she has written explain why. The teacher hands out a worksheet on static electricity. The girls copy it into their books. They cut out the pictures and stick them in, as the teacher talks about static electricity.[68]

Five Mason write notes to learn, memorize, and regurgitate in tests and examinations. They have no conception of the teacher's words/notes — i.e., syllabus content — as so many ideas to be engaged critically: to be discussed, interpreted, reflected upon, related to wider ideas or, even, *to be understood*. For them the notion (let alone the skills) of grasping underlying principles and patterns, abstracting from general to particular and vice-versa, ordering and expressing ideas, *and using the skills of reading and writing to these ends*, is non-existent. And so it is absent in their practice.

While this provides a sufficient working description of Five Mason's school literacy, the explanation from culture as to why and how their literacy is shaped and practised in that particular way tells only half the story. For in the classroom this cultural orientation to learning interacts dialectically with the pedagogy employed consistently (albeit unconsciously and unintentionally) by

Five Mason's teachers. The following passages illustrate some dimensions of the pedagogy in action.

(In an economics lesson)

Teacher	How would you measure growth in the economy?
Donna	Kilogram ... [a serious attempt at an answer based on Donna's notion of growth in other social contexts].
Teacher	(Ignoring Donna) How might the economy be expanding?
Malia	Bills expanding. [Malia knows that bills have something to do with the economy.]
Teacher	(Ignoring Malia) Look on page 14 and read the paragraph at the top.

Such instances are extremely common in Five Mason classes. Jones claims that the teachers consistently identify the girls' manifest lack of 'correct knowledge' as being in need of remedy simply by *providing* the right information: a response reinforced strongly by the girls' own expectations of and demands for such provision.

(In English)

Teacher	What does 'primitive' mean? A lot of you got this wrong, so I want you to write it in your books.
S	Not modern.
S	Ancient.
Teacher	Yes. It means 'underdeveloped', living a 'simple life'. (She write these words on the board and the girls copy.)[69]

Via such interactions — through the pedagogical *form* — the girls are being taught that they must use the teacher's words. The teacher's words, indeed her *ideas*, are not the pupils' own. They have no *meaning* for Five Mason. And so the girls 'switch off' and merely copy down the 'correct words'. This is the only strategy effectively available to them.[70] For Five Mason, the cumulative effect of the teachers' concern with their own words and knowledge is to teach/reinforce dependence. The patterns of daily practice produced in the classroom shape and perpetuate a view held by the pupils and teachers (of Five Mason) alike of how teaching and learning take place: at least for *that* setting. The process is very different within Five Simmonds' classrooms.

What we see here is the social production of a particular conception and practice of reading and writing. It is created, established, and reproduced in the dialectic between culturally acquired attitudes and dispositions and pedagogical practice, within the context of pursuing a curriculum based upon discrete subjects and organized around a specific syllabus of formal knowledge. This literacy is dysfunctional in scholastic terms. It is also *improper.*

By 'dysfunctional' I mean that it is maladapted to the girls' goal of securing scholastic success by appropriating school knowledge. This is apparent at both a specific and a more general level. Specifically, the practice of copying and reading without understanding — and in the absence of a pedagogy adapted to encouraging understanding — actually leads in many cases to the girls copying and learning *misinformation*; which further negates the possibility of understanding. In human biology and science, for example, 'diagrams were often copied painstakingly, but labelled incorrectly' — as when a teacher, presuming some understanding on the pupils' part, carelessly had an arrow going to the wrong place, or had made some other mistake. Elsewhere, notes are copied incorrectly from a teacher's words. With regard to the function of haemoglobin, Ruth writes, 'helps blood clots': whereas the teacher says, 'it helps the blood to clot'. Of the Rh. effect the teacher says, 'it affects the baby, it's jaundiced and short of red blood cells'. This is taken down as 'affects baby, yellow, short'. At a more general level, the girls' literacy is maladapted to the broad learning objectives examined by School Certificate. Their literacy is grounded in memorizing and regurgitating information. While School Certificate does, in part, reward 'absorption' and 'delivery' of content, it demands much more than that: notably, interpretation of and abstraction from the given — although by no means *structural* interpretation of social reality.[71]

These dysfunctional features of the girls' school literacy are part of what makes it an *improper* literacy. There is no potential whatsoever here for developing, refining, and employing an interpretive framework. Interpretation implies understanding, and understanding is systematically undermined here: including understanding of single and relatively straightforward ideas, let alone understanding (and interpretation) of a complex social reality. We are speaking here of literacy as the practice of entirely uncritical, unreflective, unrelational thought, which produces gross distortions in the simple transferral of information. The original ('correct') information is itself, of course, remote from the girls' experience, and quite unconnected with their existing knowledge. It is also completely divorced from anything to do with analyzing daily life in structural terms.

The very practice of literacy here is an exercise in undermining rather than enhancing control within the relations, processes, and circumstances of daily life. This is so in at least two senses. First, the girls' very practice of literacy involves them actively in producing their own failure. Their school literacy is a central component in the process of (re)producing subordination. They are destined for either low status work wherein they have minimal (or no) control or power; or else unemployment. Second, the practice of literacy here involves participation in social relations of hierarchy and domination. It confirms, reinforces, and expands the girls' ideology of authority and power relations, *and their own place within these*.

Finally, for Five Mason the practice of school literacy confirms them in their ideologies of meritocracy and equal opportunity. They see themselves as having had their chance: a perception shared by bearers of this ideology at large. They worked hard — as they understood hard work to be. This, however, was to no avail. They ascribe their failure — and prior to the actual exams, their impending/anticipated failure — to personal inability and/or lack of motivation. Ruth, for example, had wanted to become a music teacher. She failed her School Certificate exams and got a job in a fast-food shop. Why did she fail? 'Oh, I couldn't be bothered in the end. I didn't try, eh'. Repeka still wants a secretarial job. Having failed her exams she works as a packer and ushers at a local cinema. She explains her failure in terms of the exam being too hard, plus the fact that 'I played up, went out, had a good time'. Months before the exam itself, Malia says 'I wanna get School C, I just wanna get it'. When asked whether she will, she replies 'Probably . . . not'. Why not? 'I dunno. It's the brains, eh. I'll have another go next year. Probably then I might get it'.[72]

Against the Tide: Practising Proper Literacy Within Formal Education

The very problem of those research programmes which address the role of education within the overall process of social reproduction of structured domination and subordination orients us toward identifying improper literacy as prevalent within school practice.[73] Thus oriented, the radical researcher is equipped and disposed theoretically to 'affirm' this prevalence. At the same time, however, we must recognize that exceptions to the general trend toward improper literacy can and do occur. There *are* spaces within formal education in which critically consciousness and politically committed teachers may practise proper literacy with their students. I will conclude this chapter by mentioning very briefly two outstanding examples of proper literacy being pursued in formal educational settings with students from subordinate social groups. These are found in the work of Chris Searle in London's East End during the early 1970s, and Ira Shor at the City University of New York during the same period.[74] The merest sketches follow. Readers are directed to the original accounts, which are simultaneously humbling and inspirational.

Classrooms of Resistance is one of several published compilations of work produced by 11–14 year-old working-class students — many of them belonging to migrant ethnic minority groups — within English courses taught by Searle in East End schools. Searle's educational aim was to develop a programme of activity which would encourage and nurture 'the generous, empathetic, and fraternal instincts' of his pupils, and bring them 'towards literacy within a real movement of alliance with the oppressed of their own neighbourhood, country and world'.[75] He eschewed any pretence of political neutrality in his role as teacher, maintaining that education is valid only 'if it plays its part in supporting the total liberation of [humankind], and not the interests of a ruling few'. Within this ideological frame his main object was that the working-class youth in his course learn to read, write, spell, punctuate, to develop the word as a weapon and tool in ... struggles for improvement and liberation for them, and the rest of their class all over the world.[76]

Throughout these courses teacher and students together moved back and forward between three inter-related emphases: focusing on the student's own neighbourhood, and the constant attacks on the living conditions, environmental integrity, and quality of life therein; expanding the scope of class consciousness by trying to understand the conditions and plight of working people elsewhere in Britain and in the third world, and moving toward these others in solidarity; and addressing the working world of trade unionism and rank-and-file resistance on the shop floor.

The pedagogy involved discussion, research, and imaginative writing in drama or prose, relating to themes and events at each level. Themes and events centering on the local neighbourhood included land speculation, profiteering, cuts in public facilities, destruction of community life, and the undermining of class solidarity, by forces operating on behalf of elite interests 'opposed to the well-being and social and political health' of the students and their families. Events occurring at the time in Ulster, Chile, and Azania (South Africa) provided stimuli for developing an internationalist class perspective. The world of work was addressed via local and national disputes (in factories, mines, building projects, etc.), by exploring the life of the skilled and unskilled worker, and considering how workers can resist and defend themselves against exploitation and organize to improve wages and conditions. Investigation of the present was combined with study of history and tradition

> to find precedents in the past where individuals and masses of East End working people have similarly resisted or organized, or achieved advances which now benefited the [students themselves] and their families. And so local history often pushed its way into the present, as a base for contemporary action and syllabus.[77]

The opening of a luxury hotel and yacht marina on the site of the old St Catherine Docks, in the heart of the East End, provided one focus for the practice of proper literacy. The process of land speculation was explored and data on land speculators gathered, from local newspaper reports and through contact with such organizations as the East End Docklands Action Group. Such facts as the following were uncovered, discussed, and written up or used as background in pupils' written work: Taylor Woodrow rent twenty-seven acres of public land from the Greater London Council for £250,000 per year — or the equivalent of a week's income from the hotel at the time (in 1973); the project will make £200,000,000 for Taylor Woodrow — an amount that could build homes for 60,000 homeless people in the area; local people had been assured that 75 per cent of the dockland would be used for public housing, but no such development for low income families was in progress; river warehouses were being converted into luxury flats (and private profits) in Wapping; land was being sold for 'development' at prices which were beyond local community means, but low enough to ensure handsome profits for speculators and developers.

The written work of pupils which emerged out of uncovering and discussing such information spanned the range from descriptive prose to imaginative expression in poetry and political statement in comic strip form. Underlying themes included vested interest, social injustice, council cooperation with speculators, environmental pollution, lack of government action on housing shortages, luxury accommodation for the rich in an area of homelessness and unemployment, the threat of eviction as rented accommodation is sold to developers, and so on.

Rich Luxuries
Why did Taylor Woodrow build the hotel?
When there are so many people who have
    nowhere to dwell,
The Tower Hotel is only for millionaires
There is nowhere for us to live or to play.
In the Tower Hotel they have waitresses
Where we have to slave for ourselves,
They have luxuries galore
Our homes are just a bore.
They have 836 rooms in the hotel
Where we are scrambled up in about four.

Lynn Marles, 11

Wapping at Night
Wapping was a big-lighted, busy place
But buses no more
                no fights
                no lights
It's all locked behind a door.
People are sleeping
Some have stopped breathing.
                No barges
                no boats
It's all
        so quiet
The river is calm
some fish
are dead
            and
                I'm
                    Tucked
                        in
                            bed.
Peter Smith, 11[78]

167

In *Critical Teaching and Everyday Life* Ira Shor describes aspects of the pedagogy he employed with working-class students during the brief 'open admissions' era at the City University of New York. Some key elements are revealed in his description of a Utopia course. The point about Utopia is that it stimulates imaginative thought. 'It speaks to the human power to reconstruct ourselves and our social relations', providing a meeting point for creativity and politics, for imagination and action.[79] Utopia can be studied at a number of relatable levels: as a literary tradition; as a history of counter communities; as a form of critical consciousness. The approach taken in Shor's classes was to try and understand Utopian thought better through the process of teacher and students actually practising such thought. Reading and writing, then, were employed in acts of describing and analyzing aspects of social reality: by trying to understand how things came to be the way they are, and identifying problematic features within daily life. On the basis of this understanding and critique, visions of how social relations and practices might be changed for the better were constructed and practical agendas for change written up. In several instances this process issued in students taking direct action on matters affecting their interests.

The simplest pedagogical model employed in these classes was a three step problem-solving method, practised in a manner intended to dissolve as far as possible the teacher-pupil hierarchy through approximation to dialogue along the lines advocated by Freire.[80] The problems addressed comprise some feature or features of everyday life. In the first step something from daily life is observed in detail (the 'life description' step); in the second step it is investigated ('diagnosis'); and in the third it is resolved ('reconstruction'). The whole approach is characterized by its explicit concern to enhance sociological imagination: to encourage an understanding of the *structured* nature of social reality, identify particular interests being served and undermined respectively by existing structured relations and practices, and prompt a translation of this understanding and critique into social action. This is to *problematize* social reality, to take something that is everyday and present it as one aspect or facet of an overall structured social practice that serves human interests unequally, and that needs to be transformed if the interests of people at large are to be met more justly. In the 'diagnosis', students ask of the object or practice under scrutiny, 'what is its human context?', 'who benefits from it?', 'what are its social roots and consequences?' etc.[81]

Shor's example of problematizing a (fibreglass form fit) classroom chair can be used as illustration here. In the first step the chair is examined and described. Students write brief essays on the chair. Shor produces a composite description out of the individual essays of the students — enabling the group to construct a larger 'whole' out of 'parts'. On the basis of this full and careful description of a familiar object the class moves into diagnosis. The chair is hard and uncomfortable. Who would design it like that, and why? Surely it would not be students themselves, with their own interests in mind. Perhaps it has something to do with hindering relaxation, with the aim of keeping students awake and more alert in class. Bored students might doze off if they had comfortable furniture. Do the deans and presidents of the university have such chairs? Or even the teachers in their offices or at their desks? Gradually the chair appears as a symbol of oppression and inequality. Do students at Harvard have the same kind of chairs as these working-class open admission students? The chair is seen as performing an important function within the daily routines of a hierarchically and unequally ordered society. In 'reconstruction' the students design more comfortable classroom furniture; create visions of what the furniture might be like if their education formed part of a different social order. 'In their thoughts and in their writing they gain a clear image of what they would do to transform the classroom. The simple question of furniture has been turned into a politicizing issue'.[82]

Problematizing a hamburger led, among other consequences, to action based on the distinction (which surfaced in discussion) between junk food and health food. 'A class organizing committee emerged to cooperatize the college cafeteria, and have it offer a nutritious, fixed-price lunch.'[83] More generally, the nexus between motor car and hamburger was explored for the clues it gives to the social historical construction of American society, and the differences between the society that has been constructed in the US and those constructed elsewhere. This is a pedagogy for promoting historical consciousness.

> The kind of imagination which gets stimulated can serve as a base for discussing alternatives to the present society. For now, the burger and the car may be two ruling forces within daily life, but they weren't always with us and may not stay forever. At a certain point in time, society changed so as to produce hamburgers and cars, and in turn, these phenomena worked to change society. Students who gain the power to understand the transformation of society also gain the critical consciousness needed to invent their own transformations. Through our investigation, their perceptions of transport and food change. Talk emerges about non-polluting mass transit, about cooperative food service replacing the cafeteria's junk meals.[84]

There are many further dimensions and features of Shor's pedagogy, and a range of specific approaches and models which I have not the space to mention here. The Utopia course combined study of present society with investigation of Utopian communities, addressing such themes as racism, sexism, inequality, oppression, and their respective negations, along with components of everyday ideology which effectively buttress inequalities and hierarchies. These latter include such notions (which are deeply embedded in ordinary consciousness) as 'the grass is always greener', 'you can't fight city hall', and the dream of 'striking it rich'.

The kind of literacy pursued in the work of people like Searle and Shor with their students has everything to do with fostering among members of subordinate social groups a critical understanding of the relations, practices, and ideologies of daily life. It promotes a sense of group identity, and awareness of how the interests of class, race, or gender elites are opposed to their own — and how (as in the case of white and/or male students) they themselves may be implicated in the oppression of others. An important part of developing this awareness is coming to see how ideologies widely accepted by ruled groups can work against their interests and in favour of dominant interests. 'The grass is always greener', for example, is an ideological belief which helps adjust (or domesticate) a subordinate group to their own conditions and circumstances. The dream of 'striking it rich' represents to oppressed groups the one way in which they might 'make it'. That is, the way to improve their circumstances is by getting lucky — through a big win, or some other scoop of fate — rather than through struggle and action for change. Shor's students in particular spent much time exposing the interest-serving nature of such ideologies. In practising proper literacy the students in our examples came also to understand how group solidarity is broken down: how subordinated groups are divided and ruled — for example along race/ethnic, gender, skilled labour vs unskilled labour, union members vs non-union members, etc. lines — by prevailing ideologies and social practices. Further- more, the literacy they practise *actively ties* their emerging critical understanding to experiencing the kind of social relations, and engaging in the very forms of collective social action, that enhance people's control over the history that is made in their own times.

This is a literacy that is as hostile to the reproduction of patterned domination and subordination as mainstream classroom practice is to promot- ing the process of informed social transformation along genuinely egalitarian and democratic lines. While this chapter does little more than scratch the surface of its central theme, it hopefully indicates lines along which a more comprehensive investigation may proceed. Such an investigation would itself be part of the wider practice of proper literacy.

The theoretical perspective I have employed here orients us toward identifying practices and conceptions of improper literacy, and 'affirming' their prevalence within education in a context of structured domination and subordination. In chapter 5 I will apply this same perspective in the opposite direction: to identify commitment to practices and models of *proper* literacy within a revolutionary social setting aimed at replacing traditional structures of inequality and oppression with democratic and emancipatory alternatives. This will involve us in considering the nature and role of literacy in revolutionary Nicaragua.

Notes

1 APPLE, M (1981), 'Social structure, ideology and curriculum', in LAWN, M. and BARTON, L. (Eds), *Rethinking Curriculum Studies*, London, Croom Helm, p. 131 (emphasis mine).

2 For the notion of supportive rhetoric, see HARRIS (1979), *Education and Knowledge*, London, Routledge and Kegan Paul, chapter 4.

3 Compare KOZOL, (1985) *Illiterate America*, New York, Anchor and Doubleday, p. 10.

4 For Kozol's attack on measurement procedures underlying official statistics claiming near-full literacy, see his chapter 5.

5 SHOR, I. (1986), *Culture Wars*, London. Routledge and Kegan Paul.

6 *Ibid.*, p. 64.

7 Compare, for example, DALE, R. and ESLAND, G. (1977), *Mass Schooling*, Milton Keynes, Open University Press, p. 15.

8 KOZOL, *op. cit.*, p. 37.

9 The notion of functionality employed here is, clearly, an *improper* conception — as defined in chapter 2. While such functionality cannot comprise an *ideal* of attainment — in either Kozol's view or my own — it *is* useful for establishing a standard against which estimates of illiteracy can be made.

10 Many students, of course, complete a given grade of school without being able to perform at that grade level.

11 KOZOL, *op. cit.*, p. 10.

12 Cited *ibid.*, p. 58.

13 *Ibid.*, p. 57.

14 TYACK, D. (1976), 'Ways of seeing: an essay on the history of compulsory schooling, *Harvard Educational Review*, 46, 3, pp. 360–1.

15 HUNTER and HARMAN, (1979), *Adult Illiteracy in the United States*, New York, McGraw Hill, p. 31.

16 *Ibid.*, chapter 2.

17 KOZOL, *op. cit.*, p. 5.

18 *Ibid.*, p. 59.

19 HARRIS (1982), *Teachers and Classes*, London, Routledge and Kegan Paul, p. 102.

20 See COLLINS, R. (1977), 'Some comparative principles of educational stratification', *Harvard Educational Review*, 47, 1, 1–27.

21 HUNTER and HARMAN, *op. cit.*, pp. 19–20.

22 For a discussion of this theme and an overview of relevant literature, see WHITTY, G. (1985), *Sociology and School Knowledge: curriculum theory, research and politics*, London, Methuen, chapter 2.

23 Compare here, for example, SHOR (1986), *op. cit.*; KAMPF and LAUTER (1982), *The Politics of Literature: dissenting essays on the teaching of English*, New York, Pantheon Books, pp. 3–54.; SAWER, M. (Ed) (1982), *Australia and the New Right*, Sydney, Allen and Unwin.

24 SHOR, *ibid.*, pp 11 and 65. For a fascinating account of a challenge to the domination of standard over non-standard English within a revolutionary setting, compare SEARLE (1984), *Words Unchained: language and revolution in Grenada*, London, Zed Press.

25 See, for example, GOODACRE, E. (1968), *Teachers and their Pupils' Background*, London, NFER; ROSENTHAL, R. and JACOBSON, L. (1968), *Pygmalion in the Classroom*, New York, Holt, Rinehart and Winston; BERNSTEIN, B. (1971), 'On the classification and framing of knowledge', in YOUNG, M.F.D. (Ed.), *Knowledge and Control*, London, Macmillan; STUBBS, M. (1976), *Language, Schools and Classrooms*, London, Methuen; CONNELL, R. (1985), *Teachers' Work*, Sydney, Allen and Unwin.

26 For a detailed investigation of such themes, see JONES, A. (1986), *At School I've got a chance: ideology and social reproduction in a secondary school*, PhD thesis, University of Auckland.

27 HARRIS (1982), *op. cit.*, p. 102.

28 Besides individuals and groups, schools themselves may be a further legitimate beneficiary of our refusal to blame victims. For what individual schools are (or are not) and do (or fail to do) may also very much reflect *structured* inequality — resulting in, say, inferior resources, transient teachers, low morale, etc.

29 KOZOL, *op. cit.*, p. 27.

30 In the technical sense of these terms. Compare, for example, HARRIS (1982), *op. cit.*, p. 44.

31 KOZOL, *op. cit.*, p. 23.

32 SHOR (1986), *op. cit.*, p. 96.

33 Compare *ibid.* For material with an Australasian flavour bearing on this point, see SAWER (Ed), *op. cit.*, and LAUDER, H. (1986), 'The new right and educational policy in New Zealand', unpublished paper, University of Canterbury.

34 FREIRE (1985), *The Politics of Education*, London, Macmillan.

35 See SHOR (1986), *op. cit.*, for a reading of recent educational developments undertaken from this general point of view. Shor provides a valuable bibliography relating to the US scene, in the notes to his third chapter. Compare, in particular, his note 73, p. 215.

36 HIRST, (1974), *Knowledge and the Curriculum*, London, Routledge and Kegan Paul.; PETERS, R. (1965), 'Education as initiation', in ARCHAMBAULT, R. (Ed), *Philosophical Analysis and Education*, London, Routledge and Kegan Paul, pp. 87–111, (1966), *Ethics and Education*, London, Allen and Unwin, (1973), 'Freedom and the Development of the Free Man', in DOYLE, J. (Ed), *Educational Judgments*, London, Routledge and Kegan Paul, pp. 119–42, (1974), 'The Development of Reason', in his *Psychology and Ethical Development*, London, Allen and Unwin, pp. 119–50; SCHEFFLER, I. (1967), 'Philosophical models of teaching', in PETERS, R. (Ed), *The Concept of Education*, London, Routledge and Kegan Paul, pp. 120–34.

37 Compare my (1982), *Freedom and Education*, Auckland Milton Brookes, chapters 1 and 4.

38 HIRST, *op. cit.*, chapter 3.

39 For the metaphor of initiation, compare PETERS (1965), *op. cit.*

40 HIRST, *op. cit.*, p. 49.

41 Compare PETERS (1965), *op. cit.* For the original distinction between the literature and the language of disciplines, see OAKESHOTT, M. (1962), *Rationalism in Politics*, London, Methuen, especially pp. 80–110.

42 Note that this epistemological position was effectively elevated into a full *educational* position by people like Peters — insofar as the educational enterprise was equated with the development of (a very academic kind of) reason.

43 Compare FREIRE (1972), *Pedagogy of the Oppressed*, Harmondsworth, Penguin, chapter 2.

44 Compare *ibid.*, chapter 3. See also SHOR (1980), *Critical Teaching and Everyday Life*, Boston, South End, especially chapters 2 and 5.

45 For arguments concerning the ideological nature of school knowledge and the school curriculum see, for example, APPLE (1981), *op. cit.*; HARRIS (1979 and 1982), *op. cit.*; SHARP, (1980) *Knowledge, Ideology and the Politics of Schooling*, London, Routledge and Kegan Paul.; and WHITTY, *op. cit.*

46 For examples of teachers who *do* bring a well developed sociological imagination to their work, see the studies of Searle and Shor below. Their perspective differs markedly from that of the teachers at girls grammar mentioned by JONES, A. *op. cit.* When the latter engaged social issues — for example, peace/nuclear arms issues — it was typically in 'liberal' terms (comment made in conversation with this author).

47 *Ibid.*

48 *Ibid.*, p. 19.

49 OHMANN, R. (1972), 'Teaching and studying literature at the end of ideology', in *ibid.*, p. 143.

50 KAMPF and LAUTER, *ibid.*, p. 20.

51 *Ibid.*, pp. 20–21.

52 See, FRANKLIN, B. (1972), 'The teaching of literature in the highest academies of the Empire', in *ibid.*, pp. 101–29.

53 See, for example, AYNON, J. (1979), 'Ideology and United States history textbooks', in *Harvard Educational Review*, (1981), 'Social class and school knowledge', in *Curriculum Inquiry*, 11, 1; DAVIES, J. (1978), 'The H.S.C.: preparation for what?', *Radical Education Dossier*, February, 15–20; MACDONALD, M. *op. cit.*, WHITTY, *op. cit.*, chapter 2.

54 MACDONALD, G. (1976), 'The Politics of Educational Publishing', in YOUNG and WHITTY (Eds), *Explorations in the Politics of School Knowledge*, Driffield, Nafferton.

55 HARRIS (1982), *op. cit.*, p. 115.

56 *Ibid.* Comments in parentheses are mine.

57 *Ibid.*

58 See TAXEL, J. (1983), 'The American Revolution: an analysis of literary content, form and ideology', in APPLE, M. and WEISS, L. (Eds), *Ideology and Practice in Schooling*, Philadelphia, Temple University Press, for an analysis of form and content at the point where literature meets history.

59 ANYON (1979), *op. cit.*

60 MACDONALD, M. *op. cit.*, p. 170.

61 *Ibid.*, p. 171.

62 WHITTY, *op. cit.*, chapter 2, especially pp. 41–52.

63 Compare HARRIS (1982), *op. cit.*, for ideas as to how teachers may apply revolutionary teaching strategies to conventional school literatures.

64 JONES, A., *op. cit.*

65 *Ibid.*, chapter 8.

66 The cultural perception of and approach to schooling of the Five Mason girls is entirely different from that of Five Simmonds. So is the pedagogy practised in their classrooms. Compare *ibid.*, chapter 8. It should be noted that while the pedagogy employed with Five Simmonds is much more interpretive and discussive in its emphasis, it in no way fosters a proper literacy, as defined here.

67 *Ibid.*, especially chapters 2, 8, and 9.

68 *Ibid.*

69 *Ibid.*

70 *Ibid.*

71 *Ibid.*

72 *Ibid.*

73 Compare, HARRIS (1979), *op. cit.*, chapter 2, especially pp. 57–61.

74 SEARLE, (1975), *Classrooms of Resistance*, London, Writers and Readers; (1977), *The World in a Classroom*, London, Writers and Readers.

75 *Ibid.*, (1975), p. 8.
76 *Ibid.*, p. 9.
77 *Ibid.*, p. 10.
78 LYNN MARLES, in *ibid.*, p. 21. PETER SMITH, in *ibid.*, p. 29.
79 SHOR (1980), *op. cit.*, pp. 155–6.
80 FREIRE (1972), *op. cit.*, chapter 3.
81 SHOR (1980), *op. cit.*, p. 158.
82 *Ibid.*, pp. 159–61.
83 *Ibid.*, p. 163.
84 *Ibid.*, p. 166.

Chapter 5

Reading, Writing and Revolution

Introduction

The Nicaraguan revolution offers a very rich context in which we may examine the nature and role of proper literacy within an overall process of radical social change.[1] For in its widest frame the Nicaraguan revolution portrays an on-going, still-young attempt to replace established structures of domination and subordination with alternatives wherein the freedom of all to make history becomes progressively more equal. And from the time when Sandino's troops confronted US Marines through to the battles of the present day[2], the importance of reading and writing to the goal of achieving national and personal liberation has been stressed by those at the forefront of struggle in Nicaragua.

A complete study of proper literacy within the revolutionary process in Nicaragua would, then, address the period prior to 1979 (at which time the dictatorship was defeated and Somoza fled the country) as well as contemporary developments. I will be mainly concerned with aspects of the period since 1979 and must be content here with a passing reference to earlier times. The insurrection against Somoza and his National Guard was focused and led by the Sandinist National Liberation Front (FSLN), which was founded in 1961. In 1969 the Front produced its political programme for changes to be pursued upon victory. The first item on the programme's culture and education agenda was to be 'a massive literacy campaign to immediately wipe out "illiteracy"'.[3] Credit for this emphasis is attributed to Carlos Fonseca, a founder of the FSLN and its leading theoretician. Fonseca was not content, however, that the assault upon illiteracy wait until the victory over the dictatorship. On the contrary, he was committed to fostering reading and writing among illiterate people as an integral part of the struggle for popular liberation. Tomas Borge recalls a now famous conversation between Fonseca, Borge himself, and German Pomares — a peasant who had learned to read and write after joining the fight against Somoza. Borge and Pomares were training a group of peasant fighters. In

Borge's words:

> We were training them to dismantle and reassemble the Garand, the
> M-1 carbine and the .45 pistol. Carlos arrived and instructed us, 'And
> also teach them to read'.[4]

In this Fonseca was maintaining a priority established by Sandino in the 1920s
and 1930s, during his army's seven year battle against an occupying force of
US Marines. Sandino strongly encouraged his troops to learn to read and
write, and was proud of the fact that among all his officers the number of those
illiterate could 'be counted on fewer than the fingers of one hand'.[5]

It is important to grasp the context and the character of the educational
activity commended by Fonseca and practised widely among FSLN recruits
and within the many base communities. A powerful and well-organized
fighting force would be needed to defeat Somoza. This called for recruiting and
organizing large numbers of committed people who understood clearly how
and why the possibility of a viable future for themselves and their fellows
depended entirely upon overthrowing the dictatorship *and* transforming the
oppressive structures of daily life. Developing a critical understanding of daily
reality among those who suffered most within it was crucial to building and
sustaining the struggle. Barndt makes this point very well by reference to
educational activity conducted with peasants, as described by a FSLN militant.

> We would take hold of the hand of a peasant, their hands were big,
> strong, rough ... and we would ask them: 'and these callouses, where
> do they come from?' And they would respond that the callouses were
> from the machete, from working the land. And we would ask them
> that if they got callouses from working the land, why wasn't the land
> theirs, rather than the boss's? We tried to slowly awaken the peasants
> to the dream that they had.[6]

The wider educational context in which Pomares and other peasants learned to
read and write was, then, one of coming to understand their daily experience
and economic reality in terms of the structures through which they were
dominated, exploited, and oppressed by others. This, says Barndt, was *popular*
education, grounded in the interests of the poor, exploited majority.

> It posed the key contradiction for the peasant: that [they] worked
> land [they] did not own. A growing political consciousness of this
> basic inequity motivated peasants to organize in order to change it.[7]

Such examples hold important clues to understanding the pursuit and practice
of proper literacy in Nicaragua today. In order to follow these clues it is
necessary to sketch a background to the Nicaraguan revolution. Against this
background I will present two case studies which reveal and exemplify the
practice of proper literacy.

A Background to the Revolution

Situated between Honduras in the north and Costa Rica in the south, Nicaragua covers an area of approximately 57,000 square miles and has a population of almost three million people. The western half of Nicaragua can be distinguished from the eastern (or Atlantic Coast) region on geographic, historical, demographic, cultural, ethnic, linguistic and economic grounds.[8] The great majority of Nicaraguans live in the west, have Spanish-Indian ancestry, are Catholic and, in cultural terms, Hispanic. Approximately 10 per cent of the population live in the Atlantic Coast region and were responsible for 4.7 per cent of the gross domestic product in 1980. The majority here are Spanish-speaking mestizos. In addition, and importantly, various ethnic minority groups inhabit the east and north east of Nicaragua. Thee are some 70,000 Miskito, 5000 Sumu, 1500 black Carib, 700 Rama, and 26,000 Afro-European descended Creoles.

The present and future of the Nicaragua Revolution are vitally linked to the relationship between the Hispanic mainstream and the complex, distinctive reality of the Atlantic Coast. In this chapter, however, I will be focusing solely on aspects of the Hispanic mainstream. It is important that readers be aware that this *is* my focus, and that I will necessarily be by-passing much that is important to a full understanding of literacy and revolution in Nicaragua. Apart from the many wider complications — to the revolution itself and our understanding of it — presented by the diverging traditions of the two coasts, the fact is that the Nicaraguan Literacy Crusade included Miskito, Sumo, and English language programmes (as well as the major programme in Spanish), as part of the overall attempt to integrate the entire country within the revolution. Moreover, the practice of proper literacy — that is, employing reading and writing in order to understand history better, and to make better history in the light of that understanding — is an imperative for pursuing this integration in the spirit of liberation. An investigation of these themes must, unfortunately, be left for another time.[9]

Two periods are commonly distinguished within Nicaraguan history between the time that Europeans first set foot in the country and the defeat of Somoza. These are the colonial and 'independence' periods respectively.

The Colonial Period: 1522 to 'Independence'

The Spanish arrived in western Nicaragua in 1522, encountering an indigenous population of approximately one million descended from the Maya and Aztec civilizations. They defeated local resistance and soon consolidated control over the region, establishing a pattern of exploitive practices and relationships which had disastrous consequences for the Indian inhabitants and their culture.

> Superimposing themselves on the pre-existing feudal structure [the Spanish] demanded tribute in gold and, when that was depleted,

Indian slaves. Both 'commodities' were exported, the gold to Spain and the slaves to other colonies where they [quickly] perished.[10]

It was estimated that more than half a million Nicaraguan Indians were deported as slaves inside the first fifteen years of Spanish control. This slave trade, together with the introduction of European diseases to which the Indians were not immune, reduced their population to 'not more than 30,000' by 1544.[11]

The demise of the Indians all but destroyed Nicaragua's traditional economy and, with it, the traditional culture and society generally. Indian economic life had been built around labour intensive agriculture carried out by men, with women being mainly responsible for commerce. Under traditional production corn, cassava, tobacco, chili, beans, and vegetables had been grown for local consumption on family plots of communally-held land. Historical data suggests that this agricultural economy successfully met the subsistence needs of Indian communities. Moreover, the division of labour afforded women 'relative independence and participation in economic life'.[12] With colonization this agricultural model gave way almost entirely to raising cattle for hides, tallow, and salted meat. These products were sold to other colonies. The traditional emphasis and social relations of agricultural production were effectively marginalized.

The indigenous social and cultural tradition, and the roles and circumstances of women within it, were further displaced by the process of *mestizaje*: that is, the creation of a mestizo population. Apart from a few isolated instances, Spanish women colonists did not arrive in Nicaragua until some one hundred years after the men. In the interim, Spanish men depended upon Indian women to satisfy their sexual and domestic 'needs'. Haley notes that they were accustomed to taking what they wanted by force, imposing a wholly new set of power relations upon the women. Moreover, the resulting mestizo population (part Indian, part Spanish) was 'deprived of a stable place in the social order, disinherited culturally, [and] dispossessed politically'.[13] The mestizo came to form a subordinate social 'caste'. This created still further relations of domination and subordination, as mestizo men sought power and a sense of identity through ascendance over women. The measure of balance enjoyed previously by Indian women in relationship with their men was increasingly lost to them under the conditions of colonization.

Walker notes that following the exhaustion of gold and slaves Nicaragua became 'a sleepy backwater of Spain's colonial empire'. Even so, the structures of domination and subordination that were established within Nicaragua during this initial period reflect very much its colonial roots. Within Nicaragua economic and political power was concentrated in the hands of a tiny Spanish (male) elite, comprising a rural aristocracy involved in agricultural production for export and a more commercially-oriented sector. According to Walker, there was an 'ostentatious concentration of wealth in the hands of a privileged minority'. This same minority monopolized political power. In fact struggles for political dominance began to emerge *inside* the elite, between the rural aristocracy centered on Granada in the south and the commercial faction based in Leon.[14]

The history created during Nicaragua's colonial period was a history of *structured* domination and subordination. Overall it was a history of colonizer dominating over colonized. Within this, patterns of unequal power and control were established on ethnic, cultural, gender, political, and economic dimensions. Spanish ethnicity prevailed over Indian. The mestizo was created, and subsequently displaced socially and culturally. Spanish men dominated over Indian women. Mestizo men also established relations and practices of domination over women. New economic and political structures were imposed by the colonizers, and within these the Spanish elite dominated.

'Independence': from Monroe to the Somoza Solution

Patterns of structured domination and subordination were reinforced and further elaborated between 1838 (when Nicaragua became technically a sovereign state) and 1979. During this period a complex web of internal and international policies, practices, and trends combined to produce dramatic, highly visible forms of oppression in Nicaragua. The net outcome of these interacting forces was a wretched quality of life for the great majority of Nicaraguans.

The major factor here was the evolution of expansionist economic and foreign policies on the part of the US, which ensured that Nicaragua's internal politics accorded with US interests. The link between US policy and that of successive Nicaraguan administrations progressively reduced Nicaragua to the status of an impoverished, dependent neo-colony during the twentieth century. It is this aspect — which took on extreme proportions during the Somoza years — that is emphasized in much of the recent literature on Nicaragua. We must note, however, that some of the most deep-rooted and immiserating structures of oppression were established and legitimated without any obvious US policy influence. An important example here is that of legalized land seizures in the 1870s and 1880s precipitated by a coffee boom. During the first half of the nineteenth century large landowners had allowed peasant families to work parcels of land for subsistence — although the peasants were given no land title. In addition, pockets of communal land continued to be worked by Indians. With the coffee boom landowners turned from beef production to large scale coffee production. Maximizing their production and profits called for the use of land presently being worked by peasants and Indians, and for the creation of a cheap labour force. This was achieved through a series of laws which 'effectively drove peasants and Indian communal land holders off their land and turned them into an impoverished and dependent rural proletariat'. When thousands of dispossessed rebelled in 1881, 5000 were killed as government 'enforced the new "order"'.[15]

Nicaragua was decreed a sovereign state in 1838. During the next 140 years its independence was, however, essentially 'technical'. Nicaragua's politics and general daily life were shaped to a great extent by activity on the part of imperial powers to establish dominance in the Central America-Caribbean region. US President Monroe declared in 1823 that 'interference by any European power in newly emerging Latin American republics would be considered an unfriendly act toward the United States itself'. By the Monroe Doctrine the US claimed the right to 'protect' Latin America, on the assumption that the entire Americas shared a collective interest 'which the northern partner had the right to interpret'.[16] Over the following decades rivalry increased between the US and British interests in the region. Britain was the major colonial force in the Caribbean at that time and had control of Nicaragua's Atlantic Coast. Moreover, like the US itself, Britain wished to establish and control a canal route connecting the Atlantic and Pacific Oceans. Nicaragua's geography presented a viable canal prospect. Between 1850 and 1909 the two powers engaged in numerous manoeuvres to safeguard their respective interests here.

By 1900 US interests demanded more than a role as mere *protector* of the Americas. The trend was toward imperialist expansion. Pearce notes that by the 1890s the United States had a higher population than any single European nation and was outpacing Europe in steel, iron, and coal production. Moreover, 'giant monopoly firms emerged with surplus capital for export and in need of raw materials and markets'. The time had come for (neo) colonial expansion. As one US Senator put it in 1898:

> the trade of the world must and can be ours. And we shall get it. We will cover the ocean with our merchant marine. We will build a navy to the measure of our greatness. Great colonies, governing themselves, flying our flag, and trading with us, will grow about our ports of trade. Our institutions will follow ... And American law, American order, American civilization and the American flag will plant themselves on [other] shores.[17]

The implications for Nicaragua were immense. When the Liberal government of Jose Santos Zelaya opened negotiations (in 1909) with interested parties in Britain and Japan regarding a canal through Nicaragua, the US government backed a local insurrection against Zelaya, and sent troops to ensure that it would succeed. Zelaya resigned, but the Conservative government which took over was itself faced with rebellion in 1912. US Marines were sent to restore 'order', and (to this end) occupied Nicaragua until 1925. During this period the US controlled Nicaragua's affairs 'through a series of Conservative presidents [in] a symbiotic relationship' with the American administration.[18] In return for favours rendered, Washington kept the Conservatives in power. The Marines left in 1925, but returned in 1926 when fighting erupted between Liberal and Conservative forces over the outcome of a Nicaraguan election supervised by the US.

The Marines remained until 1933. This was the period of Sandino's celebrated guerrilla war against the occupiers. The failure of the Marines to defeat Sandino's army, and the considerable cost and embarrassment presented to the US by the struggle, directly produced the Somoza 'solution' to the problem of controlling the neo-colony. In 1931 a gradual withdrawal of Marines began. At the same time the US created the Nicaraguan National Guard: a powerful military unit advised, equipped, and trained by the US to maintain American order and preserve American interests in Nicaragua. Anastasio Somoza Garcia was appointed its commander when the Marines finally left in 1933.

Between 1933 and 1936 Somoza actively cultivated the loyalty of the National Guard, and in 1936 staged a coup against the elected president. His own inauguration as president, on 1 January 1937, began forty-two years of dynastic rule by the Somoza family with the backing of the National Guard. From 1937 until 1956 (when he was assassinated) Anastasio controlled Nicaragua's government either directly, as president, or indirectly via puppet presidents. From 1956 until 1963 his first son, Luis, was president. In 1967, following 4 years of control through puppets, the second son, Anastasio Somoza Debayle, assumed control. He retained power until the Sandinista insurrection drove him out in July 1979.

Besides the continuing symbiotic relationship with successive US administrations[19], the basis of control by the Somozas lay in keeping other powerful interests within Nicaragua on-side: the guard, the church, Conservative and Liberal leaders, and the commercial, agricultural, and industrial elites.[20] Given that Nicaragua has a small population, ample arable land and fertile soils to meet its domestic food needs, a climate sympathetic to agriculture, and good fishery potential, the realities of daily life which had developed by 1979 were as reprehensible as any to be found in the contemporary world.

According to an official government survey of the decade 1966 – 75, 83 per cent of Nicaraguan children suffered some degree of malnutrition.[21] Infant mortality averaged 120/1000, rising to 333/1000 in poorer neighbourhoods — such as the miserable *barrios* that had sprung up on the outskirts of Managua and other cities, as unemployed rural poor drifted to the towns in a desperate attempt to find a livelihood. Most infant deaths resulted from preventable diseases such as measles, diarrhoea, and intestinal parasites. The lack of potable water outside cities — and, even, for most city dwellers — was responsible for epidemic intestinal diseases. Living conditions were hostile to sound health. The 1971 census revealed that 47 per cent of Nicaraguan homes were entirely without sanitation — a figure increasing to 80 per cent in rural areas. In Managua, a city of 500,000 at the time, 80 per cent of houses lacked running water. More than 60 per cent of Nicaraguan dwellings had dirt floors — with consequent parasitic disorders rife among the population. Conditions generally were much worse in the countryside than in the towns.[22]

These problems were the result of the cruelly unequal distribution of resources in Nicaragua, and intensified by successive periods of economic recession during the 1970s (a legacy of the dependent economy) coinciding with increased concentration of wealth in the hands of fewer people: notably, the Somoza family itself and its closest collaborators.[23] At the time Somoza fled, his family's wealth was estimated at US $500 million. The family had holdings in more than 500 corporations, owned a newspaper, a radio station, two television stations, the national airline and steamship company, controlled two thirds of the commercial fishing, 40 per cent of rice production, and dominated sugar refining.[24] A very small minority of Nicaraguans shared in the lop-sided ownership and distribution of resources. While 1.8 per cent of landowners — fewer than 200 families — owned almost half of all farmland, 58 per cent of small farmers occupied just 3.4 per cent of the total between them. Indeed a third of all agricultural land, including the best land, was accounted for by 0.6 per cent of farms.

> Few small agricultural producers were able to survive by farming alone, but there was little steady work except for the three or four month harvest period. In 1972 the average annual income of the poorer half of the rural population was thirty-five dollars.[25]

In 1977 the per capita income for the poorer half of Nicaraguans was US $286. Meantime, for the top 5 per cent it was just under $5500. 1978 estimates suggest that at that time more than half of all rural dwellers existed on less than US $39 per year.[26] The life expectancy of Nicaraguans was the lowest in Central America, and its rate of alcoholism the highest. Booth notes that Somoza's government spent less of its budget on health and education than any other country in the region. 'Overall ... Nicaragua distributed services and wealth very unequally and ... living standards for the majority were poor, even in comparison to the rest of Central America'.[27]

Given this background it is hardly surprising to find that at the time of Somoza's flight just 5 per cent of the rural population had completed primary school, and 53 per cent of those over ten years old were illiterate. Illiteracy rates reached 90 per cent in some rural areas. Half of the existing secondary schools were private institutions, and 'even the public [secondary] schools charged fees that were beyond the reach of the average Nicaraguan'.[28] Barndt claims that only 18 per cent of all those eligible actually had access to secondary education. And in an overwhelmingly agricultural country, less than 10 per cent of secondary students prepared for work in agriculture, whilst more than half studied business.[29] Such is the logic of dependent underdevelopment. Somoza himself claimed: 'I don't want educated people, I want oxen'.[30] His wish was fulfilled — at least so far as education was concerned. The most basic literacy, let alone a sound formal education, was beyond the wildest dreams of the majority in a population where half the sick received no treatment whatsoever, and where average unemployment was 30 per cent, rising to 50 per cent seasonally. The imbalance between available labour and the demand for it, coupled with poorly developed labour organization, kept wages low — that is, where people could find work at all.

The gross facts of life at the time of the insurrection must be seen as reflections and consequences of structured domination and subordination grounded in elite interests at home and powerful interests abroad. The history created in daily life under the Somoza dynasty should not be read as the aberrant outcome merely of personal greed and corruption practised with the connivance of individuals comprising small, paid-off (and otherwise appeased and/or co-opted) elites: although this was certainly apparent. The point is that the creation and maintenance of power elites, including elites with the disposition to plunder, repress, rape, and generally dehumanize their fellows, was grounded in centuries of colonial and neo-colonial relations and practices. Hispanic Nicaragua was conceived, born, and nurtured in patterns of structured domination and control. Its underdevelopment was socially created and maintained during 450 years of colonial and neo-colonial history.

The exercise of power within the Nicaraguan social structure created dramatic patterns of inequality and oppression along economic, ethnic, political, gender and cultural lines. Huge discrepancies between people emerged in health, housing, education, income and employment, and the satisfaction of human needs and aspirations generally.[31] I have barely touched the surface of this inequality and oppression so far. Further details will emerge for key dimensions of daily life in the case studies which follow. There is, however, a crucial point to note at this stage of the argument. This is the fact that since the wretched conditions of daily life experienced by so many Nicaraguans had their origins within the very social structure itself, changing these conditions presupposed *structural* change. Improvement would not come with superficial change: such as by replacing Somoza's dictatorship with some other government equally — but, perhaps, less conspicuously — representative of minority elite interests. The very relations and practices of structured inequality had to be addressed and transformed if the people at large were to experience a real and lasting improvement in their lives.

Accordingly, the programme for change proposed by the FSLN in 1969, which has provided the political focus for revolution throughout the insurrection and after the victory, was precisely a programme for structural transformation. It was, in short, a programme for *revolution* — for *radical* social change which would 'turn social structures around'.[32] This programme addressed both international and internal dimensions of domination and subordination. When we consider some of its central planks, and the extent to which the Nicaraguan government and people together have successfully pursued these, it is easy to understand why elite interests at home and abroad have been so hostile to the Nicaraguan revolution, and so eager to fabricate propaganda to discredit it. It should be equally clear from my wider concern in this book why I seek a more sympathetic — yet optimally objective — analysis of the revolution here.

With regard to domination of Nicaragua's daily life on an international level, the FSLN promised an end to foreign policy based on the principle of submission to the US.[33] In its place would be created 'a patriotic foreign policy of absolute national independence', based on principles of mutual respect with other countries, commitment to authentic peace between nations, friendly collaboration with other people, and sovereign integrity. Economic and technical aid would be accepted from other countries only 'when this does not involve political compromises'.[34]

At the level of internal change, major policies advanced by the FSLN include the following. Political mechanisms would be established which allow 'the full participation of the entire people, on the national level as well as the local level'. The freedom of the worker–union movement to organize in the cities and countryside would be guaranteed, together with freedom to organize peasant, youth, student, women's, cultural, and other groups, to enhance participation by all in political life. In the economic sphere an agrarian reform and comprehensive labour and social security legislation were assured. Agrarian policies would be enacted to redistribute land in favour of smaller producers and the landless. They would 'turn over land to peasants, free of charge, in accordance with the principle that land should belong to those who work it'. Peasants were guaranteed rights to 'timely and adequate agricultural credit', sure markets for their production, and technical assistance. Labour and social security legislation would include a labour code, policies to end unemployment, the extension of free health care to the entire population together with health campaigns to eradicate endemic illnesses and prevent epidemics, urban and rural housing programmes, and reduced charges for water, electricity, sewerage, and other amenities. Factories and other wealth would be expropriated from Somoza and his collaborators, and control over administration and management of these enterprises given to workers. Gender relations were a further key dimension of proposed structural change. Acknowledging 'the odious discrimination that women have been subjected to compared to men', the FSLN programme assured that all efforts would be taken to establish economic, political, and cultural equality between women and men. Finally, a comprehensive revolution in education and culture was envisaged. This would begin with 'a massive campaign to immediately wipe out illiteracy', and move to develop educational programmes that would be 'free at all levels and obligatory at some'. Education would be adapted to the needs of both the nation and the individual, and scholarships granted to economically deprived students would include expenses for accommodation, books, clothing, food, and transport.[35]

Such social transformation cannot be *donated* to a people.[36] It must be won. It has to be created with their active participation, to be constantly answerable to their needs, and to grow with their own evolution in consciousness and capacity for social action. Within this essential process of participation, the practice of proper literacy (as both facilitator and outcome of social change) plays a central part. The following case studies reveal much about the character and practice of proper literacy within the Nicaraguan Revolution.

Literacy and Popular Education

Two phases of development can be distinguished here: *alfabetizacion* and *post-alfabetizacion.*[37]

Alfabetizacion

Victory over Somoza came on 19 July, 1979. Before leaving Somoza ordered his airforce to bomb Managua, the capital, and then escaped himself with all the reserves of the Central Bank less just $3.5 million. He left behind him an international debt of $1.6 billion — the highest per capita debt in Latin America. The country's infrastructure was in ruins following the civil upheaval and Somoza's last minute bombings. Buildings and factories were wrecked, crops had been neglected and destroyed, agricultural land laid waste. Nicaragua was bankrupt and there was, so to speak, no cash in the till. The human cost of the insurrection was immense. Between 40,000 and 50,000 had been killed, 100,000 injured (in a land with a total of 5052 hospital beds), and 40,000 orphaned. Most of the victims by far were young people.

No one among the victors had any experience of governing, in the conventional sense of the word. Shortly before victory, and when victory seemed imminent, a Junta of National Reconstruction was formed in exile in Costa Rica. This Junta

> created several working groups to prepare a governmental plan, as well as the plans and programmes of the various ministries. Among these was the educational working group which drafted a programme for the literacy crusade. Within days after the victory, Father Fernando Cardenal ... was charged with responsibility for the crusade.[38]

Despite the circumstances facing Nicaragua, an official announcement that the Literacy Crusade would proceed was made inside a month of Somoza's flight. The Crusade itself began eight months after victory.

The project of making Nicaraguans a literate population faced huge obstacles. In the first place, there was no money. The nation was bankrupt. Moreover, there was no local expertise — at least in terms we are familiar with — for undertaking such an exercise. Hirshon describes how a team of five young people

> with little pedagogical training but with experience in the liberation struggle set about studying different methodologies of basic adult education. They also analyzed the experiences of literacy campaigns throughout the world.[39]

There were further complications. The number of illiterate persons was not known, far less who and where they were, and who would be willing to learn. It was known only that the number was very large, and that the number of professional teachers available would be quite unable to handle the task alone. Furthermore, buildings to house literacy activity were scarce — especially in impoverished rural areas where many of the illiterate lived. Finally, given that most learners would be adults, there was the question of how they would have the time to learn. Their prior task was to rebuild the shattered economy. Production could not be reduced. If literacy learning was to occur, then it would have to proceed alongside production.

The first task was to locate the illiterate. A census was needed. This would seemingly require resources — of time, money, technology and people—that could not be afforded. There were only fifteen computers in the entire country at the time, and all were required for economic activity. In the event a successful census of Nicaraguans over ten years old was conducted in one month at a total cost of $10,000.[40] The way in which the census was carried out reveals much about the character of the Crusade as a whole and, indeed, of subsequent developments in adult education. Under the sponsorship of the Sandinista Youth Organisation, thousands of students volunteered through their schools to act as census takers. Other newly established citizen and worker organizations, notably the Rural Workers Association (in the country-side) and the Sandinista Trade Union Federation (in the cities), assisted in organizing and implementing the census. After a brief and intensive training the volunteers — mainly students — literally tramped the countryside. They recorded names, ages, occupations, educational levels, which people were interested in learning, when it would be convenient for teaching to go on, and who would be prepared to teach, at what time, on what days, and where. Results were processed by hand on the floor of an auditorium, and the analysis completed with the help of a UNESCO specialist and the Nicaraguan Institute of Statistics and Census.[41] Census results established approximately 722,000 illiterate Nicaraguans over ten years of age — a little more than half of those questioned. Clearly a vast corps of literacy teachers would be required. These teachers would face a very diverse illiterate population. Some 21 per cent of those illiterate were aged 10-14. The remainder ranged from urban *barrio* dwellers in their late teens to aged peasants living in shacks in the most remote parts of the land.

It is important to understand clearly how the assault on literacy was conceived by its architects, and what goals — in the short, medium, and long term — were set. After all, the intensive five month literacy crusade was intended only as the first step in restructuring educational life in Nicaragua. Promoting literacy means much more than simply ensuring that people can read and write (a little) on a particular day — the day of an official exam or assessment. If newly won skills are not to be quickly lost, it is necessary to establish a basis for the daily use and progressive development and refinement of these skills. From another angle, there is no real point in *making* people literate *unless* the skills they acquire have a role in enhancing their daily practice and development as human beings. It was essential, then, to develop a social and educational context in which literacy skills were objectively relevant to and functional for enhanced living, and perceived as such by those engaged in the process of becoming literate. It would be further necessary to build educational structures which would encourage and enable continuing learning after the Crusade had ended.

According to Fernando Cardenal, the Literacy Campaign co-ordinator, eliminating illiteracy would involve reducing illiteracy (from 53 per cent) to around 10-15 per cent initially, establishing a nationwide system of adult education, and expanding primary schooling throughout the country. The Crusade itself would aim to promote basic skills in reading, writing, maths and analytical thinking, together with elementary knowledge of history and civics. These goals, however, implied others within an overall process of pursuing development and independence. Under Somoza, literacy had been irrelevant for most people precisely because Nicaragua was an underdeveloped and dependent country, which was consciously and overtly governed in the interests of the few. The very *meaning* of striving for universal literacy in the Nicaraguan Revolution — indeed, the very meaning of the revolution itself — is grounded in the pursuit of development and independence: of the nation as a whole and of the people as individuals.

And so the specific pursuit of rudimentary literacy skills was seen to entail wider educational and social aims: namely,

> to encourage an integration and understanding among Nicaraguans of different classes and backgrounds; to increase political awareness and critical analysis of underdevelopment; to nurture attitudes and skills related to creativity, production, cooperation, discipline, and analytical thinking; to forge a sense of national consensus and of social responsibility; to strengthen channels of economic and political participation; to acquaint people with national development programmes; to record oral histories and recover popular forms of culture; and to conduct research in health and agriculture for future development planning.[42]

These wider goals, of course, explain why elements of analytical thinking, history, and civics were conceived as part of literacy, alongside the three Rs. For it is only if people have a clear sense of (national) history, the ability to analyze situations and problems, and some feeling of civic commitment, that the nature and problems of the past can be understood accurately and commitment to building the future in a spirit of cooperation, integration, and equality established. The new social goals, in other words, presupposed attitudes, habits, and ways of thinking that many people either did not have at all, or else had only in an embryonic way.

Success in the literacy campaign rested heavily on meeting two key needs: sufficient numbers of effective teachers, and appropriate materials and teaching methods. A teaching corps would have to be recuited and trained. Assuming an ideal ratio of one teacher to five pupils (maximum), 140,000 teachers would be required. Officials were prepared, reluctantly, to make do with fewer. In the event, some 100,000 volunteer teachers and staff members were trained during the four months leading up to the campaign. Of these, 60,000 operated in rural areas — where illness was widespread and medical treatment extremely scarce. Accordingly, in addition to being trained as literacy teachers, the volunteers were instructed in basic health care and malaria diagnosis, treatment and prevention.[43]

Who were the teachers? And how were they recruited and trained?[44] The people best placed to spend five months in rural areas without upsetting the economic and social fabric beyond a minimum were, of course, literate adolescent students. They would, however, require supervision, support, and time off school. The nation's teachers represented the most obvious source of effective supervision and support. The logical and pragmatic step was taken. Nicaragua's 10,000 teachers were redirected to the Literacy Crusade. Schools were closed for the duration of the campaign, and students invited to train and serve as literacy teachers — preferably for work in the countryside. They were promised promotion to the next school grade if they proved successful literacy teachers. Any young person aged twelve or over who obtained parental consent would spend five months in a rural area living with a campesino family and teaching basic literacy.[45] This is precisely what 50,000 young people eventually did. Others who could not leave home taught in their local area. Teachers also participated enthusiastically, and their organization (ANDEN) played an important role throughout.[46]

Training the popular literacy teachers proceeded on a multiplier effect within a workshop setting. In the first phase the seven national trainers taught eighty selected personnel: forty teachers and forty university students. Of these, forty were selected in the next phase to train approximately 600 teachers and students. They, in turn, prepared 12,000 more, mainly teachers, in late February 1980. Then in March the schools were closed, and these 12,000 conducted an eight day intensive workshop course for the many thousands of volunteers. Pupil volunteers trained eleven hours a day during this course. Volunteers who were in the workforce — factory workers, housewives, government employees, professionals, etc. — were trained outside of work hours: three hours each evening, six hours on Saturday and eight on Sunday. The literacy campaign began on 23 March, 1980.

The materials employed in the campaign were few and very simple, a priority here being to promote maximum learning at minimum expense. Each pupil received a primer-workbook — *Dawn of the People* — an arithmetic workbook — *Math and Economic Reconstruction: one simple operation* — and a pencil. Teachers had a manual which accompanied the primer — the *Teacher's Guide for Literacy Volunteers* — as well as chalk and a portable blackboard.

The primer was carefully adapted to the overall pedagogical aim, which was to promote the *active* participation of learners as far as possible within the learning process. To this end each lesson was introduced via discussion of the lesson theme by teachers and learners as a group. During each lesson pupils were involved in constructing words by combining different syllables as these were (progressively) learned. Besides serving as a medium for introducing the actual symbols of written language, the primer contained material intended to stimulate analytical thought, creative insight, historical perspective, cooperative attitudes and a sense of social commitment — in accordance with the revolutionary goal of structural change. There were twenty-three lessons organized in three broad parts:

(i)   the history and development of the revolution;
(ii) the social, economic, and cultural programmes of the revolutionary government;
(iii) civil defence.[47]

Each lesson in the primer was prefaced by a photograph and topic sentence, which jointly established a clear theme for that lesson. Each theme had an explicitly political tone: for example, 'Sandino, guide of the revolution', 'The FSLN led the people to freedom', 'Work is a right and a responsibility of every person in the land', 'the Agrarian Reform guarantees that the harvest goes to the people', 'Our democracy is the power of people belonging to organizations and participating', 'Women have always been exploited. The revolution makes possible their liberation', etc.[48] The pedagogy as a whole — its form and content — was grounded in the reality of the Nicaraguan Revolution. The actual life experience of learners was related as closely and as much as possible to the circumstances, goals, and values of the revolution as a dynamic evolving *process*. Learning was undertaken in small groups comprising a literacy teacher (a *brigadista*) and several learners.[49]

Prior to the first lesson each learner had been given a crash course in using a pencil. (Many peasants, being used to wielding machetes and other agricultural tools, experienced much difficulty at first in handling something as light as a pencil.) They had 'learned' to print the alphabet, their own name, and the name 'Carlos'. Each lesson in the primer-workbook contained dotted guidelines to assist learners with printing, until they became capable of printing unaided.

The first lesson emphasized vowels. (Its key word, 'la revolucion', includes all five vowels.) Thereafter, syllables became the basic unit of learning. The highly regular nature of Spanish allowed for a phonetic approach built around syllables extracted from key words, which were in turn extracted from the topic sentences.

> Because Spanish is such a highly regular language phonetically — one letter, one sound — a method based on syllable recognition will eventually permit the student to read virtually every word in the language.[50]

The phonetic approach has very important implications for learners being active within the learning process, as Freire (who assisted in developing the Nicaraguan programme) notes. Crucial to this active dimension is the principle of learners grasping the mechanisms of combining syllables to make words.

Once learners have grasped that this is the basis of written language they can do more than merely *follow* words in reading. They can also *construct* words and, to that extent, create their *own* texts, messages, ideas-in-print.[51] They can approach written language as active creators of words, phrases and sentences, rather than as passive recipients of a vocabulary and ideas-in-print donated by others. Thus it was that people who were illiterate a few months earlier could express, to the Minister of Education, in writing, their willingness to act as coordinators in the adult education programme that followed the literacy campaign. The pedagogical secret, so far as the *mechanics* of reading and writing were concerned, was to get the principle of word construction out of syllables grasped as quickly as possible. Thereafter literacy becomes essentially a matter of memory.[52]

Lessons were constructed along the following lines. The photograph associated with the lesson was presented, and group discussion — the dialogue—initiated by the teacher. This discussion proceeded for up to half an hour, during which the learners would ideally relate their own experience, understanding, interpretation, and aspirations to the existential situation captured in the photograph; and link this situation and their personal ideas and experiences to the revolution as an overall process. The dialogue was intended to perform, simultaneously, three main (and related) functions. First, it would involve the learners actively from the very beginning. Second, it offered teachers (to the best of their ability — which was often limited by their own inexperience and unfamiliarity with structural thought and critique) the chance to promote critical analysis by learners of their own circumstances, and their perceptions of these circumstances. At the same time, thirdly, it would ideally do this in a manner that fostered and enhanced commitment to the broad goals, values, and programmes that *were/are* the revolution. This was not a matter of discussion in a 'vacuum'. It was intended to be discussion of situations which had the potential to increase understanding of the revolution as a process, and elicit active participation in that process. The viability and legitimacy of the general programme of reordering (restructuring) society to improve life for the majority were taken as given.[53]

Where successful, dialogue would end with the teacher drawing out the topic sentence for the lesson as a conclusion from the discussion.[54] With attention focused on the topic sentence, teaching of reading and writing would begin. The lesson was structured in ten steps.[55] In the first the teacher wrote the topic sentence on the board and the learners 'read' it several times. For example, '*Carlos Fonseca dijo, "Sandino vive"*' ('Carlos Fonseca said, "Sandino lives"'). Next, the teacher isolated the key word — *vive* — wrote it on the board, and read it several times with the learners. S/he then wrote the word very slowly, emphasizing the syllables. The word was separated into syllables (vi ve), and a 'syllable family' — i.e., the consonant in a syllable combined with each of the vowels — identified for study. Learners read the syllable family in step four: va ve vi vo vu; Va Ve Vi Vo Vu. Following this the learners traced the syllable family (over the dotted lines) in their workbook and wrote it on the board. Active word construction appeared in the sixth step, with participants creating the various possible combinations of syllables and writing them as they went along. Next, variations on the syllable family were employed: the inverse (for example, av ev iv ov uv), and compound syllable groups (for example, vas ves vis vos vus). Learners then read and wrote sentences containing the syllables just learned, together with others already known. A short dictation, containing several words and at least one sentence, followed. Finally, a phrase or sentence was written very carefully for legibility.

Each lesson comprised at least two sections involving these steps, but featuring different words and syllables.[56] Working on literacy for two or three hours a day after a full quota of normal labour — the teachers in rural areas worked with peasants by day — each group could take a week or more over a single lesson. As might be expected, progress initially was slow, but became more rapid toward the end of the campaign. In very many cases learning occurred under almost impossible physical and/or emotional conditions — especially in the countryside.[57] Despite this, impressive results were achieved.

In purely numerical terms the campaign succeeded to the tune of 406,000 people passing the final (five part) examination. Relative to the elementary reading, writing, and computation skills tested, the campaign reduced illiteracy to 13 per cent. The revolutionary significance of the Literacy Crusade, however, has to do with much more than mere statistics. In educational terms, the Crusade marked the *beginning* of a process for masses of Nicaraguan adults and youth, not the end. Many wanted more — including people who remained learning until the very end but had not passed the exam. A major practical question was how to continue the education of these folk — and open it to others who had not actually taken part in the campaign — when economic resources were almost non-existent. It was at this point that the achievements of the Crusade faced their real test. For the only possible solution would involve newly literate and otherwise under-educated people assuming the major responsibility for educating themselves from then on. Whether or not they could do this would indicate how far they had been involved in pursuing and practising a liberating and empowering literacy — a *proper* literacy — during the five months of the Crusade.

The call, moreover, would be for people to create their own education in accordance with the principle of the revolution generally: namely, popular participation in a process of social change aimed at overcoming historical structures of domination and oppression. It was a call for previously uneducated and under-educated people to *educate* themselves in social relations and practices of democratic participation, by *practising* democratic relations in the process of educating themselves. A statement issued by the FSLN directorate at the completion of the Literacy Crusade affirmed that the practice of democracy is in no way confined to narrowly political terrain, and cannot be reduced to taking part in occasional elections. Rather, democracy means

the participation of the people in political, economic, social and

cultural matters. The more that people take effective part in these
spheres the greater the democracy ... Democracy implies the participation of workers in management of factories, plantations, cooperatives,
and centres of culture. In essence, democracy is the involvement of
people at large in all aspects of national life.[56]

For this to occur in Nicaragua, however, it was not enough for the
government simply to enact new laws, redistribute land, establish a social
wage, etc. — although these steps *were* necessary. In a land where so many had
been marginalized and reduced to passivity for so long, the people themselves
had to change: *within* the process of effecting social change, and as a *precondition*
of effective social change. It was the insight behind the literacy campaign itself
that an appropriate education is crucial to this process of human change. The
educative process begun in the Crusade had to be consolidated and further
developed.

It is not for nothing that it is often said: 'without education there is no
democracy'. Democracy implies participation, and participation
implies information, knowledge, understanding, and the ability to
judge, evaluate, express, criticize, construct and transform.[59]

Post Alfabetizacion

The literacy campaign of March–August 1980 evolved into the on-going
programme of Popular Basic Education (EPB), conducted within a nationwide
network of Popular Education Collectives (CEPs).[60] The basis for adult
education continuing in small groups was established in the last month of the
literacy campaign itself. As the campaign neared completion, *brigadistas* encouraged pupils to stay together as learning collectives.[61] Where *brigadistas* themselves were unable (or otherwise unwilling) to continue as popular educators
— as with most young literacy teachers from the cities who had been working
in rural areas — they invited their most advanced and/or most willing learner
to become a 'coordinator' of a new collective. The original CEPs were formed
out of two or more Sandinista Literacy Units (UAS). From every ten or so
coordinators, one would serve as a 'promoter'. These coordinators and
promoters are the 'popular teachers' of the EPB, which began in March 1981.
In the event, a large portion of the 406,000 who became literate during the
Crusade did not continue with their education — at least, not immediately.[62]
Many, however, did. In addition, others who had received a little primary
schooling under Somoza and welcomed the opportunity to study further, and
others again who, being illiterate, regretted not having taken part in the
Crusade, entered — and continue to enter — Popular Basic Education.

Adult education is constructed on a model intended to maximize dialogue
— i.e., communication rather than communiqués[63] — between the Ministry of
Education and the grassroots collectives. The guiding principle is that the

needs, challenges, and obstacles experienced by the CEPs should be as familiar to the Ministry of Education as those of the Ministry are to the collectives. Each should be equally cognisant of the aspirations and ideals, the disappointments and frustrations, of the other. The success of EPB is ultimately dependent on the willingness of people at the grassroots level to devote considerable time and energy to organizing, liaising, training, coordinating, teaching and learning. At the local level educational involvement is *entirely* voluntary.

The network of Popular Basic Education comprises five levels: national, regional, and zonal levels, promoters, and the CEPs. In diagram form the different levels and the channels of communication existing between them are as given below.

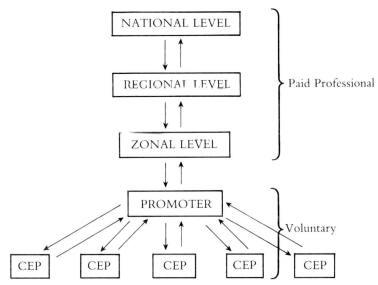

Paid professional staff are found only at national, regional and zone levels — in keeping with the need to reduce financial costs to a minimum. Nicaragua is divided into nine administrative regions and each region is further divided into zones. Zones are in turn broken into sectors, although sectors do not make up a separate administration level. Instead, the number of sectors within a zone dictates the number of paid staff allocated to that zone.

Each month there is a workshop meeting involving the national and regional levels, and a further meeting between regional and zone representatives. Zone personnel (who are expected to spend most of their time in the community rather than in the zone office!) meet with promoters twice monthly. And promoters meet with coordinators twice monthly. Each meeting at each level permits a two-way exchange of information, ideas, and views — with the intention that each level be integrated with the others and none become isolated. This way, those engaged in education within the collectives have a voice they know will be heard regularly at the official levels. The importance of this for sustaining high levels of voluntary activity is obvious.[64]

What, however, of EPB in its daily operation?

> Imagine that as night falls you turn into a popular teacher. I speak of someone like myself, who had never studied and had only been through the 'school of life'. Now, imagine thousands like me giving classes throughout the country at this very moment. They give us a little economic help, but the important thing is that the knowledge of one is also for others. And you tell me, with how much money in the world can you pay for that?[65]

EPB was conceived as a 'special elementary school' for adults; the key weapon in the 'battle for the fourth grade' in Nicaragua.[66] It has evolved as a school without walls. Learning goes on wherever there is a convenient space: in the open, in a popular teacher's home, in the trade union or agricultural cooperative office, or — where one is available — in a school room after the school day. In rural areas a candle or gas lamp provides light in winter evenings. The programme has been adapted to the rhythm of agricultural production. Semesters accord with the rural calendar. This is partly because EPB is strongest in the countryside. It is also because many urban workers who wish to take part in adult education volunteer to help with the coffee and cotton harvests.

Between 1981 and 1984 a new level of study — roughly analogous to a primary school grade — was added to the programme each semester, until the six levels which now comprise the complete EPB were in place. For those requiring it, there is a basic literacy course prior to the first level of study. The six levels of basic general education cover maths, language, natural science and social science (including history and geography). Because this is an educational programme designed mainly for working adults and intended to relate as closely as possible to their daily reality, curricula address themes and examples dealing with aspects of production. There is also an emphasis on the need to defend and further develop the attainments of the revolution so far.[67] Materials are simple and produced at minimum cost. The Ministry of Education has constructed study materials for each level. These are distributed free, together with exercise books and pencils. A radio programme designed especially for the CEPs is broadcast twice daily.

From the outset popular adult education has faced two contradictory forces. On one side is the reality of a very poor country, beleaguered economically and militarily by the US and its allies within Nicaragua, and desperately short of qualified personnel, means of communication, paper, printing facilities, classrooms, pencils, vehicles, radios, etc. On the other side there is the reality of intense pressure being applied to government by the people to deliver educationally (as well as socially, economically, etc.). The practice of Popular Basic Education within CEPs, and under the guidance of the popular teachers, has evolved in response to these contradictory forces.[68]

Promoters are responsible for three main tasks. As their name suggests, they promote involvement in EPB among people in factories, trade unions, cooperatives, communities and suburbs, and oversee the operation of the various CEPs in their charge. In addition, as noted earlier, they liaise between the professional staff at zone level and the coordinators assigned to them. Thirdly, and very importantly, they are the 'teacher of the teacher': they play the major role in helping the popular coordinators with materials and methods. Promoters generally have a small margin of educational experience over the coordinators. The idea is that this margin will enable them to help coordinators keep on top of their own learning and be able, at the same time, to provide necessary direction, impetus, and challenge to maintain the learning of others within the CEP. For the simple facts of the case are that Nicaragua's 18,000 coordinators [69] are overwhelmingly co-learners with others in the CEPs. In many cases there is very little (if anything) in educational terms, and *nothing* in occupational, cultural, economic, etc. terms, to distinguish the popular teacher from the ordinary CEP member.

The role of the coordinator is to enable learning to go on — in a spirit of mutual help, open discussion, and shared commitment — among a group of peers (the CEP) who are typically workmates in the same economic enterprise, or else are neighbours or members of the same mass organization, etc. The average size of CEPs is seven students, although some have as many as 15-20. In 1984, 43 per cent of CEPs contained individual learners working at different study levels within the EPB programme: from the introductory literacy level to the sixth level. Such 'mixed CEPs' present a major pedagogical challenge to poorly educated and scarcely trained coordinators. We should note that the (considerable) work of coordinators and promoters is unpaid. They are given a small subsidy to help with costs of getting to training and liaison workshops on weekends, and (where travel is involved) to the CEP itself. The many hours spent in preparation, meeting with higher level personnel, and becoming acquainted with materials and methods, are unpaid.

CEPs operate two hours daily after work. In some cases members are given an hour off work on pay to attend, and then continue for a further hour unpaid. In many areas the CEP is the only available educational structure. Consequently, many EPB pupils are children pursuing an education where there is no school. Elsewhere, children attend CEPs who cannot go to school because they are required for work in the family economy. Almost 25 per cent of learners in CEPs are 10-14 years old. 61 per cent of all learners are aged between 10 and 24 years. In addition, large numbers of children under 10 take part, but figures are not available here since, officially, EPB is not for *niños*. [70] A full 70 per cent of EPB students live in rural areas. Campesinos, housewives, and urban workers are the major occupational categories represented in the CEPs. One third of the learners are illiterate folk enrolled in the introductory literacy course.

Statistics pertaining to coordinators and promoters are interesting. 30 per cent of coordinators and 40 per cent of promoters are campesinos; 20 and 14 per cent respectively are housewives. A mere 5 per cent of coordinators and 12 per cent of promoters are teachers by profession. This is indeed a *people's* education. Some 10 per cent of coordinators are under 14 years old. In 1984, 56 per cent of all coordinators and 46 per cent of promoters had not completed a primary education. 21 per cent of coordinators and 16 per cent of promoters had either first learned to read in the Literacy Crusade or else had come into education through the CEPs. There are significant differences between rural and urban CEPs, reflecting the relative advantage towns enjoyed over the countryside prior to 1979. A sample of twenty-five CEPs operating in the capital, Managua, reveals a much higher average of education among popular teachers than for the nation as a whole. 73 per cent of coordinators and 100 per cent of promoters had received some secondary education. Moreover, half the promoters in the sample had studied at university. The situation in rural areas, where three quarters of the CEPs are found, is radically different — as we would expect given that only 5 per cent of folk in the countryside completed a primary education under Somoza.[71]

The most comprehensive research into *Post Alfabetizacion* in Nicaragua is found in the work of Rosa Maria Torres.[72] An Ecuadorian, Torres provides a balanced critique of the achievements and limitations of EPB. She notes that the system of collectives with their popular coordinators and promoters was intended originally as an interim measure only: to give way progressively to development of 'locales escuelas' in which the popular teachers would become 'auxiliary monitors' of professional teachers — ideally final year students from a normal (training) school. Economic circumstances, largely occasioned by the economic and military war being waged against Nicaragua, have undermined the original plan. And so popular education in Nicaragua proceeds with teachers who in most cases lack adequate preparation for such a role. This is not simply a matter of popular teachers lacking any formal pedagogical training. In addition the EPB has increasingly introduced curriculum content of which the popular teachers had little or no previous knowledge.

Popular Basic Education faces daily a wide range of further obstacles to success (in quantitative and qualitative terms alike). Many CEPs are physically isolated. This makes it difficult to maintain regular and adequate communication and support. As a result many CEPs face problems of morale. Some CEPs operate in areas of contra activity where they have become prime targets for terrorism. More than 500 people working in popular education have been assassinated since 1979.[73] Many more have been tortured and abducted. In such areas CEPs are forced either to abandon (as thousands have in the face of attack), or else to operate semi-clandestinely.[74] The need to increase production has posed a further obstacle to popular education, as workers are required to devote more time to economic activity. Heightened contra activity and the fear of full scale invasion have increased the need for regular defence training and general involvement in the Sandinista Defence Committees. This eats still more into available reserves of time and energy. Moreover, says Torres, the CEPs simply have not received the degree of support, recognition, and reinforcement they need in order to function optimally. This has been by no means a reflex of scarce resources and wider distractions alone. There have also been acknowledged shortcomings on the part of the professional administration in understanding and responding to the aspirations and circumstances of people in the CEPs.[75]

Torres claims that at the end of 1985 considerable problems and inadequacies remained in the EPB programme. In fact it is easy, she says, to get into a position of criticizing the EPB: of questioning the validity of a mass education programme that does not (and *cannot*) provide sufficient and appropriate conditions for retaining those who enrol; for ensuring the stability and permanence of CEPs; for retaining popular teachers; and for guaranteeing the quality of teaching. Drop out rates among learners, coordinators and promoters, failure rates among learners, and the rate at which CEPs dissolve before the end of a semester, can be disheartening. Consider, for example, figures for the first semester of 1983. Of 166,208 learners who began, 97,912 completed the semester and (just) 62,383 of these passed the exam. Of the 18,869 coordinators who began, 14,948 remained to the end. 3125 promoters started and 2743 completed. The semester opened with 19,056 CEPs, and closed with 14,984.

Nevertheless, Torres argues, 'democratizing education in Nicaragua meant doing it under prevailing conditions or not doing it at all'.[76] The positive reality is that for the semesters during 1982–84, the EPB produced 65,251, 62,383, 47,121, and 48,516 learners who passed their semester exams. The numbers of CEPs, promoters and coordinators remained more or less constant between the beginning of one semester and the beginning of the next. Where individual popular teachers dropped out, new ones emerged to take their place at the start of the new semester. Quite simply, for popular basic education to proceed *at all* it was necessary for campesinos to be 'transformed' into popular teachers; for classrooms without walls and equipment to be created throughout the land; for learning to go on in the absence of expertise. By the end of 1984 the first graduates of EPB emerged: adults and youth who had completed the Popular Basic equivalent of a primary education. These people represent a *total gain* for an underdeveloped, desperately poor, third world country. Their importance in revolutionary terms is incalculable.

In *The CEP: Popular Education and Participative Democracy in Nicaragua*, Torres asks to what extent EPB has actually succeeded in promoting participative democracy. She addresses this issue from three related perspectives.

(i) Has EPB helped to *democratize* education? That is, how effective are CEPs in extending education to the people?

(ii) To what extent is this education in itself a *democratic* education, within which (previous), hierarchical, assymetrical relationships and practices have begun to break down and new patterns of interaction develop among participants?

(iii) Does EPB educate Nicaraguans *for democracy*? How far does EPB help in the process of democratizing wider spheres of daily life — for example, the workplace, trade unions, families? Has it helped democratize people's personal, political, economic, social, and cultural lives?

For all its critical dimension, Torres' inquiry leaves us in no doubt that the balance of evidence lies on the side of success rather than failure on each of these dimensions. EPB has given substance to the principle of education for all who seek it: a principle systematically denied in Nicaragua prior to 1979. Moreover, this principle has been realized to an impressive extent in practice. Official figures for 1982 reveal that almost 190,000 Nicaraguans (counting popular teachers) from a total population of less than 3 million, took up the invitation to try and learn in the company of others. In the words of one woman student:

> My life has always been the chores of my house. My husband is the
> one who has worked. I have only lived raising my children, looking
> after the house, the children, the house. ... And, suddenly, one starts to
> study! A great thing, because previously I had never thought that this
> would come to our homes. It's an opportunity we'd never have
> believed we would get. And now I thank God for this cause for
> happiness.[77]

Despite the reservations that legitimately remain concerning the capacity of EPB to deliver 'quality' teaching to pupils within programmes that command their sustained interest and commitment in the face of considerable pressures and distractions in daily life, it is clear that the principle of democratizing education has been pursued to the very limits of available resources.

With regard to EPB as the practice of democratic social relations, Torres speaks of a whole new 'ideology of education' that has evolved with this programme. The function and role of *teacher* has necessarily been redefined, and the relationship between teacher and pupil transformed from a vertical to a substantially horizontal interaction. In the past, possession of knowledge was seen to set teachers and pupils apart. The teacher's knowledge provided a legitimate basis for their authority and power over pupils. With the literacy Crusade and Popular Basic Education has emerged a new set of priorities and values associated with being a teacher : to have the will and interest that others learn; to have patience and humility in interacting with learners (who, after all, are in a real sense co-learners rather than pupils when it comes to the CEPs); to teach purely out of love and respect for other people, with no material gain other than the benefits of learning oneself in the same process by which others learn. When assessing who ought to be a coordinator, most CEP students in Torres' sample emphasized these criteria over those of knowledge/ scholarship, training and experience. Knowing a little more and being able to carry others a little further was seen as the essential quality in a popular teacher. The coordinators and promoters interviewed by Torres affirmed these values, giving as their main reason for serving as popular teachers a desire to cooperate with those (others) who do not know, and expressing a sense of fulfilment when they 'can pass on the little that [they themselves] know'.[78] Some of these coordinators acknowledge that their main desire is to learn, and that serving as a coordinator allows a CEP to function and, therefore, for learning to proceed. Over half the popular teachers sampled by Torres admitted that it was common for other learners to know more about various matters arising in the learning process than they did themselves. We should remember that this was a city sample, in which popular teachers had experienced very much more formal education than their rural counterparts.

In the educational relationships of the CEP the conventional boundaries that exist between teaching and learning are to a large extent broken down, and seen by participants to be broken down. Torres claims that the reciprocal learning relationship between educator-educatee and educatee-educator espoused by Freire finds both an objective and a subjective basis in the CEP. The classical division of labour between teacher and learner is seriously challenged.[79]

Even so, the mere fact that the objective 'gap' between teacher and learner is smaller within the CEP than in typical teaching situations by no means guarantees an end to authoritarian relationships and practices. Neither, on its own, does it guarantee that learning will be 'full of participation and creativity'; that it will be critically informed. To make a successful shift from past practices steeped in pupils passively and uncritically accepting material to be memorized and repeated, and where the teacher's authority is final and ever present; to shift from this to educational practices that involve participation by all *and* promote genuinely critical understanding of and commitment to democracy, requires a positive vision and a positive ability on the part of teachers. Practising democratic pedagogy is a skill; an art. It presupposes a critical understanding of oppression and liberation. The pedagogy of educators like Searle and Shor (and, of course, Freire) is grounded in a powerful awareness of the roots and operation of inequality and hierarchy. In addition to the potentially liberating structure of the CEP, a fully democratic education here calls for special development in the consciousness of popular teachers. Nicaraguans themselves are aware that there is much to be achieved here: indeed, among teachers in the formal education system as much if not more so than among popular teachers.[80] This awareness, together with the character of the CEP itself and its popular teacher, bodes well for an enhanced democratic popular education in Nicaragua.

It is difficult to assess the precise contribution of Popular Basic Education in educating Nicaraguans *for* democracy, since activity within the CEPs — and the effects of that activity — cannot be neatly distinguished from activity in other sites of popular participation within daily life. In over 40 per cent of cases the person who is a learner or popular teacher in the CEP is also a member of one or more mass organizations: for example, Sandinista Youth, an industrial or agricultural union, the Association of Nicaraguan Women, a Sandinista Defence Committee, etc. Involvement in EPB and mass organizations is mutually reinforcing, since like EPB itself the mass organizations are structures directed toward the growth of participative democracy. Despite this complication some general comments are warranted concerning EPB and education for democracy.

First, it is clear that being literate — albeit at a level of very basic skills — greatly enhances personal involvement within the structures for cooperative and active participation established since 1979: in just the same way that the practice of literacy was vital to the life of Corresponding Societies and the labour movement. As I have insisted throughout, this literacy is not just a matter of the *mechanics* of reading and writing. It includes wider perceptions, understandings, and expectations of daily life, developed and refined by educative activity within CEPs, that shape and support the practice of literacy in wider settings (such as the agricultural cooperative or union). The actual practice of literacy by EPB learners within economic, political, cultural, etc. structures will reflect very much the values, viewpoints and relationships espoused and practised within the CEP. Similarly, the values, views and relations evident in activity within the CEP will reflect involvement in other sites of daily practice. To the extent that EPB comprises the sole or major *educational* experience of those who play an active role in democratizing social practice in Nicaragua — as it is for many — it can be seen to have enormous import in educating Nicaraguans for democracy. If we are to appreciate this more clearly, we must examine the relationship between literacy and democratic practice outside the sphere of popular education itself. To this end we will turn shortly to a discussion of women and literacy in Nicaragua.

Second, there is no doubt that the EPB programme has been very important in developing confidence among ordinary Nicaraguan people that they can tackle problems and challenges presented by daily life, and has offered ample opportunities to do just that. Popular Basic Education has done two things simultaneously here. It has given people who played an active role in the insurrection and/or in the Literacy Crusade an on-going context in which further to develop their personal and historical agency. And it has given those without any previous sense or experience of such agency a setting in which to develop it. Moreover, EPB has nurtured and engaged this agency in the face of seemingly impossible odds. Torres comments that given the objective material conditions, for EPB to have survived at all, let alone make progress, is 'an undeniable merit'. Popular Basic Education, she adds, is characteristic of the Nicaraguan revolution as a whole: 'challenging reality, and undertaking time and time again impossible tasks that become possible through the sheer attempt to carry them out'. She adds that if there is anything to be questioned here it is the will to try and do too much with the limited resources available.[81] Participative democracy is grounded in the perception on the part of ordinary people that they *can* act effectively, and in their willingness *to* act. EPB presents a classic instance of ordinary people winning this confidence and acting upon it.

Finally, EPB has reached a crossroads. In 1985 enrolment figures — with all six levels open — fell to below 80,000. Part of the drop can be explained by factors external to the programme itself. Escalation in the war, for example, meant that during 1984-5 EPB had to make do without 30 per cent of its staff, who were diverted into defence tasks. At the same time, economic measures imposed against Nicaragua have further undermined an already fragile economy (as, of course, they are intended to do).

> Family breadwinners fighting against rising inflation must often eke out their salaries with extra odd jobs. This leaves little time for classes. Education has become a luxury ... 'There comes a time when a student chooses priorities. Which is more important: studying at the popular collective, or producing my food, defending my territory? So they abandon the collective'.[82]

At the same time EPB officials openly attribute much of the fall off in enrolment to failings within the programme itself — and, in particular, failure to take sufficient account of the educational needs and aspirations of learners themselves. Evidently, the process of dialogue — of two way communication — has not yet gone far enough.

Two main contributing factors internal to EPB have been identified. One is that many potential learners have been put off by the expressly political content of EPB. The other is that EPB has apparently made too many concessions to traditional educational values. Although intended to be optimally relevant to the daily lives of workers and peasants, the programme has fallen 'into a pattern of resembling formal education ever more closely'. Rather than serving as a catalyst for transforming the rest of the educational system, it has conceded more than it should to established goals and values. Where, for instance, a campesino interested in learning maths in order to do accounts finds he is (instead) being taught isoceles triangles and square roots, he quits. EPB director, Eduardo Baez, acknowledges that formal primary education, 'rather than an adult's real needs in terms of health or production or useful knowledge', tended to dominate when the study programmes were drawn up — despite the intention to establish relevance.[83]

There is good evidence, however, that the principle of dialogue and respect for the needs and interests of learners has remained intact, despite past failings. (And let us not forget that 80,000 enrolments is still a significant — indeed, impressive — endorsement of popular education, especially given the major distractions presented by economic and defence needs.) The literacy primer is being revised and the focus on the FSLN within its content themes expunged. At the same time the study programmes for the six post literacy stages of EPB are in for a radical revision.[84] This process is just getting under way. The manner in which it is undertaken will provide an excellent index of the contribution of EPB to the further growth of participative democracy in Nicaragua. Investigation and analysis of this process must, however, wait for another occasion.

Meanwhile, I would submit that EPB is an experiment in the practice of democracy that merits critical sympathy on the part of all who are genuinely committed to fulfilment of the democratic ideal. It deserves to be understood as accurately and fairly as possible: not to be made a target of international aggression and cynicism, or overlooked out of ignorance or apathy. We are not called on to romanticize EPB; to erect it into something it is not. This is simply a call to become critically informed from a basis of openness; to seek, for as long as this is warranted, to be agents of constructive assistance rather than destructive opposition. Our praxis, as learner–educators in pursuit of liberation behoves us to learn from others as well as to teach; to accept from others as well as to advance our own judgments and practices; to listen as well as to speak; and to cooperate rather than confront. I believe that applying these values to the case of EPB will enhance education, human life, and democratic practice: here as well as there.

Women and Literacy in Nicaragua

Q.   What do you consider the single most important achieve-
       ment in the development of the feminist movement in
       Nicaragua?

A.   The Sandinista Popular Revolution, without question. —
       Angela Rosa Acevedo, National Executive Committee
       AMNLAE[85]

A very strong tradition of patriarchy evolved in Nicaragua during the colonial and neo-colonial periods. While life was wretched for the poor population generally, women bore a double yoke of oppression. Domination, exploit-ation, and degradation cut even more deeply into poor women than it did poor men.[86] Amid the lamentable living conditions suffered by the urban and rural poor, the final responsibility for keeping domestic life intact was left to women. Patriarchy, of course, cuts across social class lines. Among the wealthy elites women were regarded and treated very much as second class citizens by comparison with men. Indeed, Nicaraguan culture placed women, regardless of their social class location, in total subordination to their husbands — to the point of denying them any legal rights with regard to their children. The Law of Paternal Dominion defined the man as the sole head of the family, possessing absolute rights over children. At marriage a young woman was passed from the house of her father to that of her husband in the exact manner of property. Wider inequalities followed from this as a matter of course. In matrimonial law, for example, the term 'adultery' was interpreted as applying only to wives. Infidelity by a husband was not 'adultery' but 'concubinage'. A similar double standard applied to inheriting property. A mistress could inherit from her lover, but a wife could not inherit from hers. At least one Nicaraguan lawyer observed that under Somoza's laws it was better to be a mistress than a wife.[87] In the event of a man abandoning the family home — which was especially common among the poor, where the search for work provided an additional ground to sheer machismo for the man to wander — it was left to the wife to support and raise his children. Yet the man could legally return at any time, claim his children as property, and remove them from their mother's home.

While the culture of patriarchy imposed gender inequalities independently of wealth or class, women's oppression was certainly exacerbated by economic and political disadvantage. A woman of wealth could anticipate a patronized existence dedicated to administering the home and domestic economy, educating the children, and working for charity and the church. Among the poor, women could anticipate considerably less. Economic circumstances forced poor women to seek work wherever it was available — always in addition to their domestic tasks — and on whatever terms. Yet their work afforded them no independence, security or dignity. Possessing minimal education and/or marketable skills, city women relied on domestic work, selling in markets, or prostitution. In the countryside women, like men, relied on scarce seasonal work on the large landholdings. Wherever they worked women were paid less than men for the same work. And where women worked in the same place as their husbands they suffered the ultimate attack on their economic independence, security and dignity: the husband collected their pay.

It was recognized from the very outset of the programme for revolutionary change that Nicaraguan women suffered a special oppression of their own, in addition to that experienced by the majority of Nicaraguan people.[88] This imposed a complex agenda for social reform. It would be necessary for structural change to attack forces of *general* oppression — oppression that crossed gender lines — as well as forces of *women's* oppression in particular. This process has been set in operation, and in many ways Nicaraguan women can be seen as dual beneficiaries of revolutionary changes to date. The Agrarian Reform Law, for instance, opened for many families the immediate possibility of having some real control over their economic destinies, and for the first time since the arrival of the Spanish, women could hold land titles. The Labour Code, introduced alongside Agrarian Reform, guaranteed for the first time eight hour days, paid vacations, and equal pay for equal work. The minimum wage was raised, vacation centres for workers established, and many thousands of workers brought under the social security system.[89] These measures, and others which apply specifically to women, have begun to attack the conditions that previously undermined women's dignity, independence, and security within working life. The development of mass organizations has had the effect of drawing women into the mainstream of political activity aimed at national reconstruction.[90] These mass organizations have developed around sector interests: youth, women, local community, urban and rural working life, etc. All Nicaraguans are eligible for membership of at least one mass organization. This has created a framework through which all are encouraged to participate in the process of shaping social change; feeding their ideas and aspirations into that process. The mass organizations provide a context for dialogue between people at all levels of the decision-making process, from the ordinary citizen to government leader. They also offer an important facility for gathering information relevant to informing policy decisions. Once policy has been shaped, the different mass organizations take responsibilities for implementing, evaluating, and suggesting improvements to those programmes that relate to their sector interests.

As a sector interest Nicaraguan women have established and continue to evolve their own mass organization: namely, AMNLAE — the Association of Nicaraguan Women (named for) Luisa Amanda Espinosa.[91] Throughout the seven years of revolution so far, AMNLAE has provided the single most important structure for advancing the specific interests of Nicaraguan women. This organization, whose work began during the insurrection itself, has challenged the consciousness of women in all walks of life. It has played a key role in a number of major revolutionary developments. AMNLAE was involved in framing the Statute of Rights and Guarantees of Nicaraguans — the original written constitution of the new Nicaragua.[92] The Statute establishes the principle of equality between the sexes, and obliges the state to 'remove through all the means at its disposal, any impediments to equality among its citizens and to their participation in the social, economic, and political life of the country'.[93] Indeed, AMNLAE's influence has been present in the emergence of diverse laws and facilities intended to benefit women directly. These include: the Communication and Media Law (1979), which prohibits the use of women's bodies to promote or sell products; maternal milk banks, day care centres, and community kitchens, production cooperatives to create new jobs and leadership roles for women; provision for three months maternity leave for working mothers, etc.

AMNLAE has also been instrumental in organizing popular health campaigns for mass vaccinations (against polio, malaria, measles and tuberculosis), and for educating the population in basic hygiene and aspects of community health. In conjunction with the Ministry of Health, AMNLAE has trained some of its members to serve as public health promoters. Within the popular health campaigns the task fell to AMNLAE of recruiting and training volunteers (mostly women), arranging transport and accommodation for teams of volunteer health workers throughout the entire country, providing them with the necessary equipment, and supervising a nationwide census of factors relating to health.[94]

Because preventable diseases accounted in the past for so many deaths — especially among infants — preventive medicine and improved sanitation have assumed a central place in the on-going health care programme. The government has published more than 5 million pamphlets on health topics, and produced many billboards and posters stressing community health themes. In this way the people have been helped and encouraged to take effective action themselves against disease. Here, as in many other spheres of popular participation, a properly literate population is basic to success. And just as women have accepted the challenge generally in building the new Nicaragua, so they have been active throughout the drive for literacy itself. Moreover, the rights of women and the need for women's full and equal participation in the process of transforming social life, have been key educational themes from the time of the Literacy Crusade to the present day.

Discussion of women and literacy in Nicaragua naturally overlaps to some extent with themes that have already emerged in my account of the Crusade and Popular Basic Education. I have tried to avoid undue repetition in what follows, and trust that where there *is* repetition it helps enrich what has been said above.

The 1980 Literacy Campaign provided a very important context in which to unveil, politicize, and begin to address in social practice, multiple barriers to liberation in general and the liberation of women in particular. Three aspects especially stand out here.

(i) It offered an opportunity for people *en masse* to problematize gender oppression and exploitation as a major historical dimension of structured domination and subordination generally. The reality of women's oppression and the revolutionary commitment to overcoming traditional relations and practices which oppressed Nicaraguan women, were posed to *all* participants in the Crusade — teachers and pupils, men and women — in an attempt to stimulate among Nicaraguans at large some critical awareness of this reality and active commitment to changing it: as one *necessary* dimension of overall revolutionary change.

(ii) The literacy campaign emerged as an exercise in which women participated fully and on (at least) equal terms with men, and were *seen* to do so.

(iii) It was also a very important exercise in consolidating and enhancing social *integration* in pursuit of liberation. Maintaining a sufficient level of unity and co-operation between diverse and diverging groups of Nicaraguan people to permit genuine structural change to take place, presented a major challenge after the insurrection. Nicaraguans, quite simply, were not united under a single shared vision for the future. Massive conflicts of interest remained despite Somoza's departure. These conflicts had been masked to a large extent during the insurrection, when members of diverse and often competing interest groups with little or nothing in common other than their opposition to Somoza, forgot their differences and fought together against a common enemy under FSLN coordination. To be fighting 'with' the FSLN against Somoza in no way implied that a given individual was committed to the FSLN manifesto for social change. Indeed, the structural changes proposed by the FSLN were clearly contrary to the immediate material interests of many who fought the dictatorship. With Somoza gone there was every likelihood that these differences would quickly resurface, and once more the interests of the more wealthy and powerful would be asserted over those of the traditionally poor and weak. Yet if the fragile temporary unification of urban and rural, owner and worker, literate and illiterate, professional and peasant were lost, with it would disappear the ideal of Nicaraguans pursuing together national reconstruction in the interests of all.

Let us consider these three aspects in the context of the campaign. Lesson nineteen in the primer was based on the theme: 'Nicaraguan women have traditionally been *exploited*. The revolution now makes their liberation possible'.[95] The photograph which prefaced this lesson, and which was used to evoke the dialogue, shows an assembly of women with their arms in the air and fists clenched. Discussion proceeded from such questions as 'who might these women be?', 'what are they doing?', 'why have they organized?', 'are they protesting?', 'what might they be protesting?', 'might they have been denied their rights?', 'what *are* women's rights?', etc. Ideally the situation depicted in the photograph would be related in discussion as closely as possible to the everyday experience and aspirations of the participants themselves — whoever they were and wherever they lived. As the more formal part of the lesson unfolded, syllables in the key words yielded other evocative words. The word 'explo*i*ted', for instance, led to such words as 'cho*i*ce', 'vo*i*ce', 'jo*i*n', 'bo*i*l', and to*i*let'. These words offered direct access to an entire matrix of revolutionary ideas, values, practices and, indeed, other mass campaigns (for example, the health campaign) within the revolution. Democratic participation depends on all people — and, notably, women — having an equal *voice, joi*ning unions and other mass organizations through which they articulate and pursue their *choice*. Lesson nineteen ended with the sentence: 'Building toilets means better health".[96] During the literacy campaign men and women, *brigadistas* and learners, worked together building toilets in communities where inadequate sanitation presented a health hazard.

The lesson was constructed in a manner intended to make explicit the links between general oppression and underdevelopment in Nicaragua, and the specific oppression and underdevelopment of Nicaraguan women. And so the sentences which follow the key sentence include: 'We imported more than we exported'; 'Women participated actively during the war': 'They wanted to defend their rights'. The first sentence here is an explicit invitation to critical analysis of Nicaragua's history of underdevelopment, and to consider ways out of this historical legacy. Nicargua was poor, in large part, because it was locked traditionally into economic deficit — to the advantage of other nations. This was an important aspect of the pressing need to restructure economic life, and implied important tasks for the Nicaraguan people: for example, to increase productivity, to be willing to sacrifice certain imports, and to try to understand their personal work and economic circumstances in relation to wider economic reality. The other sentences here likewise address historical reality, although this time it is political reality impinging on *women* specifically. The obvious intent here is to shape consciousness of women's capabilities and legitimate interests. Women are to be seen, and to see themselves, as effective human agents possessing rights which others are obliged to respect. Moreover, where these rights are not upheld women will properly takes steps to ensure that in future they are. When combined with each other these sentences suggest new emphases within general revolutionary themes. The theme of women's participation contained in the second sentence can be linked to the theme of economic life in the first. This shifts the emphasis from *Nicaraguans generally* having a role in shaping economic life, to women *in particular* having this role: an important shift, bearing in mind women's traditional status within the workforce. The message is that women *could* participate effectively in the process of rescuing Nicaragua from economic deficit. After all, they *had* participated actively during the war, and the war had been successful.

At the same time as these sentences were being taught and learned, women were joining AMNLAE in increasing numbers, and AMNLAE was itself encouraging women to join the workforce.[97] Consequently, the process of becoming aware (through the literacy campaign) of revolutionary values and practices relating to women, was tied very closely to active experience of and participation in these same values and practices within daily life. This points to a crucial feature of the campaign in general; one which can again be illustrated by particular reference to women. The Crusade involved people in actively pursuing revolutionary goals and values *in the very process* of awakening critical awareness of these same values and goals. In other words, the literacy campaign was very much an *experience* of the precise goals and values it was intended to promote. By the end of the campaign women (as well as men) had not merely talked, read, and written about active participation, social unity and cohesion, critical reflection, building liberating structures, addressing oppression, etc. They had actually begun to *practise* these ideals. They had *lived* them, in the process of taking part in the campaign itself: whether as organizer, sponsor, administrator, learner, teacher, advisor, vehicle driver, etc.

Women were to the fore in every phase of the campaign. In November 1979, AMNLAE organized and sponsored a music festival to help raise funds for the Crusade. AMNLAE also actively promoted the campaign. They helped to organize literacy classes in the cities, arranging for housewives to teach in their neighbourhoods and encouraging people to enrol as learners. In many cases they had to organize child care to enable women to participate! A specially formed association of mothers joined with a network of government institutions to provide the teaching corps with food and clothing. Women had a special interest in the literacy campaign, given that a disproportionate 70 per cent of illiterate adults were women. Indeed, among the poor, three in every ten women had never attended a school at all. AMNLAE's efforts in promotion were highly successful, and almost 60 per cent of the final volunteer teaching force were women.

And so even before the teaching began, with its commitment to fostering such revolutionary values as participation, cooperation, and mutual commitment, we can see that women were already *acting* on these values in helping to establish the campaign. This tendency for revolutionary values to be present — to be practised and realized — in the very act of promoting them was, of course, writ large in the teaching/learning phase as well.

More than a fifth of the total population were actively involved in the Crusade — in one role or another — 'and through family and friends, almost the entire nation was affected by its efforts'.[98] In rural areas teachers and learners were involved in much more than the pursuit of literacy alone. *Brigadistas* and campesinos lived and worked together in the total context of rural life. Urban youth and campesino worked together by day in the fields — tending coffee plantations, milking cows, planting and harvesting crops — prior to the evening classes. In the best spirit of the revolution, this mutual engagement of town and country, young and old, male and female, often went considerably beyond the normal activities of rural life. A youth newspaper, *El Brigadista*, subsequently reported that during the five months of the campaign 'we held 2398 political and cultural meetings and 1620 rallies; harvested 17,134 manzanas (29,573 acres) of coffee, beans, corn, rice and vegetables; constructed 5195 latrines; 55 houses, 11 roads, 195 bridges, 271 schools, 14 communal baths, a canal, 53 health centres, 12 churches, 12 plazas and 28 parks'.[99] In this way theme sentences from the primer were carried into practical reality: 'Building toilets means better health'; 'Let's join together to build good roads and improve housing in our communities'; 'With everyone's help we will build playgrounds for our children'; 'The revolution builds new health centres'.

The very logic of the literacy campaign, by which widely diverse elements of Nicaraguan society participated together in a common enterprise, was a logic of unity. It was geared to promote cohesion, integration, trust, and mutual understanding and commitment. The moment by moment operation of the campaign was simultaneously *dependent upon* cooperation, integration and trust, and *evidence that* these relationships and values were in the process of being realized on a large scale. Whilst quite different people were being brought together as persons, the nation was uniting around common goals and objectives.

The literacy campaign, then, brought together old and young, urban and rural, middle class and peasant, sophisticated and simple. The experience forged strong immediate bonds of sympathy, respect and commitment, across very different peoples. The experience of a 17 year-old woman, upon arriving at the home she would teach in, was far from uncommon. Vilma Perez-Valles and her *brigadista* friends had come from comfortable homes in the city to a squalid, one-roomed shack with a dirt floor. 'There were eight children, completely nude. The pigs and cows were living with the people. There was no difference between the animals and the children. The only water was dirty!' Vilma and her friends surveyed the conditions inside the tiny house, which was lit by a single candle. 'Everything was silent as we looked at each other. One by one we began to cry. We were so sad to see with our own eyes the poverty of our people'.[100]

In the context of this shared drive for literacy it became clear to participants that being Nicaraguan meant very different things for people in different social classes, occupations, and parts of the country. Nevertheless, this shared pursuit kept before all the fact that, in spite of the differences, all were equally Nicaraguans. From this developed informed respect for differences, as well as pride in one's own way of life. Nicaraguans were different but equal. Each had their place, and within the revolution there was a mutual need of each for the other. In the words of the primer, 'There is room for all in this revolution' (from Lesson sixteen). A peasant farm worker, talking subsequently to the mother of his literacy teacher, put it more eloquently:

> Do you know that I am not ignorant any more? I know how to read now. Not perfectly, you understand, but I know how. And do you know, your son isn't ignorant any more either. Now he knows how we live, what we eat, how we work, and he knows the life of the mountains. Your son has learned to read from our book.[101]

The process of confronting (within the literacy campaign) ignorance that had for centuries sustained hierarchies, separations, disparate opportunities, and mutal suspicions, extended beyond addressing the divisions between urban and rural, old and young, traditional and modern, professional and peasant. It contributed also to breaking down perceived and lived differences and hierarchies between men and women, by establishing patterns of daily practice in which women participated on strictly equal terms with men. The whole experience of the campaign dealt a strong blow to traditional conceptions of women's role and the options available to them. Many *brigadistas* were young women from the urban middle class who had hitherto lived sheltered lives under the protection and guidance of the patriarchal family structure.[102] Their participation in the Crusade seriously challenged the necessity, relevance, and future acceptability of many constraints imposed by this structure. Contrary to parents' initial (and understandable) fears, most of these young women easily survived the rigours of life in remote and often deeply impoverished areas — where there was an ever present risk of disease and injury (and, in some places, of attacks by counter-revolutionary groups).

Moreover, the decision to separate the *brigadista* corps into squads by gender increased greatly the opportunities for female brigadistas to assume leadership roles. Miller suggests that if the squads had been mixed, 'men would probably have dominated the structure because of ingrained deference given to them'. Overall,

> the campaign experience provided young women volunteers with the opportunity to test their skills and to live independently from their families. In the process, many gained a new sense of identity and confidence and decided upon new career directions in rural development, careers that had been traditionally closed to women.[103]

Knowing that they had proved themselves responsible and effective actors in a very demanding project, young women could not simply return to the goals and expectations they held (and held of them) prior to leaving home. Many identified strongly with a revolution that offered them new challenges and possibilities. For them the future would be very different from the past. If many young women themselves immediately welcomed this possibility, it was something their parents would have to come to accept.

> Returning from the Literacy Crusade I had certain conflicts with my family; they wanted me to remain a little girl, an object. In the crusade

we women felt liberated, we all worked, we helped out in everything, and we were not under the thumb of our parents. We survived for five months alone and that gives you the experience to know how to run your own life.[104]

Often, parents came around. As one middle class mother puts it, 'the Literacy Campaign taught us what our children are capable of doing and becoming'.[105] Male peers were also forced to acknowledge the full part played by women in the campaign — although the overt chauvinism that accompanies the genuine respect and admiration conveyed in the following passage indicates something of the challenge to altering male consciousness that lay ahead.

In San Pablo ... on the border with Honduras there was a squad of women. There were many characteristics of the area which made it inappropriate for women to be assigned there. There were incursions of counter-revolutionary bands because of the nearness of the border and of the fact that it was mountainous — and it was very mountainous. The area is almost impenetrable, there are snakes, vipers, everything imaginable. But, those women, they stayed there until the end of the Crusade. They sparked the growth of the mass organizations and such things, although some male brigadistas refused to go there because they were afraid since it was on the border ... In those districts I tell you without exaggerating you have to walk eight or ten hours to get there in the rainy season — with sharp cliffs and everything. But those women got there and stayed. I tip my hat to them. We all agreed, 'Those women, they have balls'.[106]

It was not young educated middle-class women alone who began to see themselves differently, and take on new roles and pursuits as a result. This was also the experience of many working-class women, in the cities and countryside alike, who learned to read and write during the campaign. Some abandoned their traditional subservience and volunteered as coordinators in the new education collectives. Others combined this responsibility with additional new roles — in unions, with AMNLAE, in defence committees, etc. Thus 'Alva Rosa, Don Chavelo's daughter, is not only a health brigadista, but also a Popular Education Coordinator. Last year she taught two campesinos to read, and this year she's matriculated more'.[107]

The common experience of Nicaraguan women who acted in many different capacities in the literacy campaign was of being full partners in an enormously successful and important national achievement. This encouraged their subsequent involvement in the revolution process more generally. It has also prompted Nicaraguan women increasingly to identify themselves as a potent political force and to actively promote their interests as women. The emergence of this perspective on an enhanced scale has increased AMNLAE's membership and its influence within the revolution. Through AMNLAE, Nicaraguan women have made important contacts with women's organizations and concerns worldwide. This has encouraged the development of an internationalist as well as nationalist perspective among Nicaraguan women. In March 1982, AMNLAE hosted the Continental Meeting of Women.[108] This convention was attended by representatives from sixty-seven countries. Such internationalist contact not only strengthens the resolve and enriches the revolutionary vision of Nicaraguan women. It also enhances the cause of women's liberation throughout the rest of the world.

'The Nicaraguan revolution' refers not to a completed programme of social change (and still less to the realization of an *ideal* set of social conditions), but to the creation and recreation of new structures and mechanisms through which *progress* toward personal and national liberation through popular participation can continue. The various structures and mechanisms created within the revolutionary process, and through which that process is lived and expanded, include (for example), the mass campaigns (health, literacy, etc.), new laws, a new constitution, production cooperatives under worker control, a new electoral system, procedures and networks for communication between government, mass organizations and the political parties, etc. These new structures remain open to scrutiny — as part of the revolutionary process — and are retained, modified, or abandoned as required in order to maintain progress toward the goal of liberation. (As we have noted, for instance, problems are apparent within EPB. Modification is underway.) And so the revolution is dynamic rather than static, and belongs to the present and future as well as to the past. The revolution is/was not an event, but a complex on-going process. Therefore, to assess the revolution at any point in time involves looking back as well as looking ahead. Looking back we can identify and evaluate changes implemented so far: tracing objective gains which have resulted and noting whatever errors and shortcomings are evident, and problems that remain. Looking ahead involves assessing the (likely) potential of existing mechanisms, structures, programmes, etc., for progressively over-coming oppressive ideologies, relations and practices. This approach to understanding and assessing the revolution can be well illustrated by reference to matters impinging on women's liberation in Nicaragua. The important role of literacy within this context will be readily apparent.

Shortly after victory over Somoza a new constitution was framed in a process of dialogue involving the Government of National Reconstruction[109] and representatives of all the mass organizations. AMNLAE was an active partner in preparing this constitution, known as the Statute of Rights and Guarantees of Nicaraguans.[110] The original Statute has served as an interim constitution since 1979. At the time of writing a revised constitution is in the process of debate and ratification. Early in 1985 an elaborate process of evaluating and revising the 1979 constitution began. This allowed for full public participation via the seven political parties, two extra-parliamentary parties, and the full range of mass organizations.[111] All groups were invited to prepare and submit proposals for the revised constitution. These were presented to the Sub-committee of National Consultation. In the second phase (during the first half of 1986) open forums were held throughout the country to discuss a draft constitution drawn up from the proposals submitted. In all seventy-eight open public meetings were held, with due weight given to geographic region and sector interests. Each meeting was presided over by three national assembly legislators, and foreign observers were invited to take part. From these forums a revised draft was prepared. This contained 198 articles and went before the National Assembly for final approval in late 1986.[112]

Against this sketch of political process, we may return to the original Statute of 1979. This was the first legal document in Nicaragua's history to address the principle of human, political, economic, and social equality between the sexes. The deep-rooted tradition of discrimination against women in Nicaragua was a major area of concern addressed in the constitutional debate at that time. Following the enactment of the Statute a framework of far-reaching laws has emerged reflecting this concern with women's oppression. The law regulating relations between mothers, fathers and children, defines women's rights and men's obligations within the home. As a consequence, legal protection of paternal dominion has been removed, and the principle of equal responsibility for child care established. Other important laws in this area include the Nourishment Law, which guarantees protection to families abandoned by the husband, and the Adoption Law.

Recognizing that laws on their own are of little practical value without knowledge of how to gain access to the legal process and the means to do so, AMNLAE formed the Women's Legal Office in 1983.[113] The role of the Legal Office is to actively assist women in pursuing matters of family law. In addition, AMNLAE has closely monitored the legal process in terms of whether or not it has been adequate to secure those goals sought for women in the revolution and established in principle by the constitution. During 1985 the Legal Office publicly criticized the inability of existing legal arrangements to guarantee full equality for women — or, indeed, even a near approximation to it! On the basis of their investigation and critique, Legal Office lawyers drafted a proposal for constitutional change. They presented this proposal for discussion by AMNLAE members throughout the land. Widespread interest and debate ensued.

A priority stressed in the draft proposal was that urgent attention be given to 'the rights of women within the household'. Maria Lourdes Bolaños, Director of the Women's Legal Office, explained this priority by reference to common experience among her clients.

> We are confronted with some painful realities. Women mercilessly beaten; pregnant women forced to stoop and remove their husband's shoes; women denied a divorce because they cannot prove that they are abused; women who, after living for years with a man, suddenly find themselves without a roof over their heads because he has decided to end the relationship; women sexually black-mailed in order to keep their jobs; women raped by their husbands, brothers or fathers ...[114]

The Legal Office has regularly taken such cases to court. Frequently, however, it receives unsatisfactory rulings. Bolaños maintains that this is because interpretations of the law, and often the laws themselves, 'are still class oriented and sexist'.

AMNLAE has approached this failure of the legal process from two sides. First, they sought the clearest possible understanding and explanation of the problem itself. Second, they aimed to develop concrete proposals for change arising out of women's analysis of the problem. AMNLAE wanted as many women as possible to participate in this process of analyzing the problem and suggesting measures to counter it. To this end AMNLAE's draft proposal for constitutional change was produced. This draft provided a focus for discussion over several months among AMNLAE's members.

From this protracted discussion an analysis and set of concrete proposals emerged as AMNLAE's official position on weaknesses in existing legal procedures pertaining to women, and on more general changes necessary to promote equality for women within the revolution[115] Besides stressing special attention to the rights of women within the household, the AMNLAE proposal for constitutional change called for the law of the land to 'go beyond simple recognition of equality between the sexes' and institute 'preferential treatment for women under the law'. Women with dependents, it said, should have preferential access to jobs, and women generally should have preferential access to education and technical training. AMNLAE also proposed that the struggle against sexism become a constitutional subject, and 'that any apology for sexism which manifests, upholds, or reproduces prejudices against women should be an offence punishable by law'. A further major proposal was that proportional representation of the sexes in public elections be sought.[116]

Having decided as women what changes they seek, AMNLAE presented their proposals for national discussion — in public forums and within the National Assembly — as part of the process of revising the constitution. AMNLAE wants a full and continuing national debate around the theme of women's progress (or, in many cases, *the lack of it*) within the revolution: debate which draws in women who do not belong to AMNLAE as well as men. AMNLAE leaders see this wider debate as a crucial historical step. They believe that a fatal flaw in the process of developing the 1979 Statute was that good will and good intentions were not accompanied by the national debate, and other serious challenges to prevailing consciousness, necessary to make the law effective.[117] AMNLAE's initiative has proved a successful catalyst for national debate: at least among women. Women from all walks of life 'participated massively in the meetings on the political constitution, expressing

> with clarity and precision ... our demands for free choice in bearing children, respect for our physical and psychological well being, access to positions of leadership based solely on merit, [improved] access to land and land titles, the right to full employment, the protection of maternity, and equality within the couple.[118]

Official meetings between AMNLAE and the National Assembly's Sub-committee on constitutional change have taken place. AMNLAE's proposals, along with those of other mass organizations, groups and political parties, have been published and broadcast extensively throughout all media.

The picture that emerges here is one of women engaging in considerable activity, mediated by print (through reports, published critiques, discussion documents, media articles, written proposals, etc.), to assert their historical claims and challenge oppressive social relations and practices. This picture, however, requires further elaboration in order better to assess the pursuit of women's emancipation within the Nicaraguan revolution. For major practical and ideological barriers remain to women's full and equal participation as historical agents; to overcoming established patterns of domination and subordination by gender. These barriers present Nicaraguan women and men with an on-going challenge to understand gender oppression ever more critically, and to address it ever more authentically in practice. The continuing and enhanced practice of a critical and active literacy — that is, a proper literacy — is central to meeting this challenge.

A single typical example from daily life puts our picture into fuller perspective. At a recent convention of UNAG (the National Union of Farmers and Cattle Raisers) the issue of women's participation in the union appeared only at the end of the agenda, and was barely addressed. Moreover, despite the integral role played by women in the agricultural economy, 'not one woman spoke from the podium, and the number of woman delegates at the conference could be counted on one hand'. One woman delegate remarked that

> machismo still runs deep in rural areas and the campesino women are a product of that society. This explains the make-up of the [convention] and the fact that the women's issue was put on the agenda as a rhetorical formality, not as the heartfelt demand of 50 per cent of the rural population.

A second woman added that rural women are trapped in a vicious circle so far as their enhanced participation within daily life is concerned. For

> despite the fact that the whole family works, only the man is considered a member of the cooperative. That means he's the one who joins UNAG, he elects the representatives and lodges his complaints.[119]

In other words, agrarian and labour reforms — which have broadened access to land, encouraged cooperative production and worker management of cooperatives, established labour unions, etc. — the creation of mass organizations, and the enactment of a constitution, have left deep traditional structures of power by gender remarkably intact in the countryside. The principle of equal participation is *acknowledged*, but is far from actualized. Many women have, of course, experienced an improved material quality of life, together with their family and community in general. But traditional patterns of patriarchal domination, discrimination, and sexist attitudes and practices, persist. They have been tempered to a significant degree, but by no means overcome. Discussion of the Women's Legal Office suggests that much the same holds true for urban life as well.

In evaluating the revolution to date and AMNLAE's role within it, a number of Nicaraguan women note that genuine structural change impinging on women's interests has gone nowhere near far enough, and that AMNLAE itself is not well placed to speed the process along. Gioconda Belli claims that AMNLAE lacks the necessary ideological perspective to spearhead more rapid and effective change. AMNLAE *has* encouraged women to enter the workforce, to take on active roles in defence, education, and so on. It has been much less successful, however, in evolving and extending an ideological climate within which women's *real* problems can be effectively addressed. Belli claims that as women begin to get involved in the revolution, 'and increase their conscious participation as active members of society ... they have to face a complex social and family situation'. And in this situation, '*women find themselves alone in resolving their problems*'. This calls for a strong women's organization: a need, Belli claims, that AMNLAE has been unable to fulfil.

> AMNLAE had to wrestle with women's real problems if it wanted to represent them; it had to provide an answer which would transcend the mere integration of women into the workforce; it had to provide an answer to the problems arising from the very process of integration it was defending.
>
> It didn't have the answers, nor [even] the belief that a women's organization must play a persuasive role so that society develops concern for women's problems and considers them problems affecting all members of society.
>
> AMNLAE actively took on the role of organizer, but was unable to complement it by bringing women's problems to the forefront in society; what was missing was the ideological orientation required for an undertaking of this scope, which involves changing both patterns of thought and action, rather than only seeking material gains.[120]

This poses a contradiction with regard to AMNLAE's proposals for constitutional change. To the extent that Belli's critique is valid, AMNLAE has advanced proposals that stand little chance of being fully understood or implemented in practice in the immediate future. What is more, AMNLAE's *own* ideological limitations present it with the challenge of understanding (more) fully the nature and implications of the very proposals it has advanced as an organization. Given this, we must be reasonable in our expectations of what a revised constitution will accomplish with respect to women: even if it *does* incorporate the demands named in AMNLAE's proposal. The national debate called for by AMNLAE, and seen as missing from the original constitutional process six years earlier, has really just begun. And here as elsewhere, the educators (AMNLAE) must themselves be educated in the process of furthering the education of others.

What is apparent, however, *and what is surely the most important point*, is that the Nicaraguan revolution and women within it are on the right historical track. Structures and processes — for example, AMNLAE, its Legal Office, a constitution and a democratic constitutional process, etc. -— conducive to the pursuit of liberation by women are in place. Through these structures and processes the adequacy (or inadequacy) of established mechanisms, such as the law and operation of the legal system, can be continually assessed. Failings can be analyzed, and their underlying causes sought, identified, and posed as problems. These problems can then be presented for public discussion and action through the media, mass organizations, popular education, etc. Women *are* actively employing structures for popular participation in daily life to evaluate existing practices and relations, to propose changes and lobby for change, and to educate people at large for that change. In the same process, women themselves achieve a better critical understanding of their own reality and the problems they face within it. This is the very essence of the struggle for liberation; of *revolution*. Proper literacy is both a precondition and a medium of popular participation and mutual education here.

The Practice of Proper Literacy in the Nicaraguan Revolution

Proper literacy comprises practices of reading and writing which enhance people's control over their lives and their capacity for making rational judgments and decisions by enabling them to identify, understand, and act to transform social relations and practices in which power is structured un-equally. In earlier chapters I have focused on social contexts in which prevailing ideological, political and cultural conditions are hostile to the practice of proper literacy: settings in which educational and wider political structures work actively against subordinate groups acquiring and using forms of reading and writing which assist them in understanding and confronting their oppression.

The Nicaraguan revolution presents a situation which in one way is the exact opposite of our own. Official education policy in Nicaragua (and social policy generally) *has actively promoted* the acquisition and elaboration of literacy within a broad ideological framework which identifies and emphasizes the major contours of structured domination and subordination that have operated in the past. This is possible in Nicaragua because the revolutionary govern-ment — indeed, the state — is committed in principle and practice to championing the interests of those majorities who have traditionally been oppressed. Nicaraguans have been positively encouraged to acquire, employ, and expand their literacy skills in processes and settings intended to increase their critical grasp of oppressive and exploitive social relations and practices;

and to enlist their active participation in progressively replacing *the oppressive* with *the emancipatory*.

There is no other way in which to understand the Literacy Crusade of 1980 and the subsequent development of Popular Basic Education. These are mass exercises contrived to initiate participants, across traditional hierarchies of power and privilege, into a conception of social reality as structured; and, as hitherto structured in accordance with minority interests. They are an invitation to understand how history *has been made*, and how it *might be made*. It is the invitation to understand history and social reality in these terms, and to understand it ever more deeply, that lies behind the sentences and themes in the literacy primer. Compare, as typical examples: 'We are rebuilding our nation'; 'Our nation is in motion'; 'We did not want to be slaves'; 'Brave people gave their lives for our freedom'; 'Sandino planted the seed of freedom'; 'The Agrarian Reform retrieves the land for the benefit of the people'; 'They planted corn on the community land'; 'An imperialist defeat: US domination is now over. Nicaragua's resources are now ours'; 'Nicaraguan women have traditionally been exploited. The revolution now makes their liberation possible'; 'A real democracy is the expression of the power of the organized masses'; and so on.

This is not a privileged or exclusive invitation. It is open to all equally. The Crusade and EPB invite members of historically advantaged groups to set about (if they have not already) committing 'class suicide' from a position of critical awareness[121], whilst in the same process inviting historically oppressed groups to understand the possibilities for liberation that now lie within their grasp.

Of course an understanding of social reality in structural terms cannot be 'banked' into people.[122] It can only become *real* for them within a praxis. People cannot be *made* to think in structural terms; they cannot be *made* critically aware of historical process. We have to grow progressively into this awareness by actively applying a politicized awareness in our daily practice — 'trying it on against the world', as it were, in the process of coming to understand and employ it better. This is Freire's central theme. It also describes the quest of those historical and contemporary exponents of proper literacy discussed in chapters 3 and 4. The educative process involved — which comprises reflection in conjunction with action; creating/living new relations and practices in the process of trying to understand them — is long and complex. It is the first step, *and the first step only*, for a government to invite and encourage people to enter this process, and to assist them in establishing structures and mechanisms conducive to it.

An invitation to learn and employ literacy skills in pursuit of an ever more critical understanding of how history has been made and how it might be re-made is in no way the donation of a ready-packaged gift. Neither are the themes and sentences of primers and other curricular materials being used in Nicaragua presented as 'gifts' of content to be absorbed and retained. They are a stimulus to continuing discussion and understanding; an impetus to further and fuller participation in making history. Those men and women who learn to read and write in CEPs, and who use their skills within these same CEPs and/or within mass organizations, the workplace, trade unions, schools, political processes and in leisure, to enhance their understanding of and control over the creation of daily reality in accordance with the interests of all, are indeed *practising* an art: they are far from having 'perfected' it. It *never* becomes perfect, any more than we can ever become fully human.[123] Rather, we become more critically aware and more in control of history, and *maintain* ourselves in critical control, through the continuing and expanding practice of proper literacy. The future of the Nicaraguan revolution has everything to do with more and more Nicaraguans practising proper literacy more and more. Educational policies which encourage this pursuit are a necessary first step: an impetus, but no more than that. Thereafter it is an educational and educative task for active participants. Being equal to this task is the challenge that faces Nicaraguans each new day of the revolution.

Official policy bearing on the practice of reading and writing in Nicaragua provides, then, a positive stimulus to the pursuit of proper literacy. In other respects, however, the practice of proper literacy by Nicaraguans faces enormous and powerful obstacles. Among these, the single most important is the contra war, which is openly backed by the US government. This war limits to an absolute minimum the 'space' within which Nicaraguans can pursue and enhance the educational and social praxis reflected in the case studies offered above. It is important to understand here that this war is being waged on behalf of elite interests: namely, those members of traditional wealth and power elites in Nicaragua who are opposed to the revolution because it seeks to remove (the basis of) their former privilege; and international elites who benefit from the third world being maintained in dependent underdevelopment. Indeed, and uncomfortably, these people outside of Nicaragua who benefit — knowingly or unknowingly — from maintaining the third world in dependent under-development include individuals like the authors of this book: whose material standard of life is predicated at least partly on the fact that the vast majority of third world inhabitants live very badly and without control over their destiny.

This carries an important implication for the practice of proper literacy. Ultimately, for Nicaraguans to practise proper literacy it is necessary also for *us* to practice proper literacy. For unless *we* achieve a critical politics, and make the connection between waging war against a small and impoverished Central American nation and maintaining structures of domination and subordination generally, we will remain impotent to build a world that is safe for participative democracy. In the event of that failure a certain casualty will be the Nicaraguan revolution, together with our *own* historical agency.

Notes

1   'Radical' means 'of the root(s)'. Radical social change is, then, change that goes to the roots of society: to the structures and relations which shape daily practice.

2 By 'present day battles' I include Nicaragua's continuing struggle to overcome practices, ideologies, and forces *within* Nicaraguan society itself that are hostile to the pursuit of genuine structural change, as well as Nicaragua's struggle against economic and military aggression being applied by the US. The two dimensions of the current battles are, of course, very closely related.

3 Cited in HIRSHON, S. with BUTLER, J. (1983), *And Also Teach Them to Read,*, Westport, Connecticut, Lawrence Hill and Co., p. 4.

4 *Ibid.* The FSLN was, of course, named for Sandino — Nicaragua's national hero.

5 CARDENAL, F. and MILLER, V. (1981), 'Nicaragua 1980: the battle of the ABCs', *Harvard Educational Review*, 51, 1, p. 3.

6 CABEZAS, O. cited in BARNDT, D. (1985), 'Popular Education', being chapter 15 of WALKER, T. (Ed), *Nicaragua: the first five years*, New York, Praeger Press, p. 317.

7 *Ibid.*, p. 317.

8 See Centre for Research and Documentation of the Atlantic Coast (1984), *Trabil Nani* (Many Troubles), Managua; MILLER, V. (1985), *Between Struggle and Hope: the Nicaraguan Literacy Crusade*, Boulder, Westview Press, chapter 2; WALKER, T. (1985), 'Introduction' to his (Ed) *op. cit.*

9 For readers interested in issues relating to Nicaragua's Atlantic Coast I recommend the following introductory references: Centre for Research and Documentation of the Atlantic Coast, *ibid*; Bourgois, P. (1985), 'Ethnic Minorities', in WALKER, T. (Ed), *ibid.*, pp. 201–16; ORTIZ, R.D. (1984), *Indians of the Americas: human rights and self-determination*, London, Zed Press.

10 WALKER, T. *op. cit.*, p. 13.

11 ORTIZ, *op. cit.*, p. 201.

12 HALEY, E. (1983), 'Nicaragua/Women/Revolution', *Hecate*, 9, p. 82.

13 *Ibid.*

14 WALKER, T. *op. cit.*, p. 13.

15 *Ibid.*, p. 14.

16 PEARCE, J. (1982), *Under the Eagle*, London, Latin America Bureau.

17 Cited in *ibid.*, p. 9.

18 WALKER, T. *op. cit.*, p. 15.

19 Compare, BLACK, G. (1981), *Triumph of the People: the Sandinist Revolution in Nicaragua*, London, Zed Press, chapter 4; DIEDERICH, B. (1982), *Somoza: and the legacy of US involvement in Central America*, London, Junction Books.

20 BOOTH, J. (1982), *The End and the Beginning: the Nicaraguan Revolution*, Boulder, Westview Press, chapter 5, especially pp. 77–82.

21 BLACK, G. and BEVAN, J. (1980), *The Loss of Fear: education in Nicaragua*, London, World University Service, p. 17.

22 See BOOTH, *op. cit.*, chapter 5; BLACK and BEVAN, *ibid*; WEBER, H. (1981), *Nicaragua: the Sandinist Revolution*, London, Verso, chapter 1; WEISSBERG, A. (1982), *Nicaragua: an introduction to the Sandinista Revolution*, New York, Pathfinder Press.

23 BOOTH, *ibid.*, p. 80

24 WEISSBERG, *op. cit.*, pp. 8–9.

25 *Ibid.*, p. 10.

26 MILLER (1985), *op. cit.*, p. 19.

27 BOOTH, *op. cit.*, p. 85.

28 WEISSBERG, *op. cit.*, p. 10.

29 BARNDT, *op. cit.*, p. 319.
30 Cited in MILLER (1985), *op. cit.*, p. 20.
31 Compare WALKER, T. (ed), *op. cit.*, especially part IV.
32 'To revolve' means, precisely, 'to turn around'. Compare also, 'Introduction', in *ibid.*, pp. 2–11.
33 For graphic illustrations of foreign policy during the Somoza era, see *ibid.*, pp. 18–19.
34 See FSLN (1969), 'The Historic Program of the FSLN', reprinted in (1982) *Sandinistas Speak*, New York, Pathfinder Press, p. 20.
35 *ibid.*, pp. 16–17.
36 Compare FREIRE (1972), *op. cit.*
37 I am using 'alfabetizacion' here to refer to the literacy campaign. 'Post alfabetizacion' refers to the broad process of adult education that developed following the literacy campaign.
38 HIRSHON, *op. cit.*, pp. 5–6.
39 *Ibid.*, p. 6.
40 See *ibid.*, p. 10; MILLER (1985), *op. cit.*, pp. 54–8.
41 HIRSHON and MILLER, *op. cit.*
42 MILLER and CARDENAL, *op. cit.*, p. 6.
43 MILLER (1985), *op. cit.*, p. 118.
44 MILLER, *ibid.*, provides a book length account of the literacy campaign. For a wonderful account of the day to day reality of the campaign written by a participant, see HIRSHON.
45 For a literal *picture* of what this involved in practice, see *Dawn of the People: Nicaragua's literacy crusade*, Green Valley Films, Burlington, Vermont.
46 Compare MILLER (1985), *op. cit.*, p. 69, for reference to some of the tensions experienced by teachers in the campaign.
47 MILLER, V. (1982), 'The Nicaraguan Literacy Crusade', in WALKER, T. (Ed), *Nicaragua in Revolution*, New York, Praeger Press, p. 252.
48 The complete list of themes is as follows:

Lesson	Theme Sentence
1	Sandino, leader of the revolution.
2	Carlos Fonseca said, 'Sandino lives.'
3	The FSLN led the people to liberation.
4	The guerrillas overcame the genocidal National Guard.
5	The masses rose up in an insurrection made by the people.
6	The Sandinista defence committees defend the revolution.
7	To spend little, save much, and produce a lot — that is making the revolution.
8	The revolutionary workers' associations propel production forward and keep vigil over the process.
9	People, army, unity: They are the guarantee of victory.
10	The agrarian reform guarantees that the harvest goes to the people.
11	With organization, work, and discipline, we will be able to rebuild the land of Sandino.
12	1980, the year of the war against illiteracy.
13	The pillage of imperialism is over: Nicaragua's natural resources are ours.
14	The nationalization of Somoza's businesses helps us recover our wealth and strengthen our economy.

15 Work is a right and a responsibility of every person in the land.
16 The revolutionary government expands and creates health centres for the people.
17 With the participation of everyone, we will have healthy recreation for our children.
18 We are forming work brigades to construct and improve our housing.
19 Women have always been exploited. The revolution makes possible their liberation.
20 The revolution opens up a road system to the Atlantic Coast. The Kurinwás is a navigable river.
21 Our democracy is the power of people belonging to organizations and participating.
22 There is freedom of religion for all those churches that support and defend the interests of the people.
23 The Sandinista revolution extends the bond of friendship to all peoples.
From MILLER (1985), *op. cit.*, pp. 76–7.

49 Each group comprised a Sandinista Literacy Unit (UAS).
50 HIRSHON, *op. cit.*, p. 50
51 In his own practice Freire even accepted the construction of meaningless (as well as meaningful) words out of syllables, until the principle of word construction was grasped securely.
52 This phonetic approach is, naturally, less straightforward in English — a fact verified by the English language programme conducted on the Atlantic Coast as part of the literacy campaign.
53 MILLER (1985), *op. cit.*, p. 87.
54 Compare *ibid.*, pp. 83–90, for an account of the dialogue component of the lessons and the various theoretical and practical difficulties it posed.
55 *Ibid.*, p. 90.
56 See Appendix in this volume.
57 Compare HIRSHON, *op. cit.*, for a graphic account of conditions in the countryside and how these were endured by the *brigadistas*.
58 See TORRES, R. (1986), *Los CEP: educacion popular y democracia participativa en Nicaragua*, Managua, CRIES, 9.
59 *Ibid.*
60 See TORRES (1983), *op. cit.*
61 Compare HIRSHON, *op. cit.*, chapter 18.
62 TORRES (1986), *op. cit.*, p. 7.
63 Compare FREIRE (1973), *op. cit.*
64 Eduardo Baez, Vice Ministry of Adult Education, Managua, in conversation with the authors, February 1985.
65 Cited in TORRES (1986), *op. cit.*, p. 17.
66 See TORRES (1983), *op. cit.*
67 Unfortunately, the connection achieved between curricular material and daily life has not been as close as intended. See below.
68 Compare TORRES (1983), *op. cit.*
69 This is the figure for 1984 — the latest year for which I have detailed figures. The number of coordinators and CEPs would be rather lower at the present time — see below.
70 Children. Compare TORRES (1983), *op. cit.*

71 Compare TORRES (1986), *op. cit.*, pp. 4 – 8.
72 In addition to the titles already mentioned, see here (1985), *Nicaragua: revolucion popular, educacion popular*, INIES – CRIES, Managua.
73 'Teachers become targets of counter-revolution', *Times Educational Supplement*, 14 March 1986.
74 TORRES (1986), *op. cit.*, p. 16.
75 *Ibid.*, pp. 12 – 16.
76 *Ibid.*, p. 15.
77 Cited *ibid.*, p. 23. See her footnote 33.
78 Compare *ibid.*, pp. 18 – 9.
79 *Ibid.*, p. 21.
80 Compare, for example, BORGE, T. (1983), 'The new education in the new Nicaragua', in (1985), *Nicaragua: the Sandinista people's revolution*, New York, Pathfinder Press, pp. 70 – 82.
81 TORRES (1986), *op. cit.*, p. 16.
82 EDUARDO BAEZ, cited in FORD, P. (1986), 'Nicaragua: total literacy deferred', *Development Forum*, April 1986, p. 16.
83 *Ibid.*
84 Compare *ibid.*
85 In 'Striving for Equality', *Barricada Internacional*, Managua, 28 March 1985, p. 9.
86 Compare for example, HALEY'S account of the relations that have evolved between mestizo men and Nicaraguan women, *op. cit.*, p. 82.
87 See RAMIREZ-HORTON, S. (1982), 'The role of women in the Nicaraguan revolution', in WALKER, T. (Ed), *op. cit.*, p. 149.
88 That is not to say that the nature, dimensions, and depth of oppression here were well understood by Nicaraguans. See below.
89 See 'Women propose concrete changes', *Barricada Internacional*, Managua, 3 October 1985, p. 5.
90 See SERRA, L. (1982), 'The Sandinista Mass Organizations', in WALKER, T. (Ed), *op. cit.*, pp. 95 – 113.
91 From an interview recorded by the author with AMNLAE representatives, AMNLAE Office, Managua, 4 February 1985. See also RAMIREZ-HORTON, *op. cit.*
92 Framed in late 1979.
93 See 'Striving for equality', *Barricada Internacional*, *op. cit.*
94 From the recorded interview with AMNLAE representatives.
95 This is from the primer used in the English language programme on the Atlantic Coast, 106. The entire lesson is appended below. The primer reference is: Nicaraguan Ministry of Education (1980), *The Sunrise of the People*, Managua.
96 *Ibid.*, p. 111.
97 From the recorded interview with AMNLAE representatives. See also BELLI, G. 'Women in the revolution', *Barricada Internacional*, 9 October 1986, p. 9.
98 MILLER (1985), *op. cit.*, p. 200.
99 ANGUS, E. (1981), 'The awakening of a people: Nicaragua's literacy campaign', *Two Thirds*, 2, 3, 14.
100 Cited in *ibid.*
101 In MILLER (1982), *op. cit.*, p. 244.
102 Compare RAMIREZ-HORTON, *op. cit.*
103 MILLER (1985), *op. cit.*, p. 200.

104 Cited in *ibid.*, p. 203.

105 In MILLER (1982), *op. cit.*, p. 245.

106 In MILLER (1985), *op. cit.*, p. 203.

107 HIRSHON, *op. cit.*, p. 249.

108 See BORGE, T. (1982), *Women and the Nicaraguan Revolution*, New York, Pathfinder Press.

109 This was the interim government which operated between July 1979 and the general elections of November 1984. For excellent descriptions of the election process and their outcome see, Instituto Historico Centro-Americano, *Envio*, March 1984 (no. 33), August 1984 (no. 38), October 1984 (no. 40), December 1984 (no. 42), February 1985 (no. 44), April 1985 (no. 46), University of Central America, Managua, Nb English language editions of *Envio* are available.

110 See 'Women propose concrete changes', *Barricada Internacional, op. cit.*

111 See Instituto Historico Centro-Americano, *Envio*, November, 1985 (no. 53), 4b.

112 See *ibid.* See also numbers 62, August 1986, and 65, November 1986. The new Constitution was ratified by Nicaragua's president, Daniel Ortega, on 9 January 1987. See *Barricada Internacional*, 15 January 1987, and Instituto Historico Centroamericano, *Envio* January 1987 (no. 67).

113 See 'Striving for equality', *Barricada Internacional, op. cit.*

114 In 'Women propose concrete changes', *Barricada Internacional, op. cit.*

115 *Ibid.*

116 *Ibid.*

117 *Ibid.*

118 VARGOS, M. in 'Women in the revolution', *Barricada Internacional, op. cit.*

119 See 'Pending the women's issue', *Barricada Internacional*, 8 May 1986, 4.

120 In 'Women in the revolution', *Barricada Internacional, op. cit.*

121 Compare FREIRE, P. (1978). *Pedagogy in Process: letters to Guinea-Bissau*, London, Writers and Readers. See also CABRAL, A. (1969), *Unity and Struggle*, New York, Monthly Review Press.

122 Compare FREIRE (1972), *Pedagogy of the Oppressed*, Harmondsworth, Penguin, especially chapters 2 and 3.

123 Compare *ibid.*

Chapter 6

Literacy, Politics and Education Policy

Recapitulation

This book has addressed the politics of literacy. I have asked what forms reading and writing take, and what roles they play, within a social-historical setting in which human beings pursue their interests, goals, and aspirations under conditions where power is structured unequally. The whole argument has been grounded in an explicit theoretical perspective. Key axioms of this perspective include the beliefs that : power is structured unequally; competing interest groups exist within society; these groups pursue their interests from positions of greater advantage or disadvantage in terms of the structured power available to them; practices of reading and writing are integral to this social process and evolve within it.

In no way should the argument produced here be seen as *proving* the axioms in question; as establishing the theoretical perspective beyond doubt. Rather, I have aimed mainly to see what sense can be made of social reality from this perspective. What does the social practice of reading and writing look like if we investigate it in the political terms employed here?; what are the most important (or 'real') uses of reading and writing?; do these vary from conventional views of the use and value of literacy?; whose interests are best served by the ways literacy is conceived and practised?; do different peoples practice different literacies?; if so, why is this?; are some literacies preferable to others, and on what grounds?; do we have a *choice* as to how we practise reading and writing?; how wide is the choice and how might we exercise it?; how do the ways in which we teach, learn, understand, and employ literacy relate to wider dimensions of social practice (such as economic and cultural activity, legal and governmental process, etc.)? These are the sorts of questions I have tried to address. Some of them cannot even be *posed* from within the ideological and theoretical perspectives that prevail in everyday inquiry — including academic inquiry. And where others *are* addressed, they are typically given quite different answers from those suggested here. My aim will have been met if folk see fit to advance and elaborate the investigation I have attempted above: to improve and expand it, regarding the broad theoretical perspective as being sufficiently warranted to justify developing and employing it further.

The foundations of my argument were laid in chapters 1 and 2, where I tried to establish the idea that the (various) actual forms reading and writing take in daily life reflect struggle between competing interest groups within prevailing power structures. It was argued that we should try to identify and understand particular literacies in terms of their potential for either reproducing or challenging prevailing patterns of structured power and the hierarchies of interest and advantage sustained within them. Two opposing tendencies were noted. First, there is the possibility of subordinate social groups evolving and practising forms of reading and writing which assist them in undertaking effective political action aimed at structural change, whereby access to power is progressively equalized across race/ethnic, gender, cultural, social class, etc. lines. By contrast, secondly, dominant groups will retain their dominance — other things being equal — where the literacy acquired and practised by subordinate groups is rendered less effective than their own: for example, through processes which constitute the practice of reading and writing by subordinate groups as inferior, marginal, hostile to their own interests, etc. From the standpoint of subordinate social groups, these opposite tendencies are reflected in the distinction between proper and improper literacy.

The historical and contemporary cases presented in chapters 3 – 5 are an attempt to elaborate these ideas, and in particular the distinction between proper and improper literacy, within empirical settings. They speak to both of the 'options' available for literacy.[1] In the activities of the Corresponding Societies, the struggle for an authentic working-class press, and in the pedagogy employed by people like Searle and Shor, we find instances of people practising proper literacy within unsympathetic settings. Corresponding Societies and early working-class publishers were met with the full coercive power of the state. Within our own time Searle has been sacked for publishing (against the wishes of his school's governors) work written by his pupils[2], and the policy of open admissions, whereby Shor and others practised proper literacy with working-class students at the City University of New York, has been revoked. Many teachers in Britain, North America, and Australasia have been sacked, moved on, or otherwise intimidated when they have attempted to foster proper forms of reading and writing.[3] In Nicaragua the practice of proper literacy enjoys state support, but faces massive opposition from foreign interests and traditional Nicaraguan elites.[4] Turning to the other side, we find in the work of individuals like Hannah More and Sarah Trimmer, and organizations such as the SPCK and the SDUK, historical instances of improper literacy being promoted among subordinate social groups prior to the era of compulsory mass schooling. And investigation of present day schooling reveals the improper character of the literacy that is mainly practised there — although this dimension of the inquiry cries out for wider and deeper exploration. Throughout these studies the interlocking themes of competing interests and unequal access to structural power remain close to the surface: even if the exercise of power on behalf of dominant interests in our own society is much more covert than it was in the nineteenth century, and such notions as *struggle* initially seem misplaced in the context of Pacific Island pupils studying at Girls Grammar.[5]

Collectively the cases studied here represent only a tiny sample of the endless possibilities available for investigation. As in the opening two chapters, my aim has been to *employ* a particular approach to the politics of literacy — and come to understand it better by employing it — rather than trying to cover most (or even much) of the ground; far less to have the last word on the various issues raised. This all too brief investigation of a mere handful of historical and contemporary cases requires that modest conclusions only be drawn here. On the basis of my argument I would suggest that

(a) a distinction can be drawn between proper and improper literacy which is useful in investigating the politics of literacy;

(b) the diffusion of improper literacy among subordinate social groups is an important element in the process of reproducing patterned domination and subordination.

(c) attempts by oppressed groups to evolve and practise proper forms of literacy face enormous resistance/opposition from established elites;

(d) pursuit of proper literacy is a necessary and central part of political action aimed at structural change in the direction of equalizing power within the social relations and practices of daily life;

(e) while important progress has been made in the study of literacy during the past two decades, we have still much to discover about the political significance of literacy and its ideological character. Considerable work done in recent years by radical researchers bears directly on this issue. We can also learn much here from investigating literacy and education within revolutionary societies;

(f) at the same time, as far as those who seek more democratic social relations and practices are concerned, a great deal depends upon political *will*.[6] The theory (pertaining to literacy) available to members of Corresponding Societies, worker-publishers, Chartists and Sandinistas, was miniscule by comparison with that available to present day academic audiences via published documents, conferences, etc. Despite that, they *practised* proper literacy. Neither did such enemies of proper literacy as Hannah More and her ilk possess elaborate theories of reading and writing. Nevertheless, *they* practised very effective counter forms to proper literacy. As people like Freire and Kozol constantly remind us, perhaps the most important question we have to address is, 'whose side am I on?' Once this is answered a major impediment to understanding and practising proper literacy is removed — at least for those who answer the question 'properly'.

The conclusion I feel most confident drawing here is this: I am convinced that the broad framework employed in this book will repay further and deeper application. In part my confidence comes from the ease with which this political perspective delivers a coherent account of social reality and provides a satisfying explanation of much that goes on in daily life. I have, in fact, had to bypass many historical and contemporary cases of the type studied in chapters 3 – 5 because of sheer limitations on time and space. Further confidence comes from the inspiring work already done in the area of literacy studies which informs and reinforces the project I have attempted here. Most of all, though, my confidence comes from the political efficacy of the very *practice* of proper literacy: from the obvious impact that is made within daily life when proper literacy *is* practised. This is what ultimately convinces me that literacy goes to the very heart of structured domination and repression, and to attempts at overcoming it.

The impact of proper literacy in practice has both positive and negative dimensions. From a positive angle, it is amazing what is achieved in understanding social reality, and in organizing and acting to change it, when subordinated groups read and write properly. This is the clear message in every case from the Corresponding Societies to the CEPs; from students forming a committee to try and restructure their cafeteria[7] to neighbourhood literacy schemes that deliver immediate improvements in rented accommodation.[8] The empowering effect of proper literacy affirms that advantage and disadvantage indeed have structural roots which can be unearthed and 'dumped' when people determine to identify, understand, and address them collectively. What is equally instructive, this time from a negative angle, is the opposition and resentment that springs from threatened interests when oppressed groups achieve a measure (or even a hint) of proper literacy.[9] The fact that elites have such a strong intuitive feel for processes and activities that threaten their interests should encourage those who seek liberation. For once again it affirms that there *are* structural impediments to equality and social justice to be better understood and further challenged, and that literacy initiatives already underway are along the right lines — since they are touching nerves somewhere. Precisely where, and how to touch them more strongly, are matters to be pursued in ever enhanced practice of proper literacy.

By way of concluding my discussion I want briefly to suggest its relevance to a fast-growing field of academic inquiry: namely the study — and particularly, the *analysis* — of education policy.

Education Policy and the Politics of Literacy

A number of factors have merged during the 1970s and 1980s to establish education policy studies as a burgeoning area of academic interest. Silver suggests that in many cases the institutional development of education policy studies (within so many departments, units, institutes, divisions, schools, etc.) has been an attempt to compensate 'for the dwindling support for "educational foundations"': notably, history, philosophy and sociology of education, along with comparative education and educational administration.[10] Indeed, during this period the very notion of foundation *disciplines* has come under considerable attack from theorists working in epistemology, radical sociology of education, radical pedagogy, and elsewhere. Arguments that knowledge cannot be carved up into autonomous types (philosophical, historical, scientific, etc.); that people should pursue more holistic understandings of their world rather than compartmentalize knowledge and awareness; that reflection should be brought into closer relationship with action, and this is better achieved by studying issues and themes rather than academic subjects; all these, and other arguments, have contributed to a pining for more multidisciplinary approaches to academic study or, more radically, for action–research and other approximations to praxis to be employed by educationists.

Against this background, the study and analysis of education policy presented a likely academic focus in keeping with the mood of the times. In part it offered a concentration of themes, issues, and problems on which historians, philosophers, planners, comparative educators, sociologists, economists, political theorists, and others could collectively bring their skills and perspectives to bear. Moreover, considerable work had been done (since the 1950s) to develop policy *science*. This work afforded models, concepts, data, problems, and a literature which offered credibility to extending academic educational inquiry into the policy arena. Indeed, those academics (and others) who had been the 'manpower planners' and 'development specialists' of the previous decades possessed skills, experience, and a mountain of questions/issues which could inform education policy studies.

Two additional factors merit mention in relation to the recent emergence of education policy studies. First, investigation of educational policy is called out as a priority by — and, indeed, within — the radical problematics developed in sociology, education, and cultural studies over the past two decades. If education is a central site on which inequalities of power and advantage are reproduced, then education policy must reflect or otherwise involve the exercise of unequal power. How, in what directions, and in whose interests, become important and valid questions on the radical educationist's agenda. *Culture Wars* provides an excellent example of education policy studies in the radical genre and, in my view, confirms the worth of further developing that genre.

Second, in launching recently a new journal of education policy, its editors noted that

> those engaged and interested in the world of education are living through a period of policy overload and turmoil. Historically the degree of policy activity, at all levels of education, and in many different countries, is probably unprecedented for peacetime governments.[11]

Within Britain, North America and Australasia, education has been targeted for economic cuts in a time of retrenchment. At the same time, governments in these countries conceive education as 'a natural part of any strategy for economic recovery'. Consequently, educational policies are being directed toward restructuring the values, priorities and practices of formal education, with a view to bringing schools into line with 'visions' of our wider social and economic future.[12]

The direction of change and the temper of current education policy are a source of major concern to those who espouse the values of critical agency, equality, and active participation by all within a democratic way of life. There is no question that during the past decade public policy — and education policy *par excellence* — has been moving 'towards more conservative positions', and away from 'the expansive, egalitarian, meritocratic, even radical, bases of the decade from the mid-1960s'.[13] This shift defines the concern that underlies Shor's work in *Culture Wars*, and many other critical inquiries bearing on education policy.[14] In a recent paper Giroux and McLaren speak of educational 'reforms' currently proposed by conservative forces in terms of 'a retreat from democracy'. The educational ideology of the new right (or new conservatives) has effectively redefined the purpose of formal education in a way which eliminates its citizenship function 'in favour of a narrowly defined labour market perspective'. There is little concern within this ideology — which has achieved dominance in the US, and has made alarming headway in Britain and Australasia — for how 'public education could better serve the interests of diverse groups of students by enabling them to understand and gain some control over the socio-political forces that influence their destinies'. Rather, the new education discourse, and policy according with it, have made educational reform synonymous 'with turning schools into "company stores"'. School life is now assessed primarily in terms of 'its contribution to economic growth and cultural uniformity'. Accountability schemes, testing, accreditation, and cre-dentialing rule.[15] Giroux and McLaren cite a passage from Finkelstein wh·ch summarizes the present trend.

> Contemporary reformers seem to be recalling public education from its traditional utopian mission — to nurture a critical and committed citizenry that would stimulate the processes of political and cultural transformation and refine and extend the workings of political demo-cracy ... Reformers seem to imagine public schools as economic rather than political instrumentalities. They forge no new visions of political and social possibilities. Instead, they call public schools to industrial and cultural service exclusively ... Reformers have disjoined their calls for educational reform from calls for a redistribution of power and authority, and the cultivation of cultural forms celebrating pluralism and diversity. As if they have had enough of political democracy, Americans, for the first time in a one hunded and fifty-year history, seem ready to do ideological surgery on their public schools — cutting them away from the fate of social justice and political democracy

completely, and grafting them onto elite corporate, industrial, military and cultural interests.[16]

In the light of this trend, there is obviously an important place for a radically informed and critical study of education policy — and of the ideological struggles that lie behind the policy that is made, the way it is made, how it is implemented, etc. — within the activity of those educationists committed to a democratic, emancipatory ideal of education. In particular, there is a role within the struggle to bring democratic values (back) into the educational heartland for those who are interested in developing critical *analysis* of education policy.

In 'Signposts for a critical educational policy analysis', Prunty suggests that most of the hard work lies ahead of us here.[17] He argues that the literature on educational policy analysis reveals 'some disturbing trends in the current state of the field': such that policy analysis is poorly placed at present to perform the critical task required of it in the existing (reactionary) climate of educational discourse and change. Having identified the assumptions that underlie his own viewpoint, Prunty advances six necessary features of a *critical* analysis of education policy. I will outline Prunty's views, and ask how far the argument in this book can contribute to the critical policy analysis he seeks.

Some Signposts for a Critical Educational Policy Analysis

Four main failings attributed by Prunty to current analysis of educational policy are of special interest here.

(i) Most analyses fail to identify and address issues of power, control, legitimacy, privilege, equity, justice, and the dimension of values generally.

(ii) There has been a tendency for analysis of educational policy to be couched in the guise of scientific precision. As a result, value issues and the ethical and political dimensions of policy analysis have been obscured, and analysis limited largely to describing the status quo.

(iii) Emphasis has been concentrated too narrowly on the process of policy formation. Consequently, wider aspects of the policy analyst's (full) role have been downplayed. These include the tasks of advocacy, monitoring and evaluating policy, providing information for policy, and analysing policy content.

(iv) The work of policy analysts continues to have little, if any, positive impact. All too often, social problems are exacerbated by professional policy researchers.[18]

Prunty's identification of these (and other) failings, and his positive guidelines for an improved, *critical*, analysis of educational policy, are based on four suppositions. Each of these accords perfectly with the tenor of my argument throughout this book. First, given the unique role played by schools in socializing the young and transmitting, maintaining and recreating culture, educational policy analysis must relate the operation of school to that of the society overall. Next, education policy analysis cannot be value-free. After all, education itself is value-laden. It involves processes of selection, evaluation, allocation of life chances, opportunities, etc. Moreover, within existing social structures curriculum, pedagogy, and evaluation are inescapably ideological, and serve certain interests more/rather than others. Any policy analysis that fails to proceed from this insight is deficient. Third, Prunty accepts that much of the power and control exerted over classroom practice issues from and is legitimated by, education policy. Hence, education policy is inseparable from the politics of daily life. It is, in fact, a key dimension of those politics. Finally, policy generally, is best understood as the 'authoritative allocation of values'.[19] And so to ask the question, 'what counts as knowledge and culture within the schools?', is also to ask, 'whose values have been validated by education policy?' Conceiving policy as the authoritative allocation of values

> draws our attention to the centrality of power and control in the concept of policy, and requires us to consider not only whose values [and, of course, whose *interests*] are represented in policy, but also how these values have come to be institutionalized.[20]

On the basis of these suppositions and his assessment of prevailing educational policy analysis, Prunty asks how a *critical* policy analysis might be developed. He identifies six 'signposts'.

(i) Critical analysis is grounded in a genuinely democratic politics: in the analyst's commitment to pursuing a social order in which the interests of human beings at large are not compromised by the preservation of elites; where the many are *not* treated as means to the ends of the few.

(ii) Critical analysis seeks to uncover the bases of domination, repression and exploitation, that are embedded in and legitimated by educational policy. This calls for the analyst to side with the oppressed and advocate with them.

(iii) Curriculum, pedagogy, and evaluation are three 'conduits' via which those values that are institutionalized by policy are imposed upon pupils — as part of the overall process of social reproduction. And so the manner in which policy shapes what counts as valid knowledge (i.e., curriculum), as valid process for transmitting knowledge (i.e., pedagogy), and as valid attainment of knowledge (i.e., evaluation), is an important focus for critical analysis of education policy. The critical analyst pays special attention to the *process* by which certain values, ideas, and practices (with their related interests) become validated; to the principles and mechanisms by which certain views, ideas, and interests are included, *or effectively excluded*, in the process of determining 'what counts'.

(iv) A critical policy analysis must address the way in which the consciousness of oppressed groups serves the interests of their oppressors. Of special concern here is the way in which the policy process draws on beliefs and perceptions that are common among subordinate groups — for example, perceptions of powerlessness, beliefs that one is unable to take part or that it is not really one's place to contribute — to systematically exclude them from policy deliberations. Prunty calls for a 'pathology of consciousness', through which to understand such operations of oppressed consciousness. Where subordinate groups *are* accommodated to some extent within policy discussions, the workings of ideological and cultural hegemony may result in their advancing or actively supporting policy contrary to their interests.[21] A possible case here would be if working-class parents called for basics and career education at the expense of studies (in history or literature, say) which have the potential to stimulate some critical understanding of social reality.

(v) Critical policy analysis is a dialogue and a praxis. This requires the policy analyst to ensure that the process of shaping, interpreting, and implementing educational policy involves what Habermas calls *an ideal speech situation* between analyst and community (in this case subordinate social groups). Indeed, Prunty claims that policy analysts must do all they can to enable the oppressed to engage on an equal footing with more powerful social groups in the policy-making process. As an 'outsider' — in terms, typically, of social class, culture, educational experience, etc. — the analyst must commit a form of class-cultural suicide, and become a constructive catalyst (rather than an instigator) for forms of reflection and action on the part of oppressed groups aimed at framing, interpreting, and implementing policies in their interests.

(vi) The critical analyst must have a sound knowledge of the policy arena itself. This, after all, is the particular dimension of social reality they seek to influence especially, and to effect some change through. The better that social reality is understood, the better the chances are of addressing it effectively. In the case of education policy, this calls for knowledge of different kinds and levels of policy, and the relationship between them. Hence,

> an understanding of procedural policy helps to create the conditions of undistorted communication where an equitable *substantive* policy can be formed. Similarly, an appreciation of the differences between distributive, regulatory, and redistributive policies can aid the critical analyst in anticipating the winners and losers, the empowered and the constrained, and the extent to which wrongs are righted. The role of the critical policy analyst ... properly includes advocacy, and the researcher's knowing the kind of policy that will be required to redress a social injustice all the more ensures that such change can take place.[22]

A Contribution to Critical Educational Policy Analysis?

Clearly, some of Prunty's signposts are absent, or otherwise under-represented, in my argument. I do not proceed from a detailed knowledge of the policy arena. Nor do I seek to generate technical policy knowledge. This book is much more concerned with exploring a political perspective which may help us understand and evaluate better some elements of education policy. Whether or not it is helpful remains to be seen. Secondly, the present exercise is hardly a praxis : it is an academic book! Like many academic books it *calls* for praxis. It has even *described* the praxis of other people. Hopefully it manifests a little praxis as well. But it remains, essentially, an act of reflection. Its political relevance depends on its signficance for future praxis — beginning with the author's own. Next, there is no original contribution made here to the 'pathology of (oppressed) consciousness'[23], although the *role* of consciousness in maintaining structured domination and subordination is a central theme; as is the idea of pursuing liberated consciousness by consciously pursuing liberation. For a 'pathology of consciousness' we must look to and engage in the kind of inquiry undertaken by Alison Jones at girls grammar, and by many others in Britain and North America.[24] Naturally, it is within a revolutionary praxis that the pathology of oppressed consciousness is best understood and addressed; whether this be the revolutionary praxis of Corresponding Societies, culture circles, women's groups, the emerging Kohanga Reo movement in Aotearoa, CEPs in Nicaragua, or whatever. Neither, finally, have I detailed various processes and mechanisms by which some curricular, pedagogical, and evaluative forms become validated, and others marginalized; by which one *habitus* is legitimated and others subordinated. Hopefully, however, the argument in chapter 4 suggests the importance of addressing this theme in particular relation to the social construction of school literacy, and offers at least some general pointers for future inquiry.

On the other hand, Prunty's call for critical analysis *does* meet with some tangible support and elaboration here. An explicit political orientation for analysis is provided, by which to expose 'sources of domination, repression, and exploitation that are entrenched in, and legitimated by, educational policy'.[25] There are two main points to be made. First, I have tried to demonstrate the special significance of *literacy* within the politics of daily life, and thereby establish a priority for investigating educational policies which bear on the practice of reading and writing. Rather than seeing reading and writing as low level tools or skills one acquires in order to get on with 'the real business of education' — typically, studying subjects — I have emphasized that we do better to understand education as an initiation into one form of literacy or another. In this the links between one's literacy and one's consciousness, and between literacy and prevailing social structures (of domination, etc.), are paramount. We should, I suggest, try to understand curriculum, pedagogy, and evaluation as far as possible in terms of the kind of *literacy* they engender and, to that extent, the social relations and practices — the *history* — they promote.

Second, the politics of literacy — and, hence, the politics of educational policy bearing on literacy — can be usefully approached through the distinction between proper and improper literacy. A first question to be asked of an education policy will be: is this likely to encourage or discourage the practice of a proper form of reading and writing? Any policy which fails to promote proper literacy necessarily contributes to maintaining improper practices of reading and writing: it will only be a matter of degree. Policies which overtly champion basics or vo-tech propel students headlong into improper literacy. More liberal approaches to curriculum and pedagogy which stress 'balance' and 'neutrality', but fail — in the process — positively to enhance structural modes of thought and activity centering on the attempt to address patterned inequality within the relations and practices of daily life, at best maintain existing norms of impropriety. While they do not *accentuate* improper literacy, they are nevertheless impotent to transcend it. This very impotence is the Achilles heel of merely liberal conceptions and practices of education. Without a critical protective shell, liberal ideals are ready prey to forces of reaction: as the conservative reaction has demonstrated all too clearly. While policy trends from abroad find increasing favour within New Zealand, Freeman-Moir's comment from 1981 changes from a challenge to a haunting.

> Despite the collapse of school reform overseas there is little so far in New Zealand to indicate that academics teaching education in university departments even imagine that liberal theory is open to question. Instead, university teachers continue to see their task as training students to operate intelligently and efficiently within the existing system and not as constructing a critical analysis of education and of the society in which it is embedded.[26]

Those who should have been at the forefront of developing a critical education discourse have moved too slowly and (I suspect) too late. And no one else has done the job for them. If there yet remains time for us in New Zealand to learn from recent history abroad, and to prepare ourselves critically to face the tide of reaction, that time must now be very short.

During the time that may remain, the distinction between proper and improper literacy offers a basis for assessing the educational demands of would-be policy shapers in New Zealand. If the minority interests reflected in the numerous submissions, policy statements, manifestos, and other ideological pronouncements of such lobbies as the Employer's Federation, Chamber of Commerce, Concerned Parents Association, New Zealand Organization on Moral Education, Family Rights Association, Integrity Centre, the Futures Trust, and the Educational Development Association, are to be exposed and resisted, we must spell out clearly and often the political implications of the ideas and demands advanced by these groups. The policy predilections of Treasury itself must likewise be subjected to political analysis and critique. At the same time, those who seek to resist the ideology of the 'new right' (with its underlying commitment to enhancing minority interests), and to preserve whatever spaces remain in formal education for pursuing and enhancing critical understanding and commitment to democratic practice, must elaborate their politics: including their politics of literacy. This is precisely to pursue and expand opportunities for practising proper forms of reading and writing. An important part of this exercise — which is binding upon *all* in the community who are concerned that education have a democractic future, and *not* upon (a minority of) professional educators and educationists alone — will include reading and discussing work already done on trends in educational 'reform' since the early 1970s. The critiques advanced by Shor, Giroux, McLaren, Finkelstein, Aronowitz, Carnoy, Kohl, Kozol, Levin, and Apple, among others, are 'required reading' here.[27]

In accordance with Prunty's guidelines for critical analysis, my argument in this book *is* anchored in the vision of a just and democratic social order. Moreover, the relationship between the workings of education (as an identifiable site of social practice) and the wider operation of society is amplified in terms of forces working for and against the fulfilment of such a social order. I have attempted to sharpen the links between education and society by juxtaposing trends in the practice of literacy within societies like our own with recent developments in Nicaragua. Admittedly the argument is more suggestive than conclusive. What it suggests, however, has major implications for those who seek to understand and influence education policy: namely, that unless and until the interests championed by the state are truly those of the majority, education policy will necessarily promote improper literacy over proper literacy in the interests of elites. This, indeed, is practically tautological. The point of my inquiry has been to lend weight to the view that in our own society the state maintains educational activity which reproduces structured inequality — and is able to do this with considerable support (or, at least, lack of effective opposition) from disadvantaged and advantaged alike. The social production of improper literacy within education is a major factor contributing to the hegemonized consciousness by which subordinated groups support, or (at least) fail to oppose, their own subordination. By contrast, the case of Nicaragua provides some basis for believing that once control of the state falls to majority interests, educational policies aimed at promoting proper literacy and genuine forms of democratic participation can quickly and easily be put in place. Of course, implementing these policies successfully presents a tough challenge — with or without opposition on behalf of traditional elites and international vested interest. To secure appropriate policy and official goodwill is, however, a genuine revolutionary achievement.

We must have realistically low expectations of educational policy so long as the state remains the legitimating arm of structured inequality. The point of analyzing and studying education policy by those committed to proper literacy and a democratic future is that it offers an important opportunity for engaging in the historical praxis by which structures of inequality are understood and transformed, and state power is eventually enlisted in serving the interests of all on an equal basis. Understanding the options available for literacy, and why one is maintained at the expense of the other is, in my view, a necessary part of this praxis. For us, the revolutionary challenge is to build the practice of proper literacy within the process of coming to understand better the politics of literacy. Some contribution to this revolutionary praxis *can* be made by enhanced academic analysis of educational policy, and by 'policy intellectuals'[28] working within established frameworks of policy formation and implementation. Beyond this, however, we are called on to build and engage in radical politics within more informal settings.

Let me briefly note some dimensions for further research bearing on educational policy which, my argument suggests, may contribute to an informed progressive politics.

(i) We should continue to identify and scrutinize the education policy demands of conservative lobbies and interest groups within the community, and trace in detail the *political* underpinnings and implications of their demands: that is, the way in which their demands relate to structures and patterns of power and interest.[29]

(ii) We need to understand more clearly (and in detail) how the social relations and practices of the classroom contribute to disempowering children from subordinate groups, and relate this process to the inability of 'disenfranchized groups to influence the workings of the school' via educational policy.[30] The kind of research represented by 'At School I've got a Chance' is especially valuable here. For it goes to the very heart of Prunty's call for a 'pathology of consciousness', and at the same time has genuinely educative potential (of a *proper* kind) for pupils, teachers, researchers, and the community generally.

(iii) The *objective* literacy requirements of prevailing economic, educational, cultural, and political arrangements, bear futher inquiry. This involves asking to what extent, and in what detailed ways, existing modes of working, of educating and governing ourselves, and of maintaining the established balance of cultural forces within our society, effectively *presupposes* the practice of improper literacy. Obviously, a large literature already exists which is relevant to this question. There is, however, an important political end to be served in focusing this body of theory and data on the theme of *literacy* specifically. After all, the bottom line for education in a print society is that people learn to read and write. It is our *minimum* expectation of education that it enable people to read and write efficiently. There is no need to convince the public that educational policy should secure this end. Yet this minimum, conservative, taken-for-granted goal can readily be appropriated for a positive, radical educational ideal: by substituting 'properly' for 'efficiently', and then advancing the ideological view of *proper literacy* developed here. People already expect education to do a proper job of promoting literacy. Our task, as researchers committed to enhancing democracy and social justice, is to encourage a proper understanding of what this job entails, and of the constraints that currently prevent its fulfilment.

(iv) It is also worth considering what sorts of school-based remedial or intervention programmes for non-readers and 'under-achievers' are currently supported by education policy. To what extent and in what ways do these contribute to, or undermine, the practice of proper literacy? How are these programmes, and the official legitimation they enjoy, to be understood in political terms? How far are they an effective *diversion* from the real educational and (related) social issues within our society? Do they address causes or merely tinker with symptoms? How should they be described and evaluated in the light of Postman's observation that: 'it is probably true that in a highly complex society one *cannot be governed* unless one can read . . .'?[31] Are the remedial and intervention programmes available (and, in many cases, made compulsory) within schools informed by a concern for, and understanding of, wider political forces and circumstances that may give rise to difficulties with reading and writing in the first place; that may establish literacy as useless or irrelevant in the eyes of many pupils; or worse still, ensure that the literacy acquired (under compulsion) and practised by many people becomes an effective life-long instrument in the process of their own continued subordination?

Australasia, Britain, and North America are currently in a period of economic retrenchment. Education has been subject to fiscal cuts — often severe. Many of these cuts have been legitimated by conservative/reactionary ideologies which broadly accord with free market economic policies. It might prove interesting to discover which educational services to literacy enjoy continued or, even, increased support by governments seemingly committed to creating conditions under which the gap between rich and poor, controller and controlled, is widened.

(v) We should develop a comparative policy studies which juxtaposes revolutionary social goals and policies against our own. Within this process we may achieve a deeper understanding of local initiatives and possibilities, as well as those abroad, which present genuine challenges to historical structures of domination and subordination. This will help open up a dialectics of internationalism and localism. By better understanding the politics of radical social change in other countries we may better understand the requirements of radical social change at home; and vice versa. As a result, we become capable of supporting and participating in revolutionary initiatives, wherever they are taking place, and less likely unwittingly to hinder them.

Educational Policy Analysis and Political Struggle

The political perspective employed in this book supports the view that those who seriously wish to engage in critical analysis of education policy as a praxis must ultimately do so within the context of struggle by oppressed groups to understand and transform those relations and practices of daily life which oppress them. This has some important implications for 'policy intellectuals': i.e., for those who engage in policy analysis within their professional role as academics. I will conclude by noting two of these implications.

(i) One runs the risk of reifying education policy in fostering the growth of a formal literature on the subject. I am, of course, running this risk here! The more that academics write about education policy, the more we risk turning it into, and confirming it as, an *object* of scholarly inquiry. To some extent it *is* a legitimate focus for disciplined reflection. More importantly, however, education policy denotes a *process* which we must strive in action, as well as in reflection, to democratize and, where appropriate, to subvert: for example, by securing government funding for literacy projects with radical potential, and/or by radicalizing projects which have already been legitimated (and funded) through policy. An unfortunate, but almost inevitable, consequence of reifying education policy will be to alienate non-professionals from engaging it. The more we appropriate education policy for academic (and other professional-technical) treatment, the more we risk mystifying it into a domain of complexity and expertise. This is precisely the kind of process that (further) marginalizes subordinate groups from the policy arena.

An important part of the point I have tried to make by reference to Nicaragua is that educational policy is not at all mysterious or complicated *when undertaken democratically*. Indeed, when we speak of the FSLN programme for educational and cultural change, it almost seems appropriate to recognize broad *intentions* rather than policies: *decisions* rather than content. It was *decided* to launch a literacy crusade. It was *decided* to try and extend this crusade into on-going popular adult education. How this was to be done, how it was to be organized, funded, guided, etc., remained largely in the realm of the unknown at the time these decisions were taken. The very meaning and success of *policy* here necessitated the active, creative involvement of those whose interests were directly concerned by the decisions: namely, uneducated or undereducated people. *They* became creators and analysts of policy: key actors in the process of evolving, implementing, and modifying educational policy. Where shortcomings in the operation of CEPs are apparent today, it has much to do with bureaucratic and professional failure to take due account of those people who *are* the CEPs. On the other hand, much of the undeniable success of Popular Basic Education to date is attributable to the capacity of ordinary (and hitherto marginalized) people to grasp, implement, and construct-in-practice, educational *policy*. Making education policy is the democratic right of people at large, as Ernest Jones recognized so clearly prior to the enactment of compulsory mass schooling. We must ensure that in 'elevating' educational policy to the status of an academic subject, with its own 'literature' and 'language', we do not contribute to estranging people from their democratic right and impose barriers to their capacity for democratic participation — thereby becoming part of the very *problem* of oppression.

(ii) By far the greater part of critically evaluating educational policy in a praxis will occur outside of formal educational settings and roles: among community groups who organize around the experience of discrimination against them in education; within women's groups, peace groups, anti-racism groups; in workers' education associations, trade unions, and branches of political parties where commitment to working-class interests remains intact; within adult literacy initiatives; in unemployed rights centres and solidarity organizations; in groups where people come together to frame petitions, and so on. In fact, wherever groups confront educational themes which relate to their own oppression there exists the opportunity for critical analysis of educational policy as an authentic praxis.

'Analysis' here does not imply 'analyst' in any formal sense of the term. The act of (critical) analysis is simply that of breaking down elements of social reality into simpler elements so that the whole can be understood more clearly, explained more satisfactorily, and addressed more effectively in liberating action. All humans are potentially *analysts* in exactly the way that Gramsci says we are all potentially *intellectuals*.[32] The *practice* of analysis — of which we are all capable, given structures which permit it — must not be confused with the *social function* to which only a few are 'called'. Unfortunately, all too many accounts of policy analysis tacitly or overtly identify policy analysis with the social function of policy analyst.[33] This, however, could not be further from the truth. Rather, those who happen to be policy analysts by social function are only *enabled* to engage in critical analysis as praxis to the extent that they are accepted as co-strugglers by those pursuing liberation from oppression.

For critical analysis as praxis is *revolutionary* activity. In the end, those engaged in critically addressing educational policy are concerned with much more than (merely) seeking to influence official policy in ways that provide some benefit or amelioration for subordinate groups, whilst maintaining existing structures of domination and oppression substantially intact. The aim, instead, is to understand the very structures which underlie discriminatory policies — including policies which offer a semblance of reform, but which lack radical bite — in order to change the structures themselves, and not just to tinker with symptoms. In our own society the formal process of making and implementing policy is itself part of the very reality to be changed within the praxis of liberation. It is the political value for securing genuine structural change that is all-important in problematizing eduational policy, and not short term success in winning limited concessions through official policy — although any limited gains that are compatible with genuine change are to be sought and welcomed in the short run.

Consequently, at the point that really matters — in the political struggle within everyday life — policy intellectuals must become like Amilcar Cabral: genuinely *with* and *among* the people in spite of their socially created and legitimated difference. (Although it would be the least of her intentions, Hirshon portrays an excellent model of this ideal in practice in her account of the Nicaraguan literacy campaign.) Demystifying the social construction of expertise is an essential aspect of practising proper literacy in the pursuit of liberation. Being able to place one's skills in the service of subordinated groups, whilst consciously opting out of the social relations of expertise and ascribed status, is a central revolutionary demand facing academics who would align politically with the oppressed. For the very preparation and social function of the academic is simultaneously a product and a part of an educational process which is grounded in relations and practices of hierarchy and difference.

Critical analysis of educational policy is an important focus for practising proper literacy. It marks a key point at which literacy, schooling, and revolution merge. To analyze educational policy within an authentic praxis is a supreme educational calling. For as much today as in the times of Corresponding Societies and Chartists, it is in the pursuit of liberation by subordinated groups seeking to understand and transform oppressive social relations and practices that the challenge of education for democracy lies.

Notes

1   As being either integral to the social reproduction of structured inequality, or to the pursuit of liberation.
2   SEARLE, C. (1975), *Classrooms of Resistance*, London, Writers and Readers, p. 6.
3   *Ibid*. Refusal to grant tenure to such teachers has been a common ploy, especially within US universities.
4   Compare, as typical instances of *ideological* opposition to the 'new' education in Nicaragua, DORN, D. and ZAVALA CUADRA, A. (1985). 'New values in Nicaragua', *Guardian Weekly*, 6 September; and the reference to the Nicaraguan Union of Parents in Catholic Schools, *Envio*, no. 48, June 1985.
5   See chapter 4 above.
6   As opposed to merely generating more theory, data, etc. Compare KOZOL, (1985), *Illiterate America*, Chapter 2 New York, Anchor and Doubleday.
7   SHOR (1980), *Critical Teaching and Everyday Life*, Boston, South End, p. 163.
8   KOZOL, *op. cit.*,p. 45.
9   Recall here the resistance from males to the initial formation and impressive success of women's consciousness raising groups in the 1960s and 1970s. At the present time we find expressions of resentment surfacing among New Zealanders to cultural initiatives by Maori built around the practice of literacy in the Maori language within indigenous settings, and to demands that this process be present in, and enhanced through, schooling.
10   SILVER, H. (1985), 'Historian in a policy field: a British chef in Paris?', *History of Education Review*, 14, 1, p. 5.
11   (1986), 'Editorial', *Journal of Education Policy*, 1, 1.
12   *Ibid*.
13   SILVER, *op. cit.*, p. 5.
14   For an introduction to this material, see the bibliographies provided by SHOR (1986), *Culture Wars*, London, Routledge and Kegan Paul, and GIROUX, H. and McLAREN, P. (1986), 'Teacher education and the politics of engagement: the case for democratic schooling', *Harvard Educational Review*, 56, 3, pp. 213 – 38. See also GRACE, G. (1984), 'Urban Education: policy science or critical scholarship?', in his (Ed) *Education and the City*, London, Routledge and Kegan Paul, pp. 3 – 59.
15   GIROUX and McLAREN, *ibid.*, especially pp. 217–22.
16   In *ibid.*, p. 217.
17   PRUNTY, J. (1985), 'Signposts for a critical educational policy analysis', *Australian Journal of Education*, 29, 2, pp. 133 – 40.

18 See *ibid.*, pp. 133–4.
19 *Ibid.*, pp. 135–6.
20 *Ibid.*, p. 136. Comment in parentheses is mine.
21 It would be interesting, in this regard, to analyze submissions to the recent Review of the Curriculum for Schools in New Zealand. Under the guidance of a genuinely open and liberal Minister of Education, the Review sought and facilitated responses from the public at large. How far this positive encouragement to participate actually enabled subordinate groups to express hegemonized values — and how far the questionnaires themselves prompted them — strikes me as a question worth pursuing.
22 PRUNTY, *op. cit.*, 137–8.
23 *Ibid.*, 136.
24 Compare for example, CONNELL, R., ASHENDEN, D., KESSLER, S. and DOWSETT, G. (1981), Class and Gender dynamics in a ruling class school, *Interchange*, 12; FULLER, M. (1980). 'Black girls in a London Comprehensive School; in DEEM, R. (Ed), *op. cit.*; MORAN, P. (1983), 'Female Youth Culture in an Inner City School', Australian Association for Research and Education Conference Proceedings, Canberra.
25 Compare PRUNTY, *op. cit.*, p. 136.
26 FREEMAN-MOIR, J. (1981), 'Employable and quiet: the political economy of human mis-development', *New Zealand Journal of Educational Studies*, 16, 1, p. 16.
27 In addition to works already cited, see: ARONOWITZ, S. and GIROUX, H. (1985), *Education under Siege: the Conservative, Liberal, and Radical Debate over Schooling*, South Hadley, Bergin and Garvey; CARNOY, M. (Ed) (1972), *Schooling in a Corporate Society*, New York, David McKay; CARNOY, M. and LEVIN, H. (1985), *Schooling and Work in the Democratic State*, Stanford, Stanford University Press; FINKELSTEIN, B. (1984), 'Education and the retreat from democracy in the United States, 1979 – 198?', *Teachers College Record*, 86, KOHL, H. (1984), *Basic Skills*, New York; LEVIN, H. (1981), 'Back to basics and the economy', *Radical Teacher*, no. 21.
28 The term 'policy intellectuals' is employed by WILSON, J. (1981), 'Policy Intellectuals and "Public Policy"', *The Public Interest*, 64, pp. 31 – 46. For an account of policy analysis and the policy analyst which is opposed to my whole orientation here, see TROW, M. (1984), 'Researchers, policy analysts and policy intellectuals', in HUSEN, T. and KOGAN, M. (Eds), *Educational Research and Policy: how do they relate?*, Oxford, Pergamon Press, pp. 261 – 82. For recent perspectives on education policy analysis, see the Husen and Kogan collection at large.
29 For an introduction to Australasian work in this field, see SAWER, M. (Ed), *Australia and the New Right*, Sydney, Allen and Unwin; LAUDER, H. (1986); 'The new right and educational policy in New Zealand', Unpublished paper, University of Canterbury; and RYAN, A. (1986) '*For God, Country and Family': populist moralism and the New Zealand moral right*, M.A. thesis, Massey University.
30 Compare PRUNTY, *op. cit.*, p. 136.
31 POSTMAN, N. (1970), 'The Politics of reading', *Harvard Educational Review*, 40, 2.
32 GRAMSCI, A. (1971), 'The Intellectuals', in HOARE, Q. and NOWELL-SMITH, G. (Eds), *Selections from the Prison Notebooks*, London, Lawrence and Wishart, pp. 3 – 23. See also, 'On Education', in the same collection, pp. 26–43.
33 Compare, for example, TROW, *op. cit.*

Appendix

Lesson, 19 from the Primer Workbook, *The Sunrise of the People*, Ministry of Education, Managua, Nicaragua, pp. 106 – 11.

1. Let's read the sentences.   **Exercise A**

Nicaraguan women have traditionally been <u>exploited</u>.
The Revolution now makes their liberation <u>possible</u>.

2. Let's read the underlined word several times. Then, read part of the word.

exploi<u>ted</u>

exploi<u>ted</u>

3. Listen to these words. Then, read the words with the teacher.

exported	imported	defended	ended
spoiled	boiled	finished	vanished

4. Let's look at these words more carefully. Circle the parts which are the same. Underline the parts which are different.

exported	imported	defended	ended
spoiled	boiled	finished	vanished

5. Let's write these words following the dotted lines. Then, practice writing them without the dotted lines.

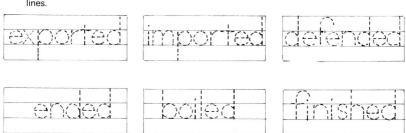

6. Let's read and write sentences containing some of these words.

We imported more than we exported.
Aid was accepted from many nations.
Women participated actively during the war.
They wanted to defend their rights.

7. Match the words in each column with the same word in the sentences.

We imported more than we exported.	more exported We than imported we
Aid was accepted from many nations.	was many from nations Aid accepted
They wanted to defend their rights.	to their wanted They rights defend

8. Write down the sentences the teacher dictates to you.

Exercise B

1. Let's read the sentences.

Nicaraguan women have traditionally been <u>exploited</u>.
The Revolution now makes their liberation possible.

2. Let's read the underlined word several times. Then, read part of the word.

<u>exploited</u>

<u>exploited</u>

3. Listen to these words. Then, read the words with the teacher.

toilet	oil	boil	voice
choice	point	join	

4. Let's look at these words carefully. Circle the parts which are the same. Underline the parts which are different.

toilet	oil	boil	voice
choice	paint	join	

5. Let's write these words following the dotted lines. Then, practice writing them without the dotted lines.

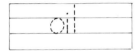  

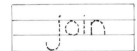 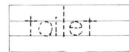 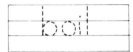

6. Let's read and write sentences containing some of these words.

The people made the choice to be free.
Let's join efforts to rebuild our country.
Building toilets means better health.
Make it a point to boil the water.

7. Match the words in each column with the same words in the sentences.

made
the
free
choice
to
The
be
people

The people made the choice to be free.

Let's join efforts to rebuild our country.

rebuild
join
Let's
country
efforts
to
our

Building toilets means better health.

means
toilets
health
Building
better

8. Write down the sentence the teacher dictates to you.

Bibliography

ALLEN, W. and McCLURE, E. (1898), *Two Hundred Years: the history of the SPCK*, London, SPCK.

ANDERSON, C. and BOWMAN, M. (Eds) (1966), *Education and Economic Development*, London, Frank Cass.

ANGUS, E. (1981), 'The awakening of a people: Nicaragua's literacy campaign', *Two Thirds*, 2, 3.

ANYON, J. (1979), 'Ideology and United States History Textbooks', *Harvard Educational Review*, 49, 3.

ANYON, J. (1981), 'Social class and school knowledge', *Curriculum Inquiry*, 11, 1.

Adult Performance Level Study (1975), *Adult Functional Competency*, Austin, University of Texas.

APPLE, M. (1981), 'Social structure, ideology and curriculum', in LAWN, M. and BARTON, L. (Eds), *Rethinking Curriculum Studies*, London, Croom Helm.

APPLE, M. (1982), 'Reproduction and contradiction in education', in his (Ed), *Cultural and Economic Reproduction in Education*, London, Routledge and Kegan Paul.

APPLE, M. (1984), 'The politics of text publishing', *Educational Theory*, 34, 4.

ARONOWITZ, S. and GIROUX, H. (1985), *Education Under Siege: the Conservative, Liberal, and Radical Debate over Schooling*, South Hadley, Bergin and Garvey.

ASPINALL, A. (1949), *Politics and the Press 1780–1850*, London, Home and Van Thal.

BAMFORD, S. (1984), *Passages in the Life of a Radical*, Oxford, Oxford University Press.

BARKER, A.G. (no date), *Henry Hetherington*, London, The Pioneer Press.

BARNDT, D. (1985), 'Popular Education', in WALKER, T. (Ed), *Nicaragua: the first five years*, New York, Praeger Press.

BARRICADA INTERNACIONAL, Managua, Nicaragua, all issues.

BATAILLE, L. (Ed) (1976), *A Turning Point for Literacy*, UNESCO.

BEE, B. (1982), *Migrant Women and Work*, Sydney, Randwick Technical College.

BEE, B. (1984), *Women's Work, Women's Lives*, Sydney, Randwick Technical College.

BENTON, T. (1974), 'Education and Politics', in HOLLY, E. (Ed), *Education or Domination? a critical look at educational problems today*, London, Arrow Books.

BERGGREN, C. and L. (1975), *The Literacy Process: a practice in domestication or liberation?*, London, Writers and Readers.

BERLIN, I. (1969), 'Two Concepts of Liberty', in his *Four Essays on Liberty*, London, Oxford University Press.

BERNSTEIN, B. (1971), 'On the classification and framing of educational knowledge', in YOUNG, M.F.D. (Ed), *Knowledge and Control*, London, Macmillan.

BLACK, G. (1981), *Triumph of the People: the Sandinist Revolution in Nicaragua*, London, Zed Press.

BLACK, G. and BEVAN, J. (1980), *The Loss of Fear: education in Nicaragua*, London, World University Service.

BOOTH, J. (1982), *The End and the Beginning: the Nicaraguan Revolution*, Boulder, Westview Press.

BORGE, T. (1982), *Women and the Nicaraguan Revolution*, New York, Pathfinder.

BORGE, T. (1985), 'The New Education in the New Nicargua', in *Nicaragua: the Sandinista people's revolution*, New York, Pathfinder.

BORGE, T. *et al* (1982), *Sandinistas Speak*, New York, Pathfinder.

BOURDIEU, P. (1977), 'Cultural reproduction and social reproduction', in KARABEL, J. and HALSEY, J. (Eds), *Power and Ideology in Education*, Oxford, Oxford University Press.

BOURGOIS, P. (1985), 'Ethnic minorities', in WALKER, T. (Ed), *op. cit.*

BOURGOIS, P. (1986), 'The Miskitu of Nicaragua: politicized ethnicity', *Anthropology Today*, 2, 2.

BOWLES, S. and GINTIS, H. (1976), *Schooling in Capitalist America*, London, Routledge and Kegan Paul.

BRIGGS, A. (Ed), (1959), *Chartist Studies*, London, Macmillan.

BROWN, P. (1918), *The French Revolution in English History*, London, Allen and Unwin.

CABRAL, A. (1969), *Unity and Struggle*, New York, Monthly Review Press.

CARDENAL, F. and MILLER, V. (1981), 'Nicaragua 1980: the battle of the ABCs', *Harvard Educational Review*, 51, 1.

CARNOY, M. (Ed) (1972), *Schooling in a Corporate Society*, New York, David MacKay.

CARNOY, M. and LEVIN, H. (1985), *Schooling and Work in the Democratic State*, Stanford, Stanford University Press.

Centre for Research and Documentation of the Atlantic Coast (1984), *Trabil Nani*, Managua, CIDCA.

CIPPOLA, C. (1969), *Literacy and Development in the West*, Harmondsworth, Penguin.

CLARKE, W. (1959), *A History of the SPCK*, London, SPCK.

COLE, G. and M. (Eds) (1944), *The Opinions of William Cobbett*, London, The Cobbett Publishing Co.

COLLET, C. (1933), *History of the Taxes on Knowledge*, London, Watts and Co.

COLLINS, R. (1977), 'Some comparative principles of educational stratification', *Harvard Educational Review*, 47, 1.

CONNELL, R. (1985), *Teachers' Work*, Sydney, Allen and Unwin.

CONNELL, R., ASHENDEN, D., KESSLER, S. and DOWSETT, G. (1981), 'Class and gender dynamics in a ruling class school; *Interchange*, 12.

CONNELL, R. ASHENDEN, D. KESSLER, S. and DOWSETT, G. (1982), *Making the Difference: schools, families, and social division*, Sydney, Allen and Unwin.

COOPER, T. (1971), *The Life of Thomas Cooper*, Leicester, Leicester University Press.

CORAGGIO, J. and IRVIN, G. (1985), 'Revolution and democracy in Nicaragua', *Latin American Perspectives*, 12, 2.

CRESSY, D. (1981), 'Levels of literacy in England 1530–1730', in GRAFF, H. (Ed.), *op. cit.*

DALE, R. and ESLAND, G. (1977), *Mass Schooling*, Milton Keynes, Open University Press.

DAVIES, J. (1978), 'The HSC: preparation for what?', *Radical Education Dossier*, February.

DEEM, R. (1978), *Women and Schooling*, London, Routledge and Kegan Paul.

DEEM, R. (Ed) (1980), *Schooling for Women's Work*, London, Routledge and Kegan Paul.

DIEDERICH, B. (1982), *Somoza: and the legacy of US involvement in Central America*, London, Junction Books.

Education Group, Centre for Contemporary Cultural Studies (1981), *Unpopular Education: schooling and social democracy in England since 1944*, London, Hutchinson.

Envio, Instituto Historico Centroamericano, Managua, all issues.

EVANS, E. (1983), *The Great Reform Act of 1832*, London, Methuen.

EVERS, C. and WALKER, J. (1982), 'The Unity of Knowledge', *Access*, 1, 2.

FINKELSTEIN, B. (1984), 'Education and the retreat from democracy in the United States, 1979 –198?', *Teachers College Record*, 86.

FLORA, J. McFADDEN, J. and WARNER, R. (1983), 'The growth of class struggle: the impact of the Nicaraguan Literacy Crusade on the political consciousness of young literacy workers', *Latin American Perspectives*, 10, 1.

FORD, P. (1986) 'Nicaragua: total literacy deferred', *Development Forum*, April.

FRANKLIN, B. (1972), 'The teaching of literature in the highest academies of the empire', in KAMPF and LAUTER, (Eds), *op. cit.*

FREEMAN-MOIR, J. (1981), 'Employable and quiet: the political economy of human mis development', *New Zealand Journal of Educational Studies*, 16, 1.

FREIRE, P. (1972), *Pedagogy of the Oppressed*, Harmondsworth, Penguin.

FREIRE, P. (1973), *Cultural Action for Freedom*, Harmondsworth, Penguin.

FREIRE, P. (1974), *Education: the practice of freedom*, London, Writers and Readers.

FREIRE, P. (1978), *Pedagogy in Process, Letters to Guinea-Bissau*, London, Writers and Readers.

FREIRE, P. (1985), *The Politics of Education*, London, Macmillan.

FULLER, M. (1980), 'Black girls in a London Comprehensive School', in DEEM, R. (ed), *op. cit.*

GIROUX, H. (1981), 'Hegemony, resistance, and the paradox of school reform', *Interchange*, 12, nos. 2 – 3.

GIROUX, H. (1982), *Ideology, Culture, and the Process of Schooling*, Lewes, Falmer Press.

GIROUX, H. (1985), 'Introduction' to FREIRE, P. *op. cit.*

GIROUX, H. and McLAREN, P. (1986), 'Teacher education and the politics of engagement: the case for democratic schooling', *Harvard Educational Review*, 56, 3.

GOODACRE, E. (1968), *Teachers and their pupils' background*, London, NFER.

GOODSON, I. (1986), 'Chariots of Fire : etymologies, epistemologies and the emergence of curriculum', ms., University of Western Ontario.

GOODSON, I. and BALL, S. (Eds) (1984), *Defining the Curriculum*. Lewes, Falmer Press.

GOODY, J. (Ed) (1968), *Literacy in Traditional Societies*, London, Cambridge University Press.

GOODY, J. and WATT, I. (1968), 'The Consequences of Literacy', in *ibid.*

GRACE, G. (1984), 'Urban Education: policy science or critical scholarship?', in his (Ed), *Education and the City*, London, Routledge and Kegan Paul.

GRAFF, H. (1979), *The Literacy Myth: literacy and social structure in the nineteenth century city*, New York, Academic Press.

GRAFF, H. (1981), 'Introduction' to his (Ed), *Literacy and Social Development in the West*, Cambridge, Cambridge University Press.

GRAMSCI, A. (1971), *Selections from the Prison Notebooks*, edited by HOARE, Q. and NOWELL-SMITH, G. London, Lawrence and Wishart.

HÄGERSTRAND, T. (1966), 'Quantitative Techniques for analysis of the spread of information and technology', in ANDERSON and BOWMAN (Eds), *op. cit.*

HALEY, E. (1983), 'Nicaragua/Women/Revolution', *Hecate*, 9.

HAMMOND, J. and B. (1930), *The Age of the Chartists*, London, Longmans Green.

HAMPTON, C. (Ed) (1984), *A Radical Reader*, Harmondsworth, Penguin.

HANS, N. (1948), *New Trends in Education in the Eighteenth Century*, London, Routledge and Kegan Paul.

HARGREAVES, D. (1980), *Adult Literacy and Broadcasting: the BBC's experience*, London, Francis Pinter.

HARRIS, K. (1979), *Education and Knowledge*, London, Routledge and Kegan Paul.

HARRIS, K. (1982), *Teachers and Classes*, London, Routledge and Kegan Paul.

HARRIS, R. (1985), 'The revolutionary process in Nicaragua', *Latin American Perspectives*, 12, 2.

HARRISON, J. (1961), *Learning and Living 1790–1960*, London, Routledge and Kegan Paul.

HEATH, S. (1980), 'The function and uses of literacy', *Journal of Communication*, 30.

HIRSHON, S. with BUTLER, J. (1983), *And Also Teach Them to Read*, Westport, Connecticut, Lawrence Hill and Co.

HIRST, P. (1974), *Knowledge and the Curriculum*, London, Routledge and Kegan Paul.

HOLLIS, P. (1970), *The Pauper Press: a study in working class radicalism in the 1830s*, London, Oxford University Press.

HOLLIS, P. (Ed) (1973), *Class and Conflict in Nineteenth Century England, 1815–1850*, London, Routledge and Kegan Paul.

HOLLY, D. (Ed) (1974), *Education or Domination?: a critical look at educational problems today*, London, Arrow Books.

HOYLES, M. (Ed) (1977), *The Politics of Literacy*, London, Writers and Readers.

HUNTER, C. ST. J. and HARMAN, D. (1979), *Adult Illiteracy in the United States*, New York, McGraw Hill.

HUSEN, T. and KOGAN, M. (Eds) (1984) *Educational Research and Policy: How do they relate?*, Oxford, Pergamon Press.

ILLICH, I. (1971), *Deschooling Society*, Harmondsworth, Penguin.

JAMES, L. (1963), *Fiction for the Working Man*, London, Oxford University Press.

JOHNSON, R. (1979), 'Really Useful Knowledge: radical education and working class culture 1790-1848', in CLARKE, J. CRITCHER, C. and JOHNSON, R. (Eds), *Working Class Culture: Studies in history and theory*, London, Hutchinson.

JONES, A. (1986), *At School I've Got a Chance: ideology and social reproduction in a secondary school*, PhD thesis, University of Auckland.

JONES, M. (1952), *Hannah More*, Cambridge, Cambridge University Press.

KAHAN, A. (1966), 'Determinents of the incidence of literacy in nineteenth-century rural Russia', in ANDERSON and BOWMAN (Eds), *op. cit.*

KAMPF, L. and LAUTER, P. (1972), 'Introduction' to their (Eds.), *The Politics of Literature: dissenting essays on the teaching of English*, New York, Pantheon Books.

KARABEL, J. and HALSEY, J. (Eds), (1977), *Power and Ideology in Education*, Oxford, Oxford University Press.

KARIER, C. et al (1973), *Roots of Crisis: American education in the twentieth century*, Chicago, Rand McNally.

KATZ, M. (1980), 'Reflections on the purpose of education reform', *Educational Theory*, 30, 2.

KELLY, G. and NIHLEN, A. (1982), 'Schooling and the reproduction of patriarchy', in APPLE, M. (Ed), *op. cit.*

KOHL, H. (1984), *Basic Skills*, New York.

KOZOL, J. (1978), *Children of the Revolution*, New York, Delta Books.

KOZOL, J. (1980), *Prisoners of Silence*, New York, Continuum.

KOZOL, J. (1985), *Illiterate America*, New York, Anchor and Doubleday.

LABOV, W. (1973), 'The Logic of non-standard English, in KEDDIE, N. (Ed), *Tinker, Tailor ... the Myth of Cultural Deprivation*, Harmondsworth, Penguin.

LANKSHEAR, C. (1982), *Freedom and Education*, Auckland, Milton Brookes.

LANKSHEAR, C. (1986), 'Humanizing functional literacy: beyond utilitarian necessity', *Educational Theory*, 36, 4.

LAUDER, H. (1986), 'The new right and educational policy in New Zealand', unpublished paper, University of Canterbury.

LAWLER, M. and LANKSHEAR, C. (1986), 'Adelante Mujer'. Con tu Participacion!: women and literacy in Nicaragua, *Landfall*, 158.

LAWN, M. and BARTON, L. (Eds) (1981), *Rethinking Curriculum Studies*, London, Croom Helm.

LAWTON, D. (1980), *The Politics of the School Curriculum*, London, Routledge and Kegan Paul.

LEVETT, A. and BRAITHWAITE, E. (1975), 'The growth of knowledge and inequality in New Zealand Society', *New Zealand Libraries*, 38, 2.

LEVIN, H. (1981), 'Back to basics and the economy', *Radical Teacher*, 21.

LEVINE, K. (1982), 'Functional literacy: fond illusions and false economies', *Harvard Educational Review*, 52, 3.

LIEBERMAN, A. and MCLAUGHLIN, M. (Eds) (1982), *Policy Making in Education*, Chicago, NSSE.

LOVETT, W. (1920), *The Life and Struggles of William Lovett*, London, Bell and Sons.

LOVETT, W and COLLINS, J. (1969), *Chartism: a new organization of the people*, Leicester, Leicester University Press.

MACDONALD, G. (1976), 'The politics of educational publishing', in YOUNG, M. and WHITTY, G. (Eds), *Explorations in the Politics of School Knowledge*, Driffield, Nafferton Books.

MACDONALD, M. (1977), *The Curriculum and Cultural Reproduction*, Milton Keynes, Open University Press.

MACDONALD, M. (1980), 'Socio-Cultural Reproduction and Women's Education', in DEEM, R. (Ed), *op. cit.*

MACDONALD, M. (1981), 'Schooling and the reproduction of class and gender relations', in DALE, R. *et al.* (Eds), *Education and the State, Vol. 2*, Lewes, Falmer Press.

MACPHERSON, C. (1977), 'Do we need a theory of the state?', *European Journal of Sociology*, 18, 2.

MACE, J. (1979), *Working With Words*, London, Writers and Readers/Chameleon.

MACKIE, R. (Ed) (1980), *Literacy and Revolution: the pedagogy of Paulo Freire*, London, Pluto Press.

MARTELL, G. (1976), 'The politics of reading and writing', in DALE, R. *et al* (Eds), *Schooling and Capitalism*, Milton Keynes, Open University Press.

MILLER, V. (1982), 'The Nicaraguan Literacy Crusade', in WALKER, T. (Ed), *Nicaragua in Revolution*, New York, Praeger Press.

MILLER, V. (1985), *Between Struggle and Hope: the Nicaraguan literacy crusade*, Boulder, Westview Press.

MILLS, C. WRIGHT (1959), *The Sociological Imagination*, New York, Oxford University Press.

MORAN, P. (1983), 'Female youth culture in an inner city school: Australian Association for Research and Education, Conference proceedings, Canberra.

MORE, H. (1830), *Collected Works*, London, Cadell.

Nicaraguan Ministry of Education (1980), *The Sunrise of the People*, Managua.

OAKESHOTT, M. (1962), *Rationalism in Politics*, London, Methuen.

OHMANN, R. (1972), 'Teaching and studying literature at the end of ideology', in KAMPF, L. and LAUTER, P. (Eds), *op. cit.*

O'NEIL, W. (1970), 'Properly literate', *Harvard Educational Review*, 40, 2.

O'NEIL, W. (1972), 'The Politics of bidialecticalism', in KAMPF, L. and LAUTER, P. (Eds), *op. cit.*

ORTIZ, R. DUNBAR, (1984), *Indians of the Americas: human rights and self-determination*, London, Zed Press.

OXENHAM, J. (1980), *Literacy: writing, reading, and social organization*, London, Routledge and Kegan Paul.

PEARCE, J. (1982), *Under the Eagle*, London, Latin America Bureau.

PEDERSON, S. (1986), 'Hannah More meets simple Simon', *Journal of British Studies*, 25.

PETERS, R. (1965), 'Education as initiation', in ARCHAMBAULT, R. (Ed), *Philosophical Analysis and Education*, London, Routledge and Kegan Paul.

PETERS, R. (1966), *Ethics and Education*, London, Allen and Unwin.

PETERS, R. (1973), 'Freedom and the development of the free man', in DOYLE, J. (Ed), *Educational Judgments*, London, Routledge and Kegan Paul.

PETERS, R. (1974), 'The development of reason', in his *Psychology and Ethical Development*, London, Allen and Unwin.

POSTMAN, N. (1970), 'The politics of reading', *Harvard Educational Review* 40, 2.

PRUNTY, J. (1985), 'Signposts for a critical educational policy analysis', *Australian Journal of Education*, 29, 2.

RAMIREZ-HORTON, S. (1982), 'The role of women in the Nicaraguan revolution', in WALKER, T. (Ed), *op. cit.*

RAPHAEL, D. (1970), *Problems of Political Philosophy*, London, MacMillan.

RORTY, R. (1980), *Philosophy and the Mirror of Nature*, Oxford, Blackwell.

ROSALDO, M. and LAMPHERE, L. (1974), *Women, Culture and Society*, Stanford, Stanford University Press.

ROSEN, H. (1972), *Language and Class: a critique of Bernstein*, Bristol, Falling Wall Press.

ROSENTHAL, R. and JACOBSON, L. (1968), *Pygmalion in the Classroom*, New York, Holt, Rinehart and Winston.

RYAN, A. (1986), '*For God, Country and Family*': populist moralism and the New Zealand moral right, M.A. thesis, Massey University.

SAVILLE, J. (1952), *Ernest Jones: Chartist*, London, Lawrence and Wishart.

SAWER, M. (Ed) (1982), *Australia and the New Right*, Sydney, Allen and Unwin.

SCHEFFLER, I. (1967), 'Philosophical models of teaching', in PETERS, R. (Ed), *The Concept of Education*, London, Routledge and Kegan Paul.

SCHOFIELD, R. (1968), 'The measurement of literacy in pre-industrial England', in GOODY, J. (Ed), *op. cit.*

SERRA, L. (1982), 'The Sandinista mass organizations', in WALKER, T. (Ed), *op. cit.*

SEARLE, C. (1975), *Classrooms of Resistance*, London, Writers and Readers.

SEARLE, C. (1977), *The World in a Classroom*, London, Writers and Readers.

SEARLE, C. (1984), *Words Unchained: language and revolution in Grenada*, London, Zed Press.

SHARP, R. (1980), *Knowledge, Ideology, and the Politics of Schooling*, London, Routledge and Kegan Paul.

SHOR, I. (1980), *Critical Teaching and Everyday Life*, Boston, South End Press.

SHOR, I. (1986), *Culture Wars*, London, Routledge and Kegan Paul.

SILVER, H. (1985), 'Historian in a policy field: a British chef in Paris?', *History of Education Review*, 14, 1.

SIMON, B. (1960), *Studies in the History of Education 1780–1870*, London, Lawrence and Wishart.

SMITH, M. (1983), 'Literature on literacy', *Media in Education*, 16, 1.

SPRING, J. (1976), *The Sorting Machine*, New York, David MacKay.

STANISLAWSKI, D. (1983), *The Transformation of Nicaragua 1519–1548*, Berkeley, University of California Press.

STREET, B. (1982), 'Literacy and Ideology', *Red Letters*, 12.

STREET, B. (1984), *Literacy in Theory and Practice*, Cambridge, Cambridge University Press.

STREET, B. (1986), 'Literacy — comparative perspectives: 'autonomous' and 'ideological' models of computer literacy', in GILL, K. (Ed), *Artificial Intelligence for Society*, New York, Wiley and Sons.

STUBBS, M. (1976), *Language, Schools and Classrooms*, London, Methuen.

STUBBS, M. (1980), *Language and Literacy*, London, Routledge and Kegan Paul.

TAXEL, J. (1983), 'The American Revolution: an analysis of literary content, form and ideology', in APPLE, M. and WEISS, L. (Eds), *Ideology and Practice in Schooling*, Philadelphia, Temple University Press.

THALE, M. (Ed) (1983), *Selection from the Papers of the London Corresponding Society 1792–1799*, London, Cambridge University Press.

THOMPSON, E. (1963), *The Making of the English Working Class*, Harmondsworth, Penguin.

TORRES, R. (1983), *La Post Alfabetizacion en Nicaragua*, Managua, INIES.

TORRES, R. (1985), *Nicaragua: revolucion popular, educacion popular*, Managua, CRIES-INIES.

TORRES, R. (1986), *Los CEP: educacion popular y democracia participativa en Nicaragua*, Managua, CRIES.

TROW, M. (1984), 'Researchers, policy analysts and policy intellectuals', in HUSEN, T. and KOGAN, M. (Eds), *Educational Research and Policy: how do they relate?* Oxford, Pergamon Press.

TYACK, D. (1976), 'Ways of seeing: an essay on the history of compulsory schooling', *Harvard Educational Review*, 46, 3.

VICINUS, M. (1972), 'The study of Nineteenth-century British working-class poetry', in KAMPF, L. and LAUTER, P. (Eds), *op. cit.*

WALKER, J. and EVERS, C. (1982), 'Epistemology and justifying the curriculum of educational studies, *British Journal of Educational Studies*, 30, 2.

WALKER, T. (Ed), (1982), *Nicaragua in Revolution*, New York, Praeger Press.

WALKER, T. (1985), 'Introduction' to his (Ed), *Nicaragua: the first five years*, New York, Praeger Press.

WALLAS, G. (1898), *The Life of Franics Place*, London, Allen and Unwin.

WEARMOUTH, R. (1948), *Some Working Class Movements of the Nineteenth Century*, London, The Epworth Press.

WEBB, R. (1955), *The British Working Class Reader*, London, Allen and Unwin.

WEBER, H. (1981), *Nicaragua: the Sandinist Revolution*, London, Verso.

WEISSBERG, A. (1982), *Nicaragua: an introduction to the Sandinista Revolution*, New York, Pathfinder.

WHITTY, G. (1985), *Sociology and School Knowledge: curriculum theory, research and politics*, London, Methuen.

WHITTY, G. and YOUNG, M. (Eds) (1976), *Explorations in the Politics of School Knowledge*, Driffield, Nafferton Books.

WICKWAR, W. (1928), *The Struggle for the Freedom of the Press*, London, Allen and Unwin.

WILDAVSKY, A. (1980), *The Art, and Craft of Policy Analysis*, London, Macmillan.

WILLIS, P. (1977), *Learning to Labour: how working class kids get working class jobs*, London, Saxon House.

WILSON, J. (1981), 'Policy intellectuals and "Public Policy"', *The Public Interest*, 64.

YOUNG, M. and WHITTY, G. (Eds) (1977), *Society, State and Schooling*, Lewes, Falmer Press.

YOUNG, M.F.D. (Ed) (1971), *Knowledge and Control*, London, Macmillan.

Index